Strategic Marketing
A European Approach

Strategic Marketing

A European Approach

Jean-Jacques Lambin

Université Catholique de Louvain
Louvain-la-Neuve, Belgium

McGraw-Hill Book Company

London • New York • St Louis • San Francisco • Auckland
Bogotà • Caracas • Lisbon • Madrid • Mexico • Milan • Montreal
New Delhi • Panama • Paris • San Juan • São Paulo
Singapore • Sydney • Tokyo • Toronto

Published by
McGraw-Hill Book Company Europe
Shoppenhangers Road, Maidenhead, Berkshire, SL6 2QL, England
Telephone 0628 23432
Fax 0628 770224

British Library Cataloguing in Publication Data
Lambin, Jean-Jacques
   Strategic Marketing: European
   Approach. – (McGraw-Hill Marketing for
   Professionals Series)
   I. Title II. Series
   658.8

   ISBN 0-07-707795-4

Library of Congress Cataloging-in-Publication Data
Lambin, Jean-Jacques
   [Marketing stratégique. English]
   Strategic marketing: a European approach / Jean-Jacques
Lambin.
       p.   cm. – (McGraw-Hill marketing for professionals series)
   Includes bibliographical references and index.
   ISBN 0-07-707795-4
   1. Marketing–European–Management.   I. Title.   II. Series.
HF5415.13.L33213   1993
658.8'094–dc20   93-21714
                                                              CIP

First-published in French as *Le Marketing Stratégique*
by McGraw-Hill France. (French edition copyright © 1989 by
McGraw-Hill France. All rights reserved.)

1234 CUP 9543

Typeset by Goodfellow & Egan Phototypesetting Ltd, Cambridge
and printed and bound in Great Britain at the University Press,
Cambridge.

Contents

Acknowledgements

This book is the English edition of the French book *Le marketing stratégique* (Paris, McGraw-Hill, second edition, 1989). This English edition has evolved from several years of research, teaching and consulting in Europe. This experience, the exchange of ideas and discussions with business professionals within various executive seminars or consulting assignments have done much to further my knowledge of the marketing process.

Several persons have directly or indirectly contributed at various stages to the development of this book: Robert Peeters (UCL, Louvain-la-Neuve) provided a review of Chapter 14; Paul Pellemans (UCL, Louvain-la-Neuve) reviewed Chapter 3 and Pol Jacobs (Volvo Trucks Belgium) was helpful in providing examples in the segmentation chapter. I am also grateful to my students—captive customers, but nevertheless attentive and demanding—to the teaching assistants of the Marketing Unit at our School (IAG), and in particular to Chantal de Moerloose who was very helpful in the revision process and efficient in detecting errors and the occasional lack of precision in the original text. For the translation, I received the assistance of Ms Shadman Mehta who provided me with an initial translation of eight chapters. Personal thanks to all of them.

Jean-Jacques Lambin
Bousval

Introduction

Why yet another introductory textbook on marketing? In other words, what distinctive qualities does this new product claim to offer? This question, central in strategic marketing, is just as relevant for an author as it is for an innovative firm.

Why this new introductory text?

A first objective is to close a cultural gap. In Europe, the marketing textbook market is largely dominated by American writers and I feel that there is a need for a text presenting the European perspective in English. In North America, the slogan 'What is good for business is good for society' is largely undisputed and, to my knowledge, there are few radicals among North American marketing academics or practitioners questioning the premises underlying the marketing discipline. Elsewhere, and in particular in European societies exposed to other social and political currents, this is not as obvious and the role of marketing is always controversial and often seriously challenged by different social groups. A first objective of this book is, therefore, to clarify the ideological foundations of marketing and to explain its role as a key determinant in a democratic economic system. This objective is particularly important for Eastern European countries which have recently chosen the road to a market economy.

A second objective of this book is to introduce upfront the strategic dimension in marketing while most introductory marketing textbooks tend to treat marketing management as a stand-alone business function and to overlook the hidden part of the marketing iceberg, i.e. the strategic choices on which marketing management decisions must be based. Similarly, most strategic marketing texts examine strategic decisions that are made at the corporate level but devote only scant attention to how these decisions are implemented at the operational level for individual brands or products. Our objective in writing this book is to propose a broader treatment of marketing integrating both its dimensions, strategic and operational. Marketing is both a business philosophy and an action-oriented process. Too often, the tendency among practitioners and the general public is to reduce marketing to its active dimension and to overlook the underlying business philosophy without which marketing is simply a set of short term selling tools.

Structure of the book

The overall structure of the book is summarized in Figure Intro.1.1. In the first chapter, we introduce a distinction between operational marketing (the action dimension) and strategic marketing (the analytical and philosophy dimension). In the new European macro-

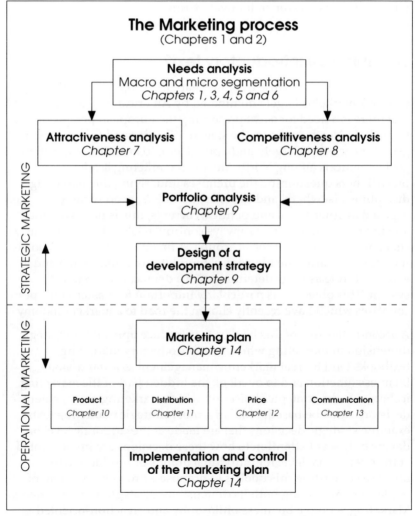

Figure Intro. 1.1 The overall structure of *Strategic Marketing*

marketing environment (Chapter 2), marketing is confronted with new challenging roles and priorities which require a reinforcement of strategic marketing and the adoption of a market orientation within the entire organization.

Strategic marketing is, to begin with, the analysis of the needs of individuals and organizations. From the marketing viewpoint, the buyer is not after a product as such, but after the solution to a problem that the product may provide. This solution may be obtained via different technologies which are themselves continuously changing (Chapter 3, 4 and 5). The role of strategic marketing is to follow the evolution of the firm's reference market and to identify various potential product markets or segments on the basis of an analysis of the needs which must be met (Chapter 6). Once the potential product markets are identified, the attractiveness of the economic opportunities must be evaluated. The appeal of a product market is quantitatively measured by the notion of market potential and dynamically measured by its economic life or its life cycle (Chapter 7). For any given firm, the appeal of a product market depends on its competitiveness, in other words, on its capacity to meet buyers' needs better than its rivals can. This competitiveness will exist as long as the firm holds a competitive advantage, either because it can differentiate itself from its rivals due to sustainable distinctive qualities, or because of higher productivity putting it at a cost advantage (Chapter 8). On the basis of this strategic audit, the market-driven firm can formulate an appropriate marketing strategy for each business unit included in its product portfolio (Chapter 9).

Operational marketing is the firm's commercial arm without which even the best strategic plan cannot lead to satisfactory results. It is an action-oriented process which is extended over a short- to medium-term planning horizon and targets existing markets or segments. It is the classic commercial process of achieving a targeted market share through the use of tactical means related to the product (Chapter 10), distribution (Chapter 11), price (Chapter 12) and communication (Chapter 13) decisions—the four Ps or the marketing mix as it is called in professional jargon. The strategic and operational marketing plan describes objectives, positioning, tactics and budgets for each business unit of the company's portfolio in a given period and geographical zone (Chapter 14).

The vigour of operational marketing is a decisive factor in the performance of the firm, especially in markets where competition is fierce. However, it is also clear that without solid strategic options, there can be no ultimately profitable operational marketing. Dynamism without thought is merely unnecessary risk. No matter how powerful an operational marketing plan is, it cannot create demands where there is no need, just as it cannot keep alive activities doomed to disappear. Hence, in order to be profitable, operational marketing must be founded upon a strategic design, which is itself based on the needs of the market and its expected evolution. The two roles of marketing are therefore closely complementary and cannot be disassociated.

There is nothing particularly sophisticated about the marketing concept and in today's European environment no one really argues with the importance of marketing. Despite this general agreement, many firms are simply paying lip service to the concept and are still limiting marketing to its operational dimension. Understanding the marketing concept is one thing; following through with the commitment to implementing this philosophy of action is quite another. A company that adopts this philosophy of action will have to set up a *market-driven organization* whose behaviour and actions are consistent with the marketing concept. Creating superior value for the buyer at a profit for the firm is much more than a marketing function. It must be the focus for the entire organization and not merely that of a single department. In other words, strategic marketing is far too important for the organization as a whole to be left to marketing people.

A European perspective

Another claim of this book is to propose to the reader a 'European Perspective' in *Strategic Marketing*. The question that comes readily to mind is then: is European marketing really different from, let's say, American or Japanese ways of conducting marketing? I strongly believe that significant differences do exist, not so much in terms of concepts or methods, but rather in terms of priorities, complexity and business philosophy. Three factors explain these differences:

- the challenge of European market integration
- European cultural diversity and pluralism
- the social accountability of European society.

European countries are confronted with a formidable challenge, the idea of unifying the European market by removing all non-tariff barriers that have existed in some countries for centuries. At a business level, European companies are analysing the impact of this market transformation, redefining their reference market, reassessing their competitiveness and determining appropriate strategies and organizational structure. In this new European context, sound strategic thinking and analysis becomes a priority preoccupation, not only for multinational firms, but for small- and medium-sized companies as well.

The European market is highly fragmented both in terms of culture and of consumer habits. The elimination of all barriers among European countries will create a borderless single market but not, however, an homogeneous single market. Cultural differences and variations in consumer attitudes across Europe will remain, even if European firms have the possibility of executing a common marketing programme throughout Europe. Thus European firms will have to cope with this cultural complexity and find adapted solutions. A level of standardization of consumer behaviour similar to the one observed in the US market will never be reached in Europe. The capacity to respect this diversity and to discover supranational segments will be a key factor to success.

European society is by far more advanced than American society in integrating individual, family and social values in economic life and public policy. The European firm has to cope with more severe societal constraints than the American firm. The slogan, largely accepted until recently by the business community—'the business of business is business'—is no longer true and the European firm cannot remain immune from societal interference and accountability. These societal constraints are the expression of new needs in society and come from public policy regulations, EC directives, green consumerists or environmentalists. They induce companies to widen the traditional marketing concept and to develop an increased consciousness of fallout generated by their marketing activity. In today's European socio-economic context, this greater societal sensitivity makes the concept of 'accountable marketing' particularly relevant.

Finally, this book offers a European perspective with the vast majority of examples and case histories being drawn from the European scene. It is also well illustrated with up-to-date European data and statistics.

Distinctive features

This text offers full coverage of both strategic marketing principles and key marketing decisions. The concluding chapter concentrates on the strategic and operational marketing plan by providing a set of questionnaires and forms which review the key concepts and issues that must be addressed in a strategic plan. In addition, other features characterize this book:

- It *discusses* the ideological foundations of marketing and its role in the turbulent environment of today's market economy.
- It *analyses* the structure of needs of both the individual consumer and of the organizational buyer.
- It *integrates* important theoretical concepts such as utility theory, buyer behaviour theory, attitude models, information theory . . . and stresses the application of this conceptual material to the realities of marketing.
- It *provides* an integrated treatment of consumer and industrial marketing underlining practical differences and conceptual similarities.
- It *offers* thorough coverage of macro and micro segmentation analyses illustrated by numerous examples taken from the European scene.
- It *gives* a general overview of the most popular market response measures provided by marketing research, void of all technical development.
- It *integrates* international and global marketing throughout the text rather than relegating it to a single chapter.
- It *contains* a section devoted to the distributor's strategic marketing, a topic often neglected in marketing textbooks.
- It is well *illustrated* with real life examples and up-to-date European data and statistics.

The target audience

This book was primarily designed for use as an introductory text in marketing by students in management and/or by business professionals who are looking for a thorough introduction to the foundations, concepts, methods and applications of marketing in both consumer and industrial markets.

More precisely, for business professionals, the book is particularly well suited for the following sub-groups:

- Marketing executives directly in charge of or participating in the development of a strategic marketing plan.
- Executives (often engineers) receiving the assignment to create or develop a marketing service or department, typically in high-tech, industrial or non-profit making organizations, where the marketing function was traditionally nonexistent or under-developed.
- Commercial executives or salespeople, having extensive field experience in selling or in advertising, and moving up to a more strategy-oriented marketing function within the firm.

- Consultants in strategic management with the mission of auditing a firm and formulating recommendations for its development.
- Executives of Eastern European and Russian companies participating in management training seminars and responsible for the restructuring of their firms.
- Experienced marketing executives who wish to structure their past experience and to gain insights into the major methods and concepts used in strategic marketing.

For students in management, the following sub-groups can be identified:

- Undergraduate students following a regular programme in Management, Applied Economics or Commercial Sciences.
- Postgraduate students holding a degree in Law, Engineering, Sociology, and attending a one-year postgraduate programme in Management.
- Post-experience students attending an MBA programme or equivalent in an International Business School.

1

The role of marketing in the firm and the market economy

Marketing is both a business philosophy and an action-oriented process. This first chapter aims to describe the *system of thought*: to clarify the ideological foundations of marketing and their main implications regarding the firm's operations and organization. As an *active process*, marketing fulfils a number of tasks necessary to the smooth functioning of a market economy. A second objective of this chapter is to describe these tasks, the importance and complexity of which have evolved with changes in technology, economics, competitiveness and the international environment. Within this framework we shall examine the implications of these environmental changes for the management of the firm, and particularly its marketing.

The ideological foundations of marketing

The term *marketing*, which has even entered the non-English vocabulary, is a word heavily loaded, debased and often misunderstood, not only by its detractors, but also by its proponents. Three popular meanings recur regularly:

- Marketing is advertising, promotion and hard selling, in other words a set of particularly aggressive *selling instruments* used to penetrate existing markets. In this first, very mercantile, sense of the word, marketing is viewed as mainly applicable to mass consumer markets and much less to more sophisticated sectors, such as high technology, financial services, public administration, and social and cultural services.
- Marketing is a set of *market analysis tools*, such as sales forecasting methods, simulation models and market research studies, used to develop a prospective and more scientific approach to needs and demand analysis. Such methods, often complex and costly, are

considered to be only available to large enterprises, and not to
small and medium-sized ones. The image projected is often that of
unnecessarily sophisticated tools, entailing high costs and little
practical value.

● Marketing is the hype, the *architect of the consumer society*; that is,
a market system where individuals are commercially exploited by
sellers. It is necessary to create new needs continuously, in order
to sell more and more. Consumers become alienated from the
seller, just as workers have become alienated from the employer.

Behind these somewhat oversimplified views there are three
characteristic dimensions to the concept of marketing: an *active*
aspect (the penetration of markets), an *analytic* aspect (the
understanding of markets) and an *ideological* aspect (a state of mind).
More often than not, the tendency is to reduce marketing to its active
dimension—that is, to a series of sales techniques (operational
marketing)—and to underestimate its analytic dimension (strategic
marketing).

Implicit in this vision of the role of marketing is the idea that
marketing and advertising are omnipotent, that they are capable of
making the market accept anything through powerful methods of
communication. Such hard selling methods are often devised
independently of any desire to satisfy the real needs of buyers. The
focus is on the needs of the seller, i.e. to achieve a sale.

The myth of the supremacy of marketing is a persistent theme,
despite the fact that there exists abundant proof to the contrary. For
example, the high proportion of new products and brands that fail
bears witness to the capacity of the market's resistance to the
allegedly seductive powers of producers.

The principle of consumer sovereignty

Although this misunderstanding goes very deep, the *theory* or
ideology which is the basis of marketing is totally different. The
philosophy at the base of marketing—what may be called the
marketing concept—rests in fact on a *theory of individual choice*
through the *principle of consumer sovereignty*. In this framework,
marketing is no more than the social expression of the principles
advocated by classical economists at the turn of the eighteenth
century translated into operational rules of management. These
principles, which were set forth by Adam Smith (1776), form the
basis of the market economy and can be summarized as follows:

> Society's well-being is the outcome, not so much of altruistic behaviour, but
> rather of the matching, through competitive exchange, of the buyer and
> seller's self-interest.

Starting from the principle that the pursuit of personal interest is an unfailing tendency in most human beings—which might be morally regrettable but remains a fact—Adam Smith suggested accepting people as they are, but developing a system that would make egocentric individuals contribute to the common good despite themselves. This is then the system of voluntary and competitive exchange, administered by the *invisible hand*, or the selfish pursuit of personal interests which in the end serves the interests of all.

Although in modern economies this basic principle has been amended with regard to social (solidarity) and societal (external effects, collective goods, Government regulations) issues, it nevertheless remains the main principle driving the economic activity of a successful firm operating in a freely competitive market. Furthermore, it is now clearer than ever before that those countries that rejected Adam Smith's ideas are now discovering, to their cost, that they have regressed economically. The recent turmoil in Eastern Europe and in the republics of the former Soviet Union gives a clear illustration of this.

At the root of the market economy we find four central ideas. These ideas seem simple, but have major implications regarding the philosophical approach to the market:

- Individuals strive for *rewarding experiences*; it is the pursuit of one's self-interest that drives individuals to produce and to work. This search is the engine of growth, of individual development, and eventually determines the overall well-being.
- *Individual choice* determines what is rewarding. This varies according to tastes, culture, values etc. Apart from respecting the ethical, moral and social rules imposed by society, no other judgement is implied as to the value or the triviality of this choice, or what might be regarded as 'true' or 'false' needs. The system is *pluralistic* and respects the diversity of tastes and preferences.
- It is through *free and competitive exchange* that individuals and the organizations they deal with will best realize their objectives. When exchange is free, it only takes place if its terms generate utility for both parties; when it is competitive, the risk of producers abusing their market power is limited (Friedman, 1980).
- The mechanisms of the market economy are based on the principle of individual freedom, and more particularly on the *principle of consumer sovereignty*. The moral foundation of the system rests on the recognition of the fact that individuals are responsible for their own actions and can decide what is or is not good for them.

The fields of marketing

Marketing is rooted in these four principles. This gives rise to a

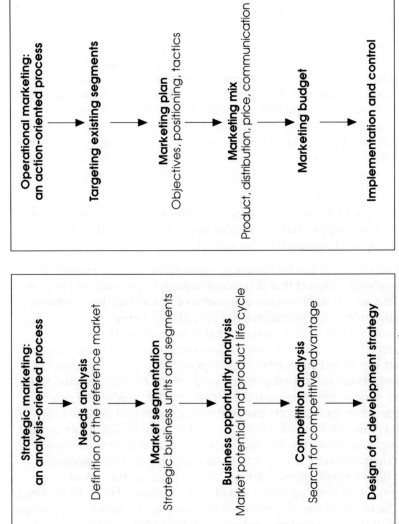

**Strategic marketing:
an analysis-oriented process**

Needs analysis
Definition of the reference market

Market segmentation
Strategic business units and segments

Business opportunity analysis
Market potential and product life cycle

Competition analysis
Search for competitive advantage

Design of a development strategy

**Operational marketing:
an action-oriented process**

Targeting existing segments

Marketing plan
Objectives, positioning, tactics

Marketing mix
Product, distribution, price, communication

Marketing budget

Implementation and control

Figure 1.1 The two faces of marketing

philosophy of action valid for any organization serving the needs of a group of buyers. The areas of marketing can be subdivided into three main fields:

- *Consumer marketing*, where transactions are between companies and end-consumers, individuals or households.
- *Organizational* or *business-to-business marketing*, where the two parties in the exchange process are organizations.
- *Social marketing*, which covers the field of activity of non-profit organizations such as museums, universities etc.

This approach implies that all activity within the organization must have the satisfaction of its users' needs as its main objective. Given that this is the best way of achieving its own goals of growth and profitability, it is not altruism, but the organization's self-interest that dictates this course of action.

Such is the ideology on which marketing is based. One can imagine that there may be a large gap between what marketing claims to be and what it is in reality. Flaws come readily to mind. Nevertheless, the successful firm must pursue the ideal of marketing. It may be a myth, but it is a *driving myth*, which must continuously guide the activities of the firm.

The two faces of marketing

The application of this philosophy of action assumes a two-fold approach on the part of the firm, as shown in Figure 1.1.

- The objectives of *strategic marketing* typically include a systematic and continuous analysis of the needs and requirements of key customer groups and the design and production of a product or service package that will enable the company to serve selected groups or segments more effectively than its competition. In serving these objectives, a firm is ensured a sustainable competitive advantage.
- The role of *operational marketing* involves the organization of distribution, sales and communication policies in order to inform potential buyers and to promote the distinctive qualities of the product while reducing the information costs. These objectives are implemented by the firm's branding policy, a key instrument for the application of the marketing concept.

We therefore propose the following definition of marketing:

Marketing is a social process, geared toward satisfying the needs and wants of individuals and organizations, through the creation of free competitive exchange of products and services that generate values to the buyer.

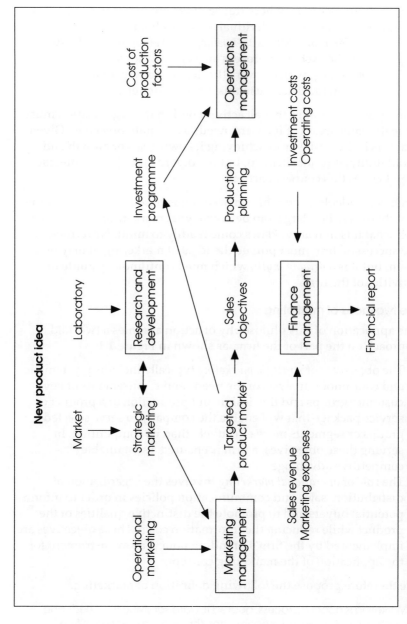

Figure 1.2 The role of marketing in the firm

The three key concepts in this definition are need, product and exchange. The notion of *need* calls into question the motivations and behaviour of the buyer, the individual consumer or the organizational client; *product* or service refers to the producers' response to market expectations; and *exchange* directs attention to the market and the mechanisms that ensure the interplay of demand and supply.

The role of marketing in the firm

The term 'marketing'—literally the process of delivering to the market—does not express the inherent duality of the process very well and emphasizes the 'active' side of marketing more than the 'analytic' side. (As an aside, we may point out that to avoid the ambiguity—and the use of an English word in the common vocabulary—the French Academy (l'Académie Française) coined the terms *'la mercatique'* and *'le marchéage'* to illustrate these two facets of marketing. In practice, however, these terms are seldom used by the French business community.) The terms strategic and operational marketing are therefore used in practice.

Operational marketing

Operational marketing is an *action-oriented process* which is extended over a short- to medium-term planning horizon and targets existing markets or segments. It is the classical commercial process of achieving a target market share through the use of *tactical means* related to the product, distribution (place), price and communication (promotion) decisions (the 'four Ps', or the 'marketing mix', as they are called in the professional jargon). The operational marketing plan describes objectives, positioning, tactics and budgets for each brand of the company's portfolio in a given period and geographical zone.

The economic role that marketing plays in the operation of the firm is shown in Figure 1.2. The main relationships between the four major managerial functions (research and development, operations, marketing and finance) are illustrated.

The main task of operational marketing is to generate sales revenues, i.e. the target turnover. This means to 'sell' and to get purchase orders by using the most efficient sales methods while at the same time minimizing costs. The objective of realizing a particular sales volume translates into a manufacturing programme as far as the operations department is concerned, and a programme of storage and physical distribution for the sales department. Operational marketing is therefore a determining factor which directly influences the short-term profitability of the firm.

The vigour of operational marketing is a decisive factor in the performance of the firm, especially in those markets where competition is fierce. Every product, even those of superior quality, must have a price acceptable to the market, be available in the network of distribution adapted to the purchasing habits of the targeted customers, and be supported by some form of communication which promotes the product and enhances its distinctive qualities. It is rare to find market situations where demand exceeds supply or where the firm is well known by potential users or where competition is non-existent.

There are many examples of promising products that have failed to prevail in the market due to insufficient commercial support. This is particularly the case in firms where the 'engineering' spirit predominates, whereby it is believed that a good quality product can gain recognition by itself, and the firm lacks the humility to adapt to the needs of customers. Latin culture is especially susceptible to this attitude: Mercury was the god of merchants as well as of thieves and Christ expelled the tradesmen from the Temple; as a result, selling and advertising are still often viewed as shameful diseases.

Operational marketing is the most dramatic and the most visible aspect of the discipline of marketing, particularly because of the important role played by advertising and promotional activities. Some firms—banks for example (Kotler, 1988, p.26)—have embarked on marketing through advertising. On the contrary, some other firms – like many producers of industrial goods—have for a long time tended to believe that marketing doesn't apply to their business, thus implicitly linking marketing to advertising.

Operational marketing is therefore the firm's *commercial arm*, without which even the best strategic plan cannot lead to satisfactory results. However, it is also clear that without solid strategic options there can be no ultimately profitable operational marketing. Dynamism without thought is merely unnecessary risk. No matter how powerful an operational marketing plan, it cannot create demand where there is no need, just as it cannot keep alive activities doomed to disappear. Hence, in order to be profitable, operational marketing must be founded upon a strategic design, which is itself based on the needs of the market and its expected evolution.

Strategic marketing

Strategic marketing is, to begin with, the analysis of the *needs* of individuals and organizations. From the marketing viewpoint, the buyer is not seeking a product as such, but wants the *solution to a problem*, which the product might provide. This solution may be obtained via different technologies, which are themselves continually changing. The role of strategic marketing is to follow the evolution of the *reference market* and to identify various existing or potential *product markets* or *segments* on the basis of an analysis of the needs to be met.

Once the product markets are identified, they represent economic opportunities whose *attractiveness* needs to be evaluated. The appeal of a product market is quantitatively measured by the notion of the *potential market*, and dynamically measured by its economic life or its *life cycle*. For a given firm, the appeal of a product market depends on its own *competitiveness*, in other words on its capacity to meet buyers' needs better than its rivals. This competitiveness will exist as long as the firm holds a *competitive advantage*, either because it can differentiate itself from its rivals due to sustainable distinctive qualities, or because of higher productivity, putting it at a cost advantage.

Figure 1.2 shows the various stages of strategic marketing in relation to the firm's other major functions. Irrespective of whether a product is *market-pull* or *technology-push*, it has to undergo the process of strategic marketing to evaluate its economic and financial viability. The interface between Research and Development, Operations and strategic marketing plays a decisive role in this respect. The choice of the product market that results from this confrontation is of crucial importance in determining production capacity and investment decisions, and hence is vital to the equilibrium of the firm's overall financial structure.

The role of strategic marketing is therefore to lead the firm towards attractive economic opportunities; that is, opportunities which are adapted to its resources and know-how, and which offer a *potential for growth and profitability*. The process of strategic marketing has a medium- to long-term horizon; its task is to specify the firm's *mission*, define objectives, elaborate a development strategy and ensure a balanced structure of the product portfolio.

The integrated marketing process

This job of reflection and strategic planning is very different from operational planning, and requires different talents in the individuals who exercise it. Nevertheless, the two roles are closely complementary in the sense that the design of a strategic plan must be done in close relation to operational marketing. Operational marketing emphasizes non-product variables (distribution, advertising and promotion), while strategic marketing tends to

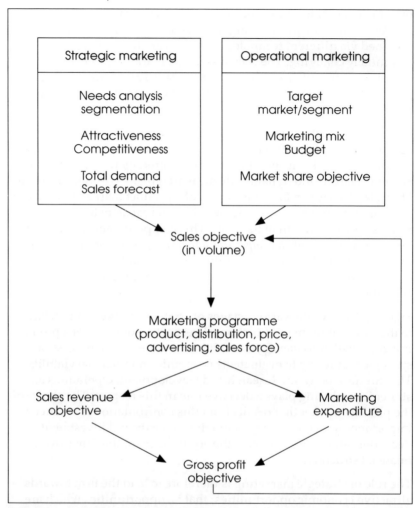

Figure 1.3 The integrated marketing process

emphasize the ability to provide a product with superior value at a competitive cost. Strategic marketing leads to the choice of product markets to be exploited in order of priority and the forecast of total demand in each of these product markets. Operational marketing, on the other hand, sets out market share objectives to reach in the target product market, as well as the marketing budgets necessary for their realization.

As shown in Figure 1.3, the comparison of the market share objective and total demand forecast in each product market makes it possible to develop a sales objective first in volume and then in terms of turnover, given the chosen pricing policy. The expected gross profit is obtained after deducting direct manufacturing costs, possible fixed costs for specific structures, marketing expenditure attributed to the sales force, and advertising and promotion as allowed for in the marketing budget. This gross profit is the contribution of the product market to the firm; it must cover overhead costs and leave a net profit.

The new role of strategic marketing

Some firms tend to confine strategic thinking to the managerial staff who support the managing director and who are based in headquarters, far from the field. But to be efficient, a strategy must be based on a deep knowledge of the market, and its implementation requires coherent plans of market penetration, as well as distribution, price and advertising policies. Without these, even the best plan has little chance of success. The chosen marketing organization must reflect this necessity and ensure that the main goals of strategic marketing are adhered to at all levels of the firm through cross-functional coordination. In large firms, a product management organization has proved to be very successful; in small or medium-sized firms, the same results can be obtained by temporary and periodic structures, such as a strategic planning task force of the key managers.

Most successful firms adopt strategic planning in one way or another. This function is clearly becoming significantly more important with the technological, economic, competitive and sociocultural changes characterizing the 1980s and '90s and the advent of the single market in Europe.

These changes emphasize the need by the firm to consolidate its strategic marketing in order (a) to base its activities on *strategic options* which are solid and well-defined, (b) to develop *systems of monitoring* the marketing environment and *analysing competitiveness*, (c) to reinforce the *capacity to adapt* to changes in the environment and (d) to regularly *re-evaluate the portfolio of businesses.*

Various empirical studies, both in Europe and in the United States, have shown the effectiveness of strategic marketing. Cooper, for example (1979), analyses the causes for the success of more than two hundred new industrial products. He finds that two out of the three key factors of success are direct results of the quality of strategic marketing: (a) superior quality from the buyer's point of view and the existence of distinctive qualities and (b) the understanding of the market and marketing know-how. It is worth noting that Booz *et al.* (1982) reached the same conclusions in their study of more than 13 000 new products. More recently, Narver and Slater (1989), using a sample of 140 strategic business units, have found that a market orientation has a substantial positive effect on the profitability of the business units studied.

Market-driven management

There is nothing particularly sophisticated about the marketing concept as stated by Ames and Hlavacels (1989, p. 30). In today's competitive environment, no one really argues with the importance of marketing. In fact, it would probably be hard to find anyone to argue against the idea that gearing all activities of a business to be responsive to customer or user needs is not only sensible, but the only way to run a business. Despite this general agreement, many companies are simply paying lip service to the concept or are not particularly happy with what marketing has done for them. Understanding the marketing concept is one thing; following through with the commitment to implementing this philosophy of action is quite another.

A company that adopts this philosophy of action will have to set up a *market-driven organization* whose behaviour and actions are consistent with the marketing concept. Creating superior value for the buyer at a profit is much more than a marketing function. It is the focus of the entire organization and not merely that of a single department. In other words, strategic marketing is too important for the organization as a whole to be left to the marketing people.

As shown by Narver and Slater (1989) and summarized in Figure 1.4, for an organization to achieve above-normal market performance it must achieve a sustainable competitive advantage which is the result of continuously creating superior value for customers. The three key behavioural components of a market-driven orientation identified are customer orientation, competitor orientation and interfunctional coordination.

- *Customer orientation* includes the organization's level of customer commitment and its efforts to create value for the customer, to understand customer needs and to anticipate new customers' problems.
- *Competitor orientation* includes understanding of competitor strengths and weaknesses, anticipation of competitors' strategies, and speed of response to competitors' actions.
- *Interfunctional coordination* refers to the dissemination of market information within the organization, functional integration in strategy formulation, and use of the perspectives and skills of departments other than the marketing department to assess customers' needs and problems.

We add a fourth component of a market-driven orientation, which is

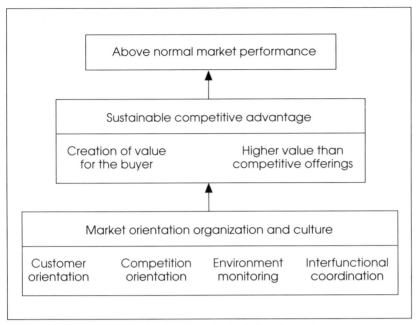

Figure 1.4 The components of a market orientation (adapted from Narver and Slater (1989))

environment monitoring, or the continuing analysis of substitute technologies, social changes and government regulations which might constitute opportunities or threats for the firm.

Thus strategic marketing covers a field which is much broader than the traditional domain of marketing management, since it includes the organizational culture and climate that most effectively encourages the behaviours that are necessary for the successful implementation of the marketing concept. We therefore propose the following definition of strategic marketing:

> The process adopted by a firm, having a market-driven orientation, to achieve above-normal market performance by continuously creating products or services which provide the buyer with a *higher quality* product than the competition.

The key concepts here are value to the buyer, competitive superiority and above-normal profit performance.

The role of marketing in a market economy

In a market economy, the role of marketing is to *organize free and competitive exchange* so as to ensure efficient matching of supply and demand of goods and services. This matching is not spontaneous and requires *liaison activities* at two levels:

- Organization of *exchange*, in other words the physical flow of goods between the manufacturing and the consumption sites.
- Organization of *communication*, in other words the flow of information to precede, accompany and follow exchange in order to ensure efficient meeting of supply and demand.

The role of marketing in society is therefore to *organize exchange and communication between sellers and buyers*. This definition emphasizes the tasks and functions of marketing, irrespective of the purpose of the process of exchange. As such, it applies to both commercial and to non-profit-making activities, and in general to any situation where free exchange takes place between an organization and the users of the products and services it offers.

Organization of exchange transactions

The organization of the exchange of goods and services is the responsibility of the distribution process, whose task is to move goods from a state of production to a state of consumption. This flow of products to the consumption state creates three types of utility, thus giving distribution a higher value added.

- *State utility*   The set of all material transformations putting goods in a consumable state: these are operations such as fragmenting, packaging, assortment etc.
- *Place utility*   Spatial transformations, such as transport, geographical allocation etc., which contribute to putting goods at the disposal of users at places of utilization, transformation or consumption.
- *Time utility*   Temporal transformations, such as storage, which make goods available at the time chosen by the user.

It is these various functions that make manufactured goods accessible and available to the targeted customers, and thus allow the actual matching of supply and demand.

Historically, these tasks of distribution have mainly been performed by autonomous intermediaries, such as sales agents, wholesalers, retailers and industrial distributors, in other words by what is called the *distribution sector*. Some functions of the distribution process have been integrated, for instance on the manufacturing side (direct marketing), on the consumption side (consumers' cooperatives), and on the distribution side (supermarkets, chainstores etc.).

Furthermore, some vertical marketing systems have been developed which group together independent firms involved at various stages of the production and/or distribution process. This is done in order to coordinate their commercial activities, to realize economies in operating costs and thus to reinforce their impact on the market. Examples include voluntary chains, retailer cooperatives and franchise organizations. In many sectors, vertical marketing systems tend to supplant the very fragmented traditional distribution channels. They form one of the most significant developments in the tertiary sector, which has helped to intensify the competitive struggle between various forms of distribution and to improve the productivity of distribution significantly.

The value added by distribution is measured by the *distribution margin*, which is the difference between the price paid to the producer by the first buyer and the price paid by the ultimate user or consumer of the product. The distribution margin may therefore include the margins of one or many distributors; for example those of the wholesalers and the retailers. Therefore, the distributive margin remunerates the functions performed by the intermediaries. In the consumer goods sectors, it is estimated that the cost of exchange, covering the whole range of tasks performed by distribution, is about 40 per cent of the retail price. The cost of distribution represents a significant part of the price paid by the buyer in all sectors of activity.

Organization of communication flows

The merging of the various practical conditions for exchange is not sufficient to ensure efficient adjustment of demand and supply. For exchange of goods to take place, potential buyers must be equally aware and informed of the existence of goods or of the combination of alternative attributes likely to meet their needs. Communication activities are aimed at accumulating knowledge for manufacturers, distributors and buyers. As shown in Figure 1.5, it is possible to distinguish seven different flows of communication in a typical market.

1 Before investing, the collection of information is initiated by the producer in order to identify the buyer's needs and wants which constitute an attractive opportunity for him or her. This is typically the role of *market research* prior to an investment decision.
2 Similarly, the potential buyer (mostly industrial) initiates a study of the possibilities offered by suppliers and invitations to tender (sourcing research).
3 After production, the manufacturer's communication programme is oriented towards distribution—a *push strategy*—with the objective of obtaining product referencing and the cooperation of distributors with regards to selling space, promotion and price.

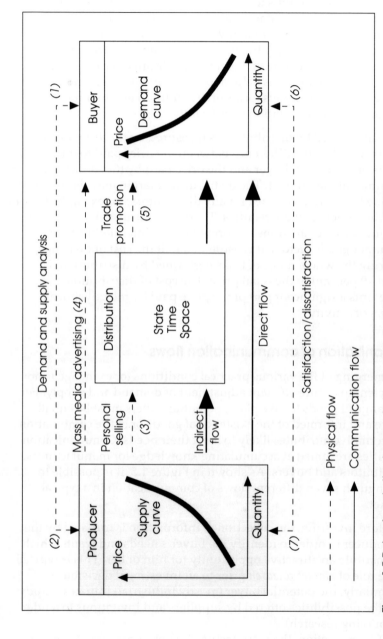

Figure 1.5 Role of marketing in a market economy (Lambin and Peeters, 1977)

4 The manufacturer initiates collection of information on all forms of brand advertising or direct selling activities aimed at making end-buyers aware of the existence of the brand's distinctive qualities: a *pull strategy.*

5 Activities of promotion and communication prompted by distributors aimed at creating store loyalty, building traffic through promotional activities, supporting proprietary brands, informing about sales terms etc.

6 After utilization or consumption of goods, the measurement of *satisfaction* or *dissatisfaction*, through surveys of consumer panels, carried out by the marketer so as to enable the firm to adjust supply to buyers' reactions.

7 After utilization or consumption of goods, *claims* and evaluations through comparative testing transmitted spontaneously by buyers, acting alone or in organized groups (consumerism).

In small markets, communication takes place spontaneously between the various parties of the exchange process. In large markets, there is a significant physical and psychological gap between the parties, and communication needs to be specifically organized.

The changing priority of marketing

Viewed from the standpoint of the organization of communication and exchange in a market economy, it is clear that, in spite of its current prominence, marketing is not a new activity, given that it covers tasks which have always existed and have always been taken care of one way or another in any system based on free exchange. Even in an autarky, founded on the most elementary form of exchange—barter—there are flows of exchange and communication, but their manifestation is spontaneous and neither requires the allocation of specific resources, nor any form of organization to ensure their functioning.

It is the complexity of the technological, economic and competitive environment that has gradually led firms first to create and then to reinforce the marketing function. Hence it is interesting to follow the history of this evolution in order to understand better the present role of marketing. One can distinguish three stages, each characterized by a priority marketing objective: passive marketing, operational marketing and active marketing.

Passive marketing: the product concept

Passive marketing is a form of organization prevalent in an economic environment characterized by the existence of a potentially important market, but where *supply is scarce*, with insufficient available production capacity to meet the market's needs. Demand is therefore higher than supply. Passive marketing, to work, also implies that needs are known and stable and that technological innovation in the reference market proceeds at a slow pace.

This type of economic situation was observed, for instance, at the beginning of this century during the industrial revolution, and more recently in the period immediately after the Second World War. This environment continues to prevail in many developing countries at present and particularly in Eastern Europe.

It is clear that in a situation characterized by scarce supply, marketing has a limited and passive role. Given that needs are known, strategic marketing is performed naturally, operational marketing is reduced to organizing the flow of manufactured goods, and promotional activity is rendered superfluous, given that the firm cannot supply the market as it would have liked. Contacts with the market are often limited to the first echelon, that is the first buyer of the product, who is usually an intermediary, wholesaler or industrial distributor. There is therefore little contact with final demand and market research is infrequent. This state of affairs is also reflected in the organization of the firm, which is dominated by the operations function, with the development of production capacity and improvement of productivity as the main priorities. Marketing is there to sell what has already been produced.

When a firm adopts the 'product concept' it is, in general, structurally organized with the following characteristics:

- A *functional disequilibrium* in the sense that, in the organizational chart, marketing does not occupy the same hierarchical level as the other functions, such as operations, finance or personnel.
- The first level of marketing is *commercial service*, in charge of sales administration and in contact with the first buyer in the distributive chain, not necessarily with the end-user.
- The product decisions are made by operations management; selling prices and sales forecasts are the responsibility of the financial department. There is typically a *dispersion of responsibilities* as far as the marketing instruments are concerned (the four Ps).

This kind of organization fosters the development of the *product concept*, based on the implicit assumption that the firm knows what is good for the buyer and the latter shares this conviction. Moreover, the managers of such firms are often convinced that they are producing a superior good and tend to take it for granted that buyers will continue to want their products. They tend to have an *inside-in perspective*, where the emphasis is placed on internal constraints and preoccupations and not on the customer's requirements or expectations.

Such a viewpoint—typical of a bureaucratic organization—is therefore completely opposed to the idea of the buyer who views a product as a solution to a problem.

This state of mind is conceivable in an environment where demand exceeds supply, where buyers are prepared to buy any kind of product if they can find it. In reality, such market conditions are exceptional, and when they prevail they are temporary. The danger of the product concept is that it makes the firm myopic in its outlook and does not encourage a proactive behaviour, i.e. one that will anticipate a change in the environment and prepare itself accordingly.

Passive marketing is a form of marketing organization which is no longer suitable for the environment facing the majority of firms in industrialized countries today. The product concept nevertheless persists in some firms, mainly among industrial firms or financial services firms, such as insurance companies. The lack of market orientation is a major cause of many bankruptcies. It is also the dominant state of mind observed among Eastern European firms, which have found themselves suddenly confronted with the formidable challenge of the market and of competition.

Until recently, the product concept also dominated in developing countries, mainly among experts of economic development. But even there marketing can play an active role and contribute towards economic development, to the extent however that such methods are now adapted to situations which are totally different from industrialized countries. See the excellent article by de Maricourt (1978) on this subject.

Operational marketing: the selling concept

Operational marketing puts the emphasis on the *selling concept*. In Western European countries this approach to management was progressively adopted by firms in the consumer goods industry during the 1950s, when demand was expanding rapidly and production capacity was available. On the other hand, although these markets were in full growth, the distributive system was often deficient and unproductive.

The following changes in the economy are the cause of this new approach to marketing management:

- The appearance of *new forms of distribution*, mainly self-service, have helped to modify the productivity of conventional distribution networks which were not adapted to the requirements of mass distribution.

- The *geographical widening of markets*, and the resulting physical and psychological gap between producers and consumers, has made it increasingly necessary to resort to means of communication such as mass media advertising.
- The development of *branding policies*, a requirement for self-service selling and a way for the firm to control its final demand.

The priority objective of marketing at this stage is to create an efficient commercial organization. The role of marketing becomes less passive. Now the task is to *find and organize markets* for the products made. At this stage, most firms concentrate on the needs of the central core of the market, with products which satisfy the needs of the majority of buyers. Markets are therefore weakly segmented and strategic decisions regarding product policy remain the responsibility of the operations department. The main function of marketing is to organize the efficient distribution of products and to manage all tasks that fall under this process of commercialization.

As far as the organizational structure is concerned, these changes in priorities translate into the creation of a *sales* or a *commercial department*, and one can observe a readjustment of functions. These sales departments are given the task of setting up a sales network, organizing physical distribution, advertising and promotion. They also manage market research programmes, which are beginning to manifest their importance, for example in analysing buying habits, the effectiveness of advertising and the impact of branding and packaging policies etc.

The selling concept

The *selling concept* is a characteristic often present in operational marketing. Its implicit assumptions are as follows:

- Consumers naturally tend to resist buying 'unsought products'.
- Consumers can be pushed to buy more by using different means of sales stimulation.
- The firm must create a powerful sales department and use substantial promotional means to attract and keep customers (Kotler, 1988).

Thus, within the firm, marketing people tend to have an *inside-out perspective*, and to give priority to the company's objectives over the customer's post-purchase satisfaction. The underlying assumption is that good selling is always 'salesperson-driven'.

Some industries which make products not naturally sought by

buyers, such as life insurance and encyclopaedias, have developed hard selling techniques, which have become popularized through various writings on the 'Art of Selling'. Furthermore, when there is extra capacity in a sector it is not unusual to see firms wanting to liquidate their stocks employing these methods by aggressively using television commercials, direct mail, newspaper advertisements etc. It is therefore not surprising to see that the public at large, as well as some firms, tends to equate marketing with hard selling or even forced selling.

During the last few years, the notion of the role of the seller has changed a lot in firms with a marketing orientation (see, for example, Miller and Heiman, 1987). The marketing concept has replaced and reversed the logic of the selling concept. As stated by the General Electric Company shortly after the Second World War,

> Rather than making what you have always made, then trying to sell it, find out what will sell, then try to make it.

In this framework, the role of the seller becomes less one of 'trying to sell' as one of 'helping to buy'. The process of selling initially bases itself on the needs of the buyer. This kind of commercial attitude can only be practical in an organization where the marketing orientation dominates. To quote Drucker (1973, pp. 64–5):

> There will always, one can assume, be need for some selling. But the aim of marketing is to make selling superfluous. The aim of marketing is to know and understand the customer so well that the product or service fits him and sells itself. Ideally, marketing should result in a customer who is ready to buy. All that should be needed then is to make the product or service available.

This ideal situation will only rarely be achieved, but it is important to remember that such is the objective of the marketing theory discussed earlier.

The risk of manipulative or wild marketing

Operational marketing has encouraged the development of the selling concept, which implies a degree of *commercial aggressiveness*, with the implicit assumption that the market can absorb everything if enough pressure is applied. Judging by the high rate of growth of private consumption and the level of household equipment purchased during the immediate post-war period, this selling policy did prove to be efficient.

However, the efficiency of the selling concept must be evaluated by keeping in mind the situation at the time, i.e. a fundamentally expanding market, weakly differentiated products, and consumers who were less experienced as buyers. The risk run by the selling

Table 1.1 Some examples of wild marketing practices

- Sales of defective or dangerous products.
- Exaggeration of the product's content through the use of flashy packaging design.
- Resorting to fraudulent practices with regard to price and delivery policies.
- Resorting to promotional techniques which exploit impulsive buyer behaviour.
- Advertisements which exaggerate the product's attributes and the promises that these attributes represent.
- Advertisements which exploit the agonies and anxieties of individuals.
- Enticing people to over-consume using hard selling methods.

In the long run, 'wild marketing' is self-destructive for a company or for a brand and goes against its best interests.

concept is to consider this commercial approach as being valid in any situation and to confuse it with the marketing concept. Levitt (1960, p. 48) compares the two concepts as follows:

> Selling focuses on the needs of the seller, marketing on the needs of the buyer. Selling is preoccupied with the seller's need to convert his product into cash; marketing with the idea of satisfying the needs of the customer by means of the product and the whole cluster of things associated with creating, delivering and finally consuming it.

An over-enthusiastic use of advertising and selling can lead to *manipulative marketing* or *wild marketing*, which tries to mould demand to the requirements of supply rather than adapt supply to the expectations of demand. Table 1.1 illustrates some examples of commercial practice which can be classified as wild marketing. The excesses of wild marketing have led to the birth of a countervailing power in the form of consumers' organizations, initiated by consumers, and in the form of legislation which increasingly reinforces the protection of consumers' legal rights, prompted by public authorities.

Active marketing: the marketing concept

The phase of active marketing is characterized by the development and/or the reinforcement of the role of strategic marketing and by the adoption of a customer orientation within the firm. Three factors are at the root of this evolution:

- Acceleration in the rate at which *technological progress* diffuses and penetrates.
- Maturity of markets and the progressive *saturation* of the needs of the core market.
- Increased *internationalization* of markets as a result of the progressive lifting of barriers to international trade.

We shall examine these three factors of change successively, as well as their implications for the marketing function in the firm.

Technological progress

One of the significant features of the period between the Marshall Plan (1947) and the creation of OPEC is the extraordinary diffusion of technological progress, which penetrated and influenced most industrial sectors within a few years. As a result, we saw, during 25 years of continuous growth, a real explosion of new products and new industries, both quantitatively and qualitatively. A large number of products that we use daily today did not exist a short while ago. Frequently it is observed that in successful companies, 40–60 per cent of their turnover comes from products which did not exist five years ago.

As far as technological progress is concerned, this period was more a period of innovation rather than a period of invention. The distinction between innovation and invention is important. *Invention* is the creative act underlying an innovation. *Innovation* is the creative and successful implementation of a concept, a discovery, or a progressive invention. Innovation is therefore the result of an explicit will to change and not the simple consequence of a stroke of good fortune. Although the pace of technological penetration accelerated rapidly during the 25 years after the Second World War, technology itself followed the path that had already been drawn previously. The new technologies of the 1950s, 1960s and 1970s were mostly based on science and knowledge developed before the First World War, with two major exceptions, computers and antibiotics. When we talk about technological progress in this period, we are essentially talking about technological extensions, developments and modifications and not about structural technological change, which is the case at the present time.

The diffusion of technological progress results from *acceleration*, generalization and systematic approach in scientific research. By acceleration, we mean that we observe an increasing rate of innovation and a shorter time frame required to pass from development to commercial exploitation on a large scale.

This evolution implies a shorter technological life for products and

Table 1.2 Shortening of the Product Life Cycle
An example: the computer market

Development phases	Average duration (months)			
	1981	**1984**	**1988**	**1991**
R&D	24	20	18	8
Market research	9	7	4	2
Expected life	88	48	24	12

(*Source:* Dataquest, April 1992, SVM 25.)

hence the time available for recovering R&D costs. Table 1.2
illustrates this point in the computer market sector.

The spread of technological progress is *generalized* throughout
sectors, firms and countries. Few sectors have been sheltered from
technological innovations, some of which are, as Schumpeter (1949)
put it 'destructive'; that is, they menace or eliminate existing
industries.

Basic sectors such as steel, leather, textiles and paper, have always
been threatened by substitutes coming from industries which are
technologically very distant. This evolution calls for a closer scrutiny
of the technological and competitive environment.

The spread of technological progress is *systematic*, in the sense that,
unlike the days when scientific research was carried out by more or
less isolated individuals, it has now become institutionalized in
firms, universities and private or public specialized centres.
Governments play a significant role in this domain, by allocating
important resources to help scientific and industrial research.

Technological innovation no longer depends on the chance of
inventions. As Ladrière (1984, p. 33) points out, innovation is the
outcome of a concerted and planned effort, which itself is directed by
some theoretical representations. There is continuity in the
elaboration of theoretical tools, which is the job of fundamental
research, and the implementation of methods that can be directly
used in the production of goods and services. Research itself is
planned according to tested methods and in terms of objectives laid
out in advance.

This technological evolution has a direct bearing on product policy
and forces the firm, for example, to review the structure of its product
portfolio at a much faster rate than before. Therefore this increased
dependence on the technological environment requires a
strengthening of the role to be played by market analysis and
environment monitoring.

Saturation of the core market

The rapid expansion of the economy during the 1960s led to a saturation of demand for products corresponding to the basic needs of the market, and this evolution is a second significant change which has contributed once again to the modification of the role of marketing in the firm. This change manifested itself with the appearance of a potential demand for products adapted more specifically to the needs of distinct groups of consumers and buyers. This evolution, which appeared at different times in different sectors, leads to market *fragmentation* and strategies of *segmentation*. As an example, let us examine the following fictitious case.

A firm is contemplating the launching of a new aperitif in the market and is wondering about the preference of potential consumers as to the degree of bitterness of the aperitif. Various tests are organized showing that the majority of consumers prefer a medium level of bitterness, as shown in the preference distribution of Figure 1.6.

The tests also show that some consumers, fewer in number, prefer a higher degree of bitterness and others a lower degree of bitterness. A situation of *diffused preferences* is typical of a latent market and the firm must decide how to position its product with respect to this dominant feature (Kuehn and Day, 1962).

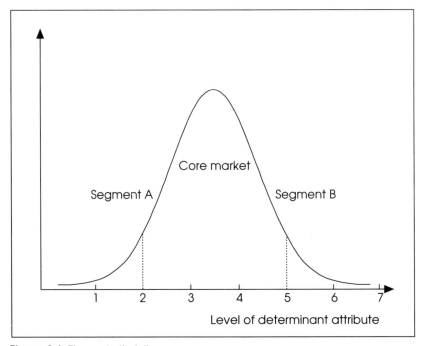

Figure 1.6 The majority fallacy

The natural tendency is to follow the *'majority rule'* and develop a product at a medium level (say level 4) of a significant product characteristic, so as to correspond to the preferences of the core of the market and thus minimize total dissatisfaction and fulfil the expectations of the greatest number. The pioneering firm thus finds access to the most important potential market and also benefits from economies of scale in production and distribution. At this stage, the firm will be exercising operational marketing to penetrate the market as rapidly as possible.

Market choices will therefore crystallize over products designed to meet the expectations of the majority. Peripheral preferences will not be met and this group of consumers will have to accept compromises. If successful, the pioneer will soon be followed by many imitators and the situation will progressively lead towards the *'majority fallacy'*, whereby all competing brands are clustered at the same medium level of the relevant product characteristic (Kuehn and Day, 1962).

The *active marketing* stage appears when the needs of the core market are saturated as a result of this situation, where a large number of competitors are making similar offers. At this stage it becomes worthwhile to rediscover the neglected differences in preferences and pay attention to the peripheral segments by launching products specially conceived to meet their needs.

In the example above, the latecomer on the market analysing consumers' preferences, makes the same observations as before. However, by launching one very smooth (level 2) and simultaneously one very bitter aperitif (level 5), the alert firm can hope to gain a total market share well over what it would gain if it launched a similar product (a 'me too') to the existing ones at level 4, where all the competing brands are clustered.

These segments are certainly smaller, but nevertheless they constitute an unexploited potential, given that these consumers have never found a product in the market corresponding to their preferences. The firm will adopt a *segmentation strategy* (based here on taste) and the market will subdivide into segments which correspond to the differentiated products. This stage, called the *segmentation stage*, requires a finer understanding from the firm of the market and of the benefits sought by different groups of buyers.

At this maturity stage of the market, product policy must therefore be increasingly based on the analysis of needs and the services expected from products. In industrialized economies, most markets adequately meet basic needs. Finding growing segments is not an easy task, but requires a deep understanding of markets, needs, users and the use of products. This knowledge can only be achieved by strengthening the 'analytic' aspect of marketing, that is by using strategic marketing and by adopting a customer orientation.

Internationalization of markets

The period now referred to as the 'Golden Sixties' corresponds to the beginning of the internationalization of markets, a process which has continued up to the 1990s. At the European level, internationalization took the form of the creation of the Common Market; at the world level it took the form of GATT (General Agreement on Tariffs and Trade) and the resulting progressive liberalization of trade, the end of the Cold War and the expansion of East–West trade. All these factors contributed to the widening markets, and, in general, to the intensification of competition and the reappraisal of established competitive positions.

Market-driven organization

The three groups of changes we have just examined all imply a consolidation of strategic marketing in the firm. As far as the organization of the firm with an 'active marketing' orientation is concerned, the significant change will be in regard to *product decisions*, which will henceforth be the responsibility of the marketing department in close liaison with the R&D department and the manufacturing department. This means that in actual practice, strategic marketing regulates product policy and decides whether products are economically viable. The idea of new products may come from anywhere: manufacturing, R&D or any other source, but it must first pass through the test of strategic marketing before adoption and manufacturing, as shown in Figure 1.7.

Firms which have adopted the marketing concept will have a marketing department whose responsibilities will comprise all the tasks that flow from operational marketing and strategic marketing (see Table 1.3), including the choice of product markets. At this stage, the market-oriented firm has an 'outside-in perspective' and places

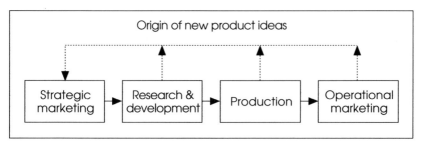

Figure 1.7 The marketing–R&D–production interface

Table 1.3 Contrasting operational and strategic marketing

Operational marketing	Strategic marketing
Action-oriented	Analysis-oriented
Existing opportunities	New opportunities
Non-product variables	Product market variables
Stable environment	Dynamic environment
Reactive behaviour	Pro-active behaviour
Day-to-day management	Longer range management
Marketing department	Cross-functional organization

priority emphasis on customers' expectations as a starting point for its product policy.

Limitations of the marketing concept

The implicit assumption at the root of the marketing concept is that *satisfying buyers' needs* is the prime objective of the firm, not because of altruism, but because it is the best way for the firm to achieve its own profit and/or growth objectives.

As in the case of the product concept and the selling concept, the marketing concept has its own limitations, of which one should be aware. An over-enthusiastic adoption of the marketing concept can lead the firm to put too much emphasis on products in high demand, or *market-pull*, at the expense of products yet unknown but *pushed by technology*. A marketing strategy exclusively guided by market wishes inevitably tends to favour minor and less revolutionary innovations than those proposed by the laboratory. Such innovations, which correspond to needs felt and expressed by the market, are by this token less risky and are therefore seen as more attractive to the firm. On the other hand, a strategy based on technological advance is more likely to lead to a breakthrough innovation and hence ensure that the firm has a long-term competitive advantage which is more difficult to catch up with (Bennett and Cooper, 1979). Most *breakthrough innovations* in fact originate from the laboratory and not from the market. It is therefore important to maintain a balance between these two strategies of product development: 'technology-push' and 'market-pull'.

Irrespective of the origin of the new product, however, the test of strategic marketing remains essential, and must take place very early in the process of new product development. The high rates of failure in products convincingly prove this assertion (Urban *et al.*, 1987, p. 41).

The practical application of the marketing concept in new product development is not without difficulty. When a new product is very innovative, potential users are often poor judges of its economic viability. Analysing a conventional market, it is very hard to establish clearly the distinction between a reaction reflecting scepticism about something too new and one that translates lack of real need or interest for the product.

> The president of Polaroid, E. Land, was in the habit of saying that given the very innovative nature of Polaroid products, conventional methods of market analysis were insufficient (Sayers, 1980, p. 69).

Strategic marketing does not necessarily suppose immediate approval by users. The guiding principle must be a *knowledge and understanding of the needs and uses* of the potential buyer. There are many ways of acquiring this understanding other than simply by questioning potential users.

This is particularly important when it comes to commercializing high-technology products. At the fundamental stage, research can be done without any preoccupation about marketing or immediate profitability. At the applied research stage on the other hand, and preferably very early in the development process, the firm must consider demand and users' points of view.

> We can establish the same kind of distinction in the field of art marketing. It is clear that an artist is not concerned about the marketing problem; he creates without worrying whether his work will please or not and this is his social function. On the other hand, the artistic director of a cultural organization has the task of detecting and presenting those creations that meet the expectations of the target public that he has chosen to reach, whoever this public may be (Searles, 1980).

Contrary to some interpretations, the application of the marketing concept doesn't mean that the firm should necessarily be led simply by demand expressed by the market and buyers, given that this demand is often for short-term and largely known needs. If the firm were to adopt this kind of vision, it would always avoid breakthrough innovations, which are precisely the ones with greatest growth and profitability.

In practice, the marketing concept is integrated differently in different firms, even if most claim to be inspired by it. In fact, as we mentioned earlier, the marketing concept is an *ideal* to be reached, rarely fully realized, but one that should nevertheless guide all the activities of the firm.

2

Marketing in a turbulent environment

Ever since the first oil shock of October 1973, firms have operated in a restrictive, highly competitive environment of economic and social turbulence, in which change is no longer accidental but has become systematic, intermittent and very largely unpredictable. What Drucker (1980) calls an 'Age of Discontinuity' is increasingly revealing itself, at least in Western Europe, as a structural transformation of the economic, competitive and sociocultural fabric. These deep modifications have forced firms to review their strategic options, to redefine their priorities and to change their managerial style. Marketing, which has also developed since the period of continuous growth of the Golden Sixties, is not immune to this reappraisal. In this chapter, we shall describe the main environmental changes observed on the European scene and their implications for marketing management in the 1990s.

The new macro-marketing environment

The underlying causes of the new challenges to be faced during the 1990s in Western Europe can be traced to several changes due to structural modifications of technology, the economy and markets, coupled with a realignment of social priorities. Today, in the 1990s, change continues at a pace which makes it safe to predict that the current escalation of turbulence will persist in the years to come. The successive oil crises of the 1970s, the stock market crash of 1987, the reunification of the two Germanies, the turmoil in Eastern Europe, the Gulf War, the second Russian revolution and the creation of the 1993 European Single Market are all examples of major modifications in a firm's macro-marketing environment. We shall briefly describe here the three major environmental changes: technological, economic and competitive.

The new technologies

Increasingly, firms are confronted with *innovation competition*, based on technical progress, which is used more and more as an offensive weapon to conquer markets. The effect of creative destruction, in the Schumpeter sense, is well known. What is new is its acceleration and geographical generalization.

The growth rate of an economy is closely related to the number of new technologies and the number of new industries that can be created with the new technologies. Unfortunately, new technologies do not appear at regular intervals. In the absence of important innovations, an economy can stagnate. This was the case during the early 1980s in Western economies and especially in Europe. Industries that served basic needs have reached saturation. These industries did not necessarily decline, but their growth slowed down. New industries emerged that cater to the affluent consumer in the form of luxury goods, recreation, travel and services. In addition to these, high-technology sectors have also developed, which constitute highways towards economic expansion. These growing markets are the stakes for which the world is engaged in battle.

Waves of inventions and innovations

We saw in the previous chapter that the growth of the last 25 years was in fact due to innovations which had been developed earlier, during the years preceding the First World War. The historical analysis of the pace at which inventions and innovations appear shows that they surge in waves with a given configuration and frequency: waves of innovation following waves of invention, with a time lag.

Marchetti (1982) studied the various innovations that have taken place in world industry during the last 200 years. His results are summarized in the graphs of Figure 2.1. The lines represent the cumulative number of inventions and innovations as a function of time. The y-axis has a logarithmic scale so that the logistic function of time can be represented by a straight line in order to facilitate visual comparison. Marchetti identifies three successive waves: the 1802 wave, from 1775 to 1828, with 21 inventions and innovations; the 1857 wave (1833–80) with 40 observations; and the 1920 wave (1905–37), with 51 data points. Comparison and analysis of the three waves highlights the following points:

- Both the sets of inventions and those of innovations are similar, in that they are *ordered*: in each wave, inventions become innovations according to the 'first come, first served' rule.
- The lag between waves, measured by the *time distance* between the

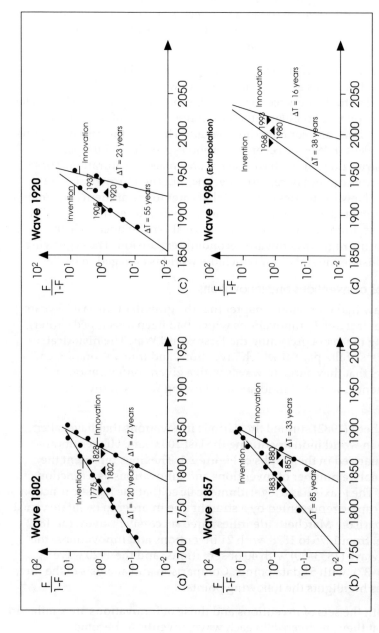

Figure 2.1 The waves of inventions and innovations (Marchetti, 1982)

central points of each wave, has remained constant, of the order of 55 years for innovations and 63 years for inventions. This corresponds to the periodicity of long cycles observed by the Russian economist Kondratiev (1935).

- The lag between the central points of inventions and innovations in each wave tends to become shorter; it is 52 years, 47 years and 33 years respectively. This reveals an *acceleration* in the passage from the laboratory to industrialization.
- The phases of inventions and innovations also tend to accelerate and cover a shorter period. As far as inventions are concerned, the duration of each wave has evolved as follows: 120, 85 and 55 years; for innovations 47, 33 and 23 years.

By extrapolating the observed regularities, Marchetti estimates the next wave to span the period from 1968–92, with the mean point in 1980. The phase is 38 years for inventions and 16 years for innovations. According to Marchetti, we are therefore at the centre of a new industrial era. As shown by the curve forecasting the 1980 wave, most of the inventions which should participate in the next great strides have already taken place.

The Kondratiev long cycle revisited

The observations on technological evolution are especially interesting since they corroborate the existence of long economic movements put forth by many economists, notably by the Russian economist Kondratiev (1935), who is considered to be the pioneer in the identification of long cycles (see box on p. 34)

The theory of long cycles is far from being unanimously accepted by economists. Some economists, like Samuelson for instance, believe that it is based on science fiction. Other economists, like Forrester (1978) or Marchetti (1982), consider it a means of visualization over the medium to long term, while keeping in mind the benefit of placing oneself in a historic perspective and at the same time being aware of the danger in extrapolating a recent past. Over the last few years, many studies have added empirical support to the ideas of Kondratiev; see Pruden (1978) and Bossier and Hugé (1981), among others.

Independently of the regularities observed by Kondratiev and Marchetti, most research on the interpretation of the economic crisis of the 1980s associates the greatest majority of the problems in Western economies over the last decade with modifications in the rate and form of technological change.

The 1980s mark the end of a growth cycle, due to the fact that the major innovations which had sparked this growth are reaching

The Kondratiev long wave

In 1926, the Russian economist Nicolas D. Kondratiev published an article, which was translated nine years later in the *Review of Economics and Statistics*. In this article, Kondratiev published a study of the capitalist economies of England, France, the USA and Germany, looking at the wholesale price level, interest rates, wages, foreign trade and the production and consumption of coal and pig iron, and the production of lead. The data permitted a study back to the early 1800s.

Kondratiev identified three *long waves* ranging from 48 years to 60 years. Updates and extrapolations of the Kondratiev wave theory identified a fourth wave with a peak in 1975. The four long waves are:

	Rise	Decline	Duration
First wave	1785–1815	1815–45	60 years
Second wave	1845–70	1870–95	50 years
Third wave	1895–1915	1915–(1945)	(60 years)
Fourth wave	(1945–75)	(1975–2005)	(60 years)

Numerous other factors have been correlated with various phases of the Kondratiev Wave:
1   During the *rise* of the long waves, years of prosperity are more numerous, whereas years of depression predominate during the downswing.
2   During the *decline* of the long waves, agriculture, as a rule, suffers an especially pronounced and long depression.
3   During the decline of the long waves, an especially large number of important discoveries and inventions in the techniques of production and communications are made, which, however, are usually applied on a large scale only at the beginning of the next long upswing.
4   At the beginning of a long upswing, gold production increases as a rule, and the world market for goods is generally enlarged by the assimilation of new and developing countries.
5   It is during the period of the rise of the long waves (i.e. during the period of high tension in the expansion of economic forces) that, as a rule, the most disastrous and extensive wars and revolutions occur.

On the whole, the post-war economic conditions are sufficiently close to the Kondratiev scenario to suggest that Western economies are in the middle of the decline phase of a fourth Kondratiev wave.

maturity; after the era of steel, the steam engine and railways, after the era of electricity, chemistry and the internal combustion engine, here we are in the era of silicon, synthetic materials, robotics, computers, astronautics, biotechnology etc. The passage from one cycle to the next is discontinuous and is characterized by a transitory period of crisis which can be fatal to those firms unable to adapt (Maisseu, 1984, p. 45).

Analogy with economic history obviously has some limits, but it is better than reading tea leaves or extrapolating the recent past.

The economic situation that we are going through corresponds to a deep-rooted phenomenon provoked essentially by the *wearing out* of the effects of conventional technologies. For most economic analysts, the only way out of the crisis is the generation of a new wave of innovations which could act as the driving force of a new expansion.

High-technology sectors

The definition of high-technology sectors rests on different criteria, the most rigorous one being the ratio of R&D spending to sales. Using a minimum of twice the average ratio observed in industry, as suggested by de Woot (1990, p. 10), we can identify six high-technology sectors:

Pharmaceuticals
Office and electronic data processing (EDP) equipment
Telecommunications
Electronics
Aircraft and aircraft parts
Rockets and spacecraft

Behind these high-technology sectors loom the great technologies of the future, or 'meta-technologies', as they are called, to denote the fact that they command a vast range of sectors and products. An important feature of the meta-technologies is the frequency with which they give rise to new technological families or clusters of products. Here again classifications vary, but there are generally agreed to be four major areas:

Information technology
Biotechnology
Optical electronics
Composite materials

Technical progress has also reached most industrial and service industries. Computer-aided manufacturing (CAM) and computer-aided design (CAD) systems have made major gains in the productivity and creativity of traditional industries, thereby giving

Table 2.1 The European Community in the triad market: selected indicators and countries (OECD, 1991)

	D	Sp	F	I	UK	B	EC12*	USA	Japan
Total population (millions, 1988)									
	61	39	56	57	57	10	324	246	123
Gross domestic product: average growth rate (%)									
1960–73	4.4	7.2	5.6	5.3	3.1	5.0	4.8	3.9	9.6
1973–80	2.2	2.1	2.8	2.8	1.0	3.1	2.2	2.1	3.7
1980–88	1.7	2.5	1.9	2.2	2.5	1.8	2.0	3.2	3.9
1988–90	4.0	4.5	3.6	3.0	2.3	3.8	3.4	2.6	5.5
Unemployment (% of total work force)									
1973	0.8	2.5	2.7	6.2	3.0	2.7	2.9	4.8	1.3
1980	2.9	11.1	6.3	7.5	6.4	8.8	6.4	7.0	2.0
1988	6.2	19.1	10.0	11.0	8.5	9.7	9.9	5.4	2.5
1990	5.1	15.9	9.0	9.9	6.9	7.9	8.4	5.4	2.1
Inflation: average growth rate of consumer price index (%)									
1960–73	3.6	6.6	4.7	4.8	4.9	5.6	4.6	3.1	6.2
1973–80	4.9	17.9	10.9	17.6	15.7	7.8	12.3	8.3	9.0
1980–88	2.5	9.8	6.9	10.5	5.8	4.9	6.8	4.6	1.8
1988–90	2.3	6.2	3.0	5.9	5.1	2.7	4.1	4.5	1.4
Public deficit (−) or surplus (+) (% GDP)									
1973	1.2	1.1	0.6	−7.9	−2.7	−3.8	−1.3	0.6	0.5
1980	−2.9	−2.6	0.0	−8.6	−3.3	−9.2	−3.9	−1.3	−4.4
1988	−2.1	−3.0	−1.8	−10.9	+1.3	−6.4	−3.7	−2.0	+1.5
1989	0.2	−2.5	−1.2	−10.1	+1.4	−6.5	—	−1.7	+2.5
Household net savings (% GNP)									
1960–69	7.6	—	11.1	15.9	4.3	—	—	6.2	11.9
1970–79	9.7	—	11.9	21.3	4.3	—	—	7.6	16.5
1980–89	8.9	—	7.9	15.9	3.7	—	—	6.0	13.1

*EC12 = Present members of the European Community, regardless of membership at the time

them new impetus for winning cost or differentiation advantages over direct competition. In the service industries, advances in computer and telecommunications have also changed the ground rules of competition and this is equally true in banking, insurance, transport and information (de Woot, 1990, p. 11).

In the face of increasingly powerful new technologies, gaining a competitive advantage depends more and more on the firm's capacity to master the mechanisms of technical progress and

Table 2.2 EC world market share in exports (EUROSTAT and OECD, 1991)

Year	Intra-EC trade excluded			Intra-EC trade included		
	EC12	USA	Japan	EC12	USA	Japan
1960	23.1	18.4	3.7	33.7	15.8	3.2
1973	21.3	15.8	8.2	38.2	12.5	6.5
1980	18.7	13.7	8.1	34.4	11.1	6.5
1988	20.4	13.2	12.0	38.5	10.2	9.2

innovation and to transform them into a significant share of the world market.

The new European economy

The effects of the technological changes on industry can be clearly seen in the light of the following facts regarding the countries in the European Community (ECOD, 1991). The data of Tables 2.1 and 2.2 are interesting in this respect. Note especially:

- *Slowed down growth,* hardly over 2 per cent per year from 1973 to 1988, compared to more than 4.5 per cent on average before 1973; growth reduced to about 3 per cent from 1988 to 1990.
- *The unemployment rate,* which had only reached about 3 per cent of the active population in 1973, went up to 10 per cent in 1983 in the seven largest industrial countries. In 1990, it was still around 8–9 per cent.
- Double digit *inflation* occurred in the European Community from 1973 to 1980, and then fell to below 6 per cent in 1988.
- *Budget deficits* have reached such proportions that they seem to forbid any new increase in public spending, especially in the USA, Italy, UK and Belgium.
- *The commercial influence* of the European Community countries has weakened. This can be witnessed in the decline in growth of exports from about 10 per cent in 1973 to below 4 per cent in 1987, as well as in the large balance of payments deficit with the rest of the world, the record being attained in 1980.
- As a result, Western Europe's market share in the world is in decline; when excluding trade within the zone, this share was only 20.4 per cent of world trade in 1988, compared with 23.1 in 1960.

From now on, European firms must operate in a much more difficult economic environment. The profound changes in the economy imply very rapid and harsh penalties for management errors, as witnessed by the spectacular rise in the number of firms going bankrupt.

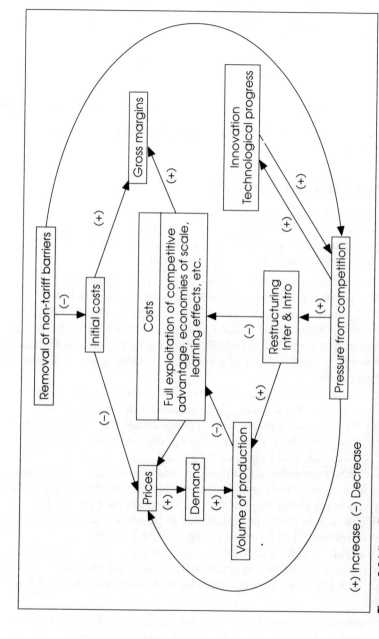

Figure 2.2 Micro-Economic effects triggered by EC market integration (Catinat and Jacquemin, 1990, p.2131)

(+) Increase, (−) Decrease

The European single market

To this macroeconomic analysis we must add a major political fact in Western Europe: the agreement of the twelve member states of the European Community to create a single market by 1992. This unique European Act, adopted by the heads of state in December 1985, and since ratified by national Parliaments, creates a *single market* extending over the whole of the Community by eliminating all non-tariff barriers between the twelve national members by the end of 1992.

The creation of this large market should not only allow for the elimination of a whole series of constraints affecting the performance of firms today, but will also result in a great shake-up by intensifying competition. According to a group of Community experts, the elimination of barriers and the resulting increased competition should have five major consequences (Cecchini *et al.*, 1988, p. 73):

- Significant reduction in costs, due to the suppression of non-tariff barriers and to better exploitation of economies of scale.
- Increased efficiency within firms and a decrease in prices as a result of competition.
- Demand increase due to lower prices and further exploitation of economies of scale.
- Adjustments between industries, with comparative advantages of some firms becoming more effective in an integrated market.
- A flow of innovations, new products and processes generated by the dynamics of the internal market.

Figure 2.2 describes the mechanisms by which such effects are to be realized. It is important to note that the gains are essentially supply-side generated. The improvements in performance would result from a response by companies reacting to changes in cost and increased competition. The increase in demand that is assumed to occur is contingent on prices falling (Catinat and Jacquemin, 1990).

Most of the projections made by the European Community would suggest that the successful integration of the European market would lead to the creation of a larger economic pie which should potentially benefit EC and non-EC firms alike.

The European Commission estimates that over five to six years, the Community's GNP could be raised by 4.5 per cent, consumer prices reduced by about 6 per cent and employment increased by 2 million. Furthermore, the European Community expects the creation of the single market to boost imports by 7 per cent and exports by 10 per cent (Cechinni, 1988, p. 98).

A Community-wide survey of firms has been done to analyse how

Table 2.3 Macro-economic indicators of Eastern European countries (1990) (OECD, IBRD, CIA, Institute of International Finance, National Westminster Bank)

	Hungary	Czechoslovakia	Poland	E Germany	Bulgaria	Romania	Yugoslavia	USSR
Population (million)	11	16	38	17	9	23	23	287
GNP per capita ($)	2621	7591	1818	12608	4744	3079	2390	4956
GDP growth 1986–88 (%)	1.5	1.5	1.0	1.5	1.9	0.1	—	—
Exports/GDP (%)	15	20	6	14	23	11	—	—
Inflation (%)	18	3	900	1	3	3	350	8
Exports to COMECON countries (% of total)	45	76	41	69	81	41	—	58
Cars per 1000	145	173	105	209	120	11	125	42
Telephones per 1000	134	226	118	211	200	130	122	115
Convertible currency external debt ($ billion)	17	7	40	21	9	2	17	38
Debt service as % of hard currency export earnings	77	16	79	30	36	17	25	20

European firms perceive the opportunities presented by the completion of the internal market. It reveals that European firms:

- Believe that the suppression of barriers will bring costs down.
- Expect their sales to go up in other countries of the Community.
- Plan to take a series of measures to improve productivity.
- Intend to increase the number of agreements of international cooperation with firms in other member states of the Community (*Economie Européenne*, No. 35, March 1988, pp. 139–43).

The expectations of firms facing the challenge of the internal market have positive implications with regard to the realization of a European global market and its expansion. The ability to master the rules of this new game obviously depends on the capacity of firms to 'think globally' and to adapt their management (marketing in particular) accordingly.

Eastern Europe: the new frontier

Suddenly, within a few months, extraordinary political and economic reforms swept Eastern Europe and the Soviet Union, focusing attention on a new market consisting of 430 million people. Many firms, be they European, American or Japanese, see a great opportunity, given the very low state of economic development of these markets (Table 2.3).

Needless to say, it is very difficult at the time of writing to formulate any prediction on what will happen in East European countries. Some very general guidelines can be proposed however.

The first thing to remember is the *diversity* of Eastern Europe, which cannot be viewed as a monolithic economic bloc as can Western Europe. The recent political events in the former USSR (and those to come) confirm that observation, as well as the data of Table 2.3. Market fragmentation and not market unity is the situation that will prevail in this part of the world for the years to come.

In view of the scale and complexity of the ongoing changes, many firms are confused, however, because they have no framework for examining the opportunities and for deciding how to respond. In fact, Eastern Europe offers three very contrasting opportunities. This section is based on the article by Pitt-Watson and Frazer (1991).

Make it here, sell it there

The greatest media coverage has been given to those companies which sell their products in the east. The most critical problem faced by these exporters is how to get money out of the country and into hard currency. If the products are not of strategic significance, barter arrangements are the only possible solution. Such arrangements are not always attractive since the products offered are generally products which do not have a market.

Make it there, sell it there

The same considerations apply to companies which invest in Eastern Europe with the intention of selling in Eastern Europe. With the exception of Russia, the domestic markets are small. Furthermore, there are many operational problems which need to be overcome: shortages of quality raw materials, complex bureaucratic approvals, inefficient pricing mechanisms and, last but not least, the lack of market orientation.

Make it there, sell it here

It seems that the greatest opportunity for many companies is to use Eastern Europe as a possible production base for sales in the West, to exploit the skills of an east European workforce and sell the output through existing marketing channels.

It follows that the greatest significance of Eastern Europe's entry into world trade is not the markets that are opened up, at least in the short term. It is the competitive industries which will develop in those countries, particularly those which can be better developed without outside assistance.

> An analogy could be drawn with Japan, whose emergence as an economic superpower was much more significant in its competitive impact on the Western electronics and motor industries, than in additional markets which it created for other Western products (Pitt-Watson and Scott Frazer, 1991, p. 18).

Before embarking on a major commitment to those countries, it is critical for Western companies to discover which industries in Eastern Europe are likely to have a sustainable competitive advantage over their foreign competitors.

The new competition

To the profound economic changes discussed above we must add changes in competitiveness resulting from the *internationalization of reference markets* at the world level in an increasing number of industrial sectors. Once again, this evolution has come about from the application of technological progress to means of transport and communication. The elimination of distances, or at least the elimination of time cost or transport cost due to geographical distance, has taken us to the stage of competitiveness at the global level in markets, products, labour costs and prices.

The new competitors

Consequently, the comparative advantages between certain regions have been reversed. This reversal has given rise to the appearance of *new competitors* for firms in industrialized countries:

- *Newly industrialized countries* (NIC), which now hold important positions in basic sectors dominated in the past by industrialized countries (steel, chemistry, textiles etc.).
- *Eastern European countries*, which are actively in competition with Western European firms in markets for basic industrial products, through barter and compensatory purchases in order to overcome shortages of hard currency. Recent changes in these countries will reinforce this trend, while at the same time presenting new opportunities for Western Europe.
- *Japanese firms*, such as Sony, Toyota, Canon, Seiko, Nikon and many others, which have acquired substantial market shares all over the world in sectors which are in high demand and which often have aggressive commercial policies (Kotler *et al.*, 1985).
- *Large distributors*, who are discovering strategic marketing and are adopting product policies to compete directly with branded products (proprietory and generic brands) more and more on the international scene.

In terms of a number of important sectors, these new rivals are in a better position for products that were traditionally part of the product portfolio of firms operating in industrialized countries.

It is within the context of such profoundly changing competition that firms must reposition themselves and find new market segments. These new market segments must provide the firm with higher value added, be better adapted to their capacities and technological edge and allow them to build a sustainable competitive advantage.

Global competitiveness

Competition is now global for a whole series of activities. This is obvious in the case of products of global 'nature', such as high-technology equipment (aerospace, aviation, telecommunication etc.) or raw materials (basic products etc.). It is less so in the case of 'universal' consumer goods, whether durable or non-durable (hi-fi, video, cameras, drinks, hamburgers, jeans etc.), and even less so in the case of services (credit cards, tourism, rentals, databanks, advisory services, recruitment etc.) (de Woot, 1990, pp. 12–13).

The industrialized countries, comprising Europe, North America and Japan in particular, form the natural reference market for firms operating in global sectors. This market includes more than 700 million inhabitants. However, this represents only 15 per cent of the

Table 2.4 Flows of Japanese direct investments in Europe (millions of US$) (Japanese Ministry of Finance)

Country	1985	1986	1987	1988	1989
UK	375	984	2 473	3 956	5 239
Netherlands	613	651	829	2 359	4 547
Luxemburg	300	1 092	1 764	657	654
Germany	172	210	403	409	1 083
France	67	152	330	463	1 136
Spain	94	86	283	161	501
Belgium	84	50	70	164	326
Ireland	81	72	58	42	133
Italy	32	23	59	108	314
Portugal	—	—	6	7	74
Switzerland	60	91	224	454	397
Austria	7	41	23	22	18
Total	1 930	3 469	6 576	9 116	14 808

world population, but two thirds of gross world production and about 85 per cent of world discretionary purchasing power (Ohmae, 1987, p. 10). As of 1989, the three combined blocs accounted for 81 per cent of the total outward stock of direct foreign investment.

Competitive advantage must be defined at the triad level. It is not enough just to do well at home any more; the firm must also perform well internationally in order to get a *leverage effect* (see Table 2.4). We can cite many reasons for the globalization of competition (de Woot, 1990, p. 12; Ohmae, 1987, pp. 10–14):

- The 700 million consumers begin to form a more *homogeneous* market as a result of communication, transport and travelling. The progressive uniformity in needs and wants is favourable to the development of a potential market for 'global' products, which is very attractive to firms because of economies of scale in production, distribution, advertising etc.
- *Diffusion of technical progress* has become so fast that it is necessary to introduce an innovation in the three large triad markets simultaneously. A delay in one of the markets exposes the firm to the possibility of being beaten by a rival who can launch a similar product and thus achieve a dominant position, which is difficult to overturn.
- The *development cost* of some equipment goods is so high that it can only be recovered at the world level.
- The *industrial fabric* has become more homogeneous, in the sense

that for many goods and services 70–80 per cent of production and consumption takes place in the countries of the triad.

To these major trends in the world economy one must add the European single market.

Warfare marketing

Another consequence of the appearance of new competitors is a reinforcement of the harshness of the competitive struggle and the necessity of a more systematic and thorough analysis of the competitive forces present. *Competitor analysis* is now a central preoccupation of strategic marketing (Porter, 1982); hence the origin of the expression *'warfare marketing'*. Ries and Trout (1986) emphasize the idea that beating the competition has become the main objective of strategic marketing. Many factors explain this evolution:

- In industrialized economies, firms are increasingly facing saturated and stagnant markets.
- In these markets, the classical marketing concept is better integrated in firms and knowledge of buyers' needs is no longer a sufficient competitive advantage.
- Products available are often of similar quality and the differences are hardly perceptible.
- Counteracting competitors' manoeuvres is therefore a key factor of success.

Warfare marketing advocates a reinforcement of the *competitor orientation* within the market-driven firm, a systematic analysis of competitive forces, and a development of attack and defence strategies, including flank and guerilla attacks inspired by military strategy. Creation and systematic exploitation of a sustainable competitive advantage have become just as necessary as the understanding of buyers' needs.

The new consumer

The mass marketing era lifted the aspirations of consumers from the materialistic needs of comfort and safety to a drive for new values. Satisfaction of 'good living' needs coupled with growth in discretionary income have changed consumer demand patterns. Having 'filled their bellies', as Ansoff put it (1984, p. 7), individuals begin to aspire to higher levels of personal satisfaction. They become increasingly discriminating in their demand for more customized services and complete information about their purchases, as well as for post-sales responsibility from the manufacturer and ecologically friendly products. They challenge the firm directly through consumerism and put pressure on governments for increased controls.

The coming of age of mass marketing

The nature of operational marketing has been changing rapidly in recent years due to the profound changes observed in industrialized countries. This trend sets the stage for new directions in distribution, selling methods and communication. Among the most critical changes are:

- Changing demography, with more single households, an increase in women in the work force, two-income families, people staying healthier and living longer etc.
- Personal time is more highly valued by well-educated consumers.
- Proliferation of weakly differentiated brands and products.
- Weakening of advertising effectiveness.
- Decline in brand loyalty.
- Rising costs of personal communication.
- Overcrowding of shopping malls and stores.
- Escalation in self-defeating promotions.

These changes have contributed to the weakening of the foundations of traditional mass marketing methods. They are simply not working very well any more. Rapp and Collins (1990) argue for a major turnaround in marketing, and predict that individualized marketing—we prefer to use the term *customized marketing*—should be substituted for mass or segment marketing.

The coming of age of mass marketing also implies placing more importance on close involvement with identified prospects and customers and replacing the marketing monologue which prevails in many market situations by a *marketing dialogue*. This can be achieved through direct marketing, interactive communication, response advertising etc. These new developments in operational marketing will be reviewed in detail in Chapters 10 and 12.

Economic and competitive changes have been accompanied by sociocultural changes. These changes, which were the socio-economic, cultural and social consequences of some marketing practices, have in turn given rise to a *reappraisal* of the classical marketing concept. The starting point of this evolution goes back to the 1970s in Europe, and it can be traced to two different movements: the consumerist and the environmentalist movements.

Consumerism

Consumerism was born out of the growing consciousness of the
excesses of operational marketing, or the practice of wild marketing
(see Table 1.1) which attempts to mould demand to meet supply
requirements rather than adapt supply to demand expectations.
Consumerism is the consequence of the relative failure of
the marketing concept. As stated by Drucker (1973, p. 85),
'. . . consumerism is the shame of marketing'.

The main arguments of the consumerist critique are as follows:

- Marketing tries to satisfy consumers' *short-term needs* at the
  expense of their *long-term well-being*.
- Products are developed in order to *favour the profit objective* of the
  firm rather than the objective of satisfying needs.
- Marketing favours the *symbolic value* of products (affective and
  emotional values) at the expense of their functional value.
- There is a fundamental *imbalance* between buyers' and sellers'
  legal rights.

It is important to emphasize that consumerism does not
fundamentally question the marketing concept, but rather demands
its full application. In fact, the consumerist movement reveals a
phenomenon of *'socialization'* or of *'unionization' of demand*, similar to
the workers' movement at the beginning of the century. This is an
important fact for the firm, as it confronts ever more involved
consumers who react to its actions in an organized manner.

Due to its countervailing power, consumerism has undoubtedly
contributed to the improvement of the ethical level of marketing
practise. It forms a pressure group that firms can hardly ignore.
Nevertheless, the objectives of consumerism have evolved clearly,
due to the pressure of change in the general economic situation. For
more about consumerism, see Aaker and Day (1982).

Environmentalism

The *environmentalist movement* reflects the new awareness of the
scarcity of natural resources and reveals a change of outlook
regarding consumption. Environmentalists question the impact of
consumption and of marketing on the environment. The reasoning is
as follows:

Each consumption has positive and negative utilities. By insisting on
increasing consumption quantitatively, marketing is instrumental in
neglecting the impact of negative consequences. These negative
consequences have a high social cost, which is also a neglected cost.

Table 2.5 Socio-economic costs of personal transportation modes
(*Le Soir*, Brussels, 16 December, 1987)

Personal transportation modes	Indirect social costs*				
	Accidents	Noise	Pollution	Total	Ratio
Cars (petrol)	1017.0	55	213	1285.0	36.4
Cars (diesel)	1017.0	55	75	1147.0	32.5
Buses	95.0	11	148	254.0	7.2
Electric trains	2.3	33	0	35.3	1.0
Diesel trains	2.3	33	44	79.3	2.2

*In Belgian francs per 1000 travellers kilometres (i.e. 1 traveller over 1000 km or 20 travellers over 50 km); traffic jam costs not included. The last column shows the ratio of each transportation mode. The train has an indirect social cost of 1 franc and the petrol-driven car has a cost of BF36.4.

> Given the scarcity of resources, it is necessary to allow explicitly for the social cost of consumption.

The data of Table 2.5 illustrate the relevance of the environmentalist reasoning in the personal transportation sector.

In contrast with consumerists, environmentalists don't accept the principle of consumer sovereignty if the application of this principle leads to the destruction of the environment. They feel that the aim of the economic system shouldn't be the satisfaction of the consumer as such, but rather the *improvement in the quality of life*. Their main concern is to protect and enhance people's living environment.

The environmentalist movement has had a great impact in many industries and is undoubtedly a factor that will deeply affect economic and industrial life. This environmental factor reflects *new needs in society*. It is no longer a protest trend, like the hippies in the late 1960s and early 1970s, but a mature trend which has spread throughout all levels of society.

Green marketing

One impact of the environmentalist movement is the emergence of a new breed of consumerists, the *green consumerists*. Green consumerists have realized that it is possible to change what they consume in a way which benefits the environment and themselves. As a result, green consumerism is putting pressure on distributors and manufacturers to switch to food products and household goods that are healthier and more environmentally friendly. They also put pressure on governments to act. Areas that seem likely to develop modified products which are environmentally safe are personal hygiene, household cleaning products (phosphate-free), food items (organic farming), recycling (paper, glass, tin etc.), toiletries and cosmetics (CFC-free sprays), recycled paper products (for household and office), packaging materials, energy efficient equipment, petrol and automobiles (lead free petrol, catalytic convertors).

The satisfaction of these needs will impose new restrictions on many firms. For others, it represents new opportunities as alert manufacturers are realizing that they can gain a competitive advantage over their rivals by adapting their products and packages in a way which is environmentally friendly.

Green marketing is the industry response to these new requirements of the market and many corporations and distributors have hurried to create ostensibly green products. However, in doing so they have often generated a great deal of confusion and, in some cases, an actual backlash towards the very products they are developing.

> According to a study by UK-based Marketing Intelligence Ltd, green products have multiplied 20 times faster than all other new packaged goods since 1986. As a result, product claims such as 'degradable', 'biodegradable', 'recyclable', 'CFC-free', 'ozone-friendly', 'environmentally friendly or safe' are appearing widely in ads and on packages (*Business International* Weekly Report, 28 January 1991).

Green consumerists argue that the lack of objective and uniform standards as to the meaning of green labels has left the environmentally conscious buyer uncertain and sceptical about green marketing in general. Green advertising campaigns are viewed as merely attention-getting devices for '. . . companies trying to hitchhike on the green bandwagon'. It is clear that a 'going green' policy should cover the entire manufacturing process and not just the advertising of the end product.

To clarify the situation, governments are introducing special product labels—eco-labels—to identify environmentally sound products for consumers and to encourage industry to design goods meeting these requirements. West Germany was the first country (in 1978) to introduce its official eco-labelling scheme (Blue Angel). Other European countries are catching on. An EC environmental labelling scheme is also expected (Potargent, 1991).

Implications for management

The arrival of affluence casts doubt on economic growth as the main instrument of social progress. In Western European countries, as well as in the USA, social aspirations have shifted from 'quantity' to 'quality' of life. The firm is now expected to be able to assume 'social accountability' as well as maintain affluence under severe constraints. The slogan, largely accepted until recently by the business community—'the business of business is business'—is no longer true and the firm cannot remain immune from societal interference.

The accountable marketing concept

The consumerist and environmentalist movements have forced some marketing theoreticians to widen the classical marketing concept in a way that puts the emphasis on the necessity to develop an increased consciousness within the firm of the sociocultural side-effects of its economic and especially its marketing activity. Thus Kotler (1979, pp. 76–86) proposed the adoption of the *societal marketing concept*. Later, Kotler stated:

> The societal marketing concept holds that the organization's task is to determine the needs, wants and interests of target markets and to deliver the desired satisfactions more effectively and efficiently than competitors in a way that preserves and enhances the consumer's and the society's well-being (Kotler, 1991, p. 29).

This concept is based on three implicit assumptions:

- Consumers' wishes do not always coincide with their long-term interests or those of the public at large.
- Consumers prefer organizations that show real concern for their satisfaction and well-being as well as the collective well-being.
- The most important task of the organization is to adapt itself to the target markets in such a way as to generate not only satisfaction, but also individual and collective well-being, in order to attract and keep customers.

Two key ideas distinguish the concept of societal marketing from that of the classical marketing concept:

- Marketing must be concerned with the *well-being of buyers* and not simply with the satisfaction of their short-term needs.
- The firm must pay attention to the side-effects of its economic and industrial activity in order to ensure the *long-term well-being of society as a whole* and not only that of individual consumers.

By adopting this wider outlook, the firm will better achieve its own growth and profit objectives.

Firms are rapidly embracing the accountable marketing concept. One example is the self-discipline code adopted in France by the French Advertisers' Association. This code forbids the use of the appeal of speed and any encouragement to use speed in car advertisements (*UDA Informations*, No. 341, December 1988).

From international to global marketing

The end of the 1980s is characterized by the completion of the process of internationalization of the world economy through *globalization*. In a growing number of activities, the geographic reference market is no longer a country or a continent, but the large industrialized countries, i.e. the triad market. Competitive advantage must now exist at this level.

Internationalization is not a new phenomenon for marketing; it has been developing since the end of the Second World War. What is new is the *interdependence of markets* as a result of globalization. Markets are no longer considered as separate entities, but more and more as a single market. In this section, we shall examine the implications of the globalization of competition for the firm's marketing management.

Standardization versus customization

Every firm must face the question of knowing how to organize in order to confront the global market in such a way as to maintain a sustainable competitive advantage. When approaching this question, two very distinct attitudes may be adopted: one which promotes the standardization of marketing activity in all markets, thus giving priority to internal performance objectives and another which, on the contrary, gives priority to *customization* of products, thus marketing to specific needs of different markets.

A *customization strategy* pinpoints existing differences between markets and does this in the spirit of the marketing concept. Three groups of factors help to differentiate markets:

- Differences in *buyer behaviour*, not only in terms of socio-demographics, income or living conditions, but especially in terms of consumption, habits, customs, culture etc.
- Differences in *market organization*, including the structure of distribution networks, the availability of media, regulations, climatic conditions, means of transportation etc.
- Differences in *competitive environment*, in terms of the degree of concentration of competition, the presence of domestic rivals, the competitive climate etc.

It is clear that there are important differences among markets and that these differences will persist in the future. These differences will have implications for the marketing strategy to be adopted.

Believers in the *standardization strategy* underline the advantages that can result from a strategy based on what is similar between markets rather than what differentiates them. The *standardization thesis*, upheld by Levitt (1983) and Ohmae (1987), is based on three hypotheses:

- World needs will become homogenized thanks to technology, transportation and communication.
- Consumers are prepared to forgo specific preferences in order to benefit from products with lower prices and good quality.
- Standardization resulting from homogenization of world markets brings about economies of scale, thus reducing the cost.

To support his thesis, Levitt mentions examples of products with high profiles such as: McDonalds, Coca-Cola, Pepsi, Revlon, Kodak, Sony, Levis etc., in addition to high-technology products which are naturally universal.

If homogenization of needs is indeed real, this does not mean that standardization is the only alternative open to the global firm. Levitt reduces global marketing to a standardization strategy. Many counter-arguments can be put forth however, which alter Levitt's arguments substantially:

- Although it is true that needs are becoming homogenized throughout the world, we are only talking about 'segments', which are found in all triad countries, with the same expectations and with slight variations. Parallel to these world segments, we also observe a *'demassification'*, or a 'personalization of consumption' giving rise to segments which are more and more specialized and which vary greatly between countries because of the greater importance of cultural and regional values.
- There is no evidence to show that consumers are becoming universally more *sensitive to prices*. Products such as Cartier watches, Louis Vuitton bags, Hermès scarves or Canon cameras, which are recognized as global products, are great commercial successes, but they are not particularly known for low prices.
- It is no longer true that economies of scale go hand in hand with frantic standardization. New production technologies have now taken industry out of the Taylor era of large manufacturing chains which produced a single product at high speed. There are now new flexible workshops with instantaneous command change and lagged differentiation techniques, which can retain the advantages of standardization while at the same time being able to customize according to personalized requirements.

However, the *problem of technical norms* remains a major handicap for standardization. In Europe, each country still has its own particular norms which force firms to manufacture many variations of the same product.

> Europe is still incapable of having identical electric plugs in all countries. The Italians, the French, and countries in Northern Europe, each have different plugs. Meanwhile in Britain, goods have to be sold without a plug because within Britain itself, there are so many different systems that the consumer must attach his own plug. As for American and Japanese norms, they border protectionism; not only does the good have to be approved, but all the substances used in it as well (Picardi, 1987, p. 115).

The 'crude' theory of standardization is therefore very doubtful and many authors have already discussed its limitations (Buzzell, 1968).

In reality, the dilemma of standardization versus customization is a false dilemma, in the sense that it poses the question of internationalization as 'all or nothing'. As suggested by Takeuchi and Porter (1986), the real question is how to reconcile the two approaches. One can concentrate on the similarities that exist between markets, which will probably exist more and more, without forgetting their differences and the corresponding need to customize. Most cases of international blunders are the outcome of a lack of cultural sensitivity and acknowledgement of values and attitudes, which means that a successful strategy in one country may prove to be bad in another.

The global marketing concept

The fundamental challenge of the globalization of markets can be summarized as follows: faced with the internationalization of markets, the firm must

- Think globally in its strategic marketing.
- Act locally in its operational marketing.

J.P. Morgan's advertising eloquently states, '. . . the key to global performance is understanding local markets'.

Global marketing implies thinking on two levels. First, consideration must be given to new segments of customers over a wider geographical market, no matter how narrow these new segments may be. Second, although those segments may be locally very narrow, their total market representation on the regional and international scale may constitute an important volume capable of generating economies of scale for the company.

Globalization in this sense applies essentially to the concept of the product and not necessarily to other tools of marketing, such as communication, price and distribution, which remain customized to local characteristics. Customization constitutes the second area of consideration. In Chapter 5 we shall examine more closely the alternatives in international segmentation (Quelch and Hoff, 1986).

It is important to realize that the global marketing concept concerns all firms and not only large international firms. The small or medium-sized firm operating in a global market must also be internationalized in such a way as to confront other competitors, i.e. as a defensive tactic (Quelch, Buzzell and Salana, 1991).

As far as marketing management is concerned, the most important implication of globalization is the necessity to define the geographic reference market as the triad countries and to elaborate active or defensive strategic options which take the new interdependence of markets into account.

The new marketing priorities

The evolution of the changing priority role of marketing is summarized in Table 2.6. The environmental changes mentioned above all imply a reinforcement of strategic marketing for companies operating in highly industrialized markets. Companies need to review their strategic options in order to face the new challenges presented by the economic, competitive and socio-cultural environment and by the internationalization of the world economy.

One can identify seven new priorities in strategic marketing:

- *Product portfolio restructuring*   To meet the new competition's challenges, Western European companies must diversify their product portfolio by evolving towards higher value added activities, based either on technological advances or on organizational know-how.
- *Customized marketing*   In affluent societies, sophisticated consumers expect to find tailor-made solutions to their problems and it is up to the firm to meet these expectations through direct response segmentation and interactive communication.
- *Competition orientation*   In stagnant and mature markets, the capacity to anticipate competitors' actions and to out-fox rivals is a key factor of success. This capacity implies the existence of a competition monitoring system.
- *Development of forecasting systems*   In a turbulent environment, traditional sales forecasting methods are ineffective and the firm must develop organizational flexibility and contingency planning systems.
- *Global marketing*   There is a growing interdependence among the countries of the triad where the industrial and cultural fabric becomes more homogeneous. Supranational segments appear which constitute market opportunities for the firm.

Table 2.6 Evolution of the priority role of marketing

Passive marketing
The firm is 'product-oriented' and has an 'inside-in' perspective.

Operational marketing
The firm is 'sales-oriented' and has an 'inside-out' perspective.

Active marketing
The firm is 'customer-oriented' and has an 'outside-in' perspective.

Accountable marketing
The firm is 'market-oriented' and has a societal perspective.

Global marketing
The firm is 'world market-oriented' and has a transnational perspective.

- *Accountable marketing* New needs are emerging in society which call for environmentally friendly products. Firms are beginning to show concern for both the individual and the collective well-being of society, instead of simply satisfying short-term needs.
- *Market-driven general management* Successful implementation of the marketing concept within the firm requires cross-functional coordination and a corporate culture which encourages the adoption of the marketing concept.

In the following chapters, we shall examine the 'how to . . . ?' issues raised by these new priorities.

Marketing and needs satisfaction

The satisfaction of buyers' needs is at the heart of a market economy and of marketing. Yet the criticism most frequently levelled at modern marketing is that it has changed the market into a mechanism that creates needs rather than satisfies them. This is an important question that cannot be evaded. It is diametrically opposed to the classical analysis of consumer sovereignty, which is the keystone of the market economy. If firms contribute to the creation of needs, then their social role is indeed indefensible. This chapter aims to try to answer this fundamental question. We shall first examine the main positions of economics and marketing theoreticians. Then we shall turn to psychology and in particular to the contributions experimental psychology has made in the study of human motivation. Finally, we shall analyse the motivation of the organizational or industrial customer which must be examined within a totally different framework from that of individual consumers.

Human needs in economic theory

The notion of need is a term that creates endless polemic because it contains elements of subjective judgement based sometimes on morality or ideology. Beyond the vital minimum that everyone accepts—but which no one tries to define—is it really necessary to vary one's food to satisfy taste, to travel out of curiosity or to have different hobbies? We must admit that, at least as far as consumer markets are concerned, these questions are not irrelevant, especially in view of the following facts: (a) the uninterrupted arrival of new products and brands on the market; (b) the continuous and spectacular presence of advertising in increasingly varied forms; and (c) the relative stability of the level of consumer satisfaction, despite the undisputed improvement in standard of living. These facts then raise the following questions:

- Do all these new products and brands really correspond to pre-existing needs?

- Would producers accept such high advertising expenditures if consumers were not allowing themselves to be influenced?
- Is the growth and economic development that marketing claims to encourage useful in the long term?

Economic theory doesn't help to answer these questions. Economists believe it is not part of their discipline to worry about what motivates an action, or to enter into introspection, which is always difficult, or especially to formulate a value judgement. It is useless to say that man strives for pleasure and avoids pain; it suffices to see that this indeed is the essence of the 'want to use' to justify its utility. The driving force, economic or otherwise, that makes an individual take an economic action, is outside the scope of economics; only the results are important. The wish to be satisfied is the only acknowledged cause of behaviour.

A need must be felt before a choice is made, which means that the scale of preferences logically precedes effective choices. If an individual is intellectually adult and reasonable, it should be possible to predict the person's behaviour, which results from rational calculation.

> The consumption choices of an individual which express his needs can be described *a priori* completely, without experimentation and on the condition that a rational behaviour, summarized by five axioms called the axioms of rationality, can be assumed (Jacquemin and Tulkens, 1988, p. 50).

The economic theory of consumer behaviour is therefore limited to the analysis of the logical implications of the hypothesis of man's rationality. The problem of motivation is totally avoided, since economists believe that the real behaviour of the consumer reflects his or her preferences and inversely that the consumer's preferences are revealed by his or her behaviour.

The weakness of the basic assumptions in economics have been underlined on many occasions. In economic theory, the concept of *rationality* is defined as equivalent to the concept of *coherence*. However, the predictive value of coherence conditions depends mainly on the existence of well known and stable preferences in the mind of the decider. But this is far from being satisfied if the original motivations are ignored, poorly known or simplified to the extreme, as is the case in economic models. How can we then be surprised by the observed difference between the 'economic person' and the 'real person'? We should nevertheless mention that, over the last few years, many efforts have been made to enrich the abstract psychology of the economic person and to come closer to the real person. Some examples are the work of Katona (1951), Abbott (1955), Becker (1965) and Lancaster (1966).

Needs, wants and demand

The biased position of neutrality taken by economists with respect to
the notion of need can also be found in marketing. Kotler (1991, p. 5)
defines need as '. . . a state of felt deprivation of some basic
satisfaction'. This is in fact the definition of a generic need. One can
imagine a generic need that corresponds to each of the tendencies
governing the life of individuals, these tendencies being necessarily
limited in number. This generic need is therefore related to human
nature and hence not created by society or by marketing; it exists
before demand, whether latent or expressed.

Kotler establishes a distinction between needs, wants and demands
(1991, p. 4). *Wants* are specific satisfiers of deeper needs. While
generic needs are stable and few, wants are many, changing and
continually influenced by social forces. Wants become *potential
demands* for specific products when backed by an ability and
willingness to buy. According to Kotler, marketing tries to influence
wants and demands by making the product attractive, affordable and
easily available. Marketing does not create needs; needs pre-exist
marketers.

> Marketers, along with other influences in society, influence wants. They
> suggest to consumers that a Cadillac would satisfy a person's need for
> social status. Marketers do not create the need for social status but try to
> point out how a particular good would satisfy that need (Kotler, 1991, p. 4).

The distinction between needs, wants and demand is important and
the three concepts are often confused. But the distinction is not
enough to close the debate on the social role of marketing. Clearly,
marketing can exacerbate needs, even if they existed before.
Furthermore, creating desires or wants that cannot be turned into
demand due to lack of purchasing power can become an important
source of frustration and malfunctioning in an economy. The
responsibility of marketing is directly implicated here, which
explains the duty to exercise restraint in its application. Various
self-disciplinary movements have seen the light of day in the USA as
well as in Europe, acknowledging the need for restraint and self-
discipline.

'False' needs versus 'true' needs

Attali and Guillaume (1974) reject the distinction between needs and
wants. They believe that *needs are generated by wants*, things that
have become normalized. They include things which no longer give
pleasure, but that would be unacceptable to do without because they
fall in the domain of the normal (Attali and Guillaume, 1974, p. 144).

It is the dynamics of wants that explains the accumulation of needs. Producers exploit the dynamics of wants to find markets allowing them to preserve their economic power.

> If social demand, which dialectically results from needs, wants and social supply, is so restricted by the constraints of the productive system, shouldn't the political control of the production of needs logically precede that of production? (Attali and Guillaume, 1974, p. 146).

This viewpoint is obviously contrary to that of orthodox economists. Rosa (1977) notes that this analysis makes the implicit assumption that there are 'real' needs and 'false' needs and that the false needs are created by society and by the producer.

> In this school of thought, there is a fundamentally unequal exchange relationship between a dominated consumer and a dominant producer; society corrupts the individual by creating artificial wants in order to better subjugate and alienate him. The conclusion that follows is simple; it suffices to make the 'good' political choice to get 'good' structures which will necessarily develop the flourishing and expression of 'real' needs (Rosa, 1977, p. 176).

This analysis, which was widespread among so-called 'left intellectuals' in Europe at one stage, has one important weakness, in that it never indicates how to distinguish true needs from false needs. Given that the vast majority of our present wants are indeed of a cultural origin, where should we draw the line, and especially who will be the enlightened dictator of consumption? Clearly it is impossible to answer these questions objectively.

> ... to substitute the disputed sovereignty of the consumer for the questionable sovereignty of a bureaucrat or of an intellectual can only create more problems than it can ever hope to resolve (Rosa, 1977, p. 159).

It should also be added that the hypothesis of consumer impotence is daily rejected by facts such as the figures available on the rates of failure of new products; more than one in two products fails to enter the market successfully. The discretionary power of the consumer is a reality and firms know it well. We must therefore recognize that the debate of 'true' versus 'false' needs can only be an ideological debate. Economists refuse to enter this debate because they know it cannot be reconciled with a scientific approach. In this kind of analysis, everything can be claimed and everything can be disclaimed according to one's point of view. Science, however, seeks objectivity and intelligibility.

Absolute versus relative needs

The interesting point about the analysis above is possibly the fact that it puts forth the cultural and social origin of our needs.

According to the dictionary, *a need is a requirement of nature or of social life*. This definition distinguishes two kinds of needs; *innate needs*, which are natural, generic or inherent in nature or the organism, and *acquired needs*, which are cultural and social and depend on experience, environmental conditions and the evolution of society.

Keynes had established a rather similar distinction between absolute needs and relatives needs. According to Keynes,

> ... those needs which are absolute in the scenes that we feel them whatever the situation of our fellow human beings may be, and those which are relative in the sense that we feel them only if their satisfaction lifts us above, make us feel superior to our fellows (Keynes, 1936, p. 365).

Absolute needs are satiable, while relative needs are not. In fact, relative needs are insatiable, because the higher the general level, the more these needs tend to surpass that level. In such conditions, producing to satisfy relative needs is tantamount to developing them. This is how individuals, even when they have in absolute terms enjoyed net improvements in their standard of living, often tend to think that their situation has deteriorated if those who normally serve as the yardstick have improved more relative to them. Cotta (1980, p. 17) writes, '. . . others' luxury becomes one's own necessity'.

The distance between reality and the level of aspiration tends to move continuously with growing dissatisfaction.

Galbraith's analysis (1971) falls within this framework. As far as he is concerned, if a need is really felt, the production of a good to satisfy this need is useful, even if the need is perfectly ridiculous. But if the wants emerge with the production, then the urgency of the wants can no longer be used to defend the urgency of production. Production only fills a void that it has itself created and then this is proof that the need is artificial and the satisfaction it will bring can only be insignificant. This is how Galbraith illustrates what he calls the 'dependence effect':

> For then the individual who urges the importance of production to satisfy these wants is precisely in the position of the onlooker who applauds the efforts of the squirrel to keep abreast of the wheel that is propelled by his own efforts (Galbraith, 1971, p. 147).

Galbraith maintains that saturation of needs is real and it is advertising which is responsible for the creation of artificial needs, '. . . to bring into being wants that previously did not exist'.

In fact, Galbraith confuses needs and demands in his analysis. Advertising can help discover an already existing need, which cannot become a demand because the product aimed at satisfying it does not yet exist. We can indeed accept that a need may exist without there being any good to satisfy it. This is the case of a *latent market*, to which we referred in the previous chapter. By making the need known, advertising creates demand, but it doesn't create the need. In other words, advertising can create a demand for a pre-existing but unidentified need.

Similarly, the notion of *'artificial' need*, used by Galbraith, leads to a judgement on the degree of marginal utility of needs. The need to acquire superior products for the sake of conspicuous consumption takes on a life of its own due to the contagious effect which characterizes this kind of need. In these conditions, we end up with a hypothesis of the *impossibility of saturation of needs* rather than a saturation hypothesis. Therefore, all that is left of Galbraith's analysis is a judgement over the degrees of marginal utility of new 'artificial' needs. Thus utility may be little but still existent. If one tries to avoid value judgements—which takes us back to the distinction between true and false needs—then the appearance of new needs can always be defended.

The distinction between absolute needs and relative needs is in fact far from being as clear cut as one might at first think. One could say, for example, that anything essential to survival is infinitely more important than any other consumption. This idea is inexact.

> To live is certainly an important objective for each of us, but suicide exists. Heroic acts too. More generally, every consumer, in his day to day search for satisfaction of various needs, takes risks that put his life in danger either immediately or in the long run. Smoking, overeating, driving, working too hard or not looking after one's health properly, travelling: these are all activities that one should avoid if survival is placed above all else (Rosa, 1977, p. 161).

Needs of a psycho-sociological origin may be felt just as strongly as the most elementary needs. For example, being deprived of intimacy and attention may provoke death or serious deficiencies in psychic and social functioning in the more extreme cases.

Despite a lack of clarity, the distinction between absolute needs and relative needs remains interesting in two respects. On the one hand, it shows that relative needs can be just as demanding as absolute needs. On the other hand, it brings to the fore the existence of a dialectic of relative needs which leads to the observation of the general *impossibility of saturation*. Even the tendency towards material comfort cannot objectively define a state of satisfaction. When an individual reaches a predefined level, he or she can then catch a glimpse of a new stage of possible improvement.

Generic versus derived needs

Abbott proposed an interesting distinction between generic needs on the one hand, and derived needs on the other (Abbott, 1955, p. 40). A *derived need* is a particular technological response (the product) to the generic need, as well as being the object of desire. For example, the car is a derived need with respect to the generic need of autonomous individual means of transportation. The same is true of the personal computer with respect to the need to process information. Saturation does not relate to the generic need, but only the derived need, in other words the dominant technological response at the time. At a given point, one may detect a tendency towards the saturation of the derived need, because of increased consumption of the good at a particular stage in its *life cycle*. The marginal utility of the derived need tends to diminish. But thanks to the impulse given by technological progress, the generic need remains insatiable, because it evolves towards higher levels due to the arrival of improved products and therefore new derived needs.

The production of goods for the satisfaction of generic needs will therefore be incessantly subject to the stimulus of its own evolution. The latter will encourage the arrival of new products on the market which are more suitable to satisfying the new level of needs. These derived needs will be saturated in their turn and be replaced by new, more developed, products. The phenomenon of relative saturation brought about by technological progress, which is the basis of the model of product life cycle discussed later on in this book, is observed for most goods and at two levels: firstly, in the improvement of technological performance of products themselves (more economical cars, more powerful computers etc.); and secondly, in the pure and simple substitution of a particular technological answer by another with higher performance (compact disc replacing long-playing records, fax replacing telex etc.). The latter form of innovation, or destructive innovation, is becoming ever more important due to the generalization of technological progress in all sectors, as we mentioned before.

Furthermore, it seems that the move to a product which is hierarchically superior tends to increase the marginal utility yet again. The decline of the marginal utility is interspersed with sudden peaks. Goods are often desired for their novelty features and the privilege of owning them, even if little is added to their performance.

Therefore, the distinction between generic and derived needs makes it clear that, although there can be no general saturation, it is perfectly possible to detect sectoral saturation. An important role for strategic marketing is thus to encourage the firm to adapt to this observed development in needs satisfaction. In this framework, it is better for the firm to define its mission by reference to generic needs rather than derived needs, given that the latter are saturable while the former are not. These are the basics of the marketing concept, described in the previous chapter.

To conclude this overview of economists' and marketing theoreticians' points of view, let us bear in mind the following propositions:

- The economist is not concerned with the problem of motivation. There are only wants and preferences. The real question, as far as he is concerned, is to know whether the consumer has *autonomy of action and decision* or not and whether his preferences have some stability or if on the contrary they are malleable (Rosa, 1977, p. 162).
- The problem is not to know whether there are true or false needs, because it is impossible to establish the distinction objectively on the one hand, and because economists refuse to make a judgement on the frivolity of choices on the other. They consider the *structure of preferences as given*.
- It is true that a great majority of our needs are cultural by origin. There is hence a *dialectic of needs*, caused by the social and cultural environment and by technological development. Like all other social forces, marketing contributes to this dialectic.
- The relative nature of many needs means that the wish to acquire superior products has a particular life of its own. *There can therefore be no general saturation*. Saturation is alien to the nature of relative needs. Their objectives are almost unlimited. By satisfying them, they become activated rather than fulfilled.
- *Technological progress* and the resulting constant renewal of products also leads to a hypothesis of impossibility of saturating generic needs, to the extent that innovations make it possible to meet these needs more and more effectively.

Finally, economists give only an incomplete answer to the following question: does society, and marketing in particular, create needs? They content themselves with the assumption that what consumers choose suits them, and they are unable to explain the real nature of consumption phenomena. To be able to distinguish between necessary needs and superfluous needs, one ought to define what should be the organic and social lives of individuals and know the structure of their motivation. We therefore need to turn to theories of human motivation in order to make some progress.

Motivation of the individual buyer

Economists, as we saw, make no distinction between what

consumers choose and what suits them, and never consider the
process of needs formation. What do individuals seek in their quest
for well-being and how does this state of well-being come about?
These two questions are never tackled by economic theory. Yet it is
clear that a more thorough analysis of consumer behaviour and the
structure of their motivation would make it easier to understand the
links that both economists and marketing try to establish between
supply and demand. Experimental psychology has made
enlightening contributions in this field and helps us discover a
whole range of general motivational orientations that determine
various individual behaviours. This section is based on the works of
Hebb (1955), Duffy (1957), Berlyne (1960), Scitovsky (1976) and
Nuttin (1980).

The 'stimulus–response' theory

A central preoccupation of the theory of motivation has been to study
why the organism moves into a state of activity. Motivation here
becomes *energy mobilization*. Originally, experimental psychology
was mostly interested in needs and drives of a purely physiological
nature, such as hunger, thirst, sex etc. In this scheme, called the
stimulus–response theory (or S–R theory) the stimulus is considered as
the active starting point of the organism's reaction. One then speaks
of *homeostasy*, which is a mechanism whereby a disorder creates an
urge giving rise to activity which restores equilibrium and thus
removes the urge. In this framework, the organism is basically
assumed to be reactive: in other words, it responds in specific ways
to stimuli. This more or less repudiates the problem of motivation.
Inactivity is supposedly the natural state of the individual.

We observe, however, that the organism doesn't always react to the
stimulus presented by its surroundings. Furthermore, it is a common
occurrence to find individuals embarking on activities that disrupt
equilibrium and setting up states of tension which would be hard to
explain if one believed the S–R theory. This theory reduces the
mechanism of motivation to a process of reducing tension and
practically ignores the *ascending phase of motivation*, that is, the
process by which new tensions or conflicts are worked out. However,
this type of behaviour is frequently observed, especially in affluent
societies, where basic needs are mostly met. A need, seen as a
homeostatic need, cannot totally explain individual behaviour.

> More mysterious than the process of *discharge* is the process that can be
> called *recharging*; and more central than the reduction of tension is the
> act by which man seeks increased responsibilities, takes bigger risks and
> finds himself new challenges (Nuttin, 1980, p. 201).

Today, experimental psychology emphasizes more and more the spontaneous activity of the nervous system and considers behavioural activity to be tied to the organism's being, just as much as physiological activity is.

The concept of arousal

Motivation theorists nowadays tend to explain behaviours in a new way, particularly because of the fact that neurophysiologists have considerably improved their knowledge of the way the brain functions and now have a completely different viewpoint. Hebb (1955, p. 246), for instance, formulates a hypothesis which is based, not on reactivity, but on the natural activity of the nervous system. Contrary to the beliefs held until then, the brain does not have to be excited from outside in order to be active and to discharge. It is not physiologically inert and its natural activity constitutes a system of self-motivation. Hebb, and also Duffy (1957, p. 267), put forth the idea that the general state of motivation can be equated with arousal, or the activity emanating from the reticular formation of the brain stem. Activity level depends on the degree of organic energy mobilized, that is on the variation in the level of arousal and vigilance. The level of arousal is measured by variations in electric current controlled with an electroencephalogram (EEG); these variations show up as waves in the EEG; the faster the electric discharge of neurons, the higher the level of arousal and the higher the frequency of oscillations in the EEG, measured in periods per second.

Scitovsky (1976) underlines the importance of the concept of arousal in understanding the reasons for a given behaviour:

> A high arousal is associated with vigilance and quick response; it makes the senses more sensitive to stimuli, increases the brain's capacity to process information, readies the muscles for action, and so shortens the total reaction time that elapses between an incoming sensation and the response through action. It makes you feel excited, emotional, anxious and tense. On the other hand, when you feel slow, less than vigilant, lax and drowsy, you are in a state of low arousal (Scitovsky, 1976, p. 19).

The increased level of arousal increases the organism's state of vigilance, thus providing favourable ground for the cerebral mechanism of stimulus–response to function rapidly and directly. The psychological measures of the level of arousal therefore provide a direct measure of the *motivational and emotional (drive) force* of a given situation for the individual (Duffy, 1957, p. 267). Also, this description of the concept of arousal suggests the existence of a continuum in the individual's level of activation.

Well-being and the optimal level of arousal

It is clear that the level of arousal has a great influence on the feeling of well-being or discomfort felt in general by people, and consequently bears on the determination of their behaviour. Excessive stimulation provokes tension, anxiety, nervousness, worry, frenzy, even panic; on the other hand stimulation which is too weak, or non-existent, brings about boredom, or a certain degree of displeasure, and creates the desire for a bigger stimulation. A job which is too simple or too monotonous can become painful if one is forced to pursue it without interruption over a long time. In fact, psychologists (Hebb, 1955, p. 250) accept that there is an *optimal level of arousal and stimulation*; optimal in the sense that it creates a feeling of comfort and well-being. Deviations below the optimum provoke a feeling of weariness, and deviations above the optimum provoke a sensation of fatigue and anxiety. Experimental observations show that, on the whole, individuals try to maintain an intermediary level of activation (Berlyne, 1960, p. 194).

We can identify here a first aspect of the general direction of motivation in individuals: *ensure comfort and prevent discomfort*. This motivation implies, on the one hand, the *reduction of tensions*, which satisfies various corporal and mental needs and reduces the level of arousal, which may be too high; on the other hand, it implies a *battle against boredom*, a behaviour which looks for stimulation and thus increases the level of arousal, which might be too low. These two types of behaviour have one thing in common: both try to fill up a gap and to *ensure a 'negative good'*, i.e. to stop pain, inconvenience and discomfort (Scitovksy, 1976, p. 69).

For economists, the reduction of arousal and tension is particularly important because as far as they are concerned almost all human activity, including consumption, is based on this process. We find here the notion of need defined by economists as simply a state of deficiency. However, the other type of behaviour, i.e. the raising of a level of arousal which is too low, is ignored by economists. This is commonly observed in more affluent economies, where prosperity has largely eliminated discomfort due to tension, but where the search for stimulation, novelty and change is becoming ever more important.

> The new consumer is also a dreamer. He buys a product, certainly to use it, but even more for the magic it offers him as premium (Séguéla, 1982, p. 50).

In some situations, finding sufficient stimulation to combat boredom can be a matter of life or death. This is true for old people for example. It is also well known that longevity is strongly related to having been able to keep a satisfying job late in life.

The need for stimulation

Berlyne's work in this area is interesting, especially because it is based on solid experimental ground. Berlyne shows that novelty (meaning anything surprising, different from past events and from what one expected) attracts attention and has a stimulating effect.

> Novelty stimulates and pleases especially when it creates surprisingness, change, ambiguity, incongruity, blurredness and power to induce uncertainty (Berlyne, 1960, p. 290).

It is as if the incongruence of the new event produces a dynamic effect which sets in motion exploratory actions.

It must, however, be made clear that the new and surprising is attractive only up to a limited degree, beyond which it becomes disturbing and frightening. Attractiveness first increases, then diminishes with the degree of newness and surprisingness. This relationship takes the shape of an inverted U-curve, known as the Wundt curve (Berlyne, 1960), shown in Figure 3.1. What is not new or surprising enough is boring, and what is too new is bewildering. An intermediate degree of newness seems to be the most pleasing.

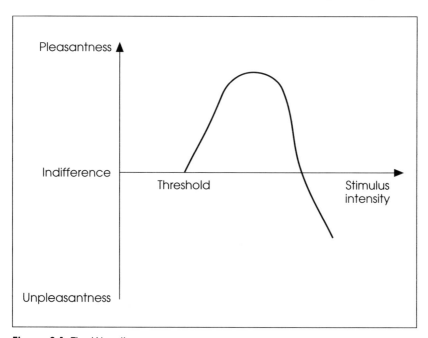

Figure 3.1 The Wundt curve

The stimulation provoked by the collative properties of goods forms an important source of satisfaction for individuals. Much of the activity of marketers, such as new product policies, segmentation and positioning, communication and promotion, focuses on meeting this expectation. For better or for worse, goods act as stimuli over the nervous system, a little bit like toys for children. The intelligence of a child can become stagnant with lack of adequate toys. In the same manner, an adult deprived of all stimuli, provided notably by the consumer society, can be overcome with boredom, depression and alienation.

> Many people feel younger when they purchase a brand new car and associate the age of their car with that of their own body. Thus buying a new car takes on symbolic proportions by representing physical rejuvenation (Valaskakis *et al.*, 1978, p. 167).

Therefore, the organism needs a continuous stream of stimuli and different experiences, just as it needs air and food. *Human beings need to need.* This basic motivation, as well as the more obvious motivation of reducing tensions, explains a large variety of individual behaviour which can only elude the deductions made by economists. The theory of 'novelty seeking' provides an explanation for consumers' actions, which introduce change, variety and novelty into their life style.

The need for pleasure

The sensation of comfort or discomfort is related to the level of arousal and depends on the latter's situation with respect to the optimum. Experimental psychologists have now proven that pleasure exists as a phenomenon different from absence of suffering or presence of comfort. The sensation of pleasure begins with variations in the level of arousal, in particular when a level of arousal which is too low or too high is approaching its optimum (Berlyne, 1960, p. 187).

Two sources of pleasure can be identified: one results from the satisfaction of a need and the resulting reduction in tension; the other comes from the stimulation itself. *Satisfaction of a need* is pleasant in itself and drives the organism to pursue its activity to the point of satiation and even beyond.

> In very poor communities, families often plunge into debt for the sake of a funeral feast or a wedding celebration. Such behaviour horrifies economists of the not-so-poor countries . . . Yet the very universality of the custom of feasting among the poor people of so many different cultures is evidence that the pleasures of a good meal for those who seldom taste

one are very great and weigh heavily against the biological needs of survival (Scitovsky, 1976, p. 66).

The economic theory of the rational behaviour of consumers implies a judicious balance between different needs and does not take into account pleasure, which can lead the individual to an allocation different from the one predicted by economic theory. It is in fact frequently observed that people behave so as to have full satisfaction from time to time, and they properly space out the moments or periods during which they completely fulfill their wants. This type of behaviour is frequently observed in industrialized countries, in the leisure sector for example, and in particular in holiday expenditure.

Note that the pleasure inherent in the satisfaction of a need implies that discomfort must precede pleasure. This common sense rule is a very old one; it was debated by the ancient Greeks. Psychiatrists call it the *Law of Hedonic Contrast*. It follows from the rule that too much comfort may preclude pleasure (a child who is nibbling all day long cannot appreciate a good meal). This fact can explain the malaise observed at times in affluent societies, when satisfaction of needs does not bring about any pleasure. By eliminating simple joys, excessive comfort forces us to seek strong sensations.

At this stage the second source of pleasure, the one resulting from the *stimulation itself*, comes into its own. Here the object of the need is not to make up for a shortage, but to contribute to the development of the individual. To quote Nuttin (1980), this is the *ascending phase of motivation*; a phase in which new tensions and discordances are established, giving individuals the *will to progress and surpass themselves*. This is Maslow's self-actualization need. People take pleasure in excitement. They get more satisfaction out of the struggle of reaching an objective than they get when they actually reach it. Once individuals have passed the moment of triumph, they almost regret having reached their goal. Most people then give themselves an even more distant objective, probably because they prefer to act and fight rather than passively observe their success (Nuttin, 1980, p. 201). In this way, individuals force their environment to stimulate them or to continue to stimulate them.

The pleasure of this type of stimulation results from the temporary tension it creates. Such pleasure is more constant and better outlasts the pleasure of comfort, because these stimulations leave more room for imagination and creativity to the individual.

> ... the object of these stimulations is almost unlimited. By meeting them, tension goes up rather than down. Thus the tendency persists beyond the point where the objective is reached (Nuttin, 1980, p. 202).

Here, we are now talking about *insatiable needs*. It is in the nature of *self-development* needs to know neither the saturation nor the periodicity of homeostatic needs.

> We see here what pleasure is and its relation to comfort: the former is the variation of the latter. If happiness is simply comfort, then it depends on the intensity of satisfied wants. Pleasure is complete when the want is a little or much more satisfied than it was. If happiness is not comfort but pleasure, then it is condemned to only live some privileged moments, prolonged with the help of memory (Cotta, 1980, pp. 11–12).

From the psychologist's point of view, seeking pleasure is an important factor in human behaviour, and it is a fundamental motivational force which must be taken into account in any analysis of individual buying behaviour.

Determinants of consumers' well-being

An overview of the major contributions of experimental psychology to the study of human motivation finally arrives at a much wider understanding of the notion of need. We started from the point of view of economists, for whom need is essentially a 'state of shortage' revealed by buying behaviour, without any explanation of the origin or the nature of motivations at the root of this state of deficiency. The absence of theory about motivations leads economists to make normative recommendations which have as much value as their starting assumptions, but which have little to do with actual observed behaviour.

Research by psychologists makes it possible to retain three general motivational directions, which can explain a large variety of behaviours and which appear to be factors that explain the individual's general well-being. These determinants can be grouped as *comfort, pleasure* and *stimulation*. Figure 3.2 explains diagrammatically the relations between these three determinants on the one hand, and their relation to individual well-being on the other.

The *three motivational forces*, determining individual well-being, can be briefly described as follows:

- The search for *comfort*, which results from two kinds of behaviour: one that reduces tensions by satisfying homeostatic needs; and one that struggles against boredom with the help of stimuli such as novelty, change, incongruity, uncertainty, risk etc.
- The search for *pleasure*, which also results from two sources: pleasure inherent in the reduction of tensions and pleasure obtained from stimuli.

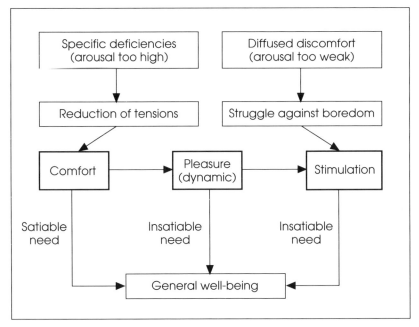

Figure 3.2 The determinants of well-being

- The search for *stimulation*, not only as a means to combat boredom, but as a goal in itself, without any other objective in mind but the tension it arouses, generating pleasure and creating the opportunity of development and actualization for the individual.

The search for comfort aims to make up for a deficiency and thus to ensure a *defensive good*; pleasure and stimulation aim to ensure a *creative good*.

By relying on this description of the major motivational forces we are in a better position to answer the questions facing marketing mentioned at the beginning of this chapter. The increased use of marketing—which takes the form of products being continually renewed, more and more subtle differentiation, sophisticated perceptual positioning, advertising suggesting elaborate life styles etc.—in reality only responds to the rise in needs of pleasure and stimulation observed in richer societies, where basic needs are well met, but where, on the other hand, needs such as novelty, surprise, complexity, and risk have become vital necessities.

The needs to try varied experiences, to live different life styles, and the possibility to try new products and to have new sources of satisfaction form an important subject matter in this type of society.

This search is endless, because there is no possible saturation in this type of need.

Some philosophers advocate rising above all wants in order to escape this endless escalation, which, far from bringing internal peace, causes worry and creates an infernal cycle. The wise Hindu Sarna Lakshman writes:

> Desire tells us: get this and then you will be happy. We believe it and we try to acquire the relevant object. If we don't get it, or if we don't get enough, we suffer. If we get it, then desire immediately suggests another objective, and we don't even see that we have been fooled (quoted by Boirel, 1977).

These philosophers are advocating the *ideal of ataraxy*, that is, the absence of turmoil as a result of the extinction of desire. The alternative to this extreme solution is *creative consumption*, that is, consumption that encourages ascending motivations of progress, self-actualization and excellence. If it is true that 'man prefers hunting to the catch', as Pascal said, then want, as being the driving force of activity, can be the first cause of satisfaction brought about by creative consumption.

Towards a comprehensive theory of consumption

The contributions of motivation theory help us to identify more general *motivational orientations* in human beings. These orientations govern a large variety of individual behaviours. These disciplinary contributions, however, provide only a general description of the needs structure, with little attempt at operationalization and no explicit reference to buying behaviour. Moreover, they tend to focus on one dimension of behaviour (economic, social, psychological etc.) and do not propose a comprehensive framework which integrates the concepts used in each contributing discipline. Several attempts have been made to develop a comprehensive multidisciplinary description of behaviour, namely by compiling lists of needs.

Typologies of human needs

Well-being means having a 'good' to satisfy each need, so a natural approach is to develop a list of needs and to compare it with available goods. The word 'goods' has here a special meaning. They are not only physical entities or services, but may be abstract, social or psychological entities, such as love, prestige etc. The seminal works of Murray (1938), Maslow (1943), Rokeach (1973) and more recently Sheth, Newman and Gross (1991) are representatives of this approach.

Murray's inventory of human needs

Murray calls a need a hypothetical construct because it is of a physiochemical nature that is unknown. It resides in the brain and is thus in a position to control all significant behaviour. In Murray's words:

> A need is a hypothetical construct that stands for a force in the brain region that organizes and directs mind and body behaviour so as to maintain the organism in its most desirable state (Murray, 1938, p. 123).

Murray gives a rather systematic inventory, classifying individuals' needs into four dimensions: *primary (viscerogenic)* and *secondary (psychogenic)* needs, according to whether they are of psychological origin or not; *positive* and *negative* needs, depending on whether the individual is attracted by the object or not; *manifest* or *latent* needs, according to whether the need drives a real or imaginary behaviour; and *conscious* or *unconscious* needs, according to whether they drive the individual to take introspective steps or not. Murray lists 37 needs covering these categories.

Murray believed that all people possess the same needs, but he recognized that the expression of them will differ from one person to another because of differences in personality and in environmental factors. Needs could be provoked by either internal or external stimuli, and they could be weak or strong at any particular time. Needs exist in three different states: (1) refractory, in which no incentive will arouse it; (2) inducible, in which a need is inactive but susceptible to excitation; and (3) active, in which the need is determining the behaviour of the organism (Murray, 1938, pp. 85–6). Thus, marketing activities could have a direct impact on inducible needs.

Maslow's need hierarchy

Maslow (1943) adopts a similar approach, grouping fundamental needs into five categories: physiological, safety, social, esteem and self-actualization needs. Table 3.1 describes these needs. Maslow's analysis, however, goes further and is not limited to a simple classification. Maslow postulates the existence of a *hierarchy of needs*, which depends on the individual's state of development.

According to Maslow, there is an *order of priorities* in needs, in the sense that we begin to try to satisfy dominant needs before going to the next category. Once the needs of a lower order have been satisfied, they allow needs of the higher order to become motivators and influence our behaviour. There is a progressive abatement in the intensity of needs already met and an increasing intensity of needs of a higher order not yet satisfied. We observe an evolution of the

Table 3.1 Maslow's hierarchy of needs (Maslow, 1943)

Physiological needs
These are fundamental; once satisfied, they cease to be determinant factors of motivation and no longer influence behaviour.

Safety needs
Physical safety, preservation of the physical structure of the organism, psychological safety, conservation of the psychic structure of personality. Need for own identity, to feel in charge of one's destiny.

Social needs
People are social animals and feel the need to fit into a group, to associate with their fellows, they feel the need to love and be loved. Mutual help, belonging and sense of community are also social needs.

Self-esteem needs
Self-esteem, personal dignity, confidence in oneself and one's own competence. The feel that one's objectives are valid. The esteem that others feel for us. The need for recognition, to be respected, to have a social status.

Self-actualization needs
These needs are at the top of the scale of human needs, and include self-realization and development; the need of people to surpass themselves; to use all their capacities and push their limits; and to give a meaning to things and find their *raison d'être*.

structure of needs depending on the individual's development as he or she goes from an overall objective of survival or living standard towards more qualitative objectives regarding life style or quality of life.

Maslow's analysis is interesting because it puts forth not only the *multidimensional structure* of needs, but also the fact that needs have different degrees of intensity in different individuals. In reality, there is always some coexistence of these categories of needs, with one category or another becoming more important according to the individual, or according to the circumstances of one particular individual.

Products to be developed for satisfying needs must therefore be planned accordingly. A good or product may have more than one role or function beyond just the basic one. Individuals use goods not only for practical reasons, but also to communicate with their environment, to show who they are, to demonstrate their feelings etc. It is important for marketing to be aware of the role played by goods and brands (Baudrillard, 1968), not simply for their functional value, but also for their emotional or symbolic values. We shall see later in this chapter that the multidimensional structure of needs also exists with the organizational customer.

Rokeach's list of values

Human values research stresses the important goals which most people seek. Values are closely linked to human needs, but exist at a more realistic level. They are the *mental representations of underlying needs*, not only of individual needs but also of societal and institutional needs. In other words, values are our ideas about what is desirable.

> A *value* is an enduring belief that a specific mode of conduct or end-state of existence is personally or socially preferable to an opposite or converse mode of conduct or end-state of existence. A *value-system* is an enduring organization of beliefs concerning preferable modes of conduct or end-states of existence along a continuum of relative importance (Rokeach, 1973, p. 5).

There are two types of values: (1) terminal and (2) instrumental. Terminal (or end-state) values are beliefs we have about the goals or end-states for which we strive (e.g. happiness, wisdom etc.). Instrumental (or means) values refer to beliefs about desirable ways of behaving to help us attain the terminal values (e.g. behaving honestly or accepting responsibility).

Since values are transmitted through cultures, most people in a given society will possess the sames values, but to different degrees. The relative importance of each value will therefore be different from one individual to another and these differences can be used as market segmentation criteria, as shown in Chapter 6 of this book. The prominence of different values can also change over time. Rokeach postulates that the total number of values that a person possesses is relatively small. In his empirical work, Rokeach identifies eighteen terminal and instrumental values (Rokeach, 1973, p. 28).

In recent years, researchers have been working to develop a short list of values that can be measured in a reliable manner. Kahle (1983) has identified eight summary terminal values:

- Self-respect
- Security
- Warm relationships
- Sense of accomplishment
- Self-fulfilment
- Being well-respected
- Sense of belonging
- Fun/enjoyment/excitement

Several researchers have found that those values relate well to various aspects of consumer behaviour or to social change.

> For example, people who value fun and enjoyment may desire a cup of coffee for its rich taste, whereas people who value a sense of accomplishment may wish to use coffee as a mild stimulant to increase productivity; and people who value warm relationships with others may want to share a cup of coffee as an aspect of a social ritual (Kahle *et al.*, 1988).

The logic of this methodology can be summarized as follows: to understand individuals' motivation, one place to start is to try to understand their values, particularly with products that involve consumer value. Also, an understanding of the way values are changing in a given society will facilitate the development of effective strategies for dealing with the dynamics of societal change.

The Sheth–Newman–Gross theory of consumption values

Applying the concept of 'value' to buying behaviour, Sheth, Newman and Gross (1991, pp. 18–25) describe market choice as a multidimensional phenomenon involving multiple values: functional, social, emotional, epistemic and conditional. They define these values as follows.

- *Functional value*   The perceived utility acquired by an alternative as the result of its ability to perform its functional, utilitarian or physical purposes. Alternatives acquire functional value through the possession of salient functional, utilitarian or physical attributes.
- *Social value*   The perceived utility acquired by an alternative as a result of its association with one or more social groups. Alternatives acquire social value through association with positively or negatively stereotyped demographic, socioeconomic and cultural ethnic groups.
- *Emotional value*   The perceived utility acquired by an alternative as a result of its ability to arouse feelings or affective states. Alternatives acquire emotional value when associated with specific feelings or when they facilitate or perpetuate feelings.
- *Epistemic value*   The perceived utility acquired by an alternative as a result of its ability to arouse curiosity, provide novelty and/or satisfy a desire for knowledge. Alternatives acquire epistemic value through the capacity to provide something new or different.
- *Conditional value*   The perceived utility acquired by an alternative as a result of the specific situation or the context faced by the choice-maker. Alternatives acquire conditional value in the presence of antecedent physical or social contingencies that

enhance their functional or social value, but do not otherwise possess this value.

These five values make *differential contributions* to specific market choices in the sense that some values can contribute more than others. Those values are also *independent*. They relate additively and contribute incrementally to choice. Although it is desirable to maximize all five values, users are often willing to accept less of one value to obtain more of another. That is why buyers are willing to trade off less salient values in order to maximize those that are most salient (Sheth *et al.*, 1991, p. 12).

Considerable overlaps are observed when comparing these summary values with the different need categories proposed by diverse disciplines. The functional value corresponds to the general motivation for comfort in Murray's viscerogenic needs and in Maslow's safety and physiological needs. The social and emotional functions correspond with Maslow's social needs of belongingness and love, with Rokeach's values of 'social recognition' and 'true friendship' and with the more general motivation for stimulation. The epistemic value is similar to Maslow's need for 'self-actualization', to Rockeach's values 'exciting life' and 'pleasure' and also to the general need for stimulation and pleasure. Previous contributions did not include the conditional value construct, which is particularly well adapted to the situation of buying behaviour. In addition, Sheth *et al.* (1991; see Chapter 5) have operationalized their theory by developing a generic questionnaire and a standardized procedure for adapting the analysis to any specific market situation.

The 'value' approach provides the market analyst with a simple but comprehensive framework for analysing the need structure of the individual buyer and for segmenting markets. The five summary values proposed by the Sheth–Newman–Gross theory will be used in the following chapters as a basis for designing operational market analysis and measurement.

Motivation of the organizational buyer

So far, our analysis has concerned only the needs and motivations of the individual as a buyer. But a large part of commercial activity, in any economy, is made up of transactions between organizations. This includes firms selling equipment, goods, intermediary products, raw materials etc. to other firms using these products in their own manufacturing process. Although the principles governing marketing are just as pertinent for firms selling industrial goods as for firms selling consumer goods, the concrete manner in which these principles are implemented may appear very different.

Distinctive characteristics of organizational marketing

The nature of demand

Industrial demand is a *derived demand*; that is, a demand expressed by an organization which uses the products purchased in its own manufacturing process, in order to meet either the demand of other organizations or the demand of the end buyer. Thus, industrial demand is part of a chain (a production chain) which depends on a downstream demand and is ultimately 'derived' from the demand for consumer goods.

Industrial demand, and particularly capital equipment demand, is *highly fluctuating* and reacts strongly to small variations in final demand (the acceleration principle).

Industrial demand is often *price inelastic*, in so far as the product represents a key component, perhaps made to exact specifications. The product is more of a necessity and there are fewer substitutes available.

The organizational customer

The industrial firm faces *multiple customers*: its direct customers and the customers of its direct customers also participating in the production chain.

The organizational customer has a *collegiate structure* at each level of the industrial chain: a group of individuals, the buying centre, who exercise different functions and roles and have distinct competences and motivations.

The customer is a *professional buyer*, technically competent; the purchase decision involves a degree of formalization not found in consumer purchasing.

Product characteristics

The product sought is generally *well defined* by the customer who knows what is wanted; specifications are clearly defined and the supplier has little room for manoeuvring.

Industrial products enter into the manufacturing process of the industrial customer and thus have a *strategic*, if not vital, importance.

Industrial products often have a very *large number of different uses*, unlike consumer goods which are almost inevitably for a specific use.

The box above describes the main characteristics of *business-to-business marketing* or of organizational marketing, grouped into three categories according to whether they relate to demand, to the industrial client or to the product.

By far the most significant feature, at least from the aspect of motivation, is the fact that the organizational customer, whose needs must be met by the supplier, is represented by a group of people called the *buying centre*. Furthermore, this collegiate structure of the industrial customer can be found at any stage of the *industrial chain* in which the customer is inserted. This is a second important feature specific to industrial marketing. The firm selling industrial goods therefore faces a double diversity of needs: those specific to the buying centre and those specific to each of the levels of the industrial chain.

The demand for industrial goods

Demand for industrial goods has the particularity of being a *derived demand*. It is demand expressed by an organization which uses the purchased products in its own manufacturing process, so as to meet the demand of other organizations or of the final consumer. It therefore expresses a demand dependent on one or many downstream demands.

The firm Polypal manufactures and sells metallic storage equipment. Such installations are purchased by firms investing in new production capacity or extending existing capacity in order to meet demand in their own markets. It is therefore in Polypal's interest first to identify developing sectors, and then to address the firms supplying the markets which would be likely to invest in storage equipment.

The demand for an industrial good is even more complex to analyse because the product is at the start of the transformation chain, far from the final demand on which it nevertheless depends. Thus it faces many echelons of successive demand, each with differentiated needs structures.

The notion of an industrial chain goes beyond a list of names by branch or by sector and makes the conventional division of the economy into primary, secondary and tertiary sectors out of date. An industrial chain consists of all the stages of production, from raw materials to satisfying the final need of the consumer, irrespective of whether this final need concerns a product or a service. There is a hierarchy of industries which are either clients or suppliers of a given firm according to whether they are upstream or downstream. The strategic force of an industrial client depends, among other things, on its ability to anticipate and control the end market of the chain in which it participates.

The following list describes the structure of a typical industrial demand (see Figure 3.3). Clearly the chain of demands may be much

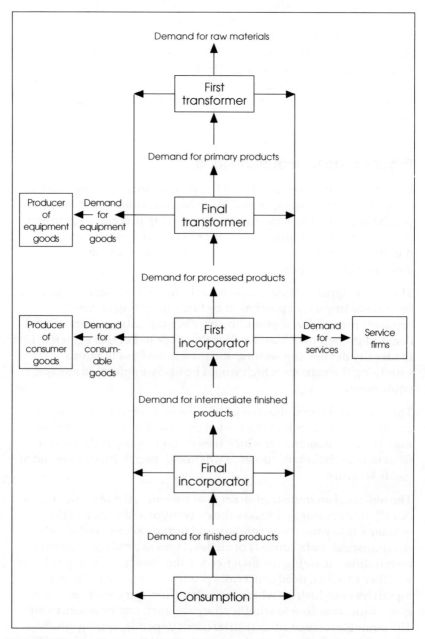

Figure 3.3 Typical structure of industrial demand: the notion of the industrial chain

longer and more complex in some cases. Without claiming this to be an exhaustive list, the following distinctions can be established.

- *First transformation*   Demand is for processed materials that are transformed into semi-finished goods, for instance, steel bars, sheets, chemicals, leather etc.
- *Final transformation*   Demand is for primary products which will be transformed into more elaborate processed products. For example, transformation of raw sheet metal into rust-proof sheet metal, either plated or pre-painted. Bekaert transforms raw steel into wires of different diameters.
- *First incorporation*   Demand is for finished goods used to manufacture more complex products which are themselves components of other products. For example, pre-painted sheet metal is used to manufacture radiators; wires are used to manufacture radial tyres.
- *Final incorporation*   Demand is for finished products incorporated in manufacturing finished products for final demand, for example, tyres and batteries, spark plugs, TV tubes, automobile windscreens etc.
- *Assemblers*   Demand is for a large variety of products which will be put together to form systems or large compounds. For example, radiators are placed with other products to form a heating system. Similarly, a system of public transport, such as an underground rail system, brings together a tremendous variety of different products.

In addition to these successive demands which follow one another in a chain, there are also lateral demands of capital equipment goods, consumable items (fuel, wrapping materials, office supplies etc.) and services (maintenance and repair, manufacturing and business services, professional services).

Therefore the industrial firm in the position of the beginning of the production chain is faced with a sequence of independent demands which finally determine its own demand. It faces two categories of clients: its *direct customers* and the *customers of its customers*. In order to apply active marketing, the firm must take into account the specific demands of its direct customers, of the intermediary customers and of those who express final demand at the end of the chain. Figure 3.4 gives example of the successive customers, direct and indirect, facing a manufacturer of heat pumps.

The buying decision centre

In an industrial firm, buying decisions, and especially the more

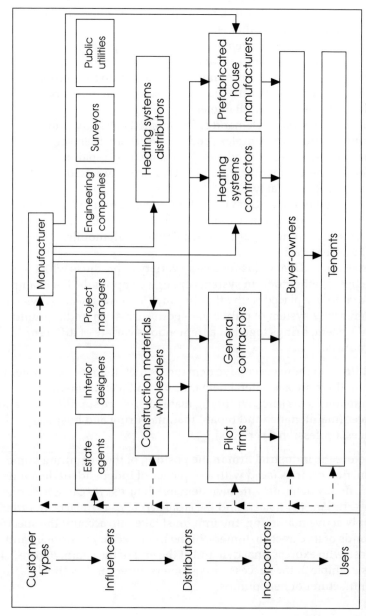

Figure 3.4 Vertical structure of the domestic heap pump market (adapted from FNGE, ESC, Lyon (1976))

important ones, are mostly taken by a group of people called the
buying group or the *buying centre*.

> The buying center is defined as consisting of those individuals who interact
> for the specific purpose of accomplishing the buying task . . . .. These
> persons interact on the basis of their particular roles in the buying process.
> The buying group is characterized by both a pattern of communication
> (interaction) and a set of shared values (norms) which direct and constrain
> the behavior of the individual within it (Webster and Wind, 1972, p. 35).

There are several distinct roles in the buying centre: users,
influencers, purchasers, deciders and gatekeepers. These individuals
are either involved in the purchase itself or are concerned about its
possible consequences on the firm's activity, and thus participate in
the purchase decision-making process in one way or another.
Understanding those roles will help one understand the nature of
interpersonal influence in the buying decision process. The buying
centre comprises individuals with different functions and therefore
with different goals, motivations and behaviours. Hence many
purchase decisions are conflicting, and they follow a complex process
of internal negotiation.

The composition of the buying centre varies with the importance of
the decisions to be made. In general, the buying centre includes the
following five roles, which can be occupied by one or several
individuals.

- *Purchasers* have formal authority and responsibility for selecting
  alternative brands and suppliers and for determining the terms of
  purchase and negotiating contracts. This is usually done by the
  purchasing manager.
- *Users* are the persons who use the product: the production
  engineer or the workers. The users can formulate specific purchase
  requirements or refuse to work with some materials. Generally
  speaking, users are better placed for evaluating the performance of
  purchased goods and services.
- *Influencers* do not necessarily have buying authority but can
  influence the outcome of a decision by defining criteria which
  constrain the choices that can be considered. R&D personnel,
  design, engineering and consultants typically belong to this
  category.
- *Deciders* have formal authority and responsibility to determine the
  final selection of brands or vendors. There is generally an upper
  limit on the financial commitment that they can make, reserving
  larger decisions for other members of the organization, for
  instance the board of directors.
- *Gatekeepers* are group members who control the flow of

Table 3.2 Decision stages and roles of the buying centre (Webster and Wind, 1972 (p. 80))

Stages in the buying process	Composition of the buying centre				
	User	Influencer	Buyer	Decider	Gatekeeper
Identification of needs	•	•			
Establishing specifications	•	•	•	•	
Identifying alternatives	•	•	•		•
Evaluating alternatives	•	•	•		
Selecting the supplier	•	•	•	•	

information into the group and who can exercise indirect influence on the buying process.

The composition of the buying centre (see Table 3.2) will vary with the complexity and the degree of uncertainty of decisions in the firm. One can distinguish three kinds of situation:

- *New task* The purchase of a new product in a new class of products for the client organization.
- *Modified rebuy* Problem and product are known, but some elements of the buyer's specifications are modified.
- *Straight rebuy* Purchase of a known product, not modified and with which the firm has extensive experience.

In the first two cases the buying centre intervenes totally. One can see that it is vital for the supplier to identify all those involved in the purchasing process, because it must identify the targets of its communication policy. It is equally important to understand how these participants interact among themselves and what their dominant motivation is (Valla, 1980, p. 28).

Needs of the buying centre

The industrial customer is therefore identified with the 'buying centre' which comprises persons from different functions in the organization, who thus have distinct personal and organizational motivations. The notion of need in industry goes beyond the conventional idea of rational choice based only on the quality–price criterion. Choices are rational, as in the case of the individual consumer, in so far as all motivations and constraints with a bearing on purchase decisions are taken into account: personal motivations, interpersonal relations, economic and organizational constraints, environmental pressures etc. As in the case of the individual consumer, need therefore has a multidimensional structure. The *overall need of an industrial customer* can be described with reference to at least five values:

- *Technology* Product specifications, state-of-the-art technology, up-to-date and constant quality, just-in-time delivery etc.
- *Finance* Price competitiveness, transfer costs, installation and maintenance costs, payment terms, delivery reliability etc.
- *Assistance* After-sales service, help for installation and operation, technical assistance and servicing etc.
- *Information* Communication, qualified sales personnel, priority access to new products, training, business intelligence etc.
- *Psycho-sociology* Reciprocal relations, compatibility of organizational forms, brand or company reputation etc.

The following (Valla, 1980, p. 25) illustrates the multidimensional nature of the industrial customer's need. The statement from the purchase manager: 'No, we won't work with this supplier any more, they are not reliable', may have different meanings:

- The quality of their products is not constant (technical value).
- Their prices are whimsical (financial value).
- They were supposed to have repaired a machine two months ago (assistance value).
- They have promised to send one of their engineers to tell us about new products being developed; we have called many times and they still haven't done it (information value).
- They treat us as insignificant (psycho-sociological value).

These few possible explanations of the attitude of the purchase manager in a medium-sized firm illustrate the variety of needs of the industrial buyer.

We note that the determinants of well-being for the industrial client are of a very different nature from those governing the well-being of the individual consumer. The structure of motivations of the industrial customer is both more complex and more simple. It is more complex because it involves an organization and different individuals operating in the organization; it is more simple because the main motivations are more objective and thus easier to identity.

However, despite the real differences that exist between the two areas, the basic ideas of marketing have the same relevance in the industrial market as they have in the consumer market: to adjust supply to the overall need of the customer. If this principle is not implemented, the penalty in the industrial market is probably paid more rapidly because of the buyer's professionalism and the fact that needs are more clearly defined.

The industrial buying process

The analysis of the buying process basically consists of identifying the specific roles played by each member of the buying centre at different stages of the decision-making process, their choice criteria, their perceptions of the performance of products or firms in the market, the weight given to each point of view etc.

As in the case of the buying decision of the individual consumer, the industrial buying process can be divided into several stages. As illustrated in Table 3.2, Webster and Wind (1972, p. 80) suggest five phases in the process:

- Identification of need.
- Determination of specifications and scheduling the purchase.
- Identification of buying alternatives.
- Evaluating alternative buying actions.
- Selection of suppliers.

Clearly, the decision of an industrial client does not always follow this process. The complexity of the decision and its degree of risk or novelty determine how formal the buying process will be. Furthermore, the decision-making and organizational processes can also vary according to the firm, both in terms of its size and its fields of activity.

One can imagine that the roles of the members of the buying centre are different at each stage of the decision-making process. The analysis of the buying process must answer the following questions:

- Who is a major participant in the decision-making process of buying a given industrial product?
- Who are the key influencers intervening in the process?
- What is the level of their influence?
- What evaluation criteria does each decision participant use?
- What is the weight given to each criterion?

This information is usually collected by survey. It helps to clarify the issue, particularly when it comes to training salespeople by helping them to understand the mechanism of the industrial buying process better.

Valla (1980, p. 27) underlines the fact that training salespeople to understand this type of analysis particularly helps them to:

- understand better the buyer's role as well as the system of motivations and constraints within which the buyer operates.

- go beyond mere contact with the purchaser by identifying other possible communication targets within the industrial client's organization.
- determine better when is the best moment to directly intervene *vis-à-vis* appropriate targets in order to increase efficiency of contacts.
- be in a better position to take advantage of opportunities when they present themselves, due to broader relations with all members of the buying centre.

We shall see in Chapter 6 that the way the buying centre functions is an important segmentation criterion in industrial markets.

4

Understanding buyer choice behaviour

Having identified the key values influencing the individual consumer's choice behaviour, as well as the multidimensional need structure of the organizational customer, we will now analyse the way in which buyers make purchasing decisions. During the last decade there have been many theoretical and empirical contributions by diverse disciplines relevant to the understanding of buying behaviour. Market analysts have models and conceptual frameworks at their disposal to help them in organizing the market information collected by the firm. This information is not always for the sake of scientific knowledge *per se*, but rather to gain a better understanding of market choice behaviour and to enhance marketing efficiency. The objective of this chapter is to review the major theoretical and conceptual contributions which could be applicable to individual as well as organizational buying decisions.

The buyer as an active decision-maker

From the marketing point of view, buying behaviour covers all activity preceding, accompanying and following purchase decisions. The individual or the organization actively takes part in the decisions in order to make choices in a systematic way, as opposed to random or stochastic selections. The purchasing behaviour is seen as a *process of problem solving*. All possible steps that may have something to do with the resolution of the problem are therefore part of the buying process. They can be grouped into five stages:

- Problem recognition
- Information search
- Evaluation of alternatives
- Purchase decision
- Post-purchase behaviour

This view of an active buyer is in total contrast to that of the passive buyer who is dominated by the unconscious and is defenceless against the selling activities of the firm and advertisers. The complexity of the decision process varies, however, with the type of buying decisions and with the risk implied by the choice.

Importance of the perceived risk

Not every purchase decision requires a systematic information search. The complexity of the approach to problem solving depends on the importance of the *perceived risk* associated with the purchase, in other words, on the uncertainty about the scope of the consequences of a particular choice. There are four kinds of risk or unfavourable consequences normally perceived by the buyer (Bauer, 1960):

- A *financial loss*, when the product is faulty and needs replacement or repair at one's own expense.
- A *loss of time*, due to hours of making complaints, returning to distributors, repairs etc.
- A *physical risk*, due to the consumption or use of products potentially harmful to one's health or the environment.
- A *psychological risk*, when a bad purchase leads to loss of self-esteem or creates general dissatisfaction.

Market research shows that buyers develop strategies and ways of reducing risk that enable them to act with relative confidence and ease in situations where their information is inadequate and the consequences of their actions are incalculable (Bauer, 1960, p. 120).

To reduce the perceived risk before the purchase decision, the buyer can use various forms of information, such as personal sources (family, neighbours, friends), commercial sources (advertising, salespersons, catalogues), public sources (comparative tests, official publications) and experimental sources (product trials, inspection). The higher the perceived risk, the more extensive the information search will be.

Problem-solving approaches

Three types of approach to problem solving can be distinguished: routine response behaviour, and limited and extensive problem-solving behaviours (Howard and Sheth, 1969).

- *Extensive problem solving* is adopted when the value of information and/or the perceived risk are high. For example, this happens in situations where the buyer is confronted with an unfamiliar brand in an unfamiliar product class. The choice criteria by which alternatives are assessed will be weak or non-existent and an

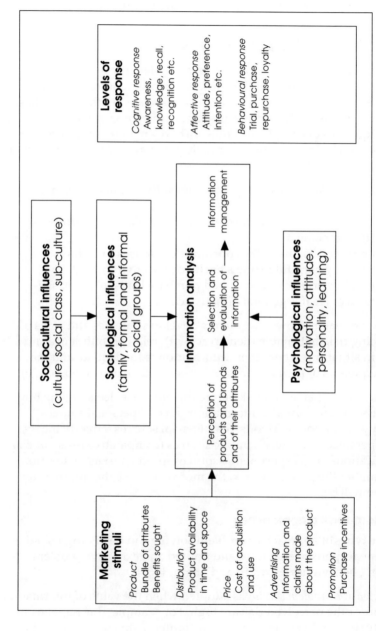

Figure 4.1 The fields of consumer behaviour analysis

intensive information search will be necessary to identify the relevant criteria.

- *Limited problem solving* applies to the situation of a buyer confronted with a new, unfamiliar brand in a familiar product class, usually where existing brands do not provide an adequate level of satisfaction. Choice criteria already exist, but there will still be a certain amount of search and evaluation prior to purchase.
- Finally, *routine response behaviour* is observed in the case where the consumer has accumulated enough experience and knowledge and has definite preferences about one or more familiar brands within a familiar product category. Here the process of choice is simplified and repetitive, with little or no prior information search. Under this situation of low involvement, considerable consumer inertia and/or brand loyalty would be expected.

Note that routine response behaviour is also observed for low-cost, frequently purchased items, be they familiar or not to the buyer. For this product category, the best information comes from buying the product, because the cost of experimenting is low. If there is dissatisfaction, the consumer will simply not re-buy the brand at the next purchase occasion. Given the low cost of error, there is no need to search diligently for information. The fields of consumer behaviour analysis are summarized in Figure 4.1.

The buyer's involvement

In recent years, the concept of *consumer involvement* has received considerable attention in the marketing literature. Involvement can be defined as '. . . a state of energy (arousal) that a person experiences in regard to a consumption-related activity' (Wilkie, 1990, p. 220). Thus involvement implies attention to something because it is somehow relevant or perceived as risky. High involvement requires high levels of prior deliberation and strong feelings, while low involvement will occur when consumers invest less energy in their thoughts and feelings. The concept of involvement, which overlaps somewhat with the above Howard and Sheth classification of problem-solving situations, is useful for analysing consumer behaviour at different levels of involvement and for deciding on the type of communication strategy to adopt in each situation. We shall return to this concept in the following chapter (see Figure 5.1, p. 122).

A rational approach to problem solving

In this framework, purchasing behaviour is neither erratic nor conditioned by the environment. It is rational in the sense of the *principle of limited rationality*, which means within the bounds of individuals' cognitive and learning capacities. The implicit assumptions are:

- Consumers make choices after *deliberation*, the extent of which depends on the importance of the perceived risk.
- Choices are based on *anticipation of future data* and not only on short-term observations.
- Choices are also guided by the *principle of generalized scarcity* according to which any human acts. Any decision has an opportunity cost.

We live in an environment where everything is scarce: not only money and goods, but also information and especially time, our scarcest resource because it is perfectly inextensible.

This approach is called a 'rational approach to problem-solving'. The use of the term 'rational' is not in contrast with the term 'emotional', which implies a value judgement on the quality of the choice. The steps undertaken are considered to be rational as long as they are *consistent* with the set objectives, whatever these objectives may be. For example, an individual for whom the social value or status effect is important is prepared to pay more for a product with the same quality. Such action is considered to be rational because the behaviour is consistent.

In other words, as long as information about the objective is sought, critically analysed and processed, behaviour is rational within the limits of the gathered information and the cognitive capability of the individual. This, however, does not exclude the existence of another, 'better' choice.

We are using here the notion of 'consistency' which is so dear to economists, with a fundamental difference. The consumer is *consistent with respect to his or her own set of axioms*, and not with respect to a set of axioms defined with no reference to specific situational context or preferences structure.

Rational behaviour does not exclude impulsive behaviour. As long as the latter is adopted deliberately, either for the simple pleasure of acting impulsively, or for the excitement of being confronted with unexpected consequences, the behaviour is said to be rational.

Rationality here implies no more than the adoption of a kind of systematic choice procedure. This could be defined as the coherent use of a set of principles forming the basis of choice. When choice is made at random, behaviour is unpredictable and erratic, and analysis is impossible. Marketing accepts the existence of the latter type of behaviour, but believes that it is not representative of actual behaviour observed in most real-life situations.

This concept of consistency of behaviour makes it possible to reconcile different disciplinary approaches (economic, psychological, sociological) in the study of buying behaviour. Marketing is interested in the real person, the individual with all his or her diversity, as illustrated by the list of values described in the previous chapter. Actual choices are influenced by several values, but the individual or the organization may very well accept a sub-optimal level of functional value, for example, in order to maximize social or epistemic value. This type of choice will be termed 'rational' because it is consistent with the personal set of values prevailing in the specific choice situation (conditional value).

Consumer behaviour in a macroeconomic perspective

Macroeconomists considered for a long time that consumers adjusted their consumption behaviour in terms of factors registered over a short period, with no explicit reference to time. However, observation of behaviour reveals that consumption is a question of habit more than anything else, its domain being certainly that of inertia, but also of expectations, predispositions and anticipations formulated in terms of longer horizons. In other words, there exists a *dynamics of behaviour* which must be taken into account when analysing and forecasting market development.

The permanent income hypothesis

A revealing example is the change of views regarding the macroeconomic theory of consumption and saving, which was dominated by the Keynesian theory up until immediately after the Second World War. According to Keynes, total consumption tends to increase with increased income, but the increased income brings about a lesser increase in consumption. In an economy where income is increasing continuously, the *average propensity to consume*, that is the share of income going to consumption, goes up at an increasingly slower rate. Logically, there should be a tendency towards saturation. In the short-run, this tendency is supposedly the result of the passive behaviour of consumers, who tend to keep their old consumption habits (Keynes, 1936, pp. 96–7). Although the economy is growing, demand stagnates in traditional sectors at consumption levels previously reached, and rejects consumption of new products. Keynes considered this consumption function to be valid in the long run too, and thus formulated his *theory of long-run stagnation* which was widely accepted during the 1940s, and he advocated using public expenditure to sustain economic growth.

Econometric studies of the consumption function, such as that of Kuznets (1946) in the USA, later contradicted Keynesian theory and showed that the propensity to consume was constant in the long-run. Given that the theory of general saturation went uncorroborated, some economists began to question the basic assumptions of the Keynesian consumption function. Such efforts culminated in the *permanent income hypothesis* (Friedman, 1957) which views consumption behaviour from a totally different perspective.

Like Keynes, Friedman accepts that the level of consumption is related to the level of income. However, he establishes a distinction between permanent and transitory income on the one hand, and permanent and transitory consumption on the other. Friedman considers that observed income and consumption are only homogeneous in appearance. They must be divided into two parts, as follows:

$$\text{Observed income} = \text{Permanent income} + \text{Transitory income}$$

and

$$\text{Observed consumption} = \text{Permanent consumption} + \text{Transitory consumption}$$

Permanent income is the income considered to be normal for the individual. It can be defined as follows:

> The constant stream of income having exactly the same present value as the variable stream of income expected by the individual within the limits of his or her planning horizon; in other words, the perpetual income stream that households expect their wealth can support.

One can imagine that permanent income is growing constantly. Transitory income, on the other hand, ensues from occasional variations in income (special economic conditions, gifts, inheritances, dividends etc.). Permanent income is not based on past data, but on an expectation of income over a given period of time. Transitory income intervenes in the short run. Indeed, over the long run, the factors that could increase it begin to reverse their effects, and must cancel out.

According to Friedman, income and consumption can only be related when the increase in income is due to an increase in permanent income. If the increase is due to transitory income, then there can be no relation between the two variables. Econometric studies in various countries have confirmed this hypothesis and have shown that consumption increases in proportion with permanent income, and hence the hypothesis that the average propensity to consume is stable can also be accepted, at least over the long run.

For example, in the 13 largest countries of the OECD, households' net savings as a percentage of national disposable income (BIS,1990, 60th report, p. 36) display the following pattern:

1960–74: 8.6 per cent
1975–79: 9.8 per cent
1980–89: 8.8 per cent

It should be noted that this parallel development has continued despite major changes in the growth of purchasing power, given that before 1973 income and consumption were growing at an annual rate of 5–6 per cent, whereas since 1974, this growth rate has gone down to 3 per cent, or even less. However, during the 1980s a declining trend in private savings has been observed in most industrialized countries (BBL, *Bulletin Financier*, September–October, 1989).

The buyer as an active decision-maker

The permanent income hypothesis is interesting from our point of view because of its assumptions about consumption behaviour. This hypothesis shows that the way in which individuals manage the allocation of their resources is not affected by deviations in current income over a short period. In reality, it seems that consumers adjust their consumption and saving behaviour as a function of their personal career, expected family events (weddings, births, children going away, retirement) and the way in which they perceive the development of their property and not in relation to immediate risks.

For the first time in neo-classical economic theory, the consumer is no longer pictured as a relatively passive being whose activity is limited to selective and timeless trade-off over essentially material choices, but as an individual whose rationality also integrates inter-temporal decisions based on expectations of future events. The consumer assumes his full role as an economic agent capable of rational choice and trade-off which goes beyond the narrow sphere of strictly market and monetary choices (Lepage, 1982, p. 15).

It is worth underlining the convergence in the points of view of behavioural theoreticians analysing the individual buying process on the one hand, and the macroeconomic analysis of aggregate consumption on the other. Both approaches lead to the same vision of the consumer: an *active decision-making agent* who makes consumption decisions on the basis of prior deliberation and of anticipations extending over a long horizon.

The buyer as a producer of satisfactions

In Chapter 3, we saw that individuals use goods to meet their needs and wants, which are expressions of their basic motivations. Let us recall that it is important that the notion of a *good* or a *product* not be limited to physical objects only. Any entity likely to provide satisfaction can be called a good. This includes people, ideas, organizations, services and not only objects.

In the search for well-being, the consumer behaves like an individual facing a decision problem and actively intervenes to solve it. Strategic marketing uses the economic theory of consumer behaviour (Abbott, 1955; Becker, 1965; Lancaster, 1966) as its conceptual framework. According to this theory, consumption is an activity where the individual chooses goods, either singly or as a combination of them, in order to 'produce' services which provide utility. From this viewpoint, goods are seen as bundles of characteristics, or *bundles of attributes* or *packages of benefits*, and the consumer as a producer of final satisfaction.

The notion of a product seen as a bundle of attributes is of central importance in strategic marketing. We will put it in operational terms in the last section of this chapter. The basic ideas of this model are very simple but extremely fertile; they constitute the theoretical foundations of benefit segmentation (Haley, 1968) and of positioning, as well as the corresponding product policies (Ratchford, 1975).

The multi-attribute product concept

The buying behaviour of consumers reflects the fact that they are motivated to seek rewarding experiences and satisfactions. The basic idea in marketing, as well as in the buyer behaviour theory, is the belief that *what the buyer is looking for is not a good, but the service or the solution to a problem that the good is likely to provide*. This simple but critical idea has important implications as far as product policy is concerned. The practical scope of the notion of product-service will become clearer in the light of the following propositions.

Proposition 1: No one buys a product *per se*. Customers buy the product or the service for what they think it will do for them.

Obviously, a car is not bought for its own sake, but for the service or the function it fulfils, namely autonomous individual transport. We are back to the distinction between a generic need and a derived need, seen in the previous chapter; one is not saturable, while the other is, particularly because of technological progress. Therefore, it is in the firm's interest to delimit its reference market with respect to the generic need or core function expected by the market when defining its mission, and not to a particular technology. For example, telex is disappearing from the market, but the need for fast communication is unchanged; nowadays it is better served by a fax.

Similarly, integrated circuits today fulfil the same functions as lamps and transistors did not so long ago, only more efficiently. This first proposition therefore advocates a *market orientation* rather than a 'product' orientation, which carries the risk of myopia, as we saw in Chapter 1.

Proposition 2: Different products can meet the same need.

In order to meet a particular need or fulfil a particular function, the buyer usually has the possibility of choosing among different products. For example, if the basic function required is interior home decoration, there are at least four substitute alternatives: wallpapers, paint, wall textiles and wood panels.

Substitute products are part of the reference market, although they may at times originate from sectors which are technologically very different. Only an analysis of the possible use of different products will allow the identification of the range of products the consumer may buy for a particular function. It is also essential to keep a close eye on the technological environment.

Proposition 3: Every product is a bundle of attributes or characteristics.

Whether it is a product or a service, every good has a basic functional value or utility—the *core service*—to which *additional services*, generating secondary utilities of various nature, may be added. Such features may include brand image, after-sales service etc., which improve or complete the core service. For instance, the basic function of toothpaste is to meet the need for dental hygiene, but it can also bring one or many additional utilities, such as decay prevention, gum protection, pleasant taste etc. Similarly, a particular model of a car may present flexibility in its use, so that the car may serve both professional as well as leisure purposes.

These additional values or *added services*, may be objective or even simply perceptual; in the latter case they result from a brand image or from an advertising positioning which creates an effect of status or esteem. Some groups of buyers may prefer a particular brand simply because it offers this type of distinctive feature which they perceive as important, especially when different competitors cater to the core function equally well. In this kind of situation, it is often the secondary features which play a determining role in the formation of preferences. A firm can therefore choose to position itself with respect to one or the other of the sought attributes, and thus to address itself to a particular group of buyers.

Proposition 4: The very same product can meet different needs.

Given that a good has many different attributes, one can imagine that the same good can meet the different needs of distinct groups of buyers, and thus fulfil different basic functions. This fact is often observed with industrial goods, which, contrary to consumer goods, often have a large number of different uses. Some examples are stainless steel, electric engines and petroleum products. The same microcomputer can meet a variety of needs of many groups of users: scientific calculations, word processing, video games or management of a small business firm. To each group of customers there corresponds a different core function. Hence, we have as many different product markets or segments as functions.

Levitt (1980, pp. 85–90) distinguishes between the notions of generic product, tangible product, augmented product and potential product. The *generic product* is the main service provided by the product; the *tangible product* is all that normally goes with the generic product (delivery times, service, image); the *augmented product* is the extras offered by the vendor and the things that give the product its distinctive features compared to its competitors; and the *potential product* is all that is potentially feasible for attracting and keeping customers.

Therefore this is similar to the notion of the product concept which views products as a bundle of attributes.

The strategies of *benefit segmentation* (Haley, 1968) consist of a systematic search for new bundles of attributes for which there is no competing offering in the market, but which meet the expectations of a specific group of buyers. A market segmentation strategy therefore begins with the identification of the benefits sought by different groups of buyers; it then goes on to the development of product concepts aimed at meeting the specific requirements or expectations of the target group of potential buyers.

Several methods have been developed to operationalize the multi-attribute product concept. The most popular method is conjoint analysis (Green and Wind, 1975) which allows the measurement of the partial utilities that the potential buyer associates with each of the characteristics or attributes. On the basis of this information, the firm can then identify the set of attributes which best corresponds to the requirements of each market segment. These methods will be presented in more detail in Chapters 5 and 10.

The dilemma of 'productivity versus diversity'

The notion of a product as a solution to a problem is therefore important for understanding segmentation strategies and the resulting proliferation of products and brands. In industrialized economies, the *logic of marketing* is based on the intensified need for novelty and change and on the growing personalization of behaviour. Taken to its extreme, the logic of marketing leads to products which are as diverse as market needs, even to the development of products tailor-made for personal preferences.

However, there exists an obvious limit to the phenomenon of segmentation, which is imposed by the *logic of production*. Multiplying the models of the same product in order to meet diverse needs endangers the productivity of the production system by reducing the economies of scale obtained in mass production. The *'productivity versus diversity' dilemma* may find a solution in new production technologies, such as flexible production systems, computerized production, robotics or new product concepts (Tarondeau, 1982) which are increasingly opening the way for reconciling these two requirements of successful management. The management of the interface between marketing, R&D and operations becomes of crucial importance in solving this kind of problem.

The domestic production function

The notion of a product as a solution to a problem underlines the fact that buyers' preferences are based directly on the satisfactions provided by goods; the overall utility level is itself derived from these satisfactions. If U_j denotes the utility function of buyer j, then we can write:

$$U_j = U_j (S_{1,j}, S_{2,j}, \dots, S_{i,j}, \dots, S_{n,j}) \tag{1}$$

where $S_{i,j}$ refers to the level of satisfaction i for each buyer. We said earlier that economic theory does not clarify the nature of these satisfactions; as far as the economist is concerned, the choices made simply reveal them. In the previous chapter, we examined the contributions made by theories of human motivation, suggesting three main motivational orientations which can explain a wide range of behaviour. Thus, from the marketing point of view, when we speak of the consumer's utility function we mean the satisfactions sought by individuals. We therefore have:

$$U_j = U_j \text{ (functional, social, emotional, epistemic, conditional values)} \tag{2}$$

Buyers will look for defensive and creative goods, in order to maximize their utility. Similarly, when defining its product policy, the firm will endeavour to develop goods that can generate the satisfactions sought by the market, so as to best realize its own objectives.

Individual consumers seek the satisfactions provided by the services of a good and, guided by their basic motivations, they actively take part in this search. Based on these ideas, the theory of domestic production, due mostly to Becker (1965) and Lancaster (1966), explains the buying behaviour by treating consumers as economic agents who produce their own final satisfactions by combining time and commodities. The uniqueness of this theory lies in the fact that in the analysis of individual choice, time (t) is also treated as a scarce resource, like all the other factors entering into the production function.

We saw that preferences relate to satisfactions which provide an overall level of utility. Let us recall expression (1):

$$U_j = U_j (S_{1,j}, S_{2,j}, \ldots, S_{i,j}, \ldots, S_{n,j})$$

There are many satisfactions which are sought and they vary with the individual (j). These satisfactions are 'produced' by the consumers themselves, through a series of personal production activities, i.e. the buying behaviour, which involves the use of commodities (x) as well as personal time (t). The productive efficiency of this domestic production depends on personal and on situational factors (E), such as the individual's competence, his or her cognitive capabilities etc., or what we called the conditional value. Therefore the domestic production function $S_{i,j}$, corresponding to a particular satisfaction S_i sought by individual j, can be written

$$S_{i,j} = S_{i,j} (x_1, x_2, \ldots, t, E) \tag{3}$$

where

$$x = \text{commodity}$$
$$t = \text{personal time}$$
$$E = \text{situational factors}$$

In this expression, commodities and time are simply 'inputs', i.e. part of the means of production, just as raw materials are part of an industrial product.

> Thus, the objective of preparing a meal is to achieve culinary satisfaction and this necessitates the use of foodstuffs in various quantities (the xs) and of time spent for shopping, preparing, actual consumption of the meal and cleaning up. The variable E, for instance, may represent the cook's culinary competence, the presence of friends to share the meal (thus increasing the consumer's satisfaction) and a possible change in technology (Rosa, 1977, p. 164).

Note that in this example, the meal may generate types of satisfaction other than just culinary: for example, the quality of the conversation exchanged during the meal may provide intellectual satisfaction. In fact, some of the participants may feel the latter more intensely than the culinary satisfaction. This brings us back to the idea that the same good can meet different needs and that individuals look for different satisfactions in the same good.

The theory continues as follows: consumers try to maximize their utility function subject to their monetary budget constraints and their time budget constraints. The monetary budget constraint of individual j can be written

$$R = \sum_{i=1}^{n} P_i x_i \qquad (4)$$

where R is monetary income and P is the market price of good i. The constraint simply implies that the total monetary expenditure resulting from the purchase of goods i should not exceed the individual's total monetary income from wages or other sources.

The time factor is taken into account because *time is our scarcest resource*, given that it cannot be expanded. Time is therefore not free in the sense that the time spent on domestic production activities is no longer available for other activities of leisure or work. There is an *option* or *opportunity cost*. When consumers spend time consuming, they cannot do other things. Economists measure this opportunity cost by the income forgone per unit of time consumed, that is by the wages the individual could have earned in employment, given his or her abilities.

Let T denote total available time (24 hours a day). The time budget constraint may be written as follows:

$$T = t(w) + \sum_{i=1}^{n} t_i \qquad (5)$$

where $t(w)$ is working time outside the home and t_i various times of 'non-work' devoted to leisure and domestic production. The sum of the times devoted to each of these activities cannot exceed the total time budget. Therefore consumer j tries to maximize the following utility function:

$$U_j = U_j [S_{1,j}(x, t, E), S_{2,j}(x, t, E), \ldots, S_{n,j}(x, t, E)] \qquad (6)$$

subject to constraints (4) and (5) above.

The satisfactions included in the utility function may be very diverse; they depend, not only on the individuals' motivations, but also on the value they place on their time, as well as their ability to generate the satisfactions they seek efficiently. The nature of the satisfactions is not to be subjected to a value judgement. *Marketing is pluralist* in its approach, in the sense that it respects the diversity of tastes and preferences. Its only reservation is that certain constraints, imposed by the social, political and moral environment which are the result of choices made by society, must be respected.

The introduction of the time factor in the domestic production function facilitates the analysis of consumption behaviour observed in opulent societies.

> In an economy, when the per capita income increases relative to the available volume of goods (because of increased labour productivity), the value of time also increases compared to the value of these goods. The increase in the relative value of time then leads to substitution effects in the domestic production function, such that the consumer is driven to using his time more economically (Rosa, 1977, p. 165).

Further analogy with production shows that it is rational for producers to save on a more costly resource and to alter their manufacturing process in such a way that the same final product is obtained with a lesser quantity of the resource which has an increased relative cost. Similarly, consumers will try to realize their preferences by means which are less time consuming.

> This is how the demand for ever faster means of transportation in rich countries is explained. Numerous services help to save time, such as those provided by fiscal experts, doctors, professors, garage owners, cookery books, frozen food, vacuum cleaners and television. Generally speaking, as the price of goods diminishes relative to time, the modern consumer uses more goods per unit of time (Rosa, 1977, p. 166).

Contrary to what some may suggest, the tendency to accumulate objects can be avoided, since these are individual choices and other forms of consumption are possible. The extreme case is the individual who chooses to live in a state of ataraxy, i.e. using no objects and devoting him- or herself to meditation and contemplation; the domestic production function for such a person will depend only on factors of circumstance (E) and on time (t).

The proposed conceptual framework is therefore quite broad and forms the *foundation of a theory of individual choice*, which can explain a wide range of behaviour, from the most pronounced materialism to extreme frugality. The observed differences in the actual behaviour of individuals simply reflect differences in motivations and in the scales of personal values. To conclude this section, we will quote the following from Abbott (1955):

> What people desire are satisfying experiences. What is considered satisfying is a matter of individual decision; it varies according to one's tastes, standards, beliefs, and objectives—and these vary greatly, depending on individual personality and cultural environment. Here is a foundation for a theory of choice broad enough to embrace Asiatic as well as Western cultures, cynics, roisterers, religious fanatics, dullards and intellectual giants alike (Abbott, 1955, p. 41).

Consumers are viewed as people with their own objectives and their own scale of values, but this doesn't rule out the possibility that they might be influenced by their cultural, social and political environment.

Modelling the multi-attribute product concept

We have seen that, from a buyer's point of view, a product or a brand can be defined as a 'bundle of attributes' which provides the buyer with the functional value or 'core service' specific to that class of product, as well as a set of secondary values or utilities which may be necessary or added. These additional services differentiate the brands and may have a determining influence on buyers' preferences. Here, we will first discuss the different elements of this bundle and then conclude with a formal model of this notion.

The core service

The core service provided by a brand corresponds to the functional value of its class of product; it is the basic and generic benefit provided by each of the brands in a given product category. For a compressor, the core service is the production of compressed air; for a toothpaste, dental hygiene; for a watch, it will be time measurement; for an airline company, the transportation from Paris to New York; for wallpaper, home decoration etc.

As underlined earlier, the core service defines the reference market in generic terms by providing an answer to the question: 'What business are we in?'. The rationale is the following:

- The buyer is not looking for a product as such, but for the core service it provides.
- The buyer can get the same core service from technologically different products.
- Technologies are moving and changing rapidly and profoundly, whereas the needs to which the core service responds remain stable.

Levitt (1980) states that in order to avoid the risk of myopia, it is in the firm's best interest to define its reference market with respect to the core service provided, rather than to a particular technology. This allows the consumer to identify the alternative solutions likely to be considered when they are confronted with a choice problem.

All brands in the same reference market provide the buyer with the same core service in a way that tends to become uniform, given that competition and the diffusion of technological progress balance out technological performance. Consequently, in a significant number of markets the core service by itself is no longer a determining factor in the buyer's decisions. The way in which the core service is provided or delivered becomes more of a deciding factor.

The peripheral services

In addition to the basic functional utility, a brand provides a series of other *utilities* or *peripheral services*, which are secondary compared to the core service, but which may prove to be decisive when competing brands tend to have even performances. These peripheral services may be of two kinds: 'necessary' services and 'added' services.

Necessary services identify with the mode of production of the core service (fuel efficiency, roominess, noise etc.) and all that normally accompanies the core service (packaging, delivery, payment terms, after sales service etc.). For example, Atlas-Copco 'oil-free' compressors produce compressed air which is totally free of oil particles; Epson printers are particularly quiet; Japanese cars are well-known for their reliability; Apple microcomputers are very user-friendly; Bang and Olufsen products have an outstanding design; Swatch has a large variety of designs, and so on.

Added services are utilities unrelated to the core service, which the brand provides as extras. Hence they constitute an important source of differentiation. For instance, Singapore Airlines offers free movies and drinks on board in economy class; some makes of car include radio equipment in their basic price; some credit cards give the right to preferential conditions in five star hotels etc.

These peripheral services themselves, whether necessary or added, form attributes which *generate satisfaction for the buyer*. These attributes may differ greatly according to the brand and can thus be used as choice criteria. Furthermore, one can imagine that different buyers attach different degrees of importance to the presence of some attributes.

Note that any brand has at least one unique feature (generally more than one), which is simply its brand name. The buyer's global perception of a brand is commonly referred to as the *brand image*.

The multi-attribute product model

Based on the above general observations, we can proceed to operationalize the multi-attribute product concept, attempting to provide predictive value as well as descriptive and explanatory value

Table 4.1 Modelling the multi-attribute product concept (Lambin, 1989)

Objective characteristics	Attributes	Evaluation of attributes		Partial utilities	Total utility
		Importance	Presence		
C_1	A_1	w_1	x_1	u_1	
C_2	A_2	w_2	x_2	u_2	
...	...	...	...	...	
C_n	A_n	w_n	x_n	u_n	U
Reality	Bundle of attributes	Priorities	Beliefs	Value system	
Technical specifications	Exploratory study	Ratio scale	Interval scale	Integrative model	

of actual buying behaviour. Table 4.1 shows the various elements which enter into the model. Combining these elements, we can derive a measure of the total utility perceived from a particular brand for a given buyer.

Let us now consider in detail the various elements that determine the global perception of a brand by an individual. The following discussion is mostly based on theoretical work by Rosenberg (1956) and Fishbein (1967).

The notion of attributes

The term 'attribute' refers to the benefit sought by the buyer; it is the atttribute that 'generates' the service and the satisfaction and thus is used as a choice criterion. Using the previous examples, it is the 'design' of a watch, the 'reliability' of a car, the 'quietness' of a printer, the 'status effect' of garments, the 'purity of compressed air' produced by a compressor etc.

As we mentioned before, the buyer generally takes many attributes into account. The overall evaluation of a brand is based on the combination of the evaluations of each attribute. These attributes can be of a functional nature (power, roominess), but also emotional or aesthetic in nature. It must be emphasized that only *relevant attributes* should be considered. Most products typically feature many functional attributes that are not pertinent to buyer decision-making in that they do not suggest meaningful benefit to the user.

Given that the desired service may have many dimensions, one should avoid defining attributes in too general terms. For instance, the attribute of 'economical' is often mentioned by potential buyers, but it is too vague a criterion and may in fact combine other attributes. When talking about a car, the advantage of being 'economical' may result from at least three micro-attributes: low price, low running costs and low maintenance costs.

Each brand can be evaluated differently on each of the micro-attributes, and it is therefore important to consider each separately.

This is also the case of the attribute 'quality', which is a *macro-attribute* covering a large number of dimensions. An attribute is in fact a discrete variable; that is, it can take on different values according to the degree of presence of the attribute in the brand being evaluated. One then considers the *level of an attribute*. Each brand constitutes a specific bundle of attributes due to the fact that the latter are present at specific levels.

The objective characteristics

These characteristics are what precede the attributes, i.e. the technical features that generate or produce the attribute. They correspond to the technical specifications of the brand or of the product. In general, several combined characteristics are required to generate the attribute. Comfort in a car results from the presence of many characteristics: independent 'four-wheel' suspension, roominess of the cabin, seat structure etc. Similarly, a supermarket is 'convenient' not only for its location, but equally for its ease of access, parking space, queueing time at cash registers etc.

If evaluation is to cover objective characteristics, it is important to avoid those which are redundant, given that some characteristics are related. For instance, the 'power' of a car depends on the size of its engine, which in turn contributes in increasing its weight and dimensions; these characteristics are therefore intercorrelated, and a judgment on one of them is enough to evaluate the others.

In general, a potential buyer is not very interested in objective characteristics, except when these reinforce the performance of the brand in the production of one of the benefits sought, or when they increase the credibility of an expected performance. For example, the plasma screen of portable microcomputers is a technical characteristic which provides the user with reading comfort; the presence of fluorine in toothpastes helps to reinforce the credibility of the function 'preventing tooth decay'; the logo of a great fashion designer is enough to create the prestige or status effect sought by some groups of buyers.

Knowledge of buyers' requirements and/or expectations gives an important incentive to research and development (R&D). Its role is to find technical characteristics which help meet market expectations yet unsatisfied, or improve performance of existing products, thus creating competitive advantage for the pioneering firm. Gore-Tex is a good example in this respect. This is a microporous membrane in expanded PTFE used in the production of sports garments, among others things. This material is ventilated and permeable with respect to perspiration, but doesn't let rain or wind through, and thus gives the user a level of comfort which is superior to any other material. The brand uses the following advertising theme: 'Waterproof garments that breath like your skin'.

The interface between R&D and strategic marketing is crucial at the stage of product concept development. This search for distinctive qualities could potentially give a new product a competitive edge.

Buyers evaluate attributes or characteristics on the basis of two kinds of consideration: the degree of importance of each attribute and the beliefs about where each compared brand or product stands on each attribute.

Importance of attributes

All attributes do not have the same importance in the eyes of the buyer. For an individual, attribute importance reflects the values and priorities that he or she puts on each of the benefits provided by the brand.

Any reasonable person wishes to obtain more in exchange for less: best service, best performance, lowest price, minimum search time, complete information etc. Since these objectives are generally unreconcilable, individuals are forced to arrive at compromises and to decide, in each specific situation, what is more important to them, given the ever imperfect information at hand.

Attributes may be important but not determinant in the choice process. *Determinant attributes* are those attributes which permit discrimination among brands. An attribute which is equally present in all the brands being compared, does not help in their differentiation and hence cannot be determinant in the choice (Myers and Alpert, 1976). The price is always an important criterion but not necessarily determinant, when, for example, all competing brands have exactly the same price.

Salient attributes are those that come spontaneously to a consumer's mind when asked to think of product attributes. These are not necessarily the most important attributes to the consumer. Attribute importance and determinance are more significant concepts than attribute salience.

The firm's knowledge of the expectations of different groups of buyers can lead to the development of new products which constitute new or improved bundles of attributes specifically designed to meet these expectations.

- Bang and Olufsen offers products designed for buyers who are particular about aesthetics and willing to pay the price.
- Fluocaril, a brand of toothpaste, emphasizes the aspect of tooth decay prevention and addresses consumers who are sensitive to medical prevention.
- The 'oil-free' compressors of Atlas-Copco are particularly suitable for manufacturing sectors where the purity of the compressed air is important in the manufacturing process (pharmaceutical products, fine textiles etc.)
- The design of Swatch watches suits buyers who like to follow the latest fashion.

Therefore, the knowledge of the attributes' relative importance can enable firms to develop *segmentation strategies*. The objective is to stick to the diversity of needs as best as possible, and avoid a situation where buyers are forced to be content with products of average performance with respect to each of the attributes.

Perceived presence of an attribute

A buyer may feel that a particular attribute is very important, but at the same time perceive a particular brand as not exhibiting that attribute well enough. Hence, measures of importance need to be complemented with measures of beliefs as to the presence of attributes.

People's perceptions are selective and relative. They are *selective* because attention is selective, given that individuals tend to filter the information to which they are exposed; some elements are retained because they fit in well with a current need or experience; others are distorted when they contradict the established framework; finally, others are rejected because they are worrying or simply disturbing (Pinson *et al.*, 1988). Furthermore, perceptions are *relative* because individuals' experiences and expectations are varied. Hence, the degree of presence of attributes is perceived differently.

Therefore individuals have perceptions about the presence of attributes in brands. These perceptions may be based on experience, collected information, friends' or neighbours' opinions, advertising or purely personal impressions. It doesn't really matter. Although they may not correspond to the brand's real nature, they do constitute the components of the brand image and of the brand equity. These perceptions form the reality with which the firm must deal, even if the true nature of the brand is different. Market research shows that respondents are able to express their views about the brands they know, and that these perceptions are measurable.

To recognize a brand, the consumer uses not only the brand name, but also other observable signals, such as packaging, design, logo, colour codes etc. These externally visible signals form an integral part of the brand's equity, given that they are used by buyers to classify brands in terms of the type of promise they represent.

Any policy of systematic imitation of the observable characteristics, aimed at maximizing similarities in order to convince buyers that the bundle of attributes and services provided is identical to those of the imitated brand, is a form of market intoxication which, from a societal point of view, is as reprehensible as false advertising or forgery. These practices, which are sometimes adopted by private brands, create confusion in the market and complicate the process of well-informed choice desired by the buyer.

Estimating values and partial utilities

The value of an attribute to an individual depends on the association of two factors entering into the evaluation. These two factors are: the importance of the attribute and its perceived degree of presence. This value is referred to as the attribute's *partial utility*; each attribute will have such a subjective value attached to it. These values are the product of the perceived degree of presence of an attribute and its importance.

A brand's *total utility* for a given buyer is then assumed to be either the sum, or the product of the partial utilities he or she attaches to each attribute.

$$U = u_1(x_1) + u_2(x_2) + \ldots + u_i(x_i) + \ldots + u_n(x_n)$$

where

U = the brand's total utility
u_i = partial utility of attribute i
x_i = perceived level of attribute i

In order to determine total utility, a model of integrating partial utilities is required. The model most often used is *compensatory* and *additive*:

- Compensatory, because a low mark given to an attribute can be compensated by a high mark given to another.
- Additive, because it is assumed that there is no interaction between attributes.

In the following chapter, we shall see that other models of integrating partial utilities can be adopted.

To estimate a brand's total and partial utilities, two estimations procedures are possible: 'compositional' or 'decompositional'.

The *compositional approach* consists of constructing the total utility score on the basis of measures of importance and beliefs on determinant attributes, obtained through surveys. Using a compensatory or non-compensatory integration model to combine these measures, a total utility score is obtained which synthesizes individuals' partial evaluations and thus reveals their preferences.

In the *decompositional approach*, respondents react to a set of product concepts, described generally in terms of characteristics. The information to be collected from respondents is limited to a ranking of preferences for the proposed product concepts. The analyst's job is then to derive the partial utilities of each characteristic level. Starting from the preferential ranking of different bundles, the underlying partial utilities are estimated by statistical inference, with the necessary constraints to reconstruct best the original preferences ranking.

In this approach, one directly estimates partial utilities which combine importance and beliefs, without being able to identify them separately. Therefore, a high level of utility can result from either a very high level of importance and a low level of perceived degree of presence, or from a low level of importance compensated by a high level of perceived degree of presence. Various other estimation methods exist. The most common and most reliable method is econometric estimation with binary variables (0,1). The next chapter will present a more detailed discussion of these methods.

The estimation of utility functions enables us to make predictions about individuals' choices when they face different brands, or different bundles of attributes. Irrespective of the approach adopted, it is important to underline the fact that buyers' preferences are observable and measurable, and tests of their predictive power have proven to be conclusive on the whole (Wittink and Walsh, 1988).

The buyer and the need for information

The theory of domestic production suggests that consumers do not buy a product, but a set of satisfaction-generating attributes, and furthermore that they actively participate in the production of the benefits sought. However, they still need to be aware of the existing possibilities for solving the problem they face. Yet, due to the constant increase in the number of products and brands available in the market, the ratio of the information held by the average

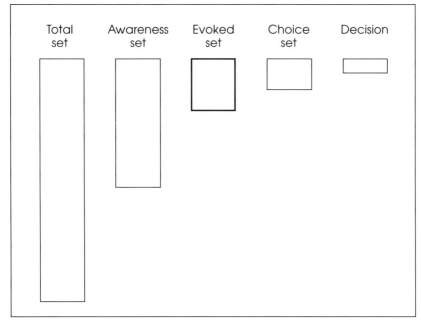

Figure 4.2 The notion of the evoked set (Howard and Sheth, 1969)

individual to total available information continues to decrease. In
most cases therefore, consumers must necessarily make decisions
based on incomplete information and on the limited number of
options they can perceive.

The *evoked set* (Figure 4.2) is the set of all alternatives that the
individual takes, or can take, into consideration at the time of
purchase (Howard and Sheth, 1969, p. 26). The evoked set can be
very different from the overall set, which includes all available
alternatives. The extent of the evoked set varies with the perceived
risk associated with the purchase decision and according to the
individual's cognitive abilities.

Given that the choice of the consumer can only be over a limited
number of alternatives which can be perceived at any given moment,
it is clear that the structure of the consumer's preferences changes
necessarily as his or her experiences reveal new characteristics and
new possibilities of choice which were unknown to the individual
before. However, this improved perception of products and their
distinctive qualities doesn't come freely; it requires doing some
research, which takes up time and implies some information cost.
In this section, we shall examine the types of information sought by
consumers and the way in which they use information from
advertising.

The costs of information

An individual facing a problem of choice, undertakes the search for information mainly to reduce uncertainty about available alternatives, their relative values and the terms and conditions of purchase. We can classify the various costs incurred by this information search into three categories (Lévy-Garboua, 1976):

- *Inspection costs*, implied by studying different markets and defining the range of possibilities (including substitutes) that the buyer could include in the set being contemplated.
- *Perception costs*, borne in view of identifying the relevant characteristics of goods included in the choice set, as well as the terms of exchange (places of purchase, price, guarantee etc.).
- *Evaluation costs*, resulting from the evaluation of how much the sought attributes are present and how authentic the market signals are about the quality of goods.

These costs are mainly in the form of time spent. But the cost of time—measured by its opportunity cost—varies from individual to individual; it also varies with factors of circumstance. For example, the cost of time is not the same during holidays as it is during a period of work. Therefore, it is not always in the consumer's interest to prolong the information search beyond a certain level. The extent of searching efforts will also vary with the degree of perceived risk in the buying decision under consideration.

The economic theory of information helps to formalize this problem, i.e. a situation where the only question is that of possible financial loss as a result of too high a purchase price. Denote by dI the additional information, dp the resulting decrease in price, q the volume of purchase and dc the change in costs allocated for obtaining this information. New information can be justified as long as the following condition is satisfied:

$$q(dp/dI) \geq dc$$

in other words, as long as the expected gain is higher than the cost of obtaining the information. From this relationship, we can deduce the following propositions (Farley, 1964):

- As the size of the purchase increases, whether in quantity or value, the importance of additional information will also increase.
- There will be a tendency to observe less inertia among large buyers than small ones.
- There will be less call for information among consumers who put a higher value on their time and assign a higher cost to extra information.

Table 4.2 Information search intensity per product category (London and della Bitta, 1984, p. 620)

Product category	Percentage of purchases by number of stores visited		
	One store	Two stores	Three stores or more
Toys	87.4	6.1	6.5
Small electrical appliances	60.0	16.0	22.0
Refrigerators	42.0	16.0	42.0
Living room furniture	22.0	13.4	62.1
New cars and major appliances	49.0	26.0	23.0

These propositions are simply the interpretation of the marginalist logic whereby the individual does a cost–benefit analysis and chooses the most satisfactory solution to him or her. Farley (1964) and Roselius (1971) have observed this kind of behaviour experimentally.

The data in Table 4.2 are from various surveys in the USA. It describes the number of retail stores visited before the actual purchase in terms of the type of product. We see that for goods with low unit costs, most buyers are happy with visiting a single sales point; for products of a higher value, the number of places visited increases (Loudon and della Bitta, 1984, p. 620).

The sources of information

The cost of perceiving attributes varies with the observable nature of products. Nelson (1970, p. 214) establishes a distinction between goods with external qualities and those with internal qualities. For the first category, the product attributes can easily be checked before purchase by simple inspection; these are products like clothing, furniture and toys for which the choice criteria can easily be verified with little cost. For products with internal qualities, however, the most important characteristics are only revealed with use, after purchase. Examples of this type of product are books, medicines, cars and computers. For this type of product, perception costs can be very high for a single individual. But the efficiency of surveying can be improved by using different sources of information, which have various degrees of reliability:

- Information sources *dominated by the producer*, in other words advertising, opinions and advice given by sellers and distributors, displays and brochures. The advantage of this kind of information is that it is free and easily accessible. The information is, however, incomplete and biased, in the sense that it emphasizes the positive qualities of the product and tends to overshadow others.

- Personal information sources, *dominated by consumers*; this is information communicated by friends, neighbours, opinion leaders or what is better known as 'word of mouth'. This kind of information is often well adapted to the needs of the future buyer. Its reliability obviously depends on that of the person transmitting the information.

- Information sources which are *neutral*, such as articles published in newspapers and reviews specializing in housing, furnishing, hunting, audio-visual and automobiles. Such publications often provide a lot of information at a relatively low cost. This category also includes publications such as official reports or reports of specialized agencies, laboratory tests and comparative tests initiated by consumer associations. The advantage of this source of information is its objectivity, its factual nature and the competence of the opinions reported.

It is worth underlining here the specific role played by consumer associations. In a situation where the perception of the attributes of a product is particularly costly, it is in the interest of the individual consumer to regroup with other consumers in order to proceed with a thorough analysis which would be impossible for an individual alone. This is a form of unionization of consumers, which constitutes a countervailing force *vis-à-vis* the firm, and has the reduction of the cost of information to the consumer as its main objective.

The most important limitation of the consumerist information is that the comparative tests generally concentrate only on criteria which determine the basic function of a product, without considering any secondary criteria such as aesthetics, attractiveness, ease of use etc. Consumerist surveys implicitly assume that only the functional value matters and not the other values that accompany it. This is a value judgement which ignores the fact that goods can generate many different satisfactions and in particular 'pleasure and stimulation' to their buyer.

> ... and what shall we say about a decorative vase, one that graces a living room even when it is empty of flowers? Can the very shape that gives it beauty be said to 'interface with its uses'? The idea that efficiency is concerned only with practical uses and not with aesthetic ones, is in itself a value judgement (Abbott, 1955, p. 45).

Despite this limitation, the use of consumerist information is becoming the second best choice for an increasing number of consumers in affluent societies, particularly as the cost of time

Table 4.3 Advertising expenditure as a percentage of
GDP 1989 (Waterson, 1992)

Spain	1.89	Austria	0.91
UK	1.29	France	0.76
Denmark	1.57	Sweden	0.85
Switzerland	1.08	Greece	0.78
Finland	1.01	Portugal	0.75
Netherlands	0.98	Belgium	0.61
Ireland	1.02	Italy	0.62
Norway	0.77	USA	1.41
Germany	0.86	Japan	0.90

increases continuously and as the number of weakly differentiated
products multiplies.

The role of advertising information

In Europe, in 1989, total media advertising expenditures represented
0.78 per cent of the gross domestic product (GDP). This is an average
rate calculated over 16 European countries. Obviously, this rate
varies from one country to another, as shown in Table 4.3. This
average rate of advertising intensity is significantly lower than the
one observed in the USA, which is 1.41 per cent of GDP.

On the whole, advertising expenditure has followed the growth
rate of GDP, and this regular increase in expenditure suggests the
efficiency of advertising for the producer. It is indeed hard to accept
that firms would comply with expenditures of this size over long
periods if it were not profitable. Consequently, we are drawn to
formulating the assumption that advertising has utility for
consumers as well, because they clearly use advertising information,
in one way or another, in their buying process.

Of course, it can be said that advertising encourages waste and can
make people buy anything. If this were really the case, the share of
advertising in the GDP would be much higher, since it would be
possible to sell more simply by advertising more. Firms which use
advertising intensively are quite aware of the deceptiveness of this
argument. Empirical studies done to measure the extent of the
economic efficiency of advertising (see Lambin , 1976) also contradict
this argument. Furthermore, the theory of encouragement to waste is
also in contradiction with the conclusions of macroeconomic studies
which show that, in the long run, the propensity to save has proved
very stable in industrial economies despite the growth of absolute
advertising intensity.

The utility of advertising, as far as the consumer is concerned, becomes more evident when one considers the objectives of communication pursued by producers who use advertising or any other form of communication with the market, such as the sales force for example. For the producer, advertising is a factor of production, like expenditures on raw materials and transport. Its purpose is to inform consumers and make them conscious of the existence of alternative solutions to their problem of choice, solutions which constitute different bundles of attributes or distinctive characteristics. As explained by Kirzner (1973, p. 155),

> ... the aim of advertising, and of sales costs in general, is to produce knowledge for consumers, in order to create demand for the product.

It makes no sense to speak of demand for a product whose existence is unknown to consumers. The producer cannot simply develop a new product; this product will only really exist when consumers have been informed of its existence. Without advertising information, the product continues not to exist, in the same way that the American continent did not exist for centuries, as far as the peoples of the western hemisphere were concerned, simply because its reality was unknown.

Information is therefore inseparable from the product itself. But informing is not sufficient; there must be communication. No matter how complete information may be, it doesn't exist, as far as the consumer is concerned, as long as it has not been perceived, understood and memorized. This explains why advertising must be attractive. In a situation where the individual is exposed to a lot of information and is constantly bombarded with advertising messages which are varied and often contradictory, the advertiser might resort to more and more aggressive means in order for an advertising message to be perceived, understood and memorized. These means may include an appeal to the imagination, to humour or to dreams, the use of slogans or images with a strong psychological content, or even call upon theatre or sports personalities to broadcast the message. All these means, which often upset the observer, are designed to make the message go through, to cut through the public's wall of indifference and thus make information more striking. Kirzner (1973, p. 162) underlines this notion as follows:

> It is not so much, perhaps, that effective communication needs to be persuasive as that it needs to be eye-catching, mind-catching, and reinforced by constant repetition.

In other words, the specific forms adopted for advertising information should not obscure the nature of its purpose, which is to reduce the perception costs to the consumer.

The value of advertising information

Given that advertising information is an information source dominated by the producer, it doesn't have the same value as other sources of information in the eyes of the consumer. It is indeed a *sales appeal*, which generates information designed to emphasize the positive aspects of the product. However, as far as the consumer is concerned, the utility of this type of information is twofold:

- On the one hand, the consumer can *get to know the distinctive qualities claimed* by the producer and to see whether what the product 'promises' corresponds to what the consumer is seeking.
- On the other hand, it helps to *save personal time*, since the information reaches him or her without the consumer having to collect it.

Lepage (1982, p. 53) underlines the fact that the important point for the consumers is that the efficiency of the advertising message intended to reach them should be higher than it would have cost them to collect the same information by other means, for example by displacing themselves. These two services performed by advertising have the effect of helping consumers to perceive opportunities of choice and of new potential forms of satisfaction at a minimum cost.

Nevertheless, one question needs to be asked: what confidence can one have in advertising information? The credibility that the consumer attaches to information from the producer differs according to the type of product. Earlier, we saw the distinction made between goods with external and internal qualities (Nelson, 1970).

For *products with external qualities*, advertising can provide credible information for consumers, because they know that the information can be objectively verified before purchase. Both consumers and advertisers know that, for this type of product, there is no room for advertising which is misleading or deceptive, because the penalty of the market is almost immediate. The same reasoning applies to products which are purchased repeatedly and have a low price; since the cost of an error of a test purchase is low, one might as well trust the advertising and follow its advice. If the product doesn't come up to expectations, it will not be bought again; the penalty is immediate.

For *products with internal qualities*, things are less evident, particularly in the case of durable goods with a long economic life where the possibility of deceiving the consumer is real. The question is to know whether the producer remains non-liable in case of deceptive advertising. In fact, as Nelson explains, this is a double-edged weapon. If a well known product proves to be of bad quality, it also becomes well known for being so. The misfortunes of some brands which have been placed on the blacklist by consumer associations show how difficult it is to regain the confidence of consumers once they have had bad experiences with a particular brand.

The role of advertising for products with internal qualities is therefore to link correctly the brand to its function and thus provide indirect information, for instance on the firm's reputation. As far as the consumer is concerned, the interesting information is to know that a given firm is advertising, hence claiming publicly the market's penalty for its products. Quoting Nelson (1974, p. 732):

> The minuscule amount of direct information from advertising for experience qualities gives the consumer an incentive to extract any conceivable indirect information that would help. Such indirect information is available from advertising. The consumer can learn what the brand advertises. I contend that this is the useful information that the consumer absorbs from the endorsements of announcers, actors, and others who are paid for their encomiums . . . . Their total informational role—beyond the relation of brand to function—is simply contained in their existence. The consumer believes that the more a brand advertises, the more likely it is to be a better buy. In consequence, the more advertisements of a brand the consumer encounters, the more likely he is to try the brand.

It seems logical indeed to assume *a priori*, that the brand offering the best guarantee is the one that has invested the most in advertising, particularly if it is a good which is bought repeatedly, and for which it is crucial, therefore, to have a high degree of loyalty.

This behaviour, which contradicts the saying *'à bon vin point d'enseigne'*, is, however, not the only possible behaviour of a consumer. It is observed that in practice, consumers tend to use many sources of information when dealing with products with internal qualities (Bucklin, 1965; Newman, 1979). It is equally for this type of product that consumerist information is mostly justified.

5

The buyer's response behaviour

The purpose of this chapter is to analyse how potential buyers choose and how they respond to marketing stimuli used by producers as part of their product, distribution, pricing and communication policy. The information collected or received by buyers during their purchasing process helps them to identify the relevant characteristics in goods and to evaluate different products or brands in their evoked set. As a result of this evaluation phase, buyers rank their preferences and decide whether or not to buy, unless situational factors intervene. Having sampled the purchased brands, buyers feel either satisfied or dissatisfied. This feeling will determine their after-purchase behaviour. This process of preference formation is analysed in its entirety by marketing researchers and this enables the firm to adapt its offerings more effectively to market expectations. In this chapter, we shall review the main concepts and methods used to anticipate and to measure market response.

The levels of market response

One can identify different ways in which potential buyers respond to perceived information and producer stimuli. Here, *'response'* means *all mental or physical activity caused by a stimulus*. A response is not necessarily manifested in external actions, but may be simply mental.

Economic theory is only interested in the act of purchase *per se* and not in the overall behavioural process which leads to purchase. From the economist's point of view, as we saw earlier, preferences are revealed by behaviour and consumer's response is the same as the demand expressed by the market in terms of quantities sold. In reality, market demand defined in this way is an 'ex-post' or historical observation, often of little practical value to the decision-maker. Market analysts hope to retrace and understand the process followed by the buyer so as to intervene in that process in a better

Table 5.1 Key measures of market response

Cognitive response
  Awareness
  Recall
  Recognition
  Knowledge
  Perceived similarity
Affective response
  Consideration set
  Attitude
  Preference
  Intention to buy
Behavioural response
  Information seeking
  Trial
  Purchase
  Loyalty

informed manner and to be able to measure the effectiveness of marketing actions. Therefore, response behaviour is a much broader notion to the marketer than it is to the economist.

The 'learn–feel–do' hierarchy

The various response levels of the buyer can be classified into three categories: *cognitive response*, which relates to retained information and knowledge, *affective response*, which concerns attitude and the evaluation system, and *behavioural* (or *conative*) *response*, which describes action: not only the act of purchasing, but also after-purchase behaviour. Table 5.1 describes the main measures currently used for each response level.

It has been postulated by practitioners in communication that these three response levels follow a sequence and that the individual, like the organization, reaches the three stages successively and in this order: cognitive (learn)—affective (feel)—behavioural (do).

This type of response model, which presupposes a *learning process*, was originally developed to measure advertising effectiveness (Lavidge and Steiner, 1961) and later extended to include the process of adoption of new products (Rogers, 1962).

> An advertising campaign supposedly first makes a person aware that a product exists, communicates information about the product, gets him to like it, then gets him to prefer it to others, penultimately moves him to the point of deciding to buy it and ultimately makes a sale (Bauer, 1960).

Palda (1966) has shown that this model is not always applicable and that uncertainty remains as to the causal links and direction existing between the intervening variables. Moreover, the learning process hypothesis implies a well thought out buying process, observed only when the buyer is heavily involved in his purchase decision. Psycho-sociologists have also shown that other sequences exist and are observed, for example, when there is *minimal involvement* (Krugman, 1965), or when there is *cognitive dissonance* (Festinger, 1957).

Although the learning process hypothesis is not generally applicable, the 'learn–feel–do' model remains valuable in structuring the information collected on response behaviours, particularly when complemented with the concepts of 'perceived risk' and of 'buyer involvement', discussed in the previous chapter.

The Foote, Cone and Belding (FCB) involvement grid

The various paths of the response process may be viewed from a more general framework which includes the degree of involvement and the perception of reality mode. Brain specialization theory proposes that anatomical separation of the cerebral hemispheres of the brain leads to specialized perception of reality: the left side of the brain (or the intellectual mode) and the right side (or the affective or sensory mode).

The left side, or intellectual mode, is relatively more capable of handling logic, factual information, language and analysis, i.e. the cognitive 'thinking' function. The right side, or affective mode, which engages in synthesis, is more intuitive, visual and responsive to the non-verbal, i.e. the 'feeling' function.

In order to provide a conceptual framework which integrates the 'learn–feel–do' hierarchy with the consumer involvement and the brain specialization theory, Vaughn (1986) presented a grid in which purchase decision processes can be classified along two basic dimensions: 'high–low' involvement and 'think–feel' perception of reality. Crossing the degree of involvement with the mode of reality perception leads to the matrix in Figure 5.1, in which we can see four different paths of the response process.

Quadrant 1 corresponds to a buying situation where product involvement is high and the way we perceive reality is essentially intellectual. This situation implies a large need for information due to the importance of the product and mental issues related to it. Quadrant 1 illustrates the learning process described earlier, where the sequence followed was 'learn–feel–do'.

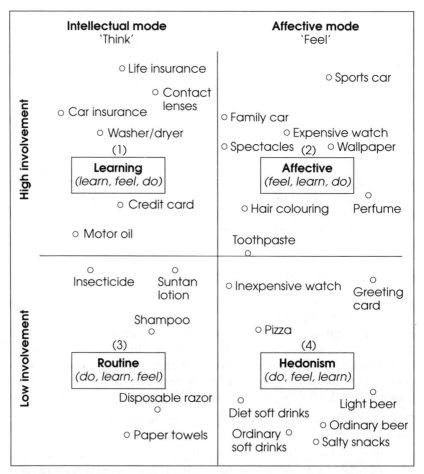

Figure 5.1 The Foote, Cone and Belding involvement grid (adapted from Ratchford (1987))

Major purchases with high prices and significant objective and functional characteristics, such as cars, electrical household goods and houses follow this process. Industrial goods also fall in this category. These factors suggest a need for informative advertising.

Quadrant 2 describes buying situations where product involvement is also high. Specific information is, however, less important than an attitude or an emotional arousal, since the product or brand choice reveals the buyer's system of values and personality and relates to the buyer's self-esteem. The sequence here is 'feel–learn–do'.

In this category, we find all products which have important social and/or emotional value, like perfumes, clothes, jewellery and motorcycles. These factors suggest a need for emotional advertising.

Quadrant 3 describes product decisions which involve minimal thought and a tendency to form buying habits for convenience. As long as the product fulfils the expected core service, we find low product involvement and routinized behaviour. Brand loyalty will be largely a function of habit. The hierarchy model is a 'do–learn–feel' pattern.

Most food and staple package goods belong in this category, which is somewhat like a commodity limbo. As products reach maturity, they are likely to descend into this quadrant. These factors suggest a need for advertising which creates and maintains habits and stimulates a reminder of the product.

Quadrant 4 illustrates a situation where low product involvement coexists with the sensory mode. Products in this category cater to personal tastes involving imagery and quick satisfaction. The sequence is 'do–feel–learn'. In this category, we find products like beer, chocolates, cigarettes, jams and fast food restaurants. For these product categories, there is a need for advertising which emphasizes personal satisfaction.

Ratchford (1987) has measured the location of 254 consumer products on this grid from a sample of 1792 adults. Figure 5.1 presents a plot of products' average scores on the 'involvement and think/feel' scales for selected product categories.

> As can be seen, the results are generally intuitive. Insurance and household appliances tend to be high involvement/think; cars tend to have both think and feel elements; food items tend to be on the 'feel' side because of sensory nature; mundane household items such as bleach and paper towels tend to be on 'low involvement/think' (Ratchford, 1987, p. 30).

An interesting observation emerging from consumer involvement analyses (see also Kapferer and Laurent, (1983)) is the large number of 'low risk–low involvement' product decisions. This fact constitutes a challenge for the firm and suggests that marketing and communication strategies must be adapted to deal with this situation where consumers just don't care very much about a large number of purchase decisions they make. The rest of this chapter will examine various measures of these three levels of market response.

Measuring the cognitive response

Cognitive response relates to knowledge, i.e. the totality of information and beliefs held by an individual or a group. Individuals store this information, which influences their interpretation of the stimuli to which they are exposed. The quantity and nature of the information retained varies according to cognitive styles (Pinson *et al.*, 1988) and perceptual capacities. *Perception* can be defined as:

> The process by which an individual selects, organizes and interprets the information inputs to create a meaningful picture of the world (Berelson and Steiner, 1964, p. 88).

Individuals will, in general, have different perceptions of the same situation, because of selective attention. Perception has a regulating function since it filters information. Some elements of information are retained either because they meet the needs of the moment, or because they come as a surprise: this is *selective perception and retention*. Other elements are perceived as altered when they contradict the specific framework of interest: this is *perceptual bias*. Finally, other elements are rejected because they are worrying or disturbing: this is *perceptual defence*.

A study done in the USA reveals, for example, that only 32 per cent of smokers have read newspaper articles suggesting a link between cigarette smoking and the development of cancer of the larynx, as opposed to 60 per cent of non-smokers.

Clearly, the first objective of producers must be to overcome perceptual resistance and to propagate knowledge about their products and about their claimed distinctive features. This first stage conditions the development of any market demand.

Several measures of the cognitive response have been developed. They can be grouped into three categories: brand awareness, advertising recall and perceived similarity.

Brand awareness

The simplest level of cognitive response is the knowledge of the existence of a product or a brand. Is the potential buyer aware of the brand existence within a given product category? Brand awareness can be defined as follows:

> The ability of a potential buyer to identify (recall or recognize) the brand with sufficient detail to propose, recommend, choose or use the brand to meet the need of a certain product category.

Thus, awareness establishes a link between the brand name and a product class. Information about brand awareness can be easily obtained by questioning potential buyers about the brands they know in the class of products under consideration. Three types of brand awareness can be distinguished:

- *Brand recognition* implies that the brand recognition precedes and

Table 5.2 Measuring brand awareness

Unaided awareness	Aided or qualified awareness
Which brands of laptop computers do you know?	Among the following brands of laptop computers, indicate the brand(s) you know:
....	Know very well: ....
....	Know by name only:.................
....	Don't know:.................................

leads to the need (I recognize brand A and I realize that I need such product category). Recognition is a minimal level of awareness which will be particularly important at the point of purchase when choosing a brand.

- *Brand recall* implies that the need for a product category precedes and leads to the brand (I need that product category, I will buy brand A). Recall is a much more demanding test.
- *Top of the mind awareness* refers to the first-named brand in a recall test. The brand is ahead of all the other competing brands in a person's mind.

Brand recall is measured by unaided awareness; brand recognition is measured by aided or qualified awareness.

Unaided awareness refers to the case where the respondent is questioned about a brand where the question makes no reference to any brand. *Aided awareness* refers to a set of brand names from a given product class which are presented to respondents, who are asked to note the ones they have heard of before. In the latter case, respondents may also be asked to specify their level of familiarity with the brand on a scale of three or five positions, as illustrated in Table 5.2. We then have a measure of qualified awareness.

The responses to these simple questions provide useful information to allow the evaluation of the *capital of goodwill* (Nerlove and Arrow, 1962) or *brand equity* (Aaker, 1991) enjoyed by the brand or by the firm. The information provided by a brand awareness analysis is used as follows.

- To determine the *brand's share of mind*, i.e. the percentage of potential buyers who name the brand or the company as the first brand or company that comes to mind in the product category.
- To identify the *triplet of the best known brands* which are in direct competition in the minds of potential customers, i.e. the number of times a brand is mentioned in an unaided recall test in first, second or third position.

- To compare the observed changes in the *recall versus recognition scores* in an unaided versus an aided recall test. Some brands or companies have a weak evocative power; a product may be easily recognized due to its obvious link with the product class, but in an unaided recall test the product scores low (see Krugman, 1986).
- To compare the correlation between the *awareness score* and *market share* of each brand with regard to the market average performance; some brands enhance their awareness better than others and are situated above the market average (see Assael and Day, 1968).
- To construct a *one-dimensional interval scale*, based on the law of comparative judgements (Thurstone, 1959). This method is used to obtain a ranking as well as measures of distance between brands in terms of awareness.
- To compare awareness scores (aided and unaided) between *different groups of buyers* and thereby identify zones of weakest awareness where remedial action should be taken.

It is worth remembering that a high awareness score is a key brand asset to the firm, which takes years to build and which requires significant and repetitive advertising investments. Brand awareness is a key component of brand equity, even if it alone cannot create sales.

In addition, apart from the identification of the brand itself, measures of knowledge may also relate to the identification of some of its characteristics, such as usual places of sale, current advertising theme and price levels.

Advertising recall

Advertising recall scores are commonly used as intermediate measures of advertising effectiveness. They are also used with different variations to measure new product acceptance. Various impact scores are available which measure the percentage of readers or viewers who correctly identify the advertisement or the message after an advertising campaign. There is a large number of variants of impact scores. The following three measures of print advertising effectiveness, obtained from interviews, recur regularly:

- *Noted score:* the percentage of readers who say they previously saw the advertisment in the magazine (ad recognition).
- *Saw—associated* or *proved name registration (PNR) score:* the percentage of individuals who correctly identify the product and advertiser with the advertisement.
- *Read most:* the percentage who say they read more than half of the written material in the advertisement.

These impact scores are collected after several exposures and are cumulative scores. Another useful impact score, called the *Beta (B) score* (Morgensztern, 1983) or day-after score, is a more revealing measure. It is defined as:

> the percentage of individuals who, when exposed for the *first time* to a new message, memorize the brand and at least one of the visual or textual elements of the advertisement.

Comparisons of Beta scores from different advertising campaigns show enormous fluctuations between campaigns with the same intensity within a medium as well as between advertising media.

Companies specializing in this kind of analysis, such as Daniel Starch in the USA, also provide 'adnorms' showing the average scores for each product category for the year. This information enables advertisers to compare their advertisement's impact to those of the competition.

The comparison of impact scores, obtained from a large number of advertisements shows that:

- The prior level of brand awareness has a significant effect on scores of advertising recall; the greater the brand awareness, the higher the impact of the message.
- Some product categories benefit from a recall above average.
- Recall measured in terms of 'saw–associated' scores is better among the upper social classes.
- Creative factors, advertisement formats, use of colour and visualization of the product in the advertisement are factors that explained the variance of observed scores (Delta 2000, 1988).

These scores are only intermediate measures of advertising effectiveness and give no indication about advertising's ultimate effectiveness, which should ideally help to produce sales. These intermediate measures are nevertheless useful since they enable advertisers to verify whether the advertisement has actually succeeded in breaking the wall of indifference of the target audience. Observed differences in recall scores can be explained by the attractiveness of the message, by the element of surprise, the incongruity and the originality. The comparison of qualitative scores (agreement, credibility, originality) shows that consumers perceive differences between advertisements by product category. These differences also exist between brands within the same class of products.

The remembering and forgetting of advertising

Studying the dynamics of recall scores provides some knowledge about the evolution of recall over time and allows the determination

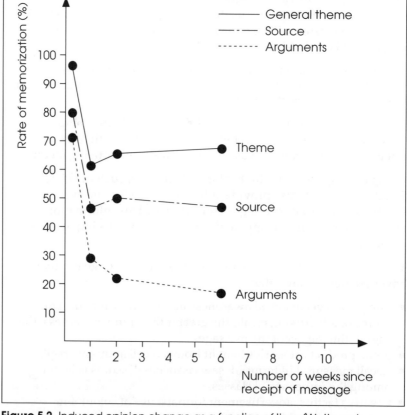

Figure 5.2 Induced opinion change as a function of time (Watts and McGuire, 1964)

of optimal advertising scheduling given the communication objective.

Experiments done in this domain (Morgensztern, 1983) have established that the proportion of individuals retaining an induced opinion change decrease geometrically over time. The rates of depreciation of recall, however, vary largely with the contents to be retained. Figure 5.2, based on an experiment conducted by Watts and McGuire (1964), illustrates this point.

> One can see that recall of the message topic drops sharply after one week (from 95 per cent to 60 per cent), but then keeps on at this level; on the other hand, recall of the arguments used in the message sees a much sharper drop in the first week (from 72 per cent to 28 per cent) and then continues to decay to reach more or less 20 per cent in the sixth week. The loss is greater. One observes a similar but less abrupt pattern for recall of the message source.

Therefore, advertisers have very little time at their disposal to get the value of the investment on communication that they have made.

The repetition of the message clearly has an effect on people's ability to remember over time. Many experiments have been carried out, namely by Zielske (Zielske, 1958; Zielske and Henry, 1980), which have underlined the relation between the change in the recall rate and different advertising schedules. In his study of 1958, Zielske measured the impact on recall of two advertising campaigns of thirteen newspaper advertisements each.

> The plan of this experiment was to expose one group of women to 13 different advertisements from the same newspaper advertising campaign at four week intervals (staggered action). Every four weeks for a year an advertisement was mailed to women in this group. A second group of women received a total of 13 advertisements, mailed one week apart (intensive action). Recall of the advertising, aided only by mention of the product class, was obtained by telephone interviews throughout the study, with no single individual being interviewed more than once.

The recall of advertising by both groups, as reported by Zielske, is shown in Figure 5.3. These data emphasize the nature of response rather than the interim decay. The following observations emerge.

- After thirteen weekly exposures (intensive action), the rate of recall registered amongst exposed households was 63 per cent; after thirteen monthly exposures, it was only 48 per cent in the other group subjected to the staggered action.
- During the period of 52 weeks, however, the average percentage of households who could recall the advertising was 29 per cent in the case of the staggered action and only 21 per cent in the other group.
- In the case of weekly exposures, four weeks after the end of the campaign the rate of recall drops by 50 per cent, and six weeks later by 66 per cent.
- The rate of forgetting decreases as the number of repetitions increases; three weeks after one exposure to the message, the recall rate drops from 14 per cent to 3 per cent, that is a depreciation rate of 79 per cent; after thirteen exposures, the recall rate drops from 48 per cent to 37 per cent in three weeks, which is a depreciation rate of only 23 per cent.

Similar results were obtained with another experiment done in 1980 (Zielske and Henry, 1980) with television advertising, again involving actions with the same intensity but different schedules. The forgetting mechanisms are very powerful and memory loss is very rapid, implying the necessity for a sufficient number of repetitions of the message.

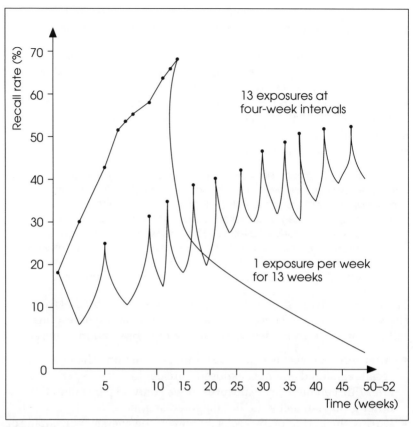

Figure 5.3 Dynamic evolution of recall as a function of time and number of exposures (Zielske, 1958)

A television campaign consisting of six repetitions in its first wave, and creating a 60 per cent rate of recall, should not be interrupted for more than three months if one doesn't want to see the rate drop below 20 per cent (Morgensztern, 1983, p. 210).

Large fluctuations will exist between different campaigns, according to their relevance and to the creative value of their messages. The same phenomenon of rapid forgetting is also observed with other media, the daily press in particular.

How to overcome buyers' wall of indifference of perceptual defence is not obvious. Yet, if this condition is not met, nothing will happen where attitude behaviours are concerned. As long as advertising information is not perceived, understood and memorized, it doesn't exist for the potential buyer. Informing is not sufficient; one must also communicate.

Perceived similarity analysis

Multidimensional scaling of perceived similarity is a method used for understanding how a brand is positioned in the minds of potential buyers vis-à-vis competing brands. This is done through the construction of perceptual maps which give a visual representation of perceived similarities among brands without formulating any prior hypotheses concerning the causes of the perceived similarities or dissimilarities. Thus, the method is a *non-attribute-based approach* which does not ask respondents to rate the brands on designated attributes, but rather asks them to make some summary judgements about the brands' degree of similarity.

For this reason, non-attribute-based perceptual maps can be considered as a form of cognitive response, even though there exists

---

Multidimensional scaling analysis: description of the estimation procedure

The objective is to develop a non-attribute-based multidimensional map to characterize the perceived relationships among a set of brands competing within a given market segment.

A representative sample of respondents is asked to rank all possible pairs of the studied brands according to their perceived degree of similarity. We thus have a triangular matrix where the entries are simple ranks, or ordered relationships by increasing dissimilarity. For N compared brands, we will have $N(N-1)/2$ different entries.

The objective of the method is to seek a configuration of points of minimum dimensionality that most nearly matches the original order of perceived distances among brands. That is a geometric configuration in which the physical distances between points are monotonic (i.e. in the same order) with the original similarity judgements.

To find this configuration, generally the computer program operates iteratively. It starts with a given (arbitrary) configuration in $N-1$ dimensions. It generates an initial solution and then assesses how well the ordering of the actual distances between the brands matches the original ranking of similarity and determines whether the fit can be improved. It then reduces the number of dimensions and repeats the process with the objective of finding the lowest dimensionality for which the monotonicity constraint is closely met.

Once the best configuration is identified, the last step is to interpret the retained dimensions and to discover the underlying macro-characteristics used by the respondents to compare the brands.

an underlying evaluation in the comparative judgements provided by the respondent.

Multidimensional scaling of perceived similarities is based on the following assumptions:

- Any product or brand (any object) is perceived by the individual as a bundle of characteristics or attributes.
- These characteristics are used as criteria for comparing brands which are part of their evoked set.
- If each of the K characteristics is geometrically represented along one axis, i.e. by one dimension of a K-dimensional space, each brand or object will represent one point in this space and the coordinates of this point will be the evaluations of the product according to each characteristic.
- In practice, it is observed that potential buyers' perceptions of products or brands are based on a small number of dimensions, rarely more than two or three, called macro-characteristics.

These privileged dimensions, or macro-characteristics, are identified and are used to compare the positioning of the different brands. Multidimensional similarity analysis finally leads to perceptual maps where each point represents a brand and the distance between points measures the approximate degree of similarity perceived by respondents. The box on p. 131 (adapted from Churchill (1987)) succinctly describes the estimation procedure followed in such analyses.

Figure 5.4 is an example of a non-attribute-based perceptual map. It depicts the market for jam in Belgium in 1978. The analysis, based on a random sample of 400 respondents, brings to the fore the existence of two dimensions in respondents' perceived similarity.

- The first dimension (horizontal) contrasts industrial jams with home-made jams. Price differences are significant between these two types of product.
- The second dimension contrasts private brands (Sarma, GB and Delhaize) with manufacturers' brands. Note that these two groups of brands have more or less the same ranking on the first dimension, implying that respondents perceive them as similar as far as this characteristic is concerned.

We have a visual representation of perceived similarities between the brands according to two dimensions which summarize the market perceptions. These results may appear trivial, in that they don't provide any new information to the manufacturer. Nevertheless, they are important because:

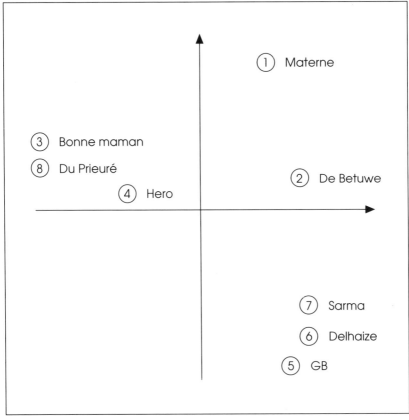

Figure 5.4 An example of a non-attribute-based perceptual map: the market for jams in Belgium (MDA Consulting Group)

- The analysis made it possible to identify the two dimensions spontaneously used by consumers when they mentally compare brands, in this example, the perception of 'industrial versus home-made' and the contrast of 'private brands versus manufacturers' brands'.
- The analysis brings to the fore the structure of the market in each subgroup by identifying whether or not the brands are perceived as direct substitutes.
- The analysis allows each firm to contrast the positioning perceived by the market with the positioning sought for the brand.

The method of multidimensional analysis does, however, have problems, which ought to be underlined.

- When the number of brands to be evaluated becomes large, the task facing respondents is very tedious. If there are 7 brands to

compare, 21 pairs of brands need to be ranked, which might overwhelm the cognitive abilities of respondents.
- Interpretation of the axes is not always obvious and normally requires additional information.

Despite these difficulties, this method of structuring the market has the following advantages:

- The method preserves the multidimensional nature of market perceptions.
- The dimensions, or comparative criteria, are not *a priori* imposed.
- Inputs are simple non-metric ranking data, which are in principle easy to obtain from respondents when the number of objects to compare is not large.

In order to be fully operational, multidimensional scaling analysis needs to be complemented with an attribute-based approach which relies on attribute-by-attribute assessments of the various brands. In general, this approach is the objective of affective response measurements (Green and Rao, 1972).

Measuring the affective response

The affective response is evaluative. It is no longer based only on simple knowledge. It also includes feelings, preferences, intentions and favourable or unfavourable judgements about a brand or an organization. Several operational measures are also available to market analysts, with attitude as a central concept.

The consideration set

The brands identified in the product category by the respondent constitute the *evoked set* of brands, as mentioned in Chapter 4 (see Figure 4.2). The choice or consideration set is more restrictive, because it only contains the brands which, from the buyer perspective, have a non-zero probability of being purchased. The distinction is quite significant; a buyer may know a brand very well without ever considering purchasing it. To identify the consideration set, additional information is necessary: identification of brands that the buyer might consider for the next purchase.

In the consumer goods sector, it is believed that the average number of known brands may vary between ten and twenty, according to the class of product, whereas the average size of the consideration set is three to five brands (Jarvis and Wilcox, 1977). The notion of the consideration set is important; there is little chance that a brand will get adopted if it is not part of this set. It is in the producer's interest to know which brands or suppliers are on the short list of potential customers.

Definition of attitude

A central notion in affective response is the concept of *attitude*. A classical definition of attitude is the one given by Allport (1935):

> The mental process by which an individual—on the basis of past experience and stored information—organizes his perceptions, beliefs and feelings about a particular object and orientates his future behaviour.

In this definition, we find the three levels of components of market response defined in the first section of this chapter.

- Attitude is based on a *series of information* about the object being evaluated, which is progressively stored by the individual (cognitive component).
- Attitude is oriented and reflects feelings, positive or negative, or *evaluation* regarding the object (affective component).
- Attitude is dynamic and is a *predisposition* to respond; as such, it has predictive value (behavioural component).

Psychosociologists (see Fishbein, 1967) also consider that attitude is *persistent*, although it can be modified; that it is *structured*, in the sense that it has internal consistency and is based on evaluative criteria; and that its *intensity* may vary widely or retain a state of neutrality.

Experimental studies in this area have shown that although measures of attitude are not infallible, they predict actual behaviours reasonably well. To be more precise, the following facts are generally accepted:

- When buyers' attitudes towards a brand become more favourable, its use tends to grow and, conversely, an unfavourable attitude heralds its decline.
- Consumers' attitudes help explain market shares held by different brands (Assael and Day, 1968).
- As the number of competing products and brands increases, the firm needs to intervene to maintain and to reinforce favourable attitudes.

Since measures of attitude are likely to be taken before a purchasing decision, they are of great importance for market analysis, as concerns diagnosis, control and prediction.

- *Diagnosis*: knowledge of a brand's strengths and weaknesses helps identify opportunities and/or threats facing a brand.
- *Control*: measures of attitudes taken 'before' and 'after' help

evaluate the effectiveness of strategies aimed at changing the attitude towards the brand.

- *Prediction*: knowledge of attitudes helps predict the market response to a new or modified product, without having to rely on ex-post observations.

Given the importance of this notion, considerable attention has been given during the last twenty years to attitude measurement issues, not only in psycho-sociology research (Rosenberg, 1956; Fishbein, 1967), but also in marketing research (Wilkie and Pessemier, 1973). The multi-attribute product concept defined in the previous chapter serves as the conceptual basis for modelling attitude. As mentioned earlier, two estimation procedures can be used for measuring a multi-attribute model: the 'compositional' approach or the 'decompositional' approach. These two approaches will be examined successively.

The compositional multi-attribute model

The multi-attribute product concept has been defined in the previous chapter. Let us briefly review the basic ideas of this notion, as they are summarized in Table 4.1.

- Individuals perceive a brand or product as a bundle of attributes.
- Each individual does not necessarily attach the same importance to attributes.
- Individuals hold certain beliefs about the degree of presence of attributes in each brand which is evaluated.
- Individuals have a utility function for each attribute, associating the degree of expected satisfaction or utility with the degree of presence of the attribute in the object.
- Individuals' attitude is structured, i.e. based on processing the stored information.

The most widely used multi-attribute model is the model developed by Fishbein (1967) and by Bass and Tarlarzyk (1969) which can be formalized as follows:

$$A_{i,j} = \Sigma \, w_{j,k} \, x_{i,j,k}$$

where

$A_{i,j}$ = attitude of individual j about brand i

$w_{j,k}$ = relative importance to individual j of attribute k

$x_{i,j,k}$ = perceived degree of presence of attribute k in brand i by individual j (score)

n = number of determinant attributes ($k=1$ to n)

This formula is a weighted average of evaluation scores. A numerical

Table 5.3 A compositional multi-attribute model

Brands of laptop computer	Attributes					Overall score*	
	Compactness	Autonomy	Power	Keyboard	Screen	Mean	Adjusted
Brand A	6	8	9	8	7	7.50	7.68
Brand B	7	8	7	8	9	7.60	7.58
Brand C	5	9	9	8	8	7.55	7.86
Brand D	7	8	9	7	9	7.85	7.95
Brand E	8	8	5	6	7	7.00	7.08
Brand F	9	2	5	6	7	5.80	5.07
Importance	0.30	0.25	0.20	0.15	0.10	1.00	—
Differentiation[†]	1.41	2.56	1.97	0.98	0.98	—	—
Determinance[‡]	0.25	0.38	0.23	0.09	0.06	1.00	—

*The mean score is calculated using the importance scores, while the adjusted mean score is determined using the determinance scores.
† Differentiation of a particular attribute is measured by the standard deviation of the scores on that attribute.
‡ Determinance is obtained by multiplying the importance score by the differentiation score and by standardizing those products to have a sum equal to 1.

example is given in Table 5.3, where five brands of laptop computer are evaluated according to five determinant attributes.

If the potential buyer evaluates brands in a linearly additive fashion, the selected laptop computer will not necessarily be the most compact nor the one with the most readable screen, the most powerful, the most convenient keyboard etc. The selected computer, however, will be that which is 'globally' best for this buyer, taking into account all of the relevant attributes and their relative importance. In this model, the multiplicative relations between importance and beliefs, the summation over all attributes and the nature of the scores show that it is a linear compensatory attitude model. This fact allows high scores in some attributes to compensate for low ratings in others.

Measuring attribute determinance

The distinction between attribute 'salience', 'importance' and 'determinance' has already been discussed in Chapter 4. Briefly,

- *Salience* corresponds to the fact that the attribute is in the respondent's mind at a given moment.
- *Importance* reflects the value system of the individual.
- *Determinance* reflects the ability of a particular attribute to discriminate among alternative brands.

Thus, determinance refers to important attributes which help to differentiate among objects being evaluated. If an important attribute is equally represented in all competing brands, it clearly doesn't allow discrimination among them, and is not a determinant in the choice. Measuring determinance implies not only a measure of importance, but also a *differentiation score*, which is a measure of perceived difference between brands with respect to each attribute.

Determinance is then obtained by multiplying scores of importance and differentiation. Differentiation may be measured by a direct question about perceived differences between brands for each attribute using, for example, a scale of 1 (no difference) to 5 (great difference). A simpler method would be a measure of dispersion for differentiation score (such as standard deviation of evaluation scores), as illustrated in Table 5.3. This method would prevent rendering the task of respondents too demanding.

Clearly, it is with respect to determinant attributes that it is interesting to situate different competing brands in the market. In the example of Table 5.3, global attitude scores are calculated first with the importance scores and then with the determinance scores. The model predicts that individual *j* will prefer computer D. But the ranking of computers B and C is modified, however, when the determinance scores are used.

Attribute-based perceptual maps

The problem of *redundancy* remains as a final question about the relevance of attributes. Two attributes are said to be redundant when there is no difference in their significance.

For example, in a study of the heavy trucks market in Belgium, two criteria of 'loading capacity' and 'engine capacity' were spontaneously evoked as important attributes. The two criteria are being used interchangeably, neither existing without the other.

If two determinant attributes are retained, but they both indicate the same characteristic, this situation is equivalent to selecting only one attribute. The analyst should establish a list of determinant but non-redundant attributes.

The method used for this purpose is factorial analysis, for example *principal components analysis (PCA)*. This method is a statistical technique which organizes and summarizes a set of data (the N determinant attributes in this case) into a reduced set of factors called the principal components or *macro-characteristics*, which are independent of each other and which contrast best the objects under study.

The output of a PCA is an attribute-based perceptual map. Each brand is positioned along the two or three retained components which can be interpreted by the correlation observed between these principal components and each attribute.

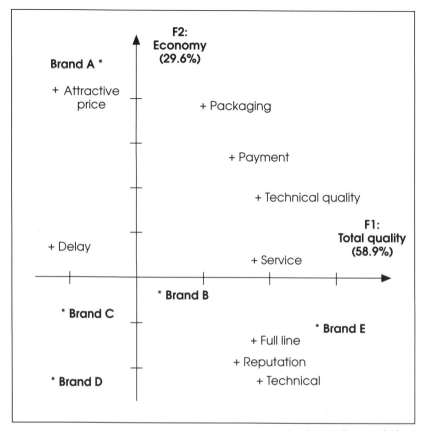

Figure 5.5 An example of an attribute-based perceptual map: the market for industrial gloves (Servais, 1988)

Studies of brand image help measure buyers' perceptions and discover market expectations. Figure 5.5 is based on buyers' perceptions of industrial distributors of safety prevention products (industrial gloves in this case) operating in the Benelux market. Application of principal components analysis on the 9 attributes retained has identified two macro-characteristics which summarize more than 88 per cent of the total information.

The first axis defines 'total quality', as perceived by respondents and regroups the following attributes: reputation, range of product, services, technical information and technical quality of products. These attributes are set against 'delivery time'. The second axis is 'economical' and is highly correlated with 'attractive prices' (Servais, 1988).

The interpretation of a perceptual map resulting from a principal components analysis is as follows:

- Two brands are close on the perceptual map if they are evaluated in the same way according to all retained attributes.
- Two attributes are close if they lead to the evaluation of brands in the same manner.

In the perceptual map of Figure 5.5, brand A is well positioned on the 'price' dimension, but poorly placed on the 'total quality' dimension, in particular because of a weakness in providing technical assistance (information and service), which is an 'added service' provided by the most quality-oriented competitors. This analysis leads to the suggestion that firm A should modify its offering and reinforce the attribute 'technical assistance' which is part of the bundle of attributes expected by customers.

Non-compensatory models of attitude

We have seen that Fishbein's model is compensatory, i.e. low points on an attribute are compensated by high points obtained for other attributes. This way of evaluating brands is not necessarily the most effective and one can imagine that an individual may face an absolute constraint on a price level. In this kind of situation, evaluation is no longer compensatory because one criterion dominates.

The box on p. 141 describes the major non-compensatory models of attitude. The most common observation is a two-stage choice procedure. At the first stage, potential buyers adopt a conjunctive model, allowing them to eliminate products not satisfying their minimal requirements. At the second stage, the remaining products are subjected to compensatory evaluation or lexicographic ordering.

Strategies for changing attitude

Knowledge of the way consumers perceive competing products in a segment is important in determining the strategy to be adopted to modify an unfavourable positioning. Six different strategies may be considered (Boyd *et al.*, 1972):

- *Modifying the product*. If the brand is not up to market expectations of a particular characteristic, the product can be modified by reinforcing the given characteristic.
- *Modifying attribute weights*. Convince the market that more importance ought to be attached to a particular characteristic that the brand exhibits well.
- *Modifying beliefs about a brand*. The market may be badly informed and underestimate some real distinctive qualities of the brand. This entails perceptual repositioning.

Non-compensatory decision and attitude models

Lexicographic model
In a lexicographic model, the buyer first *ranks criteria or attributes* in order of importance. Next, all brands or choice alternatives are compared on the most important attribute. If one brand scores higher on the most important criterion than any other brands, then it is chosen. If not (suppose it is tied with two others), then the inferior brands are eliminated and comparisons are made among the tied brands using the second most important attribute. The procedure is continued until a final superior brand remains to be chosen or until no further brands can be eliminated.

Conjunctive model
The buyer has some *minimum cut-off level* in mind for each important attribute. He or she rejects alternatives that fall below the minimum on any one of those attributes. The buyer will favour the brand(s) that exceed the minimum requirements on all important criteria. A high score on one attribute will not compensate for a below minimum level on another.

Disjunctive model
Instead of setting minimum standards on different attributes and rejecting alternatives that do not meet all those minima, the buyer sets a high standard for *one or few attributes* and then considers buying only those brands meeting or exceeding the standards on these attributes only.

- *Modifying beliefs about competing brands.* This strategy is to be used if the market overestimates some characteristics of competitors. It implies the possibility of using comparative advertising.
- *Attracting attention to neglected attributes.* This strategy usually involves the creation of a new benefit not yet considered by the target segment.
- *Modifying the required attribute level.* It is possible that the market expects a quality level which is not always necessary, at least as far as some applications are concerned. The firm can try to convince the segment that the quality offered for that particular dimension is adequate.

The major advantage of multi-attribute models over a simple overall attitude measure is in gaining an understanding of the attitudinal structure of the segment under study, in order to identify the most appropriate strategies of positioning and communication.

Measuring attitude through a decompositional approach

The compositional approach proceeds from evaluations of brands according to different attributes and builds a global utility score. The decompositional approach proceeds in the opposite direction and starts from the classification of preferences over different products or brands whose bundles of characteristics are described. From this classification, the underlying *partial utilities* of each characteristic are derived, which allows reconstitution of the respondent's order of preferences in the best possible way. Therefore, for a given buyer, the total utility of a brand is equal to the sum of its partial utilities.

In this approach, the partial utilities that buyers attach to attributes are directly estimated. These partial utilities reflect the subjective value associated with each attribute; in fact, they result from the perceived degree of presence of an attribute and its importance, without it being possible to separately identify them. Therefore, a high level of utility may be the result of either a high degree of importance and a low level of perceived presence, or a low degree of importance compensated by a high level of perceived presence. Table 4.1 discussed in the previous chapter sets out the complementarity between the compositional and decompositional approaches.

To derive partial utilities, various estimation methods are available, such as *conjoint analysis* (Green and Srinivasan, 1978) or *trade-off analysis* (Johnson, 1974).

Measuring price perceptions through conjoint analysis

In this illustrative example, the objective was to measure and compare the price sensitivities of four brands competing in the blended cigarettes segment: Marlboro, Barclay, Camel and Gauloise blonde. A cigarette brand can be defined as a bundle of seven characteristics: brand name, package content and stiffness, cigarette length, tar and nicotine content, cigarette diameter and price.

The four studied brands are different only with regard to three of these characteristics: brand, tar (T) and nicotine (N) content and price; only these characteristics are therefore determinant in the choice (Herwats, 1988).

Four levels were considered for each of these characteristics:

- Four brand names: Barclay, Camel, Marlboro and Gauloise blonde.
- Four contents of tar and nicotine. Barclay: $T = 1$mg, $N = 0.2$mg; Camel: $T = 4$mg, $N = 0.4$mg; Marlboro: $T = 9$mg, $N = 0.7$mg; Gauloise blonde: $T = 15$mg, $N = 1$mg.
- Four prices: BF57, 62, 67, 72, respectively.

Thus, altogether, the analyst can form 64 possible combinations of these components (4 × 4 × 4). Conjoint analysis is concerned with measuring the joint effect of these independent variables (the product components) on the ordering of a dependent variable, such as preference or intention-to-buy.

Given the total number of combinations, it would be too demanding a task to ask respondents to rank or rate all these combinations. The use of efficient experimental designs, such as fractional factorial designs, provides guidelines for selecting a reduced number of the 64 combinations. In this case a 4 × 4 latin square design was used and the respondents were asked to rank the 16 selected combinations from the most preferred to the least preferred. This design permits one to estimate all the main effects, while assuming the absence of significant second-order interactions among factors (Addelman, 1962). As shown in Table 5.4(a) each combination of the k variables can be described by a set of k-1 binary variables (0,1) denoting the absence or presence of the levels of each characteristic. In a linear regression model, these binary variables are used as explanatory variables for the preference ranking of each respondent. Table 5.4(a) shows the experimental design as well as data of one respondent who ranked the 16 bundles of characteristics, each bundle composed of a specific combination of variables.

For example, bundle 6 (C-62-9/0.7) is defined as follows: the brand Camel, with a price of 62, with a tar content of 9mg and a nicotine content of 0.7mg.

The analyst will normally use support material (pictures, logos etc.) to help the respondent in his or her task.

Table 5.4(b) shows the results obtained for two respondents, a Barclay smoker and a Gauloise blonde smoker. The regression results are globally statistically significant in both cases and most regression coefficients have significant t-tests. In this case, the reference bundle is bundle 1, which has the following composition: the brand Barclay at the lowest price (BF57) and the lowest tar and nicotine content (1/0.2). Given that the most preferred bundle is ranked 16th, the regression coefficients must be interpreted in terms of ranks gained or lost compared to this rank.

The *Barclay smoker* is obviously very satisfied with the reference bundle; any modification has a negative impact. Marlboro (-4.0) is the most acceptable brand, and Gauloise blonde (-12.0) is the least acceptable. This buyer is little affected by price. An increase in the price of BF5 has only a small impact (-0.25); a larger price increase induces a stronger reaction which remains small in absolute value. Similarly, the reactions to increases in tar and nicotine content are weak.

Table 5.4 Measuring price perceptions through conjoint analysis

(a)

Bundle of characteristics	Brands			Price			Content			Ranking from the respondent
	C	M	G	62F	67F	72F	4/0.4	9/0.7	15/1	
1. B-57-1/0.2	0	0	0	0	0	0	0	0	0	—
2. B-62-4/0.4	0	0	0	1	0	0	1	0	0	—
3. B-67-9/0.7	0	0	0	0	1	0	0	1	0	—
4. B-72-15/1	0	0	0	0	0	1	0	0	1	—
5. C-57-4/0.4	1	0	0	0	0	0	1	0	0	—
6. C-62-9/0.7	1	0	0	1	0	0	0	1	0	—
7. C-67-15/1	1	0	0	0	1	0	0	0	1	—
8. C-72-1/0.2	1	0	0	0	0	1	0	0	0	—
9. M-57-9/0.7	0	1	0	0	0	0	0	1	0	—
10. M-62-15/1	0	1	0	1	0	0	0	0	1	—
11. M-67-1/0.2	0	1	0	0	1	0	0	0	0	—
12. M-72-4/0.4	0	1	0	0	0	1	1	0	0	—
13. G-57-15/1	0	0	1	0	0	0	0	0	1	—
14. G-62-1/0.2	0	0	1	1	0	0	0	0	0	—
15. G-67-4/0.4	0	0	1	0	1	0	1	0	0	—
16. G-72-9/0.7	0	0	1	0	0	1	0	1	0	—

(b)

Variables	Respondent 17 (smoker of Gauloise blonde)		Respondent 86 (smoker of Barclay)	
K^*	8.25		16.0	
Marlboro	6.0	$(4.8)^\dagger$	-4.0	(4.6)
Gauloise	9.5	(7.6)	-12.0	(13.9)
Camel	8.5	(6.8)	-8.0	(9.2)
Price = BF62	-2.5	(2.0)	-0.25	(0.3)
Price = BF67	-3.5	(2.8)	-1.25	(1.4)
Price = BF72	-5.0	(4.0)	-1.50	(1.7)
Content = 4/0.4	-3.5	(2.8)	-0.75	(0.9)
Content = 9/0.7	-4.0	(3.2)	-0.75	(0.9)
Content = 15/1.0	-4.5	(3.6)	-1.50	(1.6)
R^2	0.860		0.934	
t-test	11.3		24.6	

* The reference basket included in k is price 57, content 1/0.2 and brand Barclay

$\dagger$ Student t-test between brackets

The behaviour of the *Gauloise blonde smoker* is very different. This individual seems to welcome a change in brand; after the usual brand, he or she would happily turn to Camel (+ 8.5) and then to Marlboro (+ 6.0). Compared with the other respondent, reactions to price increases are much stronger, as well as to changes in tar and nicotine content.

Similar results obtained from a larger sample of respondents allow the measurement of buyers' preferences, market segmentation with respect to price, and taste and guidelines for product development and pricing strategies.

Measuring the behavioural response

The simplest and most direct measure of behavioural response is given by sales data for the product or brand, complemented by an analysis of the market share held within each segment covered. Other types of information are useful for interpreting sales data and formulating a valid diagnostic of the positioning of the product, i.e. information about purchasing habits and also information about after-purchase behaviour.

Analysis of purchasing habits

The aim of this analysis is to establish the profile of the buying behaviour by segment of consumers within the product category being studied. Information is required on three types of behaviour: *acquisition, utilization* and *possession*. Table 5.5. presents the main elements of information being sought. These elements vary by product category and must be adapted to each particular situation.

The description of buying behaviour is facilitated by using the following basic questions: what, how much, how, where, when and who.

- 'What' allows the definition of the evoked set of brands and identification of possible substitutes.
- 'How much' provides quantitative information on the volume of purchases and consumption and on storage habits.
- 'How' highlights different ways of purchasing (hire purchase, instalment plan) and different uses to which the product is put.
- 'Where' is important for identifying the main distribution networks used, places of consumption and storing of the product.
- 'When' helps get knowledge about situational factors and consumption opportunities, as well as the rhythm of purchase and repurchase.

Table 5.5 Information on past purchasing behaviour

Questions	Acquisition	Use	Possession
What?	Regular brand Last brand purchased	Type of use Substitute products	Brand now on hand
How much?	Quantity per purchase occasion (size, units)	Consumption per week Most important use	Quantity owned now —
How?	Purchasing situation	Mode of use	Mode of storage
Where?	Usual place of purchase	Usual place of use	Usual place of storage
When?	Date of last purchase Interpurchase timing	Usual period of use	Length of storage
Who?	Person who buys	Person who uses	Person who holds

- *'Who'* aims to identify the composition of the buying centre and the role of its members.

As mentioned before, the question of the *buying centre* and its structure is fundamental in industrial marketing. It is also important regarding consumer goods, since buying decisions are hardly ever made by isolated individuals and mostly made within the family, which, in fact, constitutes a buying centre comparable to the one observed in an organization.

Knowledge of purchasing habits implies identification of the respective roles of the mother, the father and the children, and this by product category and at different stages of the buying process. These questions are important to marketers, who must adapt their product, price and communication policies to their real client (Davis and Rigaux, 1974), especially since the distribution of the roles and influence of spouses tends to change, due in particular to the rapidly changing role of women in society.

One of the first proposed typologies suggests four allocations of roles (Herbst, 1952):

- Autonomous decision by the husband or the wife.
- Dominant influence of husband.
- Dominant influence of wife.
- Synchretic decision, i.e. taken together.

The role of children is still to be taken into account. Comparison of the results of studies on the allocation of roles for various product categories shows that the influence of spouses varies greatly according to the type of product (Davis and Rigaux, 1974).

Pras and Tarondeau (1981, p. 214) emphasize that the aim of this kind of research is to define the strategies to be adopted due to a better understanding of the behaviour of the target group. Their relevance can be summarized as follows:

- Properly choose the persons to be questioned.
- Determine the content of advertising messages.
- Choose the best adapted support material.
- Adapt product conception to the needs of the person with greatest influence.
- Choose the most appropriate distribution network.

Mastering this set of information about buying habits will contribute to a significant improvement in the firm's marketing practice and thus will increase the impact of behavioural response.

Market share analysis

Company or brand sales, measured in volume or in value, are the most direct measures of the market behavioural response. Sales analysis can be misleading, however, since it does not reveal how the brand is doing relative to competing brands operating in the same reference market. An increase in sales may be due to a general improvement in market conditions and have nothing to do with the brand's performance, or the increase may be hiding a deterioration of the brand's position, for instance when it has grown less than its rivals. To be useful, sales analysis must therefore be complemented by a market share analysis, ideally in volume within each segment covered.

Calculating market shares assumes that the firm has clearly defined its *reference market*, i.e. the set of products or brands which compete with it. The method of defining a reference market is described in Chapter 6. Once the reference market has been determined, market share is simply calculated as follows:

$$\text{Market share} = \frac{\text{Brand A unit sales}}{\text{Total unit sales}}$$

The reason for measuring market share is to eliminate the impact of environmental factors which exert the same influence on all competing brands and thus allow a proper comparison of the competitive power of each. Nevertheless, the notion of market share needs to be used with caution, keeping the following considerations in mind.

- The level of market share depends directly on the choice of the basis of comparison, i.e. on the *reference market*. It is important to check that this basis is the same for all the brands.
- The hypothesis that *environmental factors* have the same influence on all brands is not necessarily verified. Some brands may be better or less well placed with respect to some environmental factors.
- When *new brands* are introduced into a market, the share of each participant must necessarily drop, without there being any bad performance, even if some brands resist the entry of a new competitor better than others.
- Market shares can sometimes fluctuate because of *accidental* or *exceptional factors*, such as a large order.
- Sometimes a drop in market share may be *deliberately provoked* by the firm because, for example, a distribution network or a market segment is being abandoned.

Irrespective of the definition adopted for the reference market, various measures of market share can be calculated.

- *Unit market share*, that is company or brand sales in volume expressed as a percentage of total sales of the reference market.
- *Value market share* is calculated on the basis of turnover rather than sales in units. A market share in value is often difficult to interpret because changes in market share reflect a combination of volume and price changes.
- *Served-market share* is calculated, not relative to the total reference market, but relative to sales in the market segment(s) addressed by the firm. Note that the served-market share is always larger than overall market share.
- *Relative market share* compares the firm's sales to that of its competitors, thus excluding the firm's own sales. If a firm holds 30 per cent of the market, and its top three competitors hold respectively 20, 15 and 10 per cent, and the 'others' 25 per cent, relative market share will be 43 per cent (30/70). If relative market share is calculated by reference to the top three competitors, then the firm's relative market share is 67 per cent (30/45). Relative market shares above 33 per cent are considered to be strong.
- *Relative market share to leading competitor* is calculated by reference to the leading competitor's sales. In the previous example, the dominant firm has a relative market share of 1.5 (30/20). The relative market share of the other firms is obtained by dividing

their market share by that of the leading competitor, i.e. 0.67, 0.50 and 0.33, respectively, in this example.

Measuring market shares can raise problems depending on the availability of the necessary information. To measure served-market share implies that the firm is in a position to evaluate total sales in each segment. Similarly, relative market share assumes knowledge of sales achieved by direct competition. Obtaining this information varies in levels of difficulty from sector to sector. In the field of consumer goods, market shares are available through syndicated consumer or dealer panels or through scanning diary panels. In the other fields, in cases where government organizations and trade associations do not provide this information, it is up to the *marketing information system* to arrange how to purchase or to create this information, which is vital for tracking sales performance.

Market share movement analysis

Consumers and dealers panels provide detailed information on market shares by region, segment, distribution network etc. Such data allow the implementation of more refined types of analysis, used to interpret gains or losses in market shares.

Parfitt and Collins (1968) have shown how to decompose market share into a number of components which help to interpret and to predict its development.

- *Penetration rate* is the share of buyers, i.e. the percentage of buyers of brand x compared to the total number of buyers in the reference product category.
- *Exclusivity rate* is defined as the share of total purchases in a product category reserved for brand x. This rate is a measure of the loyalty attached to brand x, given that buyers have the possibility of diversifying their purchases and acquiring different brands in the same product category.
- *Intensity rate* compares average quantities purchased per buyer of brand x with average quantities purchased per buyer of the product category.

A brand's market share can then be calculated from these three components. Thus,

Market share = Penetration rate × Exclusivity rate × Intensity rate

Let x denote the brand and c the reference product category to which x belongs. Let us also adopt the following notations:

N_x = Number of buyers of x
N_c = Number of buyers of c

Q_{xx} = Quantity of x purchased by buyers of x
Q_{cx} = Quantity of c purchased by buyers of x
Q_{cc} = Quantity of c purchased by buyers of c

It can be verified that

$$\text{Market share} = \frac{Q_{xx}}{Q_{cc}} = \frac{N_x}{N_c} \times \frac{Q_{xx}/N_x}{Q_{cx}/N_x} \times \frac{Q_{cx}/N_x}{Q_{cc}/N_c}$$

To express market share in value, a relative price index must be added: the ratio of the brand's average price to the average price charged by all competing brands. This definition of market share can be generally applied. It permits the identification of the possible causes of observed movements in market share. The following are possible explanations of a fall in market share:

- The brand is losing customers (lower penetration rate).
- Buyers are devoting a smaller share of their purchases of the product to this particular brand (lower exclusivity rate).
- Buyers of the brand are purchasing smaller quantities compared to the quantities bought on average by buyers of the product (lower intensity rate).

By tracking these market indicators over time, the market analyst can identify the underlying causes of market share changes and suggest corrective measures accordingly.

Measures of market share can be used from two different perspectives, as an *indicator of competitive performance* or as an *indicator of competitive advantage*. In the first case, market shares should, as much as possible, be calculated over finer divisions, i.e. by segment, by distribution network or by region. In the second case, a more aggregate basis would be more suitable because it would better reveal the strength of the market power held by the firm and the possible existence of economies of scale or of learning curve effects.

Estimating marketing response functions

A marketing response function is a relationship that links buyers' response expressed in terms of volume or market share, to one or more marketing variables. Response functions are generally obtained from historical data through econometric analysis. Quantitative estimation of response functions leads to *elasticity coefficients* measuring demand or market share sensitivity to a variation in one of the explanatory variables, such as price, advertising or household income. The notion of elasticity is defined in more detail in Appendix 5.1.

Response functions are useful because their estimations, based on

Table 5.6 Selected estimates of marketing variables elasticities

Product categories	Number of brands	Advertising elasticities*	Price elasticities*	Distribution elasticities†
Soft drinks	5	0.070	−1.419	1.181
Yoghurt	2	0.031	−1.100	—
Confectionery	2	0.034	−1.982	2.319
TV sets	4	0.122	NS	—
Cigarettes	1	0.154	−1.224	—
Bank services	5	0.003	—	0.251
Cars transported by rail	1	0.184	−1.533	—
Coffee	1	0.036	−2.933	1.868
Fruits	1	0.095	−1.229	—
Electric shavers	18	0.219	−2.460	0.909
Gasoline	19	0.024	−0.600	0.923
Shampoos	11	0.036	−1.762	—
Insecticides	9	0.058	—	—
Deodorants	11	0.054	—	—
Detergents	6	0.084	—	—
Suntan lotions	11	0.300	NS	—
Average: study 1976‡		**0.094**	**−1.624**	**1.243**
Female hygiene	6	0.010	−1.405	0.958
Dishwashers	2	0.029	−1.692	—
Detergent	1	0.049	−2.009	—
Jam	3	0.022	−2.672	2.757
Automobiles	8	0.093	−2.004	—
Average: study 1988§		**0.041**	**−1.956**	**—**
Average: 1976 and 1988		**0.081**	**−1.735**	**1.395**

Note: NS = Not Significant
* These elasticities are average elasticities
† Based on Nielsen indices of distribution coverage
‡ The observation basis is the brand per country; the countries are Belgium, France, Holland, FRG, Denmark, Italy, Norway, Sweden
§ The observation basis is Belgium

observations on different markets, different segments or different product categories, improve one's understanding of buyers' response mechanisms. Thus one progressively builds a more rigorous basis for future marketing programmes (see Assmus *et al.*, 1984).

By way of illustration, Table 5.6 presents estimates of the marketing variables elasticities for a sample of 127 brands operating on the European market and coming from 21 different product categories.

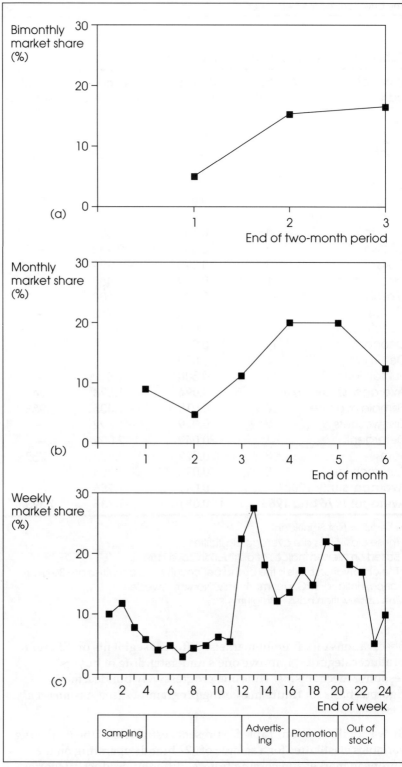

Figure 5.6 Penetration curves of a new product (Nielsen Researcher, 1981)

These elasticity coefficients observed for the distribution, price and advertising variables are directly useful for forecasting and control. They constitute good starting points for simulation exercises designed for analysing the implications of alternative marketing programs (Lambin, 1972).

In consumer markets, the use of response functions is now largely facilitated by constant improvement in databases. This development has come about as a result of technological innovation: the progressive but irreversible introduction of *scanning systems* in retail stores and increasing computerization of marketing information systems in the firm (Nielsen, 1981). Market analysts now have at their disposal more reliable information on market shares, selling prices, advertising, promotions, out-of-stocks etc. The most important change in this area is in the frequency of data, which is now available at weekly frequency rather than on a bimonthly or monthly basis. This weekly frequency gives more timely and sensitive information to assist the market analyst in assessing competitive response and brand performance. Direct causal relationships between market shares and the marketing variables can also be established.

Figure 5.6 presents the penetration curve of a new brand described successively in terms of bimonthly, monthly and weekly observations. Causal data, i.e. the marketing variables active during the launching period, are shown in the lower part of the graph, below the time scale. It is clear that bimonthly and monthly data completely mask the market response. The weekly observations, on the other hand, show the causal relationship very clearly.

Post-purchase behaviour

Having bought and used the product, the consumer or buyer develops a new attitude, based mainly on the degree of *satisfaction* or *dissatisfaction* that is felt after using the product. This positive or negative attitude will lead to a post-purchase behaviour which determines the product's acceptance and also the repeat purchase rate if it is the case of a product bought repeatedly.

The buyers' satisfaction will be a function of the degree of concordance existing between their expectations of the product on the one hand, and their perception of its performance on the other. If the result conforms with their expectations, there is satisfaction; if it is higher, satisfaction is greater; if it is lower, there is dissatisfaction. The notion of expected result goes back to Lewin's (1935) *aspiration level theory*.

Individual's aspiration levels are formed on the basis of their experiences, as well as the promises made in the firm's advertising about its products' performances. Individuals' aspirations develop differently according to their personality. Some set their aspiration level at a *minimum* which they intend to surpass. This attitude describes risk aversion. Others set their level at a *maximum*, representing an objective they endeavour to approach, but don't expect to attain. Here, aspiration level acts as a stimulus. Finally, others set their level roughly to the *average* of the results already obtained, reflecting an equality between aspiration level and realization level.

Aspirations are not static, but develop continuously. As emphasized in Chapter 3, individuals constantly seek stimulation and novelty. If successful, aspirations tend to amplify. They are also influenced by performances of other members of the group to which the individual belongs. Expectation theory therefore suggests adopting a communication policy based on the product's likely performances, and avoiding inconsiderate promises which can only create dissatisfaction, by contradicting or invalidating buyers' expectations.

Brand switching analysis

A good indicator of consumer satisfaction in a competitive market is the buyers' loyalty rate. Brand switching analysis is also useful to forecast the brand dynamic evolution. Consider the market share development of brands A, B and C, shown in Figure 5.7.

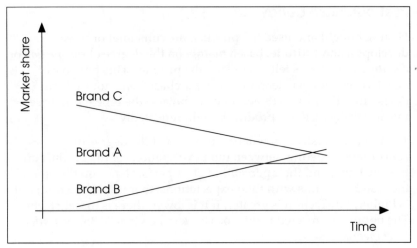

Figure 5.7 The dynamics of market share movements (Lambin and Peeters, 1977, p. 145)

The stability of brand A's market share can be interpreted in two very different ways:

- A fixed number of consumers buys the same quantity of brand A at regular intervals.
- The number of consumers dropping brand A is equal to the number of consumers adopting brand A; entry rate then compensates exit rate exactly.

On the basis of aggregate market data, it is not possible to decide which is the true state. Similarly, one could give the following explanations for brand B's growth:

- Brand B has a fixed number of loyal buyers to whom new buyers are added at a regular pace.
- Entry rate is higher than exit rate.
- The number of brand B's buyers remains unchanged, but some of them are purchasing an increased quantity per buying occasion.

Here again, the available information does not permit us to discriminate between these possible explanations.

To keep the analysis simple, let us limit ourselves to a market composed of two competing brands. As shown in Figure 5.8, each particular purchasing act, viewed in a dynamic perspective, can be described in terms of three origins and three destinations. For each brand, we can thus define a loyalty rate and an attraction rate. These switching rates an be defined as follows:

- The *loyalty rate* is the percentage of buyers who, having purchased brand A in the previous period (t-1), continue to buy brand A in the current period (t).

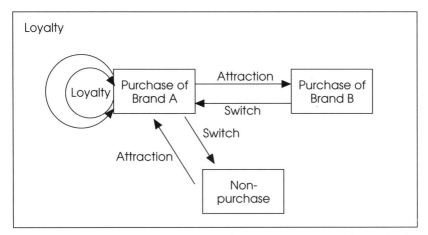

Figure 5.8 The brand switching dynamic (Lambin and Peeters, 1977, p. 146)

Table 5.7 Example of brand switching analysis: the heavy duty truck market (MDA Consulting Group, Brussels)

Brand replaced in period *t*	Brand purchased in *t*+1 (%)						Market share in *t* (%)
	Daf	Mercedes	Renault	Scania	Volvo	Others	
Daf	56.2	15.3	1.3	2.3	11.4	13.5	7.6
Mercedes	8.2	59.5	2.4	2.3	11.1	16.5	16.3
Renault	9.0	9.2	53.0	5.0	1.2	22.6	3.2
Scania	8.1	13.3	0.0	65.6	6.1	6.9	3.3
Volvo	16.5	12.9	1.2	1.7	60.0	7.7	6.2
Others	11.7	17.1	4.8	2.9	10.3	53.2	63.4
Market share in *t*+1 (%)	14.6	23.2	5.3	4.8	13.2	38.9	100.0

- The *attraction rate* is the percentage of buyers who, having purchased a competing brand in period *t*-1, purchase brand A in period *t*.

These proportions, called *transition probabilities*, can be estimated through survey or on the basis of panel data. To illustrate, the transition probabilities observed in the Belgian market among six makes of heavy trucks are presented in Table 5.7.

These transition probabilities allow the market analyst to explain market share movements over time, to describe the underlying competitive dynamics and to formulate predictions on market developments assuming that the observed transition probabilities will remain unchanged within a reasonable planning horizon.

If α denotes loyalty rate and β attraction rate, brand A's market share in future period $t+1$ will be

$$MS\,(t-1) = \alpha\,MS\,(t) + \beta[1 - MS(t)]$$

Brand A's long-run or equilibrium market share, $MS(e)$, can be calculated from the following expression,

$$MS(e) = \frac{\text{Attraction rate}}{(1 - \text{loyalty rate}) + (\text{attraction rate})} = \frac{\beta}{(1 - \alpha) + \beta}$$

Note that equilibrium market share is independent of the initial market share. It describes the brand's trajectory, assuming constant transition probabilities. This type of dynamic analysis is particularly useful at the launching stage of a new product.

Appendix 5.1: Defining the notion of elasticity

The elasticity of demand, with respect to a marketing variable, measures the responsiveness of the quantity demanded for a product or a brand to a change in the level of the marketing variable.

Specifically, if we consider price (p) as the marketing variable under study, price elasticity is defined as the rate of percentage change in quantity (q) demanded relative to the percentage change in price, or

$$\varepsilon_{q,p} = \frac{\% \text{ change of } q}{\% \text{ change of } p} = \frac{\delta q/q}{\delta/p} = \frac{\delta q}{\delta p} \frac{p}{q}$$

For the generally assumed case, demand increases as price decreases.

Demand is said to be 'elastic' with respect to price, if the ratio is greater than one in absolute terms; it is 'inelastic' if price elasticity is less than one.

Elasticity is normally not the same at each level of the marketing variable. When the response function is as follows,

$$q = a\,p^{\beta}$$

the exponent β is the elasticity assumed constant between two levels ($q1,p1$) and ($q2,p2$). It can be determined as follows:

$$\varepsilon_{q,p} = \frac{\log(q_1/q_2)}{\log(p_1/p_2)}$$

If the response function is

$$q = a + b \ln s$$

where s is the advertising expenditure, the elasticity coefficient is variable and is given by

$$\varepsilon_{q,s} = \frac{\beta}{q}$$

A distinction must be made between short- and long-term elasticity. If the dynamic advertising response function is as follows:

$$Q = a + \beta \sum_{i=0}^{\infty} \lambda^{i} S_{t-i}$$

the cumulative advertising elasticity is equal to

$$\varepsilon_{q,p} = \frac{\beta}{1-\lambda} \times \frac{S}{Q}$$

where λ denotes the rate of the implied geometric progression. Other forms of the response functions are of course possible.

6

Needs analysis through market segmentation

One of the first strategic decisions a firm has to make is to define its reference market and to choose the customer segment(s) to target. This choice implies the splitting of the total market into groups of customers with similar needs and behavioural or motivational characteristics, and which constitute distinct market opportunities. A firm can elect to serve all possible customers or to focus on one or several specific segments within the reference market. This segmentation of the reference market is generally done in two steps, corresponding to different levels of total market disaggregation. The first step, called *macro-segmentation*, has the objective of identifying 'product markets', while in the second step, called *micro-segmentation*, the goal is to uncover customer 'segments' within each product market previously identified. Using this mapping of the reference market, the firm will then evaluate the attractiveness of each product market and/or segment (see Chapter 7) and assess its own competitiveness (see Chapter 8). This chapter describes a general methodology for segmenting a market and also presents alternative ways of international segmentation.

Macro-segmentation analysis

In the majority of markets, it is almost impossible to satisfy all customers with a single product or service. Different consumers have varying desires and interests. This variety stems from diverse buying practices and basic variations of customers' needs and the benefits they seek from products. Increasingly, therefore, companies have found it essential to move away from mass marketing toward target marketing strategy, where the focus is on a particular group of customers. This identification of target customer groups is market segmentation, where the total market is disaggregated into subgroups, with similar requirements and buying characteristics. Knowing how to segment a market is one of the most important skills a firm must possess. Segmentation defines what business the firm is in, guides strategy development and determines the capabilities needed in the business unit.

Defining the reference market in terms of 'solution'

Implementing a market segment strategy should begin with a business definition statement that reveals the true function or purpose of the firm in a customer-oriented perspective. Three fundamental questions should be addressed:

- What business(es) are we in?
- What business(es) should we be in?
- What business(es) shouldn't we be in?

To answer these questions in a customer-oriented perspective, the business definition should be made in generic terms, i.e. in terms of the 'solution' sought by the customer and not in technical terms, to avoid the risk of myopia. The rationale behind the 'solution approach' has been explained in Chapter 4. It can be summarized as follows:

- To the buyer, the product is what it does.
- No one buys a product *per se*. What is sought is a solution to a problem.
- Different technologies can produce the same function.
- Technologies are fast changing, while generic needs are stable.

It is therefore important for the market-oriented firm to define its reference market in terms of a generic need, rather than in terms of a product. Here are some examples of market reference definitions.

- Derbit Belgium is operating in the European roofing market and manufactures membranes of APP-modified bitumen. The company defines its market as follows: 'we are selling guaranteed waterproof solutions to roofing problems in partnership with exclusive distributors and highly qualified roofing applicators'.
- Otis Elevators serves two closely related markets: (a) the design, manufacture and installation of elevators, escalators and moving sidewalks and (b) the subsequent servicing of the equipment. Their business definition is: '. . . our business is moving people and materials horizontally and vertically over relatively short distances', and '. . . when elevators are running well, people do not notice them . . . our objective is to go unnoticed'.
- Sedal, a small French company manufacturing ventilation metallic grids, defined its business as the 'air and temperature control' business and expanded its offerings to air ventilation and air conditioning systems.

- Bata used to see itself as a 'leather' specialist. The company now defines its business as a shoe specialist, using plastic, textile or leather as basic material.

Ideally, the business definition should be stated in terms narrow enough to provide practical guidance, yet broad enough to stimulate imaginative thinking, such as openings for product line extensions or for diversification into adjacent product areas. At the Grumman Corporation, the guidelines for the mission statement advise:

> We should be careful not to confine the market boundaries by our existing or traditional product participation. The market definition analysis is purposely meant to create an outward awareness of the total surrounding market, and of its needs and trends that may offer opportunity for, or on the other hand challenges to, our current or contemplated position (Hopkins, 1982, p. 119).

The business definition is the starting point for strategy development. It helps identify the customers to be served, the competitors to surpass, the key success factors to master and the alternative technologies available for producing the service or the function sought.

Conceptualization of the reference market

As suggested by Abell (1980), a reference market can be defined in three dimensions: customer group, or *'who'* is being satisfied; customer functions or needs, or *'what'* is being satisfied; and the technologies used to meet the needs, or *'how'* customer needs are being satisfied. We thus have a three-dimensional framework, as shown in Figure 6.1. To segment the market, the first step is to identify the relevant criteria for describing each of these three dimensions.

Functions. We refer here to the need to be fulfilled by the product or the service. Examples of functions would be home interior decoration; international transportation of goods; waterproof roof protection; rust prevention; teeth cleaning; deep versus shallow drilling; diagnostic imaging etc.

Functions have to be conceptually separated from the way the function is performed (i.e. the technology). The dividing line between 'functions' and 'benefits' is not always clear, as functions are narrowly subdivided or as assortments of functions are considered, for example, teeth cleaning plus decay prevention, shampoo with anti-dandruff treatment. Thus, functions can also be defined as a package of benefits sought by different customer groups.

Customers. We describe the different customer groups that might buy the product. The most common criteria used are households versus

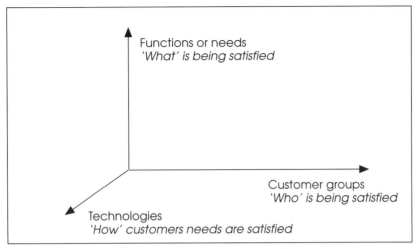

Figure 6.1 Market boundaries definition (Abell, 1980)

industrial buyers, socio-economic class, geographic location, type of activity, company size, OEM versus user, decision-making unit etc. In most situations, several criteria are required.

At this level of macro-segmentation, only broad customer characteristics are retained. For consumer goods, more detailed criteria are often necessary, such as age group, benefits sought, life style, purchase behaviour etc. This is the object of micro-segmentation.

Technologies. These describe the alternative ways in which a particular function can be performed for a customer. For example, paint or wallpaper for the function of home interior decoration; road, air, rail or sea for international transportation of goods; bitumen or plastic for roof protection; toothpaste or mouthwash for teeth cleaning; X-ray, ultrasound or computerized tomography for diagnostic imaging etc.

As underlined above, the technology dimension is dynamic, in the sense that one technology can displace another over time. For example, X-rays are displaced by ultrasound, nuclear medicine and CT scanning as alternative imaging diagnostic techniques. Similarly, electronic mail tends to displace printed materials in the field of written communication.

Market boundary definitions

Using this framework, we may distinguish between a 'product market', a 'market' and an 'industry' (Figure 6.2).

- A *product market* is defined by a specific customer group seeking a

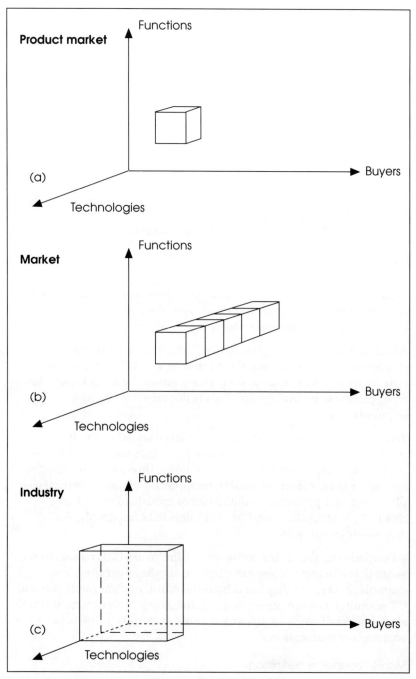

Figure 6.2 Defining the reference market (Abell, 1980)

specific function or assortment of functions based on a single technology.

- A *market* is defined by the performance of given functions in given customer groups, but including all the substitute technologies to perform those functions.
- An *industry* is based on a single technology, but covers several businesses, i.e. several functions or assortments of functions and several customer groups.

These alternative boundaries definitions correspond to different market coverage strategies, each having their own merits and weaknesses.

The *industry* definition is the most traditional one, but also the least satisfactory because it is supply-oriented and not market-oriented. From a marketing point of view, this definition of the reference market is much too general, since it includes a large variety of functions and customer groups. In the household appliances industry, for example, this would include microwave ovens and laundry irons, two very different products in terms of growth potential and of customers' behaviour characteristics.

However, most industrial and foreign trade statistics are industry-based and it is therefore difficult to avoid industry definitions completely.

The *market* definition is very close to the generic need concept and has the merit of emphasizing the existence of substitute technologies for performing the same function. A technological innovation can dramatically change existing market boundaries. The monitoring of substitute technologies is enhanced by this reference market definition. The major difficulty stems from the fact that the technology domains involved may be very different.

> Customers with a need for a 6 mm hole will normally use a metal twist drill, but some segments are finding lasers or high-pressure water jets to be a better solution. Also, companies that refine cane sugar wrestle with this question often. Their product is a sweetener, but the needs of soft drink and candy manufacturers for sweetening can be satisfied with sugar made from corn (fructose) or sugar beets. Depending on market conditions, these alternatives may be cheaper. Should they offer all sweetening materials? (Day, 1990, p. 27).

The market definition is very useful for giving directions to research and development and for suggesting diversification strategies.

The *product market* definition is the most market-oriented definition. It corresponds to the notion of 'strategic business unit' (SBU) and is very close to the real world market. This market definition automatically dictates four key elements of the firm's strategic thrust:

- The customers to be served.
- The package of benefits to be provided.
- The competitors to surpass.
- The capabilities to acquire.

This partitioning of the total reference market into product markets will guide the market coverage decisions and will determine the type of organizational structure to adopt.

One shortcoming of this market definition is the difficulty of finding appropriate market measurements, most government statistics being industry-based and not market-based.

Development of a macro-segmentation grid

Once the relevant segmentation variables are identified, the next task is to combine them for developing a segmentation grid. To illustrate this process, let us consider the market of heavy duty trucks. The identified segmentation variables are the following:

- *Functions:* regional (distribution and construction), national and international transport of goods.
- *Technologies:* air, rail, water and road (below and above 16 tons).
- *Customers:* types of activity: own account and professional transporters; size of fleet: small (1–4 trucks), medium (4–10 trucks) and large (>10 trucks).

If we consider all possible combinations, we have here a total of 108 (3 × 4 × 3 × 3) possible segments. Ignoring transportation modes other than road transportation (below and above 16 tons), the number of potential segments remains very great. In developing an operational segmentation grid, the following rules should be adopted.

- The analyst should start with the longest list of segmentation variables to avoid overlooking meaningful criteria.
- Only those variables with a truly significant strategic impact should be isolated.
- The number of variables can be reduced by collapsing together variables that are correlated.
- Some cells are generally infeasible combinations of segmentation variables and therefore can be eliminated.
- Some segments can be regrouped if the differences among them are not really significant or their size too small.
- The segmentation grid should include potential segments as well and not only segments that are currently occupied.

Table 6.1 Macro-segmentation of the truck market (% total truck population) (Lambin and Hiller, 1990)

Activity/functions	Fleet size and weight						Total
	Small (1–4)		Medium (4–10)		Large (>10)		
	<16t	>16t	<16t	>16t	<16t	>16t	
Own account transporters							
Distribution	7.3*	4.5	1.1	1.8	0.4	2.1	17.2
Construction	0.1	1.1	0.9	1.4	1.7	1.6	6.8
National	4.7	1.6	1.4	3.8	1.7	3.6	16.8
International	1.3	0.9	0.2	1.3	—	1.4	5.1
Others	—	0.6	0.3	—	2.5	—	3.4
Professional transporters							
Distribution	1.1	0.8	0.9	1.6	—	1.6	6.0
Construction	0.2	1.6	—	0.4	—	1.2	3.4
National	1.4	1.5	1.4	3.0	2.5	8.5	18.3
International	0.2	0.7	0.5	6.1	0.4	14.7	22.6
Others	—	0.4	—	—	—	—	0.4
Total	16.3	13.7	6.7	19.4	9.2	34.7	100.0%

* Read as: 7.3% of all truck registrations were less than 16 tons GVW, fleet owner-operators engaged in distribution

In the case of Volvo Trucks, the final segmentation grid retained comprises (4 × 3 × 2) = 24 potential segments, as shown in Table 6.1. Re-examination of the segmentation grid suggested the regrouping of the most similar segments that must be served together, to retain eventually four major segments which altogether represent 70.4 per cent of the total truck population in the Belgian market. For an example of application of this procedure in the oil drilling equipment market, see Porter (1985, pp. 248–55).

Testing the macro-segmentation grid

To verify the usefulness of the grid, the company's customers and direct competitors should be located in the different segments. The objective is to evaluate the potential of each segment in terms of size and growth, and to measure the market share held by the firm within each segment. The questions to examine are the following:

- Which segment(s) display the highest growth rate?
- What is our present market coverage of the market?
- Where are our key customers located?
- Where are our direct competitors located?
- What are the requirements of each segment in terms of service, product quality etc.?

The answers to these questions will help the firm to define its market coverage strategy and also to regroup segments having the same requirements and/or the same competitors.

Finding new segments

The segmentation grid should include potential segments as well and not only currently occupied segments. Potential segments may suggest new market penetration strategies. For example, in the heavy duty trucks case, renting companies should be added among the customer groups. In some countries, there is a potential for direct sales through this specialized customer group.

In searching for potential new segments, the following questions should be considered:

- Are there other technologies to perform the required functions?
- Could additional functions be performed by an enhanced product?
- Could the needs of some buyers be better served by reducing the number of functions and possibly lowering the price?
- Are there other groups of buyers requiring the same service or function?
- Are there new channels of distribution that could be used?
- Are there different bundles of products and services that could possibly be sold as a package?

Finding new ways to segment the market can give the firm a major competitive advantage over rivals.

Reference market coverage strategies

Reference market coverage decisions will be made on the basis of the 'attractiveness/competitiveness' analysis of the different product markets (see Chapter 9). Different market coverage strategies can be considered by the firm.

- *Focused strategy*. The market boundaries are defined narrowly in terms of functions, technology and customer groups. This is the strategy of the specialist seeking a high market share in a narrow niche.
- *Functional specialist*. The firm serves a single or narrow set of functions but covers a broad range of customers. The market boundaries are defined narrowly by function, but broadly by customer group. Firms manufacturing intermediate components fall in this category.
- *Customer specialist*. The market boundaries are defined broadly by function but narrowly by customer group. The focus is on the

needs of a particular group of customers. Companies specializing in hospital equipment belong to this category.

- *Full coverage*. The market boundaries are defined broadly by function and customer group. The firm covers the whole market. A steel company is a good example of this kind of market.
- *Mixed strategy*. The firm is diversifying its activities in terms of functions and/or customer groups.

In most cases, market coverage strategies can be defined in only two dimensions, functions and customer groups, because in general only one technology is mastered by the firm, even if substitute technologies exist. For example, jam is in direct competition with melted cheese and chocolate paste. Because manufacturing requirements are so different, none of the firms operating in the sector of fruit transformation also has industrial operations in these adjacent sectors.

In some cases, however, firms define their businesses in terms of several substitute technologies, such as General Electric in the diagnostic imaging market (see Abell, 1980, Chapter 5).

In a given sector of activity, business definitions may differ from one competitor to another. A firm specializing in a particular function can be confronted by a rival specializing in a particular customer group interested in the same function. The first competitor will probably have a cost advantage over the second one, who will be probably more efficient in terms of distribution or customer service. The competitor analysis system should help identify the distinctive qualities of direct competitors.

Changes in market boundaries

Under the pressure of technological progress and changing consumption habits, definitions of market boundaries keep on changing along any one of three dimensions: functions, technologies or customers.

- *Extension to new customer groups* through a process of adoption and diffusion, for example, adoption of microcomputers in the class room.
- *Extension to new functions* through a process of systematization and through the creation of products to serve a combination of functions, for example, telephone sets combined with a fax and with an automatic answering device.
- *Extensions to new technologies* through a process of technological substitution, for example, electronic mail replacing printed mail.

These changing forces explain the changing profiles of product life cycles, a key criterion for assessing the attractiveness of product markets. The product life cycle (PLC) model will be analysed in the next chapter.

Micro-segmentation analysis

The objective of micro-segmentation is to analyse the diversity of customers' requirements in a more detailed way within each of the product markets (or macro-segments) identified at the stage of macro-segmentation analysis. Within a particular product market, customers seek the same core service, for instance, time measurement in the watches market. However, keeping in mind the multi-attribute product concept, the way the core service is provided and the secondary services that go with the core service can be very different. The goal of micro-segmentation analysis is to identify customer groups searching for the same package of benefits in the product. This can lead to a differentiation strategy to obtain a competitive advantage over rivals by doing a better job of satisfying customer requirements.

Market segmentation versus product differentiation

A distinction should be clearly made between segmentation and differentiation, two key marketing concepts.

Product differentiation provides a basis upon which a supplier can appeal to selective buying motives. Chamberlin (1950, p. 56) has defined this concept in the following way:

A general class of product is differentiated if any significant basis exists for distinguishing the goods (or services) of one seller from those of another. Such a basis may be real or fancied, so long as it is of any importance whatever to buyers, and leads to a preference for one variety of a product over another.

The products are differentiated if the consumer believes that they are different.

While product differentiation is based on distinctions among products, market segmentation is based on distinctions among prospects that constitute the market (Smith, 1956). Recognition of the heterogeneity of customers has led firms to appeal to segments of what once might have been considered a homogeneous market. Generally, segmentation is viewed as a process of market disaggregation. It may be useful to view it as a process of consumer aggregation.

The firm could consider each buying unit as a segment. However, at least some economies of scale should be possible if these buying units were clustered into fewer groups. Buying units are aggregated in segments in such a way that there is a maximum homogeneity of demand within segments and maximum heterogeneity of demand between segments. Continuation of the aggregation process eventually leads to the formation of a single segment: the market as a whole. The firm must determine the level of aggregation which will generate the optimal profits (Dalrymple and Parsons, 1976, p. 143).

Thus, product differentiation is a supply concept, while market segmentation is a demand concept.

Steps in market segmentation

The implementation of a micro-segmentation analysis consists of four basic steps:

- *Segmentation analysis*, or subdividing product markets into distinct groups of potential buyers having the same expectations or requirements (homogeneity condition), and being different from customers who are in other segments (heterogeneity condition).
- *Market targeting*, or selecting particular segment(s) to target, given the firm's strategic ambition and distinctive capabilities.
- *Market positioning*, or deciding how the firm wants to be perceived in the minds of potential customers, given the distinctive quality of the product and the positions already occupied by competitors.
- *Marketing programming*, aimed at target segments. This last step involves the development and deployment of specific marketing programme(s) specially designed for achieving the desired positioning in the target segment(s).

The first step, segmentation analysis, can be implemented in four different ways:

- *Descriptive segmentation*, which is based on socio-demographic characteristics of the customer irrespective of the product category.
- *Benefit segmentation*, which considers explicitly the product category and the person's system of values.
- *Life style segmentation*, which is based on socio-cultural characteristics of the customer, irrespective of the product category.
- *Behavioural segmentation*, which classifies customers on the basis of their actual purchasing behaviour in the marketplace.

Each of these segmentation methods has its own merits and weaknesses, which will be discussed in the following sections.

Descriptive or socio-demographic segmentation

Socio-demographic segmentation is an indirect segmentation method. The basic assumption embedded in this buyers classification is the following: 'People having different socio-demographic profiles also have different needs and expectations regarding products and services'.

This is obvious in many fields. Women and men have different needs for products like clothes, hats, cosmetics, jewellery etc., and similarly for teenagers or senior citizens, for low and high income households, for rural versus urban households, and so on. Thus, socio-demographic variables are used as proxies for direct needs analysis.

The most commonly used variables are: sex, age, income, geographic location, education, occupation, family size and social class, all variables which reflect the easily measurable vital statistics of a society.

Frequently, a socio-demographic segmentation combines two or three variables, as shown in Figure 6.3, where the consumer banking market is analysed using sex, family life cycle and employment as segmentation variables. In total, 42 (7 × 3 × 2) theoretical segments are identified, each with possibly different financial needs. In this case, there may be some degree of overlap, e.g. both male and female may be part of the household (with or without children) and both may be working. An examination of each possible segment can be made in terms of its viability. A particular service can be developed to meet each viable segment, and a communication strategy chosen which will convey the information to the segment.

Usefulness of socio-demographic data

The *merits* of socio-demographic segmentation are its low cost and ease of application. In most markets, information on socio-demographic variables is readily available in published sources. In addition, consumer panels use these criteria in their monthly or bimonthly reports on a similar basis across the main European countries.

Also, in recent years significant socio-demographic changes have been observed in industrialized countries. Among these changes are:

- Declining birth rate.
- Increase in life expectancy.
- Increasing number of working women.
- Postponement of the age of marriage.
- Increasing divorce rate.
- Increasing numbers of single parent families.

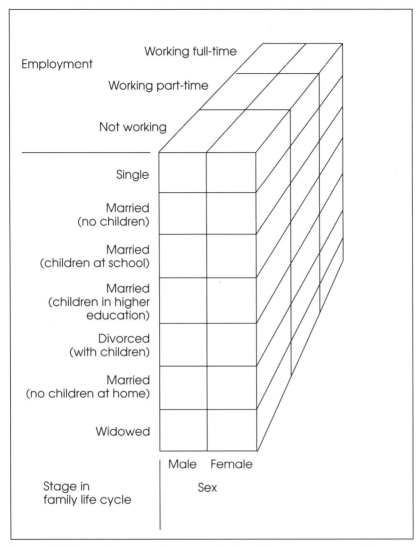

Figure 6.3 Socio-demographic segmentation of the consumer banking market (Yorke, 1982)

These changes all have direct implications on the demand structure and on consumer purchase behaviour. They create new market segments and new requirements in existing segments. Examples are:

- The *senior citizens* (over 65) segment for banking services, recreational activities, medical care etc.
- The segment of *single-adult households*, i.e. the unmarried, divorced, widowed or single parent families.
- The *dual-income households* having higher discretionary income.

- The segment of *working women* for all time-saving goods and services, like microwave ovens, catalogue shopping, easy-to-prepare foods, fast-food restaurants etc.

The changes observed during the last twenty years in the socio-demographic profile of the European Community are presented in Table 6.2.

Several uses are currently made of socio-demographic data, namely:

- To describe and better understand present customers.
- To have the ID profile of a target segment.
- To select media having a higher probability of reaching a target group.
- To identify prospective buyers of a new product.

Limitations of descriptive segmentation

Socio-demographic segmentation (as well as behavioural segmentation) is *ex-post analysis* of the kind of people who make up specific segments. The emphasis is on describing the characteristics of segments rather than on learning what causes these segments to develop. This is why it is called 'descriptive segmentation'.

Another major weakness is the *declining predictive value* of socio-demographic segmentation in industrialized countries as, increasingly, different persons adopt the same consuming behaviour with the growing standardization of consumption modes across social classes. In other words, the fact of belonging to the upper class does not necessarily imply any more the existence of a purchase behaviour different from a middle class person. Today, two consumers of the same age, same family structure and same income may have extremely different behaviours and attitudes, reflected in different buying habits, product preferences and sometimes completely opposite reactions to advertising. Socio-demographic segmentation must be complemented by other methods to understand and predict buyers' behaviour.

Benefit segmentation

In benefit segmentation, the emphasis is placed on differences in peoples' values and not on differences in socio-demographic profiles. Two persons identical in terms of socio-demographic profiles may have very different *value systems*. Moreover, the same person having different experiences with products can hold different values towards each product that is purchased. For example, a person who buys a refrigerator because it is the cheapest available may want to buy the most expensive TV set simply because of its superior design.

Table 6.2 Changes in the socio-demographic profile of the
European Community (EUROSTAT, 1991)

Total population		
	1980: 279m	1990: 327m
Persons aged 60 and over		
	1980: 17%	2010: 27%
Persons under 20 years old		
	1980: 30%	2010: 20%
Life expectancy (years)		
	1960: 67.3 (M)	1988: 72.0 (M)
	72.7 (F)	78.6 (F)
Infant mortality rate (per 1000 live births)		
	1960: 34.8	1988: 8.2
Foreign population		
	Extra-EC: 2.5% or 7.9 million	
	Intra-EC: 1.5% or 4.9 million	
Number of households		
	111.5 million private households	
	2.8 persons per household	
Number of one-person households		
	22.3% of total households	
Average age of first marriage		
	1950–70: 25.6 (M)	1987: 27.1 (M)
	23.0 (F)	24.6 (F)
Number of divorces ($\times$ 1000)		
	1960: 125.3	1988: 534.2
Activity rate for women (% of active population)		
	1983: 46.6%	1988: 51.0%

Or, the individual who pays a high price for a bottle of wine may
own a very cheap watch.

Thus, as discussed in Chapter 3, the value or the benefit sought in
purchasing a particular product is the critical motivational factor to
identify. The objective of benefit segmentation is to explain
differences in preferences and not simply to give ex-post
descriptions of purchase behaviours.

A classic example of benefit segmentation analysis is due to
Yankelovich (1964) in the watches market. His approach discloses
three distinct segments, each representing different values attributed
to watches by each of three different groups of consumers.

- *Economy segment.* This group wants to pay the lowest possible
  price for any watch that works reasonably well. If it fails within a
  year, they will replace it (23 per cent of buyers).

- *Durability and quality segment.* This group wants a watch with a long life, good workmanship, good material and good styling. They are willing to pay for these product qualities (46 per cent of buyers).
- *Symbolic segment.* This group wants useful product features and meaningful emotional qualities. The watch should suitably symbolize an important occasion. Here, a well known brand name, fine styling, a gold or diamond case, and a jeweller's recommendation are important (31 per cent of buyers).

Without such an understanding, the demographic characteristics of the buyers were most confusing. It turns out, for example, that the most expensive watches are being bought by people with both the highest and the lowest incomes. On the other hand, some upper income consumers are no longer buying costly watches, but are buying cheap, well-styled watches to throw away when they require servicing. Other upper income consumers, however, continue to buy fine, expensive watches for suitable occasions (Yankelovich, 1964).

At one time, most watch companies were oriented almost exclusively toward the third segment, thus leaving the major portion of the market open to attack and exploitation. The US Time Company, with the brand Timex, took advantage of this opening and established a very strong position among buyers in the first two segments.

Benefit segmentation (Haley, 1968) requires obtaining detailed information on consumer value systems. Each segment is identified by the benefits it is seeking. It is the total package of benefits sought which differentiates one segment from another, rather than the fact that one segment is seeking one particular benefit and another a quite different benefit. Individual benefits are likely to have appeal for several segments. In fact, most people would like as many benefits as possible. However, the relative importance they attach to individual benefits when forced to make trade-offs can differ a lot and, accordingly, can be used as an effective criterion in segmenting markets. Thus, opportunities for segmentation arise from *trade-offs* consumers are willing to make among the benefits possible and the prices paid to obtain them.

Thus, the multi-attribute product concept (see Chapter 4) is the implied behavioural model in benefit segmentation. Its implementation requires the following information from a representative sample of target consumers.

- The list of attributes or benefits associated with a product category.
- An evaluation of the relative importance attached to each benefit.
- A regrouping procedure of consumers with similar rating patterns.

Table 6.3 Benefit segmentation of the toothpaste market (adapted from Haley (1968))

Benefits sought	Benefit segments			
	Sensory	Sociables	Worriers	Independents
Flavour, product appearance	***	*	*	*
Brightness of teeth	*	***	*	*
Decay prevention	*	*	***	*
Low price	*	*	*	***

Note: *** = Most important

● An evaluation of the size and profile of each identified segment.

Thus, in the toothpaste market, the attributes identified through consumer research and their relative importance (*) are presented in Table 6.3. Supplementary information has also been collected about the people in each of these segments. Four segments were identified (Haley, 1968):

● The *decay prevention segment* contains a large number of families with children. They are seriously concerned about the possibilities of cavities and show a definite preference for fluoride toothpaste.
● The *sociables segment*, which comprises people who show concern for the brightness of their teeth, is quite different. It includes a relatively large group of young married couples. They smoke more than average and their life style is very active.
● The *sensory segment* is particularly concerned with the flavour and the appearance of the product. In this segment, a large portion of the brand deciders are children. Their use of spearmint toothpaste is well above average.
● The *independent segment* is price-oriented and shows a dominance of men. It tends to be above average in terms of toothpaste usage. People in this segment see very few meaningful differences between brands.

Benefit segmentation has important implications for the product policy of the firm. Once marketing understands the expectations of a particular consumer group, new or modified products can be developed and aimed at people seeking a specific combination of benefits.

Limitations of benefit segmentation

The greatest difficulty in applying this approach lies in the selection of the benefits to emphasize, mainly in the consumer goods markets.

Table 6.4 Hi-fi chains market: benefit segments and principal benefits sought

The technicians
- Mean to enjoy high-fidelity sound in its technical aspects.
- Look for the quality and purity of the sound.
- Mostly interested by the technical features without being necessarily qualified.

The musicians
- Mean to enjoy music.
- Look for the spirit of the music, its musical space and colour.
- Mostly interested by the musical interpretation without having necessarily a great musical culture.

The snobs
- Mean to show their resources, taste and aesthetic sense.
- Look for prestige, demonstration effects and social integration.
- Often poorly informed, tend to buy what is known and safe.

The others

When market analysts ask consumers what benefit they want in a product, they are not likely to provide very new information about product benefits, since they are not highly introspective. If direct market analysis is supplemented with information about consumers' problems, however, new insights can be obtained. For example, in the toothpaste market, protection of gums is a new benefit promoted by brands having adopted a paramedical positioning. This is the outcome of dental hygiene analysis conducted with the dental profession.

Another difficulty of benefit segmentation stems from this fact: if we are gaining in understanding of consumer preferences, we are losing in terms of knowledge of the socio-demographic profiles of different customer groups. How do we reach, selectively, the 'worriers'? Thus, additional information must be collected to be able to describe these segments in socio-demographic terms.

Benefit segmentation analysis requires the collection of primary data, always a costly exercise. In addition, sophisticated multivariate measurement techniques (cluster analysis) must be used to identify the different customer groups. In some cases, however, interesting insights on benefits sought can be obtained through qualitative research, as illustrated in Table 6.4 in the hi-fi chains market.

Segmenting markets with conjoint analysis

The method of conjoint analysis has been described in Chapter 5. As explained, the focus of conjoint analysis is on the measurement of buyer preferences for product attribute levels and of the buyer

Table 6.5 Benefit segmentation through conjoint analysis: book review example (adapted from Roisin (1988))

Attributes	Segment 1 (35.5%)	Segment 2 (21.0%)	Segment 3 (11.3%)	Segment 4 (32.2%)
Content				
Book review	−7.1	1.2	−6.2	−1.8
Book guide	−7.4	−7.9	2.9	−3.1
Present content	0	0	0	0
Literary news	0.3	−2.1	−6.8	−3.3
Price Range:	7.7	9.1	9.7	3.3
BF100	0.5	0.6	0.3	1.1
BF142	0	0	0	0
BF200	−0.7	−0.6	−0.4	−1.0
Range:	1.2	1.2	0.7	2.1

benefits generated by the product attributes. Since measurements are made at the individual level, if preference heterogeneity exists the market analyst can detect it and regroup individuals displaying the same utilities.

An empirical example will clarify the methodology. The application involves a bimonthly books magazine which publishes new book reviews, book guidance and advice, book digests and short articles. The editor is considering three alternative modifications of the editorial content:

(a) Concentrating on book reviews and analyses and dropping all the other editorial sections (*book review*).
(b) Concentrating on guidance and advice on a larger number of books using standardized evaluation grids (*reader's guide*).
(c) Limiting the number of book reviews, but adding a section on literary news with interviews of authors and special topical sections (*literary news*).

A 'do nothing' alternative is also considered, i.e. to keep the present editorial content unchanged. As to the selling price, three levels are considered: the present price of BF142, an increased price of BF200 and a decreased price of BF100, the number of pages remaining unchanged (30 pages). A questionnaire was mailed to 400 respondents selected among a group of readers and 171 valid questionnaires were used to estimate the utility functions. A cluster analysis programme was then used to regroup the respondents having the same utilities. As shown in Table 6.5, four different segments were identified.

- In *segment 1*, the respondents seem to be happy with the present editorial content. They react very negatively to the first two alternatives, and positively, but without enthusiasm, to the 'literary news' concept.
- In *segment 2*, there is a clear preference for the 'book reviews' concept and a negative attitude towards the other two editorial concepts.
- In *segment 3*, it is the 'reader's guide' concept which is preferred, the other two being clearly rejected.
- In *segment 4*, the present editorial content is the best alternative, but the range of utilities is also the smallest.

Thus in terms of benefits sought, the four segments are very different. As to the prices, the largest price sensitivity is observed in segment 4, as evidenced by the range, while segments 1 and 2 react in a very similar way, segment 3 being the least price sensitive. Analysis of the composition of these four segments showed that segment 4 was largely composed of librarians, while high school teachers were an important group in segment 3.

For a review of the contributions of conjoint analysis in market segmentation, see Green and Krieger (1991).

Behavioural segmentation

Usage segmentation attempts to classify consumers on the basis of their actual purchase behaviour in the market place. As such, it is also a descriptive and ex-post segmentation method. The criteria most commonly used are product usage, volume purchased and loyalty status.

- *Product-user segmentation*. A distinction can be made between users, non-users, first users, ex-users, potential users, and occasional versus regular users. A different selling and communication approach must be adopted for each of these user categories.
- *Volume segmentation*. In many markets, a small proportion of customers represents a high percentage of total sales. Often, about 20 per cent of the users account for 80 per cent of total consumption. A distinction between heavy, light and non-users is often very useful. Heavy users, or key accounts, deserve special treatment.
- *Loyalty segmentation*. Among existing customers a distinction can be made between hard-core loyals, soft-core loyals and switchers. Markets like cigarettes, beers and toothpaste are generally brand-loyal markets. Keeping loyal customers is the objective of relationship marketing. Appropriate marketing strategies can be

be developed to attract competitors' customers or to increase the loyalty of switchers.

Sociocultural or life style segmentation

As mentioned above, socio-demographic criteria are losing predictive value in affluent societies as consumption patterns become more and more personalized. Individuals from the same socio-demographic groups can have very different preferences and buying behaviour, and vice versa. Sociocultural segmentation, also called *life style* or *psychographic segmentation,* seeks to supplement demographics by adding such elements as activities, attitudes, interests, opinions, perceptions and preferences to get a more complete consumer profile. It attempts to draw human portraits of consumers adding detail at the less obvious levels of motivation and personality. Wells and Tigert make the following points:

> Demographics have been and continue to be extremely useful, but they are unsatisfying. They lack color. They lack texture. They lack dimensionality. They need to be supplemented by something that puts flesh on bare statistical backbone (Wells and Tigert, 1971, published in Wells, 1974, p. 37).

The basic objective is to relate personality-type variables to consumer behaviour. Life style descriptors are used as proxies for personality traits.

'Life style' refers to the overall manner in which people live and spend time and money. A person's life style (or psychographic profile) can be measured and described in a number of ways:

- At a superficial level, but directly observable, consumers' life styles are reflected by the *products and services purchased* and by the way in which buyers are using or consuming them.
- At an intermediate level, a person's *activities, interests* and *opinions* are revealing of her or his value system.
- At the most stable and persistent level are the person's *value system* and *personality traits* which are, of course, more difficult to measure.

Valette-Florence (1986) suggests defining a person's life style as the interaction of these three levels: the group of persons having a similar behaviour at each of these levels is homogeneous in terms of life style. Thus a life style is the outgrowth of a person's value system, attitudes, interests and opinions (AIO) and of the individual's consumption mode. It describes the sort of person she (or he) is and at the same time it differentiates her (or him) from other persons.

Life style studies can be conducted at one of these three levels.

Table 6.6 Life style dimensions (Plummer, 1974)

Activities	Interests	Opinions	Demographics
Work	Family	Themselves	Age
Hobbies	Home	Social issue	Education
Social events	Job	Politics	Income
Vacation	Community	Business	Occupation
Entertainment	Recreation	Economics	Family size
Club membership	Fashion	Education	Dwelling
Community	Food	Products	Geography
Shopping	Media	Future	City size
Sports	Achievements	Culture	Life cycle

The closer we are to actual purchase decisions the easier are the measurements, but also the more volatile are the conclusions. The largest majority of empirical life style studies have been conducted at the AIO level, where research measures (a) people's *activities* in terms of how they spend their time; (b) their *interests*, what they place importance on in their immediate surroundings; (c) their *opinions* in terms of views of themselves and the world around them; and (d) some basic *demographic* characteristics such as their stage in life cycle, income, education and where they live. Table 6.6 lists the elements included in each major dimension of life style.

Life style studies provide a broad everyday view of consumers, a living portrait which goes beyond flat socio-demographic descriptions and helps understand actual consumer behaviour.

Technique of life style segmentation

In a typical life style study, a questionnaire is developed containing a set of statements measuring the life style dimensions relevant to the product category under study. Each dimension is measured by several statements or propositions to which respondents indicate the extent of their agreement or disagreement on a five point Likert scale ranging from: 'definitely disagree' to 'definitely agree'. Examples of life style statements are presented in Table 6.7. If the relevant dimension is 'price conscious', then it will be measured by consumers agreeing or disagreeing with 5 or 6 statements similar to the one presented in Table 6.7, under the dimension 'price conscious'.

Typically several different statements are introduced into the questionnaire to measure the same dimension. Approximately 200 to 300 AIO statements may be included. In addition to the AIO statements, information is also collected on product usage and on demographic characteristics.

Table 6.7 Examples of general life style statements (Wells and Tigert, 1971)

- I find myself checking the prices in the grocery stores even for small items (price conscious).
- An important part of my life and activities is dressing smartly (fashion conscious).
- I would rather spend a quiet evening at home than go out to a party (homebody).
- I like to work on community projects (community minded).
- I try to arrange my home for my children's convenience (child oriented).

Armed with these three sets of data (AIO statements, product usage and demographics), the market analyst constructs user profiles. The analysis involves relating levels of agreement on all AIO items with the levels of usage of a product and with demographic characteristics. The procedure is the following.

- Factor analysis is used to reduce the set of statements to a summary set of factors.
- Each respondent's scores on the factors are computed.
- Respondents are then clustered into segments that are relatively homogeneous using a cluster analysis programme.
- The clusters are then labelled by the factors which most typify each cluster.
- Finally, the segments are cross-tabulated with demographic and usage variables to help characterize the identified segments.

An example of general life style segmentation of the European market is presented in Figure 6.4.

Benefits of life style segmentation

General or situation-specific life style studies can be conducted. *General life style studies* classify the total population into groups based on general life style characteristics, such as 'receptivity to innovation', 'family centred', 'ecological sensitivity' etc. Each sub-group represents a different pattern of needs, and market analysts can discern which types of consumers are strong prospects for their products, what other things appeal to these prospects and how to communicate with them in the most effective way.

From a more dynamic point of view, the changing weight of existing socio-cultural profiles in the total population can be evaluated and emerging socio-cultural trends identified. This approach is useful to detect leading indicators of change. In Europe, the group Europanel

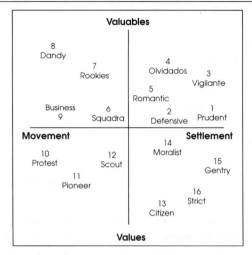

Figure 6.4 European life style segmentation (Winkler, 1991)

1 **Prudent**
Retirees resigned to their fate,
seeking security

2 **Defensives**
Younger inhabitants of small towns
seeking protection and support in
their traditional family structures

3 **Vigilante**
Frustrated blue-collar workers
trying to preserve their identities

4 **Olvidados (left out)**
Retirees and housewives threatened
and left-out by society's growing
complexity; seek protection

5 **Romantic**
Sentimental, romantic young nest
builders seeking modern progress
and a secure life for their families

6 **Squadra (team player)**
Tolerant suburban young couples seeking
a secure life of sports and leisure;
smaller group gives feeling of security

7 **Rookies**
Working class youth, excluded in their
own eyes, seeking integration via money-
making/consumption; frustrated by low
education

8 **Dandy**
Hedonistic group 'show-offs'
with modest income and concern
for outward appearances

9 **Business (sharks)**
Spendthrift, well-educated,
ambitious young wolves, seeking
leadership in a competitive society

10 **Protest**
Intellectual young critics seeking
to revolutionize society

11 **Pioneer**
Young well-off, ultra-tolerant
intellectuals seeking social justice

12 **Scout**
Tolerant middle-aged conservatives
seeking orderly social progress

13 **Citizens**
Community organizers seeking leadership
in social activities

14 **Moralist**
Quiet, religious citizens seeking a
peaceful future for their children

15 **Gentry**
Law and order conservatives belonging
to old money established élite

16 **Strict**
Repressive puritans

(GFK) has developed a general typology of 16 European socio-style profiles. In the USA, the VALS programme was created by SRI International with eight consumer segments (VALS-2). The 16 Euro-styles identified in the European market by the Europanel Group are presented in Figure 6.4.

The map of Figure 6.4 shows the 16 Euro-styles in two dimensions. The first may be described roughly as the willingness to accept new ideas or to try new things (movement versus settlement); the second opposes an orientation towards material goods (valuables) and towards ethics (values). A third dimension opposing rational and emotional behaviour has been observed but is not represented here.

> Thus people in type 8 (Dandies), which is close to the upper left-hand corner of the map, are materialistic and adventurous. People belonging to type 16 (Strict), near the bottom right-hand corner of the map, are more interested in ethical issues than material considerations and are very conservative in attitude (Winkler, 1991, p. 9).

Having this map, it is possible to overlay the pattern of product (or brand) usage or attitude and to compare the kinds of people being heavy users of the product category and/or of the brand.

In *product-specific life style* studies, the objective is to understand consumer behaviour related to a particular product or service. The AIO statements are then more product-specific. To illustrate, here are examples of AIO statements adapted to the credit cards market:

- I like to pay cash for everything I buy.
- I buy many things with a credit card or a charge card.
- In the past year, we have borrowed money from a bank or finance company.
- To buy anything other than a house or a car on credit is unwise.

Life style research methodology also has some important advantages over motivation research and depth interviews: (a) samples are large; (b) conclusions do not rely heavily on interviewer interpretation of relatively unstructured responses; (c) data are easily analysed by a variety of well understood statistical methods; and (d) less highly trained interviewers can be employed.

Problems in life style research

Life style research was at one time very popular in marketing research, particularly among advertising people, although several researchers have very early expressed considerable reservations as to its validity and predictive value. A certain number of methodological issues are still unresolved.

- To date, there is *no explicit theoretical model* which specifies the key concepts of life style to be explored and their hypothesized relations to purchase behaviour. In most cases, it is a trial-and-error procedure which is adopted.
- As a consequence, the *selection of life style dimensions* and indicators is largely based on intuition, hunches and the researcher's imagination. Life style researchers do not agree on

what variables should be included. The end result is a very large number (up to 300) statements included in the questionnaire, a way out facilitated by increasing computer capacities.

- Life style analyses belong to the class of causal studies, since the objective is to explain why people behave as they do. To demonstrate the existence of a causal relationship requires a *well-conceived experimental design* and careful testing of the observed relationship. Evidence of a relationship does not necessarily imply causality. Spurious correlations as well as spurious non-correlations exist and the lack of prior research design can cause faulty interpretation of data.
- Traditionally, the association between life style data with variables like product usage, brand loyalty etc. are examined by direct cross-tabulations, while the *multivariate nature of data* suggest the use of multivariate statistical techniques.
- Questions are also raised regarding the *reliability of the measuring instrument*. Can we expect reliable and valid responses from a questionnaire which takes several hours to complete and may lead to boredom or fatigue?

For a systematic analysis of the methodological issues raised by life style research and for the remedies suggested, see Green and Wind (1974) and Valette-Florence (1986, 1988). For an empirical validation of life style studies in the French market, see Kapferer and Laurent (1981).

Several of the methodological issues raised here are critical and question the internal and external validity of general life style studies. This means that its users must make special efforts to be careful in measurements, statistical analyses and interpretations of results if they are to uncover valid information on consumer behaviour. It is up to the market analyst to verify whether the basic validity conditions are indeed fulfilled.

Industrial markets segmentation

Conceptually, there is no difference between industrial and consumer market segmentation, but the criteria used to segment the market vary greatly. The same distinction between macro- and micro-segmentation can be made. Macro-segmentation involves dividing the market into subgroups based on overall characteristics of customer organizations, i.e. organizational demographics. Micro-segmentation criteria pertain to characteristics of the decision-making process and to the structure of the decision centre.

The simplest way to segment industrial markets is to use broad descriptive characteristics, such as industrial sectors (NACE or SIC

Table 6.8 Major bases for industrial segmentation: the nested approach (Shapiro and Bonona, 1983)

Organizational demographics
Industry sectors
Company size
Geographic location
Operating variables
Technology
User/non-user status
Customer capabilities
Purchasing approaches
Decision centre organization
Purchasing policies
Purchasing criteria
Situational factors
Urgency
Application
Size of order
Personal characteristics
Motivation
Buyer and seller relationship
Risk perceptions

category), company size, geographic location or end-market served. This information is easily accessible since this type of data is readily available through government agencies, who publish detailed industrial classifications. Benefit segmentation is also easier in industrial markets than in consumer markets, because users are professional people who have less difficulty in expressing their needs and in qualifying the relative importance of different product attributes.

Shapiro and Bonona (1983) have expanded the use of macro- and micro-segmentation into what is called a *'nested approach'*. This method assumes a hierarchical structure of segmentation bases which move from very broad or general bases to very organization-specific bases. Rather than a two-step process, the nested approach allows three, four or five steps. The list of segmentation criteria is presented in Table 6.8.

Implementation of a segmentation strategy

Having completed the market segmentation analysis, management has to make decisions regarding the segments to target and regarding the positioning to adopt within the targeted segments. The final stage is to define the type of marketing programme to adopt within each chosen segment.

Market targeting strategies

Having analysed the reference market's diversity, the next task is to decide what type of market coverage strategy to adopt. This point has already been discussed. The options open to the firm are of three types: undifferentiated, differentiated or focused marketing (Smith, 1956).

By adopting an *undifferentiated marketing strategy*, the firm ignores market segment differences and decides to approach the entire market as a whole and not take advantage of segmentation analysis. It focuses on what is common in the needs of buyers rather than on what is different. The rationale of this middle-of-the-road or standardization strategy is cost savings, not only in manufacturing, but also in inventory, distribution and advertising. In affluent societies, this strategy is more and more difficult to defend as it is rarely possible for a product or a brand to please everyone.

In a *differentiated marketing strategy*, the firm also adopts a full market coverage strategy, but this time with tailor-made progammes for each segment. This was the slogan of General Motors, claiming to have a car for every 'purse, purpose and personality'. This strategy enables the firm to operate in several segments with a customized pricing, distribution and communication strategy. Selling prices will be set on the basis of each segment's price sensitivity. This strategy generally implies higher costs, since the firm is losing the benefits of economies of scale. On the other hand, the firm can expect to hold a strong market share position within each segment. Differentiated marketing does not necessarily imply full market coverage. The risk may be to over-segment the market, with the danger of cannibalism among the excess brands of the same company.

In a *focused marketing strategy*, the firm is concentrating its resources on the needs of a single segment or on a few segments, adopting a specialist strategy. The specialization can be based on a function (functional specialist) or on a particular customer group (customer specialist). Through focused marketing, the company can expect to reap the benefits of specialization and of improved efficiency in the use of the firm's resources. The feasibility of a focused strategy depends on the size of the segment and on the strength of the competitive advantage gained through specialization.

The choice of any one of these market coverage strategies will be determined (a) by the number of identifiable and potentially profitable segments in the reference market and (b) by the resources of the firm. If a company has limited resources, a focused marketing strategy is probably the only option.

Requirements for effective segmentation

To be effective and useful a segmentation strategy should identify segments that meet four criteria: differential response, adequate size, measurability and accessibility.

- *Differential response.* This is the most important criterion to consider when choosing a segmentation strategy. The segments must be different in terms of their sensitivity to one or several marketing variables under the control of the firm. The segmentation variable should maximize the behavioural difference between segments (heterogeneity condition) while minimizing the differences among customers within a segment (homogeneity condition).
- *Adequate size.* Segments should be defined so that they represent enough potential customers to provide sufficient sales revenue to justify the development of different products and marketing programmes. A trade-off must be made here between two logics: the logic of marketing, which tries to meet the needs of the market through narrow definition of segments, and the logic of production, which emphasizes the benefits of economies of scale through standardization and long production runs.
- *Measurability.* Before target segments can be selected, the size, the purchasing power and the major behaviour characteristics of the identified segments must be measured. If the segmentation criteria used are very abstract, such information is hard to find. For example, if the prospects are companies of a certain size, it would be easy to find information about their number, location, turnover etc. But a segmentation criterion like 'innovativeness of companies' does not lend itself to easy measurement and the firm would probably have to conduct its own market survey. Abstract criteria are often used in benefit and life style segmentations, while descriptive segmentation is based on more concrete and observable criteria.
- *Accessibility.* This refers to the degree to which a market segment can be reached through a unique marketing programme. There are two ways to reach prospects: controlled coverage and customer self-selection. Controlled coverage is very efficient because the firm reaches target customers with little wasted coverage of indviduals or firms who are not potential buyers. Customer self-selection involves reaching a more general target while

Table 6.9 Comparative evaluation of segments

	Segment 1	Segment 2	Segment 3	Segment 4
Demographics	————	————	————	————
Benefits sought	————	————	————	————
Buying behaviour	————	————	————	————
Success factors	**Importance of success factors**			
Product features	————	————	————	————
Price	————	————	————	————
Services	————	————	————	————
Delivery	————	————	————	————
Assistance	————	————	————	————
Economic factors				
Size in volume	————	————	————	————
Average price	————	————	————	————
Growth rate	————	————	————	————
Life cycle phase	————	————	————	————

relying on the product's and advertising's appeal to the intended target group. These consumers select themselves by their attention to the advertisements. A controlled coverage approach is economically more advantageous.

The main characteristics of each segment can be summarized in a segmentation analysis grid, as shown in Table 6.9

Product positioning strategies

Selection of the positioning strategy provides the unifying concept for the development of the marketing programme. Positioning indicates how the firm would like to be perceived in the minds of target customers. Positioning can be defined as follows:

> Positioning is the act of designing and communicating the firm's offer so that it occupies a distinct and valued place in the target customers' mind (Ries and Trout, 1981).

Positioning is mostly relevant when coupled with a segmentation analysis which requires a positioning by segments instead of a single positioning for the total market. Positioning strategy is the operational way to implement a differentiation strategy.

The typical questions to address here are the following:

- Which are the distinctive features and/or benefits, real or perceived, considered as the most important from the buyer's point of view?

- Which are the perceived positions of the main competing brands according to these features and/or benefits?
- Given the strengths and weaknesses of our brand and the positions already occupied by competing brands, what is the best positioning to adopt?
- What is the most appropriate marketing programme for achieving the chosen positioning?

Thus, not all brand or product differences are meaningful to buyers. As discussed in Chapter 8 (see p. 257), the source of differentiation should be 'unique', 'important' to the buyer, 'sustainable', 'communicable' and 'affordable'.

Alternative bases for positioning

Wind (1982, pp. 79–80) has identified six alternative bases for positioning. These are:

- Positioning on product features.
- Positioning on benefits, on problem solution or needs.
- Positioning for specific usage occasion.
- Positioning for user category.
- Positioning against another product.
- Product class dissociation.

Other positioning bases exist, such as, for example, life style positioning.

Selecting a positioning basis

When selecting a positioning basis, a certain number of conditions must be carefully met:

- To have a good understanding of the *present positioning* of the brand or firm in the customers' minds. This knowledge can be acquired through brand image studies, as described in Chapter 5.
- To know the present positioning of *competing brands,* in particular those brands in direct competition.
- To select one positioning and to identify the most relevant and credible *arguments* which justify the chosen positioning.
- To evaluate the potential *profitability* of the contemplated positioning, while being suspicious of false market niches invented by advertising people or discovered through an unvalidated qualitative study.
- To verify whether the brand has the required *personality potential* for achieving the positioning in the minds of consumers.
- To assess the *vulnerability* of the positioning. Do we have the resources required to occupy and to defend this position?
- To ensure *consistency* in the positioning with the different

marketing mix instruments: pricing, distribution, packaging, services etc.

Once the positioning strategy is adopted and clearly defined, it is much simpler for marketing people to translate this positioning in terms of an effective and consistent marketing programme.

Attribute-based perceptual maps

When the number of benefits to consider is large, attribute-based perceptual maps are useful to identify the different packages of benefits and to describe the perceived positioning of the major competing brands. To illustrate, we refer to a study of the Belgian toothpaste market aiming to verify the way consumers perceive a brand extension of the brand Signal, called Signal-plus. In this analysis, 24 product benefits were identified through unstructured group discussions:

Good for children	Traditional
Protects gums	Prevents tartar
Prevents decay	Fresh breath
Expensive	Pleasant texture
Sold in pharmacy	Economical
Much advertised	Unpleasant taste
Whitens teeth	For the whole family
Cavity protection	Strong taste
Young	Pleasant advertising
Medical	Friendly
Funny colours	Less effective than claimed
With fluoride	Attractive packaging

A representative sample of 130 respondents in the 12–30 age group were exposed to the 12 brands and asked to rate the twelve leading brands of toothpaste by simply noting their perceptions as to the absence or presence (0,1) of each particular benefit in each brand. These data were fed into a computer programme called Factorial Correspondence Analysis (ANAFACO) to determine the association of the benefits with the brands.

The two-dimensional map identified is presented in Figure 6.5, which provides management with a picture of the market for all competing brands and for the benefits associated with the brands.

- *Segment 1* regroups the medical brands perceived as giving 'gum protection', being 'sold in pharmacies', 'expensive' and with 'unpleasant taste'.
- *Segment 2* regroups the cosmetic brands, emphasizing 'fresh breath', being 'friendly', with a 'pleasant taste', 'attractive packaging' and 'pleasant texture'.
- *Segment 3* regroups the anti-cavity brands and emphasizes 'white

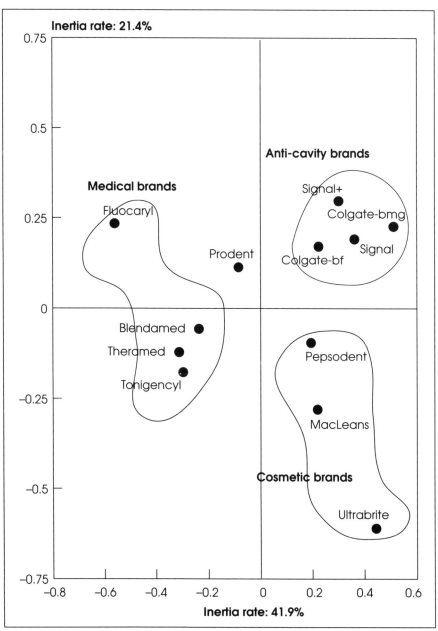

Figure 6.5 Product positioning analysis: the toothpaste market in Belgium, 1985

teeth', 'good for children', 'pleasant colours', 'with fluoride', 'pleasant advertising'.

The promise in segment 3 is more friendly than in segment 1 but is coupled with a more serious promise: cavity prevention.

Thus, this type of perceptual map permits management to evaluate the way segments perceive the different brands and whether the intended positioning has been reasonably well achieved.

International segmentation

With the globalization of the world economy, opportunities are growing to create demand for universal products. International segmentation is a way in which a global approach can be adopted to sell a physically similar product worldwide. The objective is to discover in different countries and/or regions groups of buyers having the same expectations and requirements *vis-à-vis* products, despite cultural and national differences. Those segments, even if they are small in size within each country, may represent in total a very attractive opportunity for the international firm. To adjust to local differences, the physical product can be customized through services, accessories or inexpensive product modifications. The potential for globalization is not the same for each product category and different approaches can be adopted. For a review of the literature in this topic, see Hassan and Katsanis (1991).

Identification of global market segments

Global market segmentation can be defined as the process of identifying specific segments, whether they be country groups or individual buyer groups, of potential customers with homogeneous attributes who are likely to exhibit similar buying behaviour. There are three different approaches for global segmentation: (a) identifying clusters of countries that demand similar products; (b) identifying segments present in many or most countries; and (c) targeting different segments in different countries with the same product (Takeuchi and Porter, 1986, pp. 138–40).

Targeting country clusters

Traditionally, the world market has been segmented on geographic variables, i.e. by regrouping countries that are similar in terms of climate, language, religion, economic development, distribution channels etc. Products rarely require modification or tailoring for every single country, except for such things as labelling and the language used in the manuals and catalogues. On the European scene, natural clusters of countries would be, for example, the Nordic countries (Denmark, Norway, Sweden and maybe Finland); the Germanic countries (Germany, Austria, part of Switzerland); the Iberian countries etc. With this country segmentation strategy, products and communication would be adapted for each group of countries.

Within the European Community, an argument in favour of this country approach lies in the very high diversity of the different countries, as evidenced by the comparison of their socio-demographic profiles. See the social portrait of Europe recently published by the EC (EUROSTAT, 1991).

However, this approach presents three potential limitations: (a) it is based on country variables and not on consumer behavioural patterns, (b) it assumes total homogeneity within the country segment, and (c) it overlooks the existence of homogeneous consumer segments that might exist across national boundaries. With the growth of regionalism within Europe, the second assumption becomes a more and more limiting factor.

Selling to universal segments across countries

As discussed in Chapter 2, several trends are influencing consumption behaviour on a global scale and many consumer products are becoming more widely accepted globally, such as consumer electronics, automobiles, fashion, home appliances, food products, beverages and services. Many of these products respond to needs and wants that cut across national boundaries.

Thus, even if product needs overall vary among countries, there may be a segment of the market with identical needs in every country. The challenge facing international firms is to identify these 'universal' segments and reach them with marketing programmes that meet the common needs of these potential buyers. These universal segments are most likely to be high-end consumers, sport professionals, executives of multinational companies or, in general, sophisticated users, because these groups tend to be the most mobile and therefore the most likely to be exposed to extensive international contacts and experiences.

A growing market segment on a global scale is composed of consumers aspiring to an 'élite life style'. This élite, in Tokyo, New York, Paris, London, Hong Kong, Rio de Janeiro etc, is the target of brands that fit the image of exclusivity, like Mercedes, Gucci, Hermès, American Express, Gold Card, Chivas, Godiva etc.

Such high-end brands can be targeted internationally to this universal segment in exactly the same way that they are currently positioned in their respective home market.

This international segmentation strategy is illustrated in Figure 6.6(a). The size of universal segments can be small in each country.

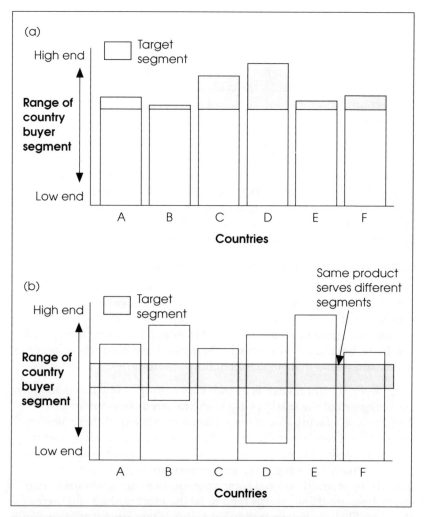

Figure 6.6 International segmentation: two different market positioning strategies: (a) universal segment positioning across countries; (b) diverse segment positioning across countries (Takeuchi and Porter, 1986 (Michael E. Porter, ed., *Competition in Global Industries*, Boston, MA: Harvard Business School Press, 1986. © 1986 by the President and Fellows of Harvard College. Reprinted by permission.))

What is attractive is the cumulative volume. For example, the Godiva pralines are present in twenty different countries all over the world, sometimes with modest market shares. It is nevertheless the world leader chocolatier.

Targeting diverse segments across countries

Even if product needs vary among countries, the same product can sometimes be sold in each country but in different segments, by adopting different market positioning based on non-product variables such as distributive networks, advertising and pricing. This approach is illustrated in Figure 6.6(b).

> The positioning adopted for the Canon AE-1 provides a good example of this international segmentation approach. The AE-1 was targeted towards young replacement buyers in Japan, upscale first-time buyers of 35 mm single-lens reflex cameras in the USA, and older and more technologically sophisticated replacement buyers in Germany. Three different marketing programmes were developed for Japan, the USA and Europe (Takeuchi and Porter, 1986, p. 139).

This approach requires important adaptations of communication and selling strategies which contribute to increasing costs or at least to preventing cost decreases as a consequence of standardization.

Of the three segmentation approaches, universal segmentation is the most innovative and also most likely to give the firm a significant competitive advantage, because product and communication can be standardized and transferred among countries. This gives the brand a reputation and a coherence in image and positioning which is internationally reinforced. The diverse segmentation approach has the merit of taking into consideration differences in consumer behaviour among countries and of introducing adaptations to accommodate these differences. On the other hand, because of these country to country adaptations, the brand image in each country will probably be different.

The case of universal segments

The global approach in segmenting world markets looks for similarities between markets. The traditional international approach is multi-domestic, i.e. it tends to ignore similarities. The global approach actively seeks homogeneity in product, image, marketing and advertising message, while the multi-domestic approach maintains unnecessary differences from market to market. The goal, however, is not to have a uniform product line worldwide. Rather the goal is to have a product line that is as standardized as possible, while recognizing that allowances for some local conditions are both necessary and desirable.

The case of Black & Decker provides a good illustration of this strategy (Farley, 1986). Black & Decker is established in 50 countries and manufactures in 25 plants, 16 of which are outside the USA. It has a very high level of brand awareness worldwide, sometimes in the 80–90 per cent range. For Black & Decker the potential economies of scale and cost savings of globalization were considerable. The challenges to be overcome were the following:

- Different countries have different safety and industry standards that make complete standardization impossible.
- European and American consumers have very different responses to product design and even to colours.
- Consumers use the products in different ways in different countries. For example, Europeans are more power-oriented in their electric tools than Americans (Farley, 1986, p. 69).

As a consequence of this diversity, the multi-domestic organization approach produced staggering product proliferation. The company had hundreds of products worldwide and relatively few interchangeable among countries. As a result of the globalization approach implemented between 1980 and 1990, Black & Decker has developed global products. The rule now is that any new product must be designed for a world market. People within the organization are expected to think 'world product' first; anything else has to be justified.

Trade-off between standardization and customization

In the largest majority of market situations, some degree of adaptation will be necessary. The essence of international segmentation can be summarized as follows: *think of global similarities and adapt to local differences*. This perspective should help management to determine similarities across national boundaries while assessing within-country differences. The different strategies susceptible to adoption, depending on the diversity of expectations and cultural background, are presented in Table 6.10. Three types of product policy can be considered:

- *Universal product*: the physical product sold in each country is identical except for labelling and for the language used in the manuals.
- *Modified product*: the core product is the same, but some modifications are adopted, such as voltage, colour, size or accessories, to accommodate government regulations or to reflect local differences in taste, buying habits, climate etc.
- *Country-tailored product*: the physical product is substantially tailored to each country or group of countries.

The financial and cost implications of these alternative product policies are, of course, particularly important.

Establishing a world brand

Not every product has the same global vocation, and some products may be easier than others to develop as world brands. Several brands are on the market and recognized as world brands: Coca-Cola, Marlboro, Kodak, Honda, Mercedes, Heineken, Swatch, Canon,

Table 6.10 Strategies of international segmentation (Blanche, 1987)

Global marketing strategies	Expectations of segments			
	Homogeneous		Similar	Different
	Same culture	Different culture	Same culture	Different culture
1 Unchanged product and operational marketing	1	—	—	—	—
2 Unchanged product and adapted operational marketing	—	2	2	2	—
3 Adapted product and operational marketing	—	—	—	3	3
4 New product and specific operational marketing	—	—	—	—	4

Gucci, British Airways, Perrier, Black & Decker, Hertz, Benetton, McDonalds, Godiva and many others. It is worth noting that the popularity of these brands is independent of the attitude towards their country of origin.

In reality, the universal vocation of a product is closely linked to the universality of the benefit sought. To the extent that a product is a proven success in meeting the needs of a particular group of buyers in a given country, it is logical to expect a similar success with the same group of people in another country, provided of course the product is adapted to local consuming habits or regulations. In other words, as suggested by Quelch and Hoff (1986), the driving factor in moving toward global marketing should be 'the efficient worldwide use of good marketing ideas rather than scale economies from standardization'.

The closer is the product to the *high-tech/high-touch poles*, the more universal is the product. These two product categories have in common the fact of (a) being high-involvement products and of (b) sharing a common language (Domzal and Unger, 1987, p. 28).

- *High-tech products* appeal to highly specialized buyers who share a common technical language and symbols. This is the case among computer users, tennis players and musicians, who all understand the technical aspects of the products. This is true for heavy machinery, computer hardware and financial services, but also for personal computers, video equipment, skiing equipment etc. The mere existence of a common 'shop talk' facilitates communication and increases the chance of success as global brands.
- *High-touch products* are more image-oriented than product features-oriented, but they respond to universal themes or needs, such as romance, wealth, heroism, play etc. Many products, like fragrance, fashion, jewellery and watches, are sold on these themes.

For these two product categories, buyers all over the world are using and understanding the same language and the same symbols. Worldwide brand standardization appears most feasible when products approach either end of the high-tech/high-touch spectrum (Domzal and Unger, 1987, p. 27).

7

Market attractiveness analysis

The output of a segmentation analysis takes the form of a segmentation grid displaying the different segments or product markets which belong to the reference market. The next task is to assess the business opportunity of each of these segments in order to decide which segment(s) to target. Attractiveness analysis has the objective of measuring and forecasting the size, life cycle and profit potential of each segment or product market. Measuring the sales potential of a market is the responsibility of strategic marketing. These market projections will then be used by general management to calibrate investments and production capacity. Market potential forecasting and measurement is a key input for these decisions. The objective of this chapter is to review the major concepts of demand analysis and to describe briefly the main sales forecasting methods.

Basic concepts in demand analysis

At its simplest level, the demand for a product or service is the quantity sold. Upfront, it is important to distinguish clearly between two levels of demand: primary demand, or total market demand, and company demand (also called selective demand).

The *primary demand* for a particular product is the total sales volume bought by a defined customer group, in a defined geographic area, in a defined time period, and in a defined economic and competitive environment. The term 'product category need', or 'category need' is also commonly used. Thus, primary demand measurement implies prior definition of the segment or product market. Also, it is a function of both environmental and of total industry marketing efforts.

Company demand is the company or brand's share of primary demand. It, too, is a response function. Its determinants are environmental factors and company (or brand) marketing factors.

The notion of market potential

Market potential represents the upper limit of demand in a defined period of time. The relationship between primary demand and total industry marketing efforts is depicted in Figure 7.1(a). The response function is S-shaped with total demand on the vertical axis and total marketing efforts on the horizontal axis. The curve of Figure 7.1(a) is defined for a constant macro-environment. Typically, the relationship is not linear. Some minimum level of demand (Q_0) will occur at zero marketing effort; as the total marketing pressure on the market increases, sales also increase, but at a decreasing rate. Beyond a certain level of marketing intensity, primary demand reaches an

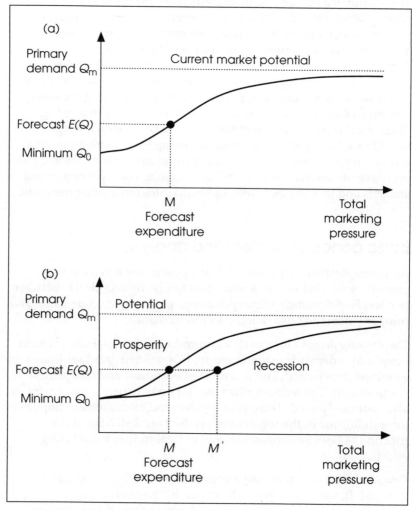

Figure 7.1 The current market potential

upper limit (Q_m) called the saturation level or the current market potential.

Expansible versus non-expansible primary demand

The gap between the minimum (or present) level of primary demand and its maximum level reflects the size of the market opportunity. In the first part of the curve, demand is said to be *expansible*: i.e. the level of primary demand is easily affected by the size and intensity of total marketing efforts. Primary demand elasticity is high and each firm contributes to the development of the total market. In the upper part of the response curve, demand becomes inelastic and the market is said to be *non-expansible*. Further increase in marketing intensity has no impact on the size of the market, which has reached its maturity stage.

Thus, in a non-expansible market the size of the market is fixed. Any sales increase in favour of a particular firm necessarily implies a market share gain.

Absolute versus current market potential

A distinction must be made between two notions of market potential: the 'absolute' market potential and the 'current' market potential.

> *Absolute market potential* corresponds to the total sales level (in volume or value) that would be observed if every potential user consumed the product at the optimum frequency rate and at the full rate per use occasion.

Thus, the absolute market potential (AMP) defines the upper limit of the market size under the somewhat artificial assumption of optimum market coverage. The concept is useful, however, for assessing the size of a business opportunity and for estimating the growth opportunity in a particular market given the present level of demand.

Three assumptions are made concerning usage of the product in order to derive the absolute market potential.

- Everyone who could reasonably be expected to use the product is using it.
- Everyone who is using it is using it on every useful occasion.
- Every time the product is used, it is used to the fullest extent possible (i.e. full dosage, full serving etc.).

An example of estimation of absolute market potential is presented in Table 7.1.

The absolute market potential is time-dependent, as illustrated in

Table 7.1 Estimating industry absolute market potential for mouthwash (Weber, 1976, p. 66)

Number of potential users
Assume that everyone 5 years and older is a potential user.
Approximately 90 per cent of the US population.
US population: 222 million.
Number of potential users: 90% × (222 m) = 200 million.
Number of use occasions per year
Assume that each potential user can use mouthwash twice a day.
Number of use occasions per year:

$$200 \text{ million people} \times 2/\text{day} \times 365 \text{ days}$$
$$= 146 \text{ billion use occasions per year}$$

Full use on each occasion
Assume that full use (or full dosage) is 1 oz per use.
The absolute market potential is therefore 146 billion oz per year, an average of 16 oz per bottle.
Result: 9.125 billion bottles per year.

Figure 7.2(a). Its evolution over time is caused by external factors like change in consumption habits, cultural values, disposable income, technological changes, level of prices, government regulations etc. The firm has no direct control over these factors, yet they have a decisive influence on the development of the market. Occasionally, firms are indirectly able to influence these external causes (through lobbying, for instance), but their power is limited. Most of the firm's efforts, therefore, are directed toward the anticipation of changes in the environment.

The current market potential is described in Figure 7.2(b). It can be defined in the following terms.

Current market potential is the limit approached by primary demand as total industry marketing efforts tend towards infinity, in a given environment and in a given time period.

In Figure 7.2(b), the current market potential corresponds to the saturation level Q_m. This level is not static, however. First, it evolves over time under the influence of diffusion and contagious (or contagion) effects, and tends towards its upper limit, which is the absolute market potential. Second, it also evolves under the pressure of environmental factors. The dependence of the current market potential on the environment is illustrated in Figure 7.1(b).

Two scenarios (or market demand functions) are represented in Figure 7.1(b): a scenario of prosperity and a scenario of recession.

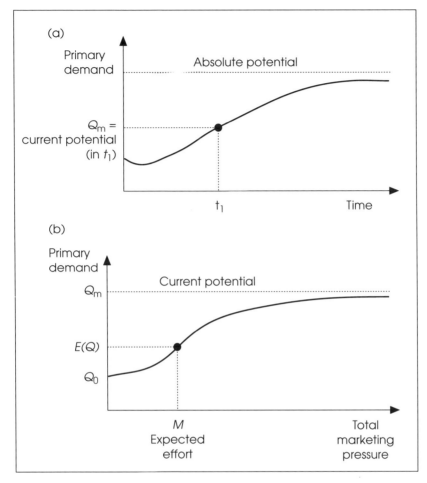

Figure 7.2 Current versus absolute market potential

Under the prosperity scenario, the forecast or expected level of total sales is $E(Q)$, assuming the level M for total industry marketing effort. Now, if the recession scenario prevails, to achieve the same sales volume, total marketing effort should be at the level M' and not M.

Firms cannot do much about the prevailing market scenario, except to try to anticipate future environment conditions as best as possible. In the turbulent environment of the 1990s this is a particularly difficult task and many firms are systematically developing alternative scenarios to increase their capacity to react quickly to a sudden crisis in the environment.

The determinants of demand

As already underlined, market demand is not a fixed number but a function which relates the level of sales to its causes, termed demand determinants. The causes of sales are twofold: external or uncontrollable causes and internal or controllable causes.

As indicated in Chapter 1, the *controllable factors* fall into four basic categories, popularly known as the 'four Ps' (McCarthy, 1960) or the marketing mix: product, place, price and promotion. This set of marketing factors constitutes the total offering of the firm to the buyers in hopes of meeting their needs at a profit. They are the main determinants of company demand.

As for the *uncontrollable factors*, they constitute the constraints to be dealt with in the market place, which the firm does not control. These constraints can be grouped in five broad categories termed the 'five Cs' (Wilkie, 1985): customer, competition, company, channel, conditions.

- *Customer constraint*: the firm must understand its buyers to develop a marketing mix program that appeals to them.
- *Competition constraint*: competitors are also striving to convince the same buyer group, and the firm must have a competitive advantage over its rivals.
- *Company constraint*: the marketing program must be adapted to the strengths and weaknesses of the firm.
- *Channel constraint*: the channel consists of independent wholesalers, distributors and retailers who behave in their own self-interest but who are the necessary partners of the firm.
- *Conditions constraint*: this last constraint refers to a host of economic, social, political and weather conditions.

It is up to the market analyst to identify and to understand these constraints as best as possible, in order to adapt the marketing mix to best account for them.

Structure of primary demand

Demand analysis, measurement and forecast is the primary responsibility of market research. The goal is to estimate in quantitative terms the size of the market potential and the current level of demand, and to formulate forecasts of its future development over a number of years. Aggregate estimates of total demand are rarely available and the role of the market analyst is to identify and estimate the key components of market potential. The structure of demand is different for consumer products (durable or non-durable goods), for industrial goods and for services.

Demand for consumer goods

Demand estimates are usually based on two factors: the number of potential users (n) and the rate of purchase (q). Thus, we have

$$Q = n \times q$$

where Q designates total demand in units. Similarly, total sales revenue will be given by

$$R = n \times q \times p$$

where R denotes total sales revenue and p the average price per unit.

Demand for non-durable consumer products

If the consumer good is not linked to the use of a durable good, total demand can be estimated in the following way.

- Number of potential consuming units.
- Proportion of customers using the product (market occupation rate).
- Size or frequency of purchase (market penetration rate).

The absolute market potential is determined by assuming a 100 per cent occupation rate and the optimum penetration per use occasion. The current level of primary demand implies data on current purchasing behaviour. These data can sometimes be obtained from trade associations, from government publications or through primary market research. A major problem in measuring current demand is the degree to which purchase rates vary among different buyer groups. Only primary sources of market research, such as consumer panels, can provide this type of data.

If the consumer good is linked to the use of a durable good (soap and washing machines, for instance), the equipment rate of households must also be considered, in addition to the utilization rate of the equipment. We thus have,

- Number of potential consuming units.
- Household rate of equipment.
- Equipment utilization rate.
- Consumption rate per use occasion.

Here also, the absolute market potential can be determined assuming a 100 per cent equipment rate, an average utilization rate and an average consumption rate which is technically defined in most cases. As for the estimation of the level of current market demand, primary market research data are necessary.

Demand for consumer durable goods

In this case, a distinction must be made between first equipment demand and replacement demand. The components of *first equipment demand* are:

- The number of effective users and rate of increase of their equipment rate.
- The number of new users and equipment rate of these new using units.

The diffusion rate is an important factor in the growth of first equipment demand within the target population. The analysis of penetration curves for similar products is very useful in this respect.

Replacement demand is more complex to estimate. The following components of replacement demand must be identified and estimated:

- Size of the current population.
- Age distribution of the current population.
- Service life of the equipment (technical, economic or fashion obsolescence).
- Scrappage rate.
- Substitution effect (new technologies).
- Mortality rate of users.

Replacement demand is directly dependent on the rate at which owners scrap a product because of wearing out or obsolescence. Market analysts can estimate scrappage rates either by examining the technical service life of a product or the historical long-term rate of voluntary scrappage.

If historical data on scrappage rates can be calculated from a sample of users, market analysts can use actuarial methods to estimate the replacement potential for products of different ages.

The demand for consumer services

The demand for services can be estimated as described above for consumer goods. Services, however, have three major characteristics that greatly impact the marketing management of them.

Intangibility of services

Services are immaterial. They exist only once produced and consumed. They cannot be inspected before purchase and the selling activity must necessarily precede the production activity. As the consumer goods firm, the service firm is selling a promise of satisfaction. But contrary to a consumer good, the service sold has no physical support except the organizational system of the service firm when visible to the customer. Thus, from the buyer's point of view the uncertainty is much larger and the communication role of the firm is to reduce that uncertainty by providing physical evidence, signs, symbols or indicators of quality. On this topic, see Levitt (1981) and Zeithaml, *et al.* (1990).

Inseparability of services

Services are produced and consumed at the same time, and the customer participates in the process of the service production. The implication is twofold here. First, the service provider necessarily has a direct contact with the customer and is part of the service. There is a large human component involved in performing services. Thus, standardization is difficult because of the personalized nature of services. Second, the client participates in the production process and the service provider-customer interaction can also affect the quality of the service. On this topic, see Eiglier and Langeard (1987).

Perishability of services

Since services are intangible, they cannot be stored. The service firm has a service production capacity which can be used only when demand is expressed. Demand peaks cannot be accommodated and the potential business is lost. Similarly, if an airliner takes off with 20 empty seats, the revenue that these 20 seats could have produced is also lost forever. Thus, a key challenge for service firms is to better synchronize supply and demand by reshaping supply or by reshaping demand through pricing incentives and promotions.

An implication of these characteristics is the difficulty of maintaining a constant level of quality of the services. Services' total quality control is a major issue for the service firm. The components of service quality are described in Chapter 10 (see also Lambin, 1987).

The demand for industrial goods

We have seen in Chapter 3 that the industrial demand is actually *derived* from the consumer market place. Thus, industrial marketers must be cognizant of conditions in their own markets, but must also be aware of developments in the markets served by their customers and by their customers' customers. Of course, many industrial products are far removed from the consumer and the linkage is difficult to see. This separation becomes more apparent as the number of intermediate customers increases between a given manufacturer and the end user. In other cases, the linkage is quite clear, such as the impact of automobile sales on the steel industry.

Thus, if consumers are not buying homes, autos, clothing, stereos, educational or medical services, there will be less need for lumber, steel, cotton, plastics, computer components and hospital forms. Consequently, industry will require less energy, fewer trucking services and not as many tools or machines (Morris, 1988, p. 390).

The planning task can become quite complex when a manufacturer's output is used in a wide variety of applications.

The demand for industrial consumable goods

We have here products which are used by the industrial firm but not incorporated in the fabricated product. The components of demand are the following:

- Number of potential industrial users (by size).
- Proportion of effective users (by size).
- Level of activity per effective user.
- Usage rate per use occasion.

The usage rate is a technical norm easy to identify. The number of companies classified by number of employees, payroll, value of shipments etc. can be obtained in the Census of Manufacturers.

> The Cleanchem Company has developed a water treatment chemical for paper manufacturers. Total paper shipments in the north-east region represent a value of $700 million. Data found in trade reports and information received from local water utilities show that paper mills use 0.01 gallons of water per dollar of shipment value. Cleanchem engineers recommend a minimum of 0.25 ounces of the water treatment chemical per gallon of water and 0.30 ounces per gallon of water to be optimal. The absolute market potential is estimated to range between 1 750 000 ounces ($700 million times 0.01 times 0.25) and 2 100 000 ounces. These estimates must be adjusted for the activity level of paper mills (Morris, 1988, p. 183).

The current proportion of effective users in this example is the major source of uncertainty.

The demand for industrial components

Industrial components are used in the product fabricated by the customer. Thus their demand is directly related to the volume of production of the client company. The components of their demand are the following:

- Number of potential industrial users (by size).
- Proportion of effective users (by size).
- Quantity produced per effective user.
- Rate of usage per product.

Producers of automobile parts are a good example of a sector that responds to this type of demand. A fluctuation in consumer demand for automobiles will eventually result in a variation of the demand for their components. Thus a careful observation of the evolution of demand for the end product is imperative for the producer of industrial components that wishes to predict its own demand.

The demand for industrial equipment

Here we have products such as industrial machines or computers that are necessary to the production activity. They are durable goods and thus the distinction between primary and replacement demand is important. *Primary equipment demand* is determined by the following factors:

- Number of companies equipped (by size), increase of the production capacity.
- Number of new-user companies (by size), production capacity.

Replacement demand is determined by the following factors:

- Size of the existing population.
- Age distribution and technology level of the population.
- Distribution of the product life span.
- Rate of replacement.
- Effect of product substitution.
- Effect of reduction of production capacity.

The acceleration effect

The demand for industrial equipment is directly related to the production capacity of the client companies, and thus even a small fluctuation in final demand can translate to a very large variation in the demand for industrial equipment. This phenomenon is known as the *'acceleration effect'*.

For example, suppose that the life span of a population of machines is ten years. If the demand for the consumer goods produced by these machines increases by 10 per cent, 10 per cent of the existing population will need to be replaced, and an additional 10 per cent production capacity will be needed to meet the increased demand. Thus the demand for the machines will double. If the demand for the consumer goods decreases by 10 per cent, the required production capacity will only be 90 per cent, and thus the 10 per cent that fail will not need to be replaced. Thus the demand for the machines falls to 0.

The volatility of the demand for industrial equipment means that for accurate demand forecasting, companies must analyse both their own demand and the final demand of the companies they supply. The date in Figure 7.3 show evidence of an 'acceleration effect' in three different markets.

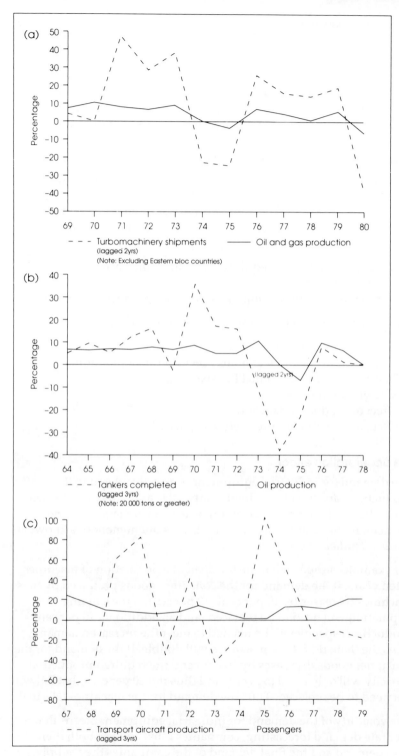

Figure 7.3 The acceleration effect in three different markets (Bishop *et al.*, 1984)

Marketing implications of industrial derived demand

In addition to the difficulty of forecasting sales, derived demand also has implications for operational marketing. The dynamic industrial firm may decide to target its selling efforts not only on the immediate customer but also towards indirect customers further down the production chain.

Thus Recticel has advertised the benefits of its polyurethane foam to armchair and sofa distributors and to the general public as well. Its goals are twofold here: first to encourage end-users and distributors to place demands upon various furniture manufacturers to begin using the Recticel foam as a component in their production process; and second, to provide promotional efforts for furniture manufacturers currently using Recticel's product.

By focusing efforts further down the industrial chain, the industrial firm is adopting a *'pull strategy'* which complements more traditional selling efforts targeted at direct customers (push strategy). To limit their dependence on direct customers, dynamic industrial firms have to adopt a proactive marketing behaviour and to play an active role in demand stimulations at each level of the industrial chain.

Growth opportunity analysis

The gap between the current and the absolute level of primary demand is indicative of the rate of development or underdevelopment of a product market. The larger the gap, the greater is the growth opportunity; conversely, the smaller the gap, the closer the market is to the saturation level.

Weber (1976) has developed a framework, called gap analysis, to analyse the gaps between absolute market potential and current company sales. Four growth opportunities are identified as shown in Figure 7.4: the usage gap, the distribution gap, the product line gap and the competitive gap. The *competitive gap* is due to sales of directly competitive brands within the product market and also to substitute products. The other gaps present growth opportunities that will be briefly reviewed below.

Usage gaps

The *usage gap* is due to insufficient use of the product. Three types of usage gap can be identified:

- The *non-user gap*, i.e. the customers who could potentially use the product but are not using it.
- The *light user gap*, i.e. the customers who use the product but do not use it on every use occasion.

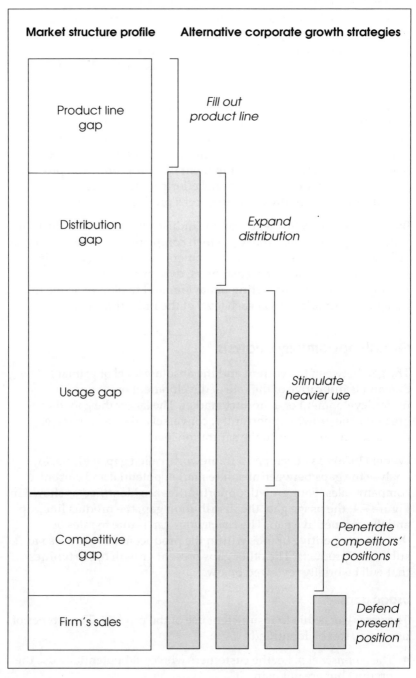

Figure 7.4 Growth opportunity analysis (Weber, 1976)

- The *light usage gap*, i.e. the customers who use the product but by less than a full use on each use occasion.

A strategy aiming at closing these gaps will contribute to the development of primary demand and will therefore benefit all competing firms as well.

Distribution gaps

The *distribution gap* is due to absence or inadequate distribution within the product market. Three types of distribution gap can be observed.

- The *coverage gap* exists when a firm does not distribute the relevant product line in all geographic regions desired.
- The *intensity gap* exists when a firm's product line is distributed in an inadequate number of outlets within a geographic region where the firm has distribution coverage.
- The *exposure gap* exists when a firm's product lines have poor or inadequate shelf space, location, displays etc. within outlets where the firm does have distribution for the product.

Sales of a particular product line can be adversely affected by any or all of these three different distribution gaps. Before adopting new product lines, the firm should try to close these distribution gaps.

Product line gaps

The product line gap is caused by the lack of a full product line. Seven types of product line gap could exist:

- *Size-related product line gaps.* Product 'size' can be defined along three dimensions: 'container size' for consumables like soft drinks or detergents, 'capacity' for durables like refrigerators or computers and 'power' for automobile engines or industrial machinery.
- *Options-related product line gaps.* Optional features can be offered by a firm desiring to cater to specific demands of individual customers. Automobiles serve as one good example. By offering a large number of options, car manufacturers can produce a large number of cars, each one in some way different from every other one.
- *Style, colour, flavour and fragrance-related product line gaps.* Style and colour can be important for clothing, shoes, appliances, automobiles etc.; flavours and fragrances can become important means of expanding product lines in food and drink products, tobaccos, toiletries etc.
- *Form-related product line gaps.* One form of a product may be more attractive for customers than another. Possible dimensions of form

include method or principle of operation (petrol versus electric mowers), product format (antacids: chewable, swallowable liquid, effervescent powder or tablets); product composition (corn oil, vegetable oil margarine) and product containers (resealable, returnable, throwaway bottles, easy-open cans).

- *Quality-related product line gaps.* Price lining is a popular practice used by marketers to provide consumers with a choice of products differentiated by overall quality and prices. Sporting goods manufacturers market tennis rackets and golf clubs in a range from beginners' models (low price) up to professional models (high price).
- *Distributor brand-related product line gaps.* Many manufacturers realize a significant proportion of their sales through selling to retailers who then put their own brand names on the products, like Saint Michael for Marks and Spencer in the UK. For manufacturers who recognize the private brand market as a separate segment, private brands can account for product line gaps.
- *Segment-related product line gaps.* As discussed in Chapter 6, a firm can adopt different market coverage strategies. A firm has a product line gap for any segment for which it does not have a product.

Each of these identified product line gaps constitutes a growth opportunity for the firm through innovation or product differentiation.

The types of development strategies to be considered to close these gaps are briefly presented in Figure 7.4. Those strategies will be described in more detail in Chapter 9. In addition to these development strategies operated by the firms, one must add the natural changes in the size of the industry market potential, which is linked to the product life cycle.

The product life cycle

In attractiveness analysis, market potential analysis is a first, and essentially quantitative, step. The analysis must be completed by a study of the product life cycle, or the evolution of the potential demand for a product or service over time. An essentially dynamic concept borrowed from biology, the product life cycle (PLC) model takes the form of an S-shaped graph comprising five phases. The first phase is a take-off, or introductory phase, followed by an exponential growth phase, a shake-out phase, a maturity phase and a decline

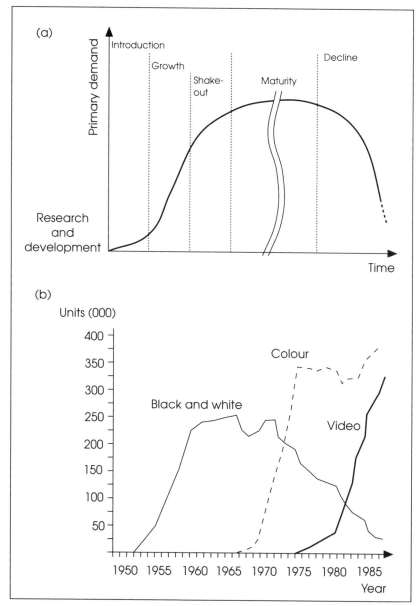

Figure 7.5 (a) Idealized representation of the product life cycle. (b) The product life cycle of television in Belgium

phase. Figure 7.5(a) presents an idealized representation of the product life cycle, while Figure 7.5(b) portrays the life cycle of audio-visual products in Belgium, and in particular black and white TV.

The determinants of the product life cycle

Before moving to an explanation of the product life cycle, its stages and its marketing implications, it is important to explain what type of products should be dealt with in a life cycle analysis. Should it be a category of products (typewriters), a particular type of product within the category (electric typewriters), a specific model (portable electric typewriters) or a specific brand (Canon)? While a life cycle analysis at any level can have value if properly conducted, the most useful level of analysis is that of a *product market*.

A product market lends itself best to a life cycle analysis because, as we saw in the previous chapter, it best describes buying behaviours in a particular product category and it most clearly defines the frame of reference: *a product seen as a specific package of benefits, targeted to a specific group of buyers*. The same product can very well have different life cycle profiles in different geographic markets or different segments within the same market. Every product market has its own life cycle which reflects not only the evolution of the product, largely determined by technology, but also the evolution of primary demand and its determinants.

Once the level of analysis has been determined, the question becomes whether the product life cycle profile is to be treated as an independent variable determined by non-controllable factors or as a dependent variable determined by the marketing efforts of the company. In the first case, the product life cycle determines the strategies adopted at the different phases. In the second case, the strategies adopted must shape the life cycle (Dhalla and Yuspeh, 1976). The response to this question is different for the analysis of a product market or of a specific brand.

The product market life cycle model

For a product market, primary demand is the principal driving force and its determining factors are both non-controllable environmental factors and industry's total controllable marketing variables. One of the most important non-controllable factors is the *evolution of technology*, which pushes towards newer, higher performance products, and makes older products obsolete. A second factor is the evolution of production and consumption norms, which makes certain products no longer suitable for the market and calls for others. Thus, the PLC model portrays the sales history of a particular product technology, which constitutes one specific solution (among many others) for a specific group of buyers to a market need.

These factors exist in all business sectors, which does not however exclude the possibility that certain better protected product markets have a much longer life cycle than others. The life cycle remains largely influenced by industry marketing efforts, particularly when the market is expanding. Dynamic companies are the driving force in a market, guiding its evolution, development and eventual relaunch sparked by modifications to the product. The product life cycle is thus not fixed, and research in the field has identified a great variety of life cycle patterns (Cox, 1967; Swan and Rink, 1982).

The brand life cycle model

For a particular brand, selective demand is the driving element. It is determined by the evolution of the reference market, but with an added competitive factor: the share of total marketing efforts for the particular brand compared with other competing brands. Thus it is perfectly possible to find a brand in decline in an expanding market, or vice versa.

> The CEO of Procter and Gamble does not believe in the product life cycle model, and cites as an example the brand Tide, launched in 1947 and still in a growth phase in 1976. In reality, the product was modified 55 times in its 26 year existence to adapt to market changes including consumption habits, characteristics of washing machines, new fabrics, etc. (Day, 1981, p. 61).

It is clear that the life cycle of a brand is essentially determined by factors under the control of the company: the marketing strategy adopted and the amount of effort dedicated to it. Hinkle (1966) studied the historical evolution of 275 brands of food, cosmetic, and household items, and found in the majority of cases a bimodal profile. There was a first cycle, followed by a relaunch of the product, as shown in Figure 7.6 (see also Figure 7.7). In the following

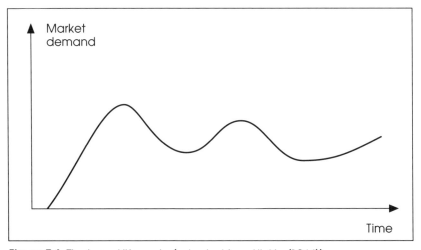

Figure 7.6 The brand life cycle (adapted from Hinkle (1966))

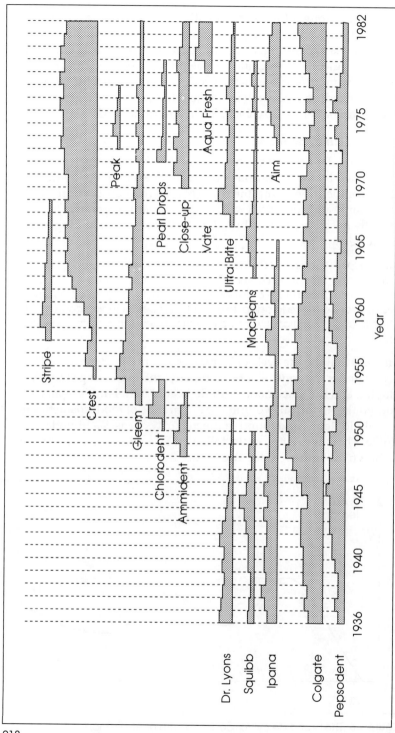

Figure 7.7 Examples of brand life cycles: the toothpaste market in the USA (Nielsen Researcher, 1984)

paragraphs, we will refer to the life cycle of a product market and no longer to that of a specific brand.

Strategic implications of the product life cycle

As product markets grow, mature and decline over time, marketing strategy must evolve to the changing buyer's behaviour and competitive environment. To say that a product has a life cycle implies four things:

- The economic and competitive environment is different at each phase.
- The priority strategic objective must be redefined at each phase.
- Products' cost and profit structures are different at each phase.
- The marketing program must be adapted in each stage of the PLC.

The shortening of the product life cycle is a major challenge for the innovative firm, which has less and less time to achieve its objectives.

The introductory phase

In the introductory phase, the market is often (not always) characterized by a slow growth of sales because of various environmental factors. The first of these is the *technology uncertainty*, which is often not yet entirely mastered by the innovating company. In addition, the technology may be still developing or evolving in reaction to the first applications, and thus the producer cannot yet hope to produce at maximum efficiency.

Distributors are a second environmental force, and can be very reluctant at this stage to distribute a product which has not yet proven itself on the larger market. In addition, an industrial distributor will need to familiarize itself with the product, its technical characteristics and its principal functions, which will additionally slow the process.

The *potential buyers* make up a third environmental factor. They can often be slow to change their consumption or production habits because of switching costs and caution towards the innovation. Only the most innovative of consumers will be the first to adopt the new product. This group constitutes a rather small initial segment for a product in the introduction phase, and is thus another contributing factor to slow sales.

A final environmental force is the *competition*. Typically, the innovating company is without direct competition for a period of time, depending on the strength of the patent protection if any. Substitute product competition can still be very strong, however, except in the case of breakthrough innovation. This phase is often characterized by a high degree of uncertainy because current and potential competitors are not well known, the market is poorly defined and information is scattered.

Internal company factors which also characterize the introduction phase include highly negative cash flows, large marketing expenses, high production costs, and often large research and development costs to be amortized. All of these factors put the new product in a very risky financial position. For this reason, the shorter the introduction phase of the product, the better for the company's profitability.

The *length of the introductory phase* of the PLC is a function of the rapidity of adoption of the less innovative potential buyers, which is influenced by various factors:

- Importance to the buyer of the new product's benefits.
- Presence or absence of adoption costs to be supported by the buyer.
- Compatibility of the product with current modes of comsumption or production.
- Observable nature of the new product's benefits.
- Possibility of trying the new product.
- Competitive pressures inducing buyers to adopt the innovation.

Given these factors, the company's highest priority strategic objective is *to create primary demand* as rapidly as possible and thus to keep the introduction phase as short as possible. These objectives include:

- Creating awareness of the product's existence.
- Informing the market of the new product benefits.
- Inducing potential customers to try the product.
- Securing channels for current and future distribution.

Thus the marketing strategy in the early phase of the PLC typically stresses market education objectives.

To respond to these priorities, the *marketing programme* in the introduction phase will tend to have the following characteristics:

- A basic, core version of the product.
- An exclusive or selective distribution system.
- A high price elasticity situation.
- An informative communication programme.

Several alternatives exist as to the types of launching strategies, particularly in terms of pricing: the dilemma of 'skimming versus penetration' pricing will be discussed in more detail in Chapter 12.

The growth phase

If the product successfully passes the test of its introduction to the market, it enters the growth phase. This phase is characterized by growth of sales at an accelerating rate. The causes of this growth are the following:

- The first satisfied users become repeat customers and influence other potential users by word of mouth; thus the rate of occupation of the market increases.
- The availability of the product due to wider distribution gives the product more visibility, which then further increases the product's diffusion in the market.
- The entrance of new competitors increases the total marketing pressure on demand at a moment when it is expansible and strongly elastic.

An important characteristic of this phase is the regular decrease of production costs due to the increase in the volume produced. An effect of experience also begins to be felt. Prices have a tendency to decrease, which allows the progressive coverage of the entire potential market. Marketing expenses are thus spread over a strongly expanding sales base, and cash flows become positive.

The characteristics of the *economic and competitive environment* change markedly:

- Sales are growing at an accelerating rate.
- The target group is now the segment of early adopters.
- New competitors enter the market.
- The technology is well diffused in the market.

To meet these new market conditions, the *strategic marketing objectives* are changed as well. They now include:

- Expanding the size of the total market.
- Maximizing the occupation rate in the market.
- Building a strong brand image.
- Creating brand loyalty.

To achieve these new objectives, the *marketing programme* will also be modified, as follows:

- Product improvements and features addition strategy.
- Intensive distribution and multiple channels strategy.
- Price reductions to penetrate the market.
- Image building communication strategy.

This primary demand development strategy requires important financial resources, and, if the cash flows are positive and profits rising, the equilibrium breakeven point is not necessarily reached yet.

At this time, there is no intensive competitive rivalry in the product market, since the marketing efforts of any firm contribute to the expansion of the total market and are therefore beneficial for other firms (cross-elasticity is positive).

The shake-out phase

This is a transitory phase where the rate of sales growth is decelerating, although primary demand is still growing. The target group is now the majority of the market. The weakest competitors start dropping out, as the result of successive decreases in the market price, and the market is becoming more concentrated. The key message of the shake-out phase is that things will be more difficult in the market because of the slowing down of total demand. Competing firms are led to redefine their priority objectives in two new directions.

- First, the strategic emphasis must shift from developing primary demand to building up or maximizing *market share.*
- Second, *market segmentation* must guide the product policy to differentiate the firm from the proliferation of 'me too' products and to move away from the core market. The majority rule has become the majority fallacy.

The new *priority objectives* are:

- To segment the market and to identify priority target segments.
- To maximize market share in the target segments.
- To position clearly the brand in consumers' minds.
- To create and maintain brand loyalty.

To achieve these objectives, the *marketing programme* will stress the following strategic orientations:

- Product differentiation guided by market segmentation.
- Expansion of distribution to get maximum market exposure.
- Pricing based on the distinctive characteristics of the brands.
- Advertising to communicate the claimed positioning to the market.

The shake-out period can be very short. The competitive climate becomes more aggressive and the key indicator of performance is market share.

The maturity phase

Eventually, the increase of primary demand slows down and stabilizes at the growth rate of the real GNP or the rhythm of demographic expansion. The product is in the phase of maturity. The majority of products can be found in this phase, which usually has the longest duration. The causes of this stabilization of the global demand are the following:

- The rates of occupation and penetration of the product in the market are very high and very unlikely to increase further.
- The coverage of the market by distribution is intensive and cannot be increased further.
- The technology is stabilized and only minor modifications to the product can be expected.

At this stage, the market is highly segmented as companies try to cover all the diversity of needs by offering a wide range of product variations. Over the course of this phase the probability of a technological innovation to relaunch the PLC is high, as everyone in the industry tries to extend the life of the product.

The trends observed in the shake-out period have materialized and the characteristics of the economic and competitive environment are the following:

- None-expansible primary demand growing at the rate of the economy.
- Durable goods demand is determined by replacement demand.
- Markets are highly segmented.
- The market is dominated by a few powerful competitors and the market structure is oligopolistic.
- The technology is standardized.

The firm's *priority objective* is to defend, and if possible to expand, market share and to gain a sustainable competitive advantage over direct competitors. The tools to be used for achieving this objective are basically of three types:

- To differentiate the products through quality, features or style improvements.
- To enter new market segments or niches.
- To gain a competitive advantage through the non-product variables of the marketing mix.

The slowing of the market growth certainly has an impact on the competitive climate. Production capacity surpluses appear and contribute to the intensification of the competitive situation. Price competition is more frequent, but has little or no impact on total demand, which has become inelastic to price. It will only affect the market share of the existing competitors. In as much as the industry succeeds in avoiding price wars, this is the phase where profitability

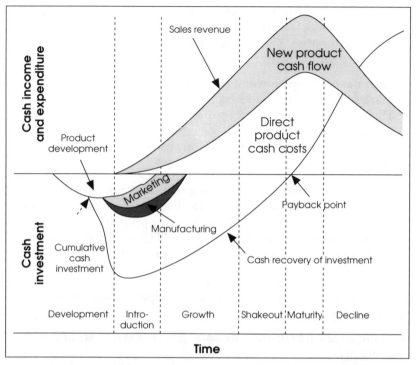

Figure 7.8 Financial flows and the PLC (adapted from Sizer (1972))

is highest, as shown in Figure 7.8. In theory, this profitability will be as strong as the market share retained is high.

The decline phase

The decline phase is characterized by a structural decrease in demand for one of the following reasons:

- New, more technologically advanced products make their appearance and replace existing products with the same function.
- Preferences, tastes, or consumption habits change with time and render products outdated.
- Changes in the social, economic and political environment, such as modifications in environmental protection laws, make products obsolete or simply prohibited.

As sales and potential profits decrease, certain companies disinvest and leave the market, while others try to specialize themselves in the residual market. This represents a valid option if the decline is progressive. Except in a turnaround of the market, which is sometimes observed, the abandon of the technologically outdated product is inevitable. (In Table 7.2 the reader will find a product— life cycle evaluation grid.)

Table 7.2 Product life cycle evaluation grid (Taylor, 1986, p. 28)

Market characteristics	Phases of the product life cycle				
	Introduction	Growth	Shake-out	Maturity	Decline
Primary demand					
Slow growth	*	−	−	*	−
Fast growth	−	*	−	−	−
Slowing down	−	−	*	−	−
Decreasing	−	−	−	−	*
New competitors					
Some	−	−	−	−	−
Many	−	−	−	−	−
Few	−	−	−	−	−
Even fewer	−	−	−	−	−
Real prices					
Stable	−	−	−	−	−
Decreasing	−	−	−	−	−
Erratic	−	−	−	−	−
Range of products					
Increasing	−	−	−	−	−
Few changes	−	−	−	−	−
Decreasing	−	−	−	−	−
Distribution					
Low growth	−	−	−	−	−
Fast growth	−	−	−	−	−
Few changes	−	−	−	−	−
Decreasing	−	−	−	−	−
Product modifications					
Few	−	−	−	−	−
Many	−	−	−	−	−
Very few	−	−	−	−	−
Communication content					
Core service	−	−	−	−	−
Main attributes	−	−	−	−	−
New uses	−	−	−	−	−
Secondary attributes	−	−	−	−	−

Limits of the product life cycle model

The life cycle model is not unanimously accepted among market analysts and certain of them recommend the complete abandon of the concept (Dhalla and Yuseph, 1976). Several legitimate criticisms should lead to a nuanced use of the model, though its utility remains nonetheless important.

Circular reasoning

The first criticism is methodological. It holds that the product life cycle model uses circular reasoning: its phases are defined by the rate of growth of sales, then the phases are used to predict sales (Hunt, 1983). This purely endogenous definition is indeed very unsatisfactory. It is from the comprehension of the driving forces of the PLC model that one can formulate predictions. The potential explanatory variables are known, yet the measure of their influence is, all the same, difficult to establish. By accumulating empirical observations, one can progressively improve this comprehension. For empirical studies of the PLC model, see notably Cox (1967), Polli and Cook (1969), Rink and Swan (1979), Swan and Rink (1982) and Tellis and Crawford (1981).

Deterministic model

A second criticism questions the deterministic nature of the model, which assumes the existence of a predefined sequence of phases in time. The company which considers the life cycle as inevitable risks acting in such a manner that the life cycle becomes a self-fulfilling prophesy (Dhalla and Yuspeh, 1976). The company's strategy should rather be to try to affect the life cycle to its greatest advantage. This criticism is based on an assumption that the life cycle is in fact a dependent variable, entirely determined by the actions of the company. This problem has already been discussed above. It stems from the fact that the life cycle model has been applied both to brands and to product markets. It is certain that on the brand level, uncontrollable factors have relatively less impact; however, on the level of a product category or of a product market, the dependence of primary demand on environmental factors is important and cannot be overlooked in a strategic analysis.

Diversity of actual PLC profiles

A third source of difficulty comes from the fact that available experimental observations show that the PLC profile does not always follow an S-curve as suggested by the model. Rink and Swan (1979) identified as many as twelve different profiles. Sometimes products escape the introduction phase and enter directly into growth; others skip the maturity phase and pass directly from growth to decline; still others skip decline and find a new vigour after a brief slowdown etc. (see Figure 7.9). Thus there is not only one type of evolution that will invariably intervene, and it is often difficult to determine in

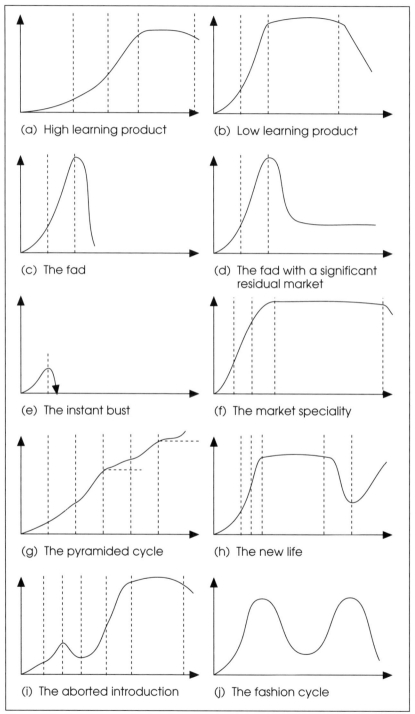

(a) High learning product

(b) Low learning product

(c) The fad

(d) The fad with a significant residual market

(e) The instant bust

(f) The market speciality

(g) The pyramided cycle

(h) The new life

(i) The aborted introduction

(j) The fashion cycle

Figure 7.9 Common variants of the product life cycle (Wasson, 1974)

which phase a product is currently situated. This difficulty reduces the utility of the concept as a planning tool, and even more so as the duration of the phases varies from one product to another, not to mention from one country to another for the same product. In 1960, most of the European producers of TV sets had planned their production capacity for colour TV (at that time in the introductory phase) by reference to the PLC of colour TV in the USA, which had a very long introductory phase. In Europe, however, the market penetration was very rapid, the European market and environment being very different.

The different profiles observed can be explained by the evolution of the following explanatory factors: technology, consumption habits, and company dynamism. The PLC model does not exempt the market analyst from a systematic analysis of the driving forces at the origin of these changes. The obvious difficulty is to determine, before the facts, the type of evolution that will prevail.

The PLC model as a conceptual framework

Another explanation of the observed differences in the profiles comes from the fact that companies can act upon the pattern of the PLC profile by innovating, repositioning the product, promoting its diffusion to other groups of consumers, or modifying it in various manners. Throughout the life cycle, the dynamic firm will try to pursue the following objectives:

- Shortening the introduction phase.
- Accelerating the growth process.
- Prolonging the maturity phase.
- Slowing the decline phase.

The ideal profile of a product life cycle is one where the development phase is short, the introduction brief, the growth phase rapid, the maturity phase long and the decline long and progressive.

The initiatives taken by an innovating firm can thus modify the life cycle profile of a product market. A classic example of a life cycle with successive product relaunches is the nylon industry, where the growth phase was prolonged several times due to successive technological modifications (Yale, 1964). It is clear that if all the competitors in a product market consider maturity or decline inevitable, the phases risk being realized sooner than expected.

More than a planning tool, the life cycle model is a *conceptual framework* for analysing the forces which determine the attractiveness of a product market and which provoke its evolution. Markets evolve because certain forces change, provoking pressures or inciting changes. Porter calls these forces the evolutionary process.

Instead of attempting to describe industry evolution, it will prove more fruitful to look underneath the process to see what really drives it . . . . The evolutionary processes work to push the industry toward its potential structure, which is rarely known completely as an industry evolves. Imbedded in the underlying technology, product characteristics, and nature of present and potential buyers, however, there is a range of structures the industry might possibly achieve, depending on the directions and success of research and development, marketing innovations and the like (Porter, 1980, p. 163).

These changing forces are important to identify, and for that purpose the product life cycle model is useful (Levitt, 1965).

Methods of forecasting the product life cycle

The application of the PLC model implies the ability to formulate forecasts of the evolution of primary demand in a given product market, be they qualitative or quantitative. This problem has become particularly complex in Western economies because of the turbulence of the environment and the radical nature of the changes observed over the course of the last decade. In light of these difficulties and the importance of forecasting errors, certain analysts came to speak of the futility of forecasting. In reality, forecasting is an inevitable task that all companies must perform, whether explicitly or implicitly. The objective of this section is to describe the problems of forecasting demand and the conditions that must be fulfilled for the application of the principal forecasting methods.

Typology of forecasting methods

The different forecasting methods can be classified with reference to two dimensions: the degree of interpersonal objectivity of the forecasting process and the extent of its analytical nature. At the two extremes of these dimensions are subjective or objective methods and heuristic and analytical methods.

The first dimension opposes quantitative to qualitative methods, where the roles of intuition, creativity and imagination are dominant.

- *Subjective methods.* The process used to formulate a forecast is not explicit and is inseparable from the person making the forecast.
- *Objective methods.* The predictive process is clearly defined and can be reproduced by other people, who would necessarily come up with the same forecast. The methods used here are quantitative.

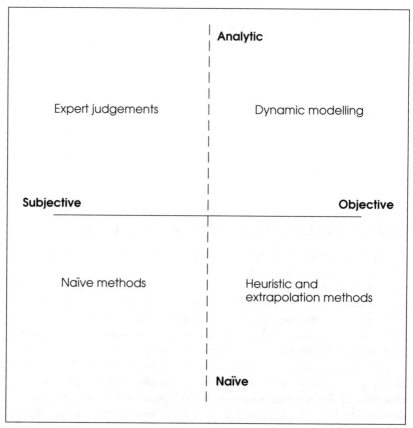

Figure 7.10 Typology of demand forecasting methods

The second dimension deals with the analytical character of the forecasting approach, which opposes extrapolation methods to explanatory methods, be they qualitative or quantitative.

- *Analytic methods.* The explanatory factors of demand are identified and their probable future values predicted; one then deduces the probable value of demand, conditional upon the realization of the established scenario.
- *Heuristic methods.* The forecast is based essentially on rules of thumb or extrapolation of historical facts, and not on an identified causal structure.

As shown in Figure 7.10, the intersection of these two dimensions allows one to classify the different demand forecasting methods into four categories. In what follows, we shall briefly review the main methods used, neglecting the case of naïve methods.

Forecasting methods based on expert judgements

When the forecast formulated does not rest on objective data but rather on the judgements of managers or consumers, the forecasting methods used are said to be expert judgement-based. The 'expert' is assumed to base his or her judgement on a group of explanatory factors, to estimate their chances of occurrence and their likely impact on the level of demand.

Thus, underlying this approach there is a *causal structure*, a set of judgements upon the explanatory factors of demand and their probability of occurrence, in the framework of one or several scenarios. This causal structure is unique to the expert, and another expert confronted with the same problem could come up with different conclusions using the same information. The expert approach presents the advantage of allowing exchange and confrontation of ideas, because of the existence of an explicit causal structure. The three judgement-based methods most often used are: management judgements, sales force estimates and buyers' intentions.

Management judgements

The forecast is determined by the *vision, intuition* or *imagination* of the individual who formulates it. Managers are asked to give their best guesses or estimates, with their degree of uncertainty taking, for example, the form of probabilities.

This approach is, to a certain degree, always present in a company. It is frequently observed in organizations dominated by managers who orient their actions only on the basis of their own views. The value of this approach will obviously depend on the values of the experience and the intuition of the managers. The major disadvantage of this approach is its difficulty of communication and the absence of any possibility of verification or disproval. One way to reduce the subjectivity of individual judgement is to have a *panel of managers* who discuss possible forecasts and try to reach a consensus. A somewhat better way to arrive at subjective estimates is to use the *Delphi method*.

Under this procedure, the judgements of individuals in a group of experts are solicited anonymously (usually by questionnaire). Then the median judgement is computed and communicated to the individuals in the group, who are again asked to make a new judgement. In practice, it has been found that such a procedure quickly leads to a consensus, typically within two rounds.

The Delphi method has been applied with some success in marketing. Its major drawback lies in the biasing influence of the feedback. An alternative is to obtain independent estimates from several individuals and to average them to yield an aggregate forecast.

Decision support systems have been developed in recent years to assist management in making judgement-based decisions and forecasts.

Sales force estimates

Sales people are in general very knowledgeable about future potential sales to existing customers and can provide useful estimates of the untapped market potential in their own territory as well. The simplest way to proceed is to ask sales people for overall sales estimates in their territories for each product under a set of assumptions regarding the level of marketing support. Management then adds up the estimates to arrive at a total for the firm.

The main shortcoming of this approach is the *vested interest problem* since sales people may systematically underestimate sales in order to keep their quota low and to appear subsequently as high sales achievers. Several remedial actions can be taken to improve the reliability of the sales estimates.

- Asking sales people to assess their own degree of uncertainty (or confidence) in their estimates. This information can then be used to qualify the forecast.
- Combining each sales person's estimate with an estimate provided by the regional sales manager.
- Applying a correction factor to each person's estimate based on his or her history of over- or under-reporting.

Involving the sales force in the sales forecasting process is important for motivating the sales force and for gaining acceptance of the sales quotas. It is also interesting to have sales forecasts available at very disaggregate levels, such as region, territory, customer etc.

Buyers' intentions surveys

A last judgemental method is to estimate demand directly on the basis of stated intentions to purchase provided by buyers. Buyers' intentions can be analysed at two different levels: (a) the general level of buyers' expectations and confidence about their present and future personal finance and/or about the economy or (b) the level of a specific product class or a brand. In the European Community two general surveys of buyers' intentions are periodically carried out.

The first is the EC quarterly survey on consumers' sentiments or confidence about the economy and about their personal economic situation. Consumers are also asked to express their intentions to purchase major durable goods within the next three months. These

Table 7.3 Typical question on buyers' intentions

Do you intend to buy a new car within the next six months?					
No chance	Slight possibility	Fair possibility	Good possibility	High probability	Certain
(0)	(0.20)	(0.40)	(0.60)	(0.80)	(1.00)

data are then used to construct an *index of consumer confidence* which can be used as an early indicator of shifts in retail sales (Eurobaromètre, 1992).

In the field of industrial goods, central banks within the EC are conducting monthly surveys among industrial firms regarding their expectations and/or intentions about investment, employment, production capacity utilization and current state of orders and shipments for both domestic and international markets. These data, available for each major industrial sector, are used to construct an *index of industry confidence*, which has proved to be a reliable early indicator of economic recession or recovery. Firms are using this information to anticipate shifts in the level of demand.

Various firms carry on their own surveys of consumer intentions, especially when testing a new product concept (see Chapter 10). A typical question on buyers' intentions looks like the one presented in Table 7.3.

The frequencies observed for the two upper classes of this purchase probability scale can be used to generate potential market estimates and/or brand shares.

When one comes to intentions about the purchase of a specific good or brand, specific intentions surveys have been found to be of more limited value than general surveys. Intentions are not always related strongly to behaviour, except when *advanced planning* is required, as is the case for major product or service purchases, such as automobiles, housing, holiday trips etc.

Subjective methods have obvious limitations, but they nevertheless provide a useful starting point in demand estimation. However, they should be used conjointly with more objective methods.

Heuristic and extrapolation forecasting

When the analytic structure of the forecasting process is weak, but when the forecast rests on objective market data, the methods used are said to be heuristic methods. They are either rules of thumb, loosely based on empirical data, or extrapolations of current sales.

The chain ratio method

This method is an extension of the absolute market potential given earlier in this chapter, which calls for identifying all potential buyers (n) in the product market or segment and for assuming optimum use (q) of the product by each potential user. Two examples of application have been provided, one for a consumer good (see Table 7.1) and one for a consumable industrial good (see pp. 208–9). The determination of the current level of primary demand in these two examples would require estimates of the current occupation rates.

The chain ratio method involves the use of successive adjusting percentages to break down the absolute potential to come to the demand for a particular product or brand. To illustrate, let us consider the case of a company selling a compound to be used in conjunction with the usual water-softening chemicals used for treating water in boiler systems. The market is dominated by a monopolist, but many factories are still non-users of the compound. To determine the expected sales volume of this new compound in a particular geographic area, an estimate can be made by the following calculations.

Water consumption by factories equipped with boiler systems = 7 500 000 hl
Softener use ratio per litre of water = 1%.
Percentage of factories using water-softening products = 72%.
Compound use ratio per litre of softener = 9%.
The *current market potential* is
7 500 000 hl × 0.01 × 0.72 × 0.09 = 486 000 litres
Percentage of factories using the chemical compound = 54%
The current level of *primary demand* is
7 500 000 hl × 0.01 × 0.72 × 0.09 × 0.54 = 262 440 litres

If the target market share for Company A is 40 per cent, the expected sales volume in this particular area will be 104 976 litres.

The difficulty of this method is the choice of the different multipliers if no primary research data is available. Moreover, error in any one multiplier will carry throughout the analysis, given the dependency of each level on preceding levels. The way out is to adopt different multipliers to generate, not a single estimate, but a range of estimates. In any case, this method should be used along with other procedures or complementary analyses.

Buying power index

In the field of consumer goods a popular technique is the buying power index (BPI) method. The objective is to measure the attractiveness of a market by a weighted average of the three key components of any market potential, i.e.

- The number of potential consuming units.
- The purchasing power of these consuming units.
- The willingness to spend of these consuming units.

Indicators of these components are identified by region, province, district, community or city and a weighted average index is computed for each area.

Two approaches are possible here: to use a standard buying power index developed by marketing research companies or to develop an index tailored to the specific products and market of a particular firm.

Standard BPIs are in general based on the three following indicators: total population, per capita income and retail sales. The relative buying power of any area *i* is given by

$$BP_i = 0.5(C_i) + 0.3(Y_i) + 0.2\,(W_i)$$

where

C_i = percentage of total population in area i
Y_i = percentage of income originating from area i
W_i = percentage of retail sales in area i

The weights adopted in the BPI equation are those used by the *Sales & Marketing Management* magazine which, in the USA, publishes BPIs in July of each year. They are derived empirically through regression analyses and they apply mainly to mass products moderately priced. Other weights can be adopted if necessary, as well as additional indicators. Similar BPIs are published by Chase Econometrics for the main regions of the EC, and by Business International (1991) for 117 countries throughout the world.

Tailor-made BPIs would typically keep the same three basic components of buying power, but would include indicators more directly related to the business plus possibly other indicators to reflect competitive conditions or local characteristics. An example of a tailor-made BPI is presented in Table 7.4.

The market studied is the soft drink market. The indicators used to compute the buying power index are number of households with children, private disposable income, and number of hotels, restaurants and cafés within each area. These data, expressed in percentages of the total, are available for 14 sales territories. The buying power index is a simple average of the three percentages of each territory. Its predictive value has been verified by correlating the BPI with product category sales in each area.

In Table 7.4, the BPI is used to assess the market penetration of brand A within each area. To estimate potential sales of each territory, the BPI is multiplied by the expected national sales for the brand. Other

Table 7.4 Sales performance evaluation per territory

Territory	Brand A sales	Percentage of total sales	Buying power index (%)	Performance index
1	2533	3.53	4.31	0.82
2	8458	11.80	7.84	1.51
3	3954	5.52	5.89	0.94
4	19 619	27.37	20.28	1.35
5	3780	5.27	4.75	1.11
6	3757	5.24	13.24	0.40
7	5432	7.58	8.74	0.87
8	3701	5.16	3.97	1.30
9	3028	4.22	3.19	1.32
10	3820	5.33	9.16	0.58
11	2433	3.39	3.70	0.92
12	5736	8.00	8.32	0.96
13	2569	3.58	2.96	1.21
14	2861	3.99	3.65	1.09
Total	71 681	100.00	100.00	—

strategic goals or local conditions must, of course, be considered. Some firms also use the BPI as a guide to allocate their total advertising budget among the different sales territories.

Trend decomposition and extrapolation

The purpose of trend analysis is to decompose the original sales series into its principal components, to measure the past evolution of each component and to project this evolution into a near future. It is evident that this projection has no meaning beyond the short term, that is the period of time for which one can consider that the characteristics of the phenomenon being studied do not change measurably. However, these conditions exist rather often in practice, because inertia also exists in the environment. Five different components can be identified in a typical sales time series:

- A *structural component*, i.e. the long-term trend, generally linked to the life cycle of the product market.
- A *cyclical component*, represented by fluctuations around the long-term trend, provoked by medium-term changes in economic activity.
- A *seasonal component*, or recurrent short-term fluctuations due to diverse causes (weather, holidays, calendrial structure etc.).
- A *marketing component*, reflecting short-term promotional actions, temporary price cuts or out-of-stock situations.
- An *erratic component*, which reflects the impact of complex

Table 7.5 Seasonally adjusted quarterly sales: an example

Quarter	1987	1988	1989	1990	1991	1992	Seasonal index
1	105	106	112	121	124	130	0.908
2	101	111	115	117	125	127	0.996
3	100	110	110	117	129	132	1.153
4	108	110	117	118	122	124	0.943

phenomena, poorly understood, unpredictable and non-quantifiable.

For each component, a parameter is estimated on the basis of the regularities observed in the past: long-term average growth rate, short-term fluctuations, seasonal coefficients and special events. These parameters are then used to generate a sales forecast, assuming that their past values will remain unchanged during the next period.

Exponential smoothing

This approach forecasts sales as a weighted average of sales observed in a number of past periods, with the largest weights being placed on sales observed in the most recent periods. The sales forecast for the next period is given by

$$\bar{Q}_t = \alpha \, Q_t + (1-\alpha) \, \bar{Q}_{t-1}$$

where

$\bar{Q}_t$ = smoothed sales for the current period
α = smoothing constant, where $0 < \alpha < 1$
Q_t = current sales in period t
Q_{t-1} = smoothed sales as computed in period $t-1$

The smoothing constant is a number between 0 and 1 and must be selected by the market analyst. Low values of α are appropriate when sales change slowly, whereas high values are relevant for rapid changes in sales. Computer programs are available to select the best value of α by trial and error on historical data.

To illustrate, let us examine the data presented in Table 7.5. Quarterly sales in volume have been seasonally adjusted. The objective is to find the optimal value for α, the smoothing constant. The data of 1992 are used to test the predictive value of the model.

To forecast sales for the first quarter of 1992, we need the smoothed sales as estimated for the preceding periods. For example, the smoothed sales for the first quarter of 1988 are then:

$$\bar{Q}_{88} = (0.10) \, (106) + (0.90) \, (105) = 105.1$$

where seasonally adjusted sales for 1987 have been used for the smoothed sales because the latter are not available when one begins exponential smoothing. Similarly, for the other quarters we have successively:

$$Q_{89} = (0.10)\,(112) + (0.90)\,(105.1) = 105.9$$
$$Q_{90} = (0.10)\,(121) + (0.90)\,(105.9) = 107.3$$
$$Q_{91} = (0.10)\,(124) + (0.90)\,(107.3) = 109.0$$

Thus, the forecast for the first quarter of 1992 is based on past sales and is equal to

$$E(Q_{92}) = Q_{91} = 109.0$$

Note that the sales forecast is always included between current sales and smoothed sales for the current period.

The error of forecasting can be computed as

$$\text{Forecasting error} = \frac{109.0 - 130}{130} = 16.2 \text{ per cent}$$

This is a very large prediction error, which can be caused by the small value of the smoothing constant a since, in this example, sales are rapidly increasing. A value of 0.80 for a gives smoothed sales for 1991 equal to 128.60, reducing the forecasting error to 1.1 per cent, a much better performance.

A large number of different techniques exist, incorporating more than one smoothing constant. For an overview of these methods, see Makridakis and Wheelwright (1973). The main shortcoming of exponential smoothing methods is their inability to really 'forecast' the evolution of demand, in the sense that they cannot anticipate a turning point. At most, they can rapidly integrate a modification in sales. This is why these methods are termed 'adaptive forecasting models'. For numerous management problems, this 'after the fact' forecast is nonetheless useful since the causes of sales tend to operate in a regular manner. Thus, the use of previous sales levels as predictors of future levels often works satisfactorily.

Dynamic modelling

'Objective' and 'analytical' forecasting methods are the most advanced methods, scientifically speaking. They are based upon the construction of explicative mathematical models, which allow the simulation of market situations in alternative scenarios. In its basic philosophy, mathematical modelling is very similar to the expert approach described above: identifying a causal structure, constructing one or several scenarios and deducting the probable level of demand in each of them. The difference comes from the fact that *the causal structure was established and validated experimentally in objectively observable and measurable conditions.* The strength of this approach is that the model becomes an instrument of discovery and exploration of numerous and varied situations that the human mind could not exhaustively explore.

It is important to note that this approach is only valid as long as the causal structure identified remains stable. Forecasting with an explicative model thus also implies an extrapolation, but of the second degree. In a rapidly and profoundly changing environment, a mathematical model is incapable of anticipating the effect of a change of which the cause has not been taken into account in the model. A mathematical model thus lacks the ability to improvise, and cannot adapt to a profoundly modified environment, whereas an expert can.

The majority of forecasting errors are due to the fact that, at the moment of formulation of the forecast, it has been implicitly considered that the current tendencies will more or less maintain themselves in the future. This is rarely the case in the reality of social and economic life.

> In 1983 and 1984, 67 new types of business personal computers were introduced to the US market, and most companies were expecting explosive growth. One industry forecasting service projected an installed base of 27 million units by 1988; another predicted 28 million units by 1987. In fact, only 15 million units had been shipped by 1986. By then, many manufacturers had abandoned the PC market or gone out of business altogether. The inaccurate suppositions did not stem from a lack of forecasting techniques. Instead, they shared a mistaken fundamental assumption: that relationships driving demand in the past would continue unaltered. The companies didn't foresee changes in end-user behaviour or understand their saturation point (Barnett, 1988, p. 28).

History can be an unreliable guide as domestic economies become more international, new technologies emerge and industries evolve. These abilities of anticipation must be developed and this assumes a good comprehension of the key driving factors and of the vulnerability of the company to environmental threats.

The necessity of an integrated approach

The examination of the different possible forecasting approaches has shown the advantages and limitations of each. In reality, the approaches are very complementary and a good forecasting system should be able to make use of all of them.

In a turbulent environment, it is clear that intuition and imagination can be precious instruments of perception of reality and

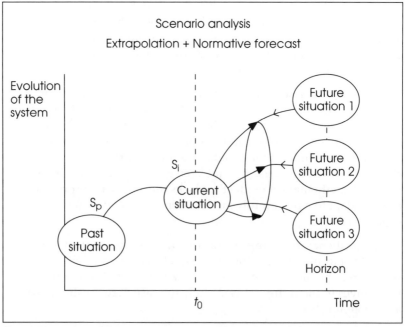

Figure 7.11 The scenario approach (de Boisanger, 1988)

complementary to quantitative approaches, which, by definition, rely solely on observed facts. In addition, a purely qualitative approach runs certain risks, and as much as possible the intuitions and visions should be analysed in the light of the facts available. What is important is thus the confrontation of these two approaches.

The integration of the different methods evoked by the scenarios method is a good manner in which to approach a forecasting problem. A *scenario* can be defined as follows:

> a presentation of the key explanatory factors to be taken into consideration, and a description of the manner(s) in which these factors could affect demand.

A scenario is thus different from a forecast. A forecast is more a judgement which tends to predict a specific situation and which is to be taken or left on its own value. A scenario, on the other hand, is an instrument which is conceived for analysis and reflection, and namely:

- To give a better understanding of a market's situation and its past evolution.
- To sensitize the company to its interactions with the environment.
- To evaluate its vulnerability to threats.
- To identify possible lines of action.

Thanks to this sensitization, the method allows the company to improve its anticipation capability and to develop its flexibility and adaptability (de Boisanger, 1988, p. 63). A scenario should be regarded together with other scenarios: one basic scenario and other alternative scenarios based on key factors, as illustrated in Figure 7.11.

This approach, which is based upon the conviction that the future can never be completely measured and controlled, presents several advantages for management:

- Firstly, it sensitizes the company to the uncertainties which characterize any market situation; in a turbulent environment, sound management implies the *ability to anticipate* the evolution of the environment.
- The scenario method facilitates *integration of the different forecasting approaches,* qualitative or quantitative.
- The practice of this approach introduces more flexibility in management and induces the company to develop alternative plans and a system of *contingency planning* (see Chapter 14).

The spectacular development of microcomputer technology has largely facilitated the application of this method, notably in allowing its decentralization within the company.

8

Competitiveness analysis

Having evaluated the intrinsic appeal of the product markets and segments in the reference market, the next stage of strategic marketing is to analyse the climate or the *competitive structure* of each of the product markets, and then evaluate the nature and intensity of the *competitive advantage* held by the various competitors in each market. A product market may be very attractive in itself, but not so for a particular firm, given its strengths and weaknesses and compared to its most dangerous competitors. Therefore, the aim of measuring business competitiveness is to identify the kind of competitive advantage that a firm or a brand can enjoy and to evaluate to what extent this advantage is sustainable, given the competitive structure, the balance of existing forces and the positions held by the competitors.

The notion of competitive advantage

Competitive advantage refers to those characteristics or attributes of a product or a brand that give to the firm *some superiority over its direct competitors*. These characteristics or attributes may be of different types and may relate to the product itself (the core service), to the necessary or added services accompanying the core service, or to the modes of production, distribution or selling specific to the product or to the firm.

When it exists, this superiority is relative and is defined with respect to the best-placed competitor in the product market or segment. We then speak of the most dangerous competitor, or the *priority competitor*.

A competitor's relative superiority may result from various factors. Generally speaking, these can be classified into two main categories, according to the competitive advantage they provide. They can be internal or external.

A competitive advantage is *external* when it is based on some distinctive qualities of the product which give *superior value to the buyer*, either by reducing its costs or by improving its performance.

An external competitive advantage gives the firm increased *market power*. It can force the market to accept a price above that of its priority competitor which may not have the same distinctive quality. A strategy based on an external competitive advantage is a *differentiation strategy*, which calls into question the firm's marketing know-how, and its ability to better detect and meet those expectations of buyers which are not yet satisfied by existing products.

A competitive advantage is *internal* when it is based on the firm's superiority in matters of cost control, administration and product management, which bring *value to the producer* by enabling it to have a lower unit cost than its priority competitor.

Internal competitive advantage results from better *productivity*, thus making the firm more profitable and more resistant to price cuts imposed by the market or by the competition. A strategy based on internal competitive advantage is a *cost domination strategy*, which mainly calls into question the firm's organizational and technological know-how.

To succeed with an external advantage strategy, the price premium the customer is willing to pay must exceed the cost of providing that extra value. Similarly, a cost strategy must offer acceptable value to customers, so that prices are close to the average of competitors. If too much quality is sacrificed for achieving a low-cost position, the price discount demanded by customers will more than offset the cost advantage.

These two types of competitive advantage have distinct origins and natures, which are often incompatible because they imply different abilities and traditions. Figure 8.1 shows the two aspects of competitive advantage, which can be expressed as questions.

- *Market power*: to what extent are buyers willing to pay a price higher than the price charged by our direct competitor?
- *Productivity*: is our unit cost higher or lower than the unit cost of our direct competitor?

The horizontal axis in Figure 8.1 refers to maximum acceptable price and the vertical axis to unit cost. Both are expressed in terms of percentages compared to the priority competitor.

- Positioning in the upper left quadrant and lower right quadrant are extreme cases, disastrous or ideal, respectively.
- Positioning in the lower left quadrant implies cost domination.
- Positioning in the upper right quadrant implies successful differentiation.

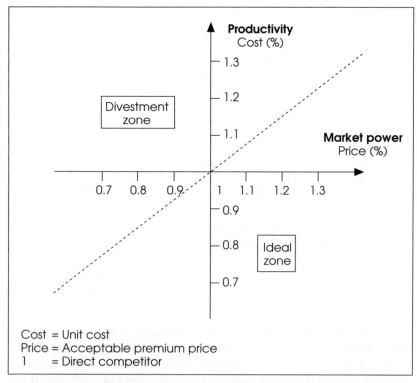

Figure 8.1 Competitive advantage analysis

The purpose of measuring business competitiveness is to allow the firm to find its own position on these axes and to deduce its strategic priority objectives for each of the products of its portfolio. To find the position along the market power axis, the firm will use information provided by brand image studies which, as seen in Chapter 5, help measure the brand's perceived value and estimate price elasticities. As for the productivity axis, the experience law can be used when applicable (see pp. 261–73) or else the firm can use information provided by the marketing intelligence unit which has, among other things, the task of monitoring competition.

Forces driving industry competition

The notion of extended rivalry, due to Porter (1980), is based on the idea that a firm's ability to exploit a competitive advantage in its reference market depends not only on the direct competition it faces, but also on the role played by rival forces, such as potential entrants, substitute products, customers and suppliers. The first two forces

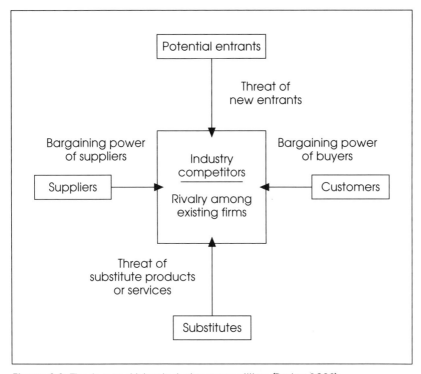

Figure 8.2 The forces driving industry competition (Porter, 1980)

constitute a direct threat; the other two an indirect threat, because of their bargaining power. It is the combined interplay of these five competitive forces, shown in Figure 8.2, which determines the profit potential of a product market. Clearly, the dominant forces determining the competitive climate vary from one market to another. Using Porter's analysis, we will examine the role of these four external competitive forces successively. The analysis of rivalry between direct competitors will be left for later in this chapter.

Threat of new entrants

Potential competitors, likely to enter a market, constitute a threat that the firm must limit and protect itself against, by creating barriers to entry. Potential entrants can be identified as follows:

- Firms outside the product market which could easily surmount the barriers to entry.
- Firms for which entry would represent a clear synergy.
- Firms for which entry is the logical conclusion of their strategy.
- Clients for suppliers who can proceed to backward or forward integration (Porter, 1980, p. 55).

The importance of the threat depends on the *barriers to entry* and on the strength of reaction that the potential entrant can expect. Possible barriers to entry are as follows:

- *Economies of scale.* These force the entrant to come in at large scale or else risk having to bear a cost disadvantage.
- *Legal protection* obtained through patents, as we have seen in the case of the conflict between Kodak and Polaroid.
- *Product differentiation* and brand image, leading to a high degree of loyalty among existing customers who show little sensitivity to newcomers.
- *Capital requirements*, which can be considerable, not only for production facilities, but also for things like inventories, customer credit, advertising expenses, start-up losses etc.
- *Switching costs*, that is, one-time real or psychological costs that the buyer must bear to switch from an established supplier's product to that of a new entrant.
- *Access to distribution channels*: distributors might be reluctant to give shelf space to a new product; sometimes the new entrant is forced to create an entirely new distribution channel.
- *Experience effects* and the cost advantage held by the incumbent, which can be very substantial, especially in highly labour-intensive industries.

Other factors which may influence the entrant's degree of determination are the expectation of sharp reactions from existing firms and of the dissuasive nature of the retaliations they may organize. The following factors will in particular influence the degree of deterrence in the response:

- A history and reputation of aggressiveness *vis-à-vis* new entrants.
- Degree of commitment of established firms in the product-market.
- Availability of substantial resources to fight back.
- Possibility of retaliation in the entrant's home market.

Put together, sustainable entry barriers and the ability to respond are the elements that determine the entry deterring price.

Threat of substitute products

Substitute products are products that can perform the same function for the same customer groups, but are based on different technologies. Referring back to the distinctions made in Chapter 6, substitute products go hand in hand with the definition of a market which is the 'set of all technologies for a given function and a given customer group'. Such products are a permanent threat because a substitution is always possible. The threat can be intensified, for instance, as a result of a technological change which modifies the substitute's quality/price as compared to the reference product market. Prices of substitute products impose a ceiling on the price firms in the product market can charge. The more attractive the price–performance alternative offered by substitutes, the stronger the limit on the industry's ability to raise prices.

Clearly, substitute products that deserve particular attention are those that are subject to trends improving their price–performance trade-off with the industry's product. Moreover, in such a comparison, special attention needs to be given to switching costs (real or psychological) which can be very high and, as far as the buyer is concerned, offset the impact of the price differential.

Identifying substitute products is not always straightforward. The aim is to search systematically for products that meet the same generic need or perform the same function. This can sometimes lead to industries far removed from the main industry. It would be insufficient simply to look at the uses made in the major customer groups, because the information risks appearing too late. Therefore it is necessary to have a permanent monitoring system of major technological developments in order to be able to adopt a proactive rather than a reactive behaviour.

Bargaining power of buyers

Buyers have a bargaining power *vis-à-vis* their suppliers. They can influence an activity's potential profitability by forcing the firm to cut prices, demanding more extensive services, asking for better credit facilities or even by playing one competitor against another. The degree of influence depends on a number of conditions (Porter, 1980, pp. 24–7):

- The buyer group is concentrated and purchases *large volumes* relative to seller sales; this is so for large distributors, and, in France, for large shopping centres.
- The products that buyers purchase from the industry represent a significant fraction of their *own costs*, which drives them to bargain hard.
- The products purchased are standard or *undifferentiated*. Buyers are sure that they can always find alternative suppliers.
- The buyers' *switching costs*, or costs of changing suppliers, are few.
- Buyers pose a *credible threat of backward integration*, and are therefore dangerous potential entrants.
- The buyers have *full information* about demand, actual market prices and even supplier costs.

These conditions apply equally to consumer goods as well as industrial goods; they also apply to retailers as against wholesalers, and to wholesalers as against manufacturers. Such a situation, where buyers' bargaining power is very high, is seen in Belgium and France in the food sector, where large-scale distribution is highly concentrated and can even dictate its terms to manufacturers (Bialobos, 1982).

These considerations underline the fact that the choice of buyer groups to sell to is a crucial strategic decision. A firm can improve its competitive position by a *customer selection policy*, whereby it has a well-balanced portfolio of customers and thus avoids any kind of dependence on the buyer group.

Bargaining power of suppliers

Suppliers can exert bargaining power because they can raise the prices of their deliveries, reduce product quality or limit quantities sold to a particular buyer. Powerful suppliers can thereby squeeze profitability out of an industry unable to recover cost increases in its own prices. For instance, the increase in the price of basic steel products, imposed in Europe between 1980 and 1982 by the Davignon plan, contributed to profit erosion in the downstream steel transformation sector. Intense competition prevented firms in this sector from raising their prices.

The conditions making suppliers powerful are similar to those making buyers powerful (Porter, 1980, pp. 27–9):

- The supplier group is dominated by a few companies and is more concentrated than the industry it sells to.
- It is not facing other substitute products for sale to the industry.
- The firm is not an important customer of the supplier.
- The supplier's product is an important input to the buyer's business.
- The supplier group has differentiated its products or has built up switching costs to lock the buyers.
- The supplier group poses a credible threat of forward integration.

Note that the labour force used in a firm must also be recognized as a supplier. As such, and according to its degree of organization and unionization, labour exercises a significant bargaining power which can greatly affect potential profits in an industry.

These four factors of external competition, together with rivalry among existing firms within the same product market, determine a firm's potential profitability and market power. By way of

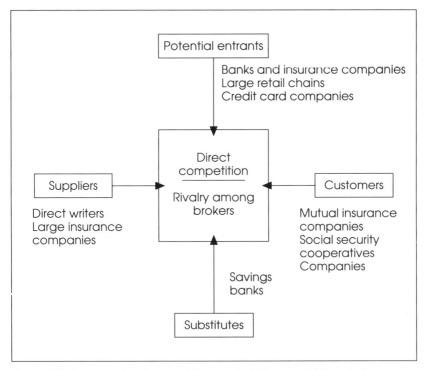

Figure 8.3 An example of competition analysis: the market for private insurance brokers (MDA Consulting Group)

illustration, the results of a competitive structure analysis in the private insurance brokerage market is presented in Figure 8.3.

Achieving competitive advantage through market power

The intensity and form of the competitive struggle between direct rivals in a product market varies according to the nature of the actual competitive structure. This defines the degree of interdependence between rivals and the extent of *market power* held by each competitor. To analyse a particular market situation, it is convenient to refer to the various competitive structures proposed by economists, for which numerous theoretical and empirical studies exist. Four competitive structures are generally distinguished: pure (or perfect) competition, oligopoly, monopolistic (or imperfect) competition and monopoly. We will examine each of these alternatives successively and underline the expected competitive behaviour in each case.

Pure or perfect competition

Perfect competition is characterized by the existence in the market of a large number of sellers facing a large number of buyers. Neither of the two groups is powerful enough to influence prices. Products have clearly defined technical characteristics, are perfect substitutes and sell at the market price, which is strictly determined by the *interplay between supply and demand*. In this kind of market, sellers have no market power whatsoever, and their behaviour is not affected by their respective actions. Key features are therefore the following:

- Large number of sellers and buyers.
- Undifferentiated and perfectly substitutable products.
- Complete absence of market power for each player.

This kind of situation can be seen in industrial markets for unbranded products, and in the 'commodities' market, such as soft commodities and the minerals and metals market. These are normally organized markets (terminal markets) such as the London Metal Exchange (LME) or the various commodity futures exchange.

In a perfectly competitive market, the interplay between supply and demand is the determinant factor. As far as the firm is concerned, price is given and the quantity supplied is the variable of interest. The demand function is therefore an inverse function of the form

$$P = f(Q)$$

where the market price, P, is the dependent variable and quantity, Q, is the independent variable.

To improve performance, the firm's only possible courses of action are either to modify its deliveries to the market, or to change its production capacity upward or downward, depending on the market price. In the short term, it is essential for the firm to keep an eye on competitors' production levels and on new entrants in order to anticipate price movements.

In the long term, it is clearly in the firm's interest to release itself from the anonymity of perfect competition by differentiating its products to reduce substitutability, or by creating switching costs to the buyers in order to create some form of loyalty. One way of achieving this, for example, is to exercise strict quality control accompanied by a branding policy. A number of countries exporting food products follow this kind of strategy to maintain their product's price and demand levels: Columbian coffee, Spanish oranges, Cape fruits and Swedish steel are attempts at this type of differentiation. Another way is to develop, downstream in the industrial chain, higher added value activities incorporating the commodity, with the objectives of stabilizing the level of demand and gaining protection from wild price fluctuations.

Oligopoly

Oligopoly is a situation where the number of competitors is low or a few firms are dominant. As a result rival firms are highly interdependent. In markets concentrated in this way, each firm knows well the forces at work and the actions of one firm are felt by the others, who are inclined to react. Therefore, the outcome of a strategic action depends largely on whether or not competing firms react. The box on p. 252 describes the notion of reaction elasticity, which measures the force of the reaction (Lambin, 1976).

The more undifferentiated the products of existing firms, the greater the dependence between them will be; in this case we talk about *undifferentiated oligopoly*, as opposed to *differentiated oligopoly*, where goods have significant distinctive qualities of value to the buyers. Oligopolistic situations tend to prevail in product markets having reached the maturity phase of their life cycle, where total demand is stagnant and non-expansible.

The mechanisms of a price war

In undifferentiated oligopoly, products are perceived as 'commodities' and buyers' choices are mainly based on price and the service rendered. These conditions are therefore ripe for intense price competition, unless a dominant firm can impose a discipline and force a leading price.

This situation is one of *price leadership*, in which the dominant firm's price is the reference price used by all competitors. On the other hand, if price competition does develop, it generally leads to reduced profitability for everyone, especially if total demand is non-expansible. *A price war* then gets under way, as follows:

- A price cut initiated by one firm creates an important market share movement due to buyers attracted by the reduced price.
- The firm's market share increases. Other firms feel this immediately, given that their own shares drop. They begin to adopt the same price cut to overturn the movement.
- Price equality between rivals is restored, but at a lower level, which is less profitable for all.
- Since total demand is non-expansible, the price cut has not contributed to increasing the market size.

Lack of cooperation or discipline causes everyone's situation to deteriorate. The decision tree in Figure 8.4 describes the sequence of

Reaction elasticity defined

Reaction elasticities measure the intensity of competitive reaction to a decision taken by a rival firm. Denoting by i the firm initiating the change, and by r the reacting firm, we have the following function:

$$M_{r,t} = f(M_{i,t})$$

where M designates a marketing variable and t the period.

This function assumes an instantaneous reaction, which is more likely to occur in the case of price modifications than for non-price variables, where an adjustment period is necessary, for instance for quality change, creation of a new advertising campaign etc.

In the general case, we will have

$$M_{r,t} = f(M_{i,t-k})$$

The reaction elasticity is defined as

$$\varepsilon_{r,i} = \frac{\% \text{ variation of } M_r}{\% \text{ variation of } M_i}$$

The interpretation of the order of magnitude of a reaction elasticity is straightforward.

- An elasticity close to 0 implies a lack of reaction from rivals; we have here independent competitive behaviour.
- An elasticity included between 0.20 and 0.80 implies a partial adaptation.
- An elasticity included between 0.80 and 1.00 implies a quasi-full adjustment.
- An elasticity larger than 1 is revealing of an escalation strategy or overreaction among rivals.

Retaliation strategies can be complex and based on different marketing factors (direct versus indirect reaction) or based on a single or on several marketing variables (simple versus multiple reactions).

actions and reactions, as well as the main demand concepts involved at each mode.

In a non-expansible market, competition becomes a zero sum game. Firms seeking to increase sales can only achieve it at the expense of direct competitors. As a result, competition is more aggressive than when there is growth, where each firm has the possibility of increasing its sales by simply growing at the same pace as total demand, that is with constant market share.

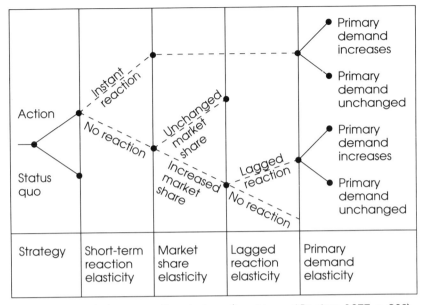

Figure 8.4 Structuring a reaction strategy (Lambin and Peeters, 1977, p. 282)

Alternative competitive behaviours

In a stagnant oligopolistic market, explicit consideration of competitors' behaviour is an essential aspect of strategy development. *Competitive behaviour* refers to the attitude adopted by a firm in its decision-making process, with regards to its competitors' actions and reactions. The attitudes observed in practice can be classified into five typical categories.

- *Independent behaviour* is observed when competitors' actions and/or reactions are not taken into account, either implicitly or explicitly, in the firm's decisions. This attitude is observed in particular with regard to operational decisions, and is sometimes seen even in the case of strategic choices, in firms with a dominant market position.
- *Cooperative behaviour* corresponds to a confident or complaisant attitude which seeks, tacitly or explicitly, understanding or collusion rather than systematic confrontation. Tacit agreement is frequently seen between medium-sized firms; explicit or cartel agreement, on the other hand, takes place more between large firms in oligopolistic markets which are not subject to competition regulations or which are controlled very little in this respect.
- *Follower behaviour* is based on an explicit consideration of competitors' actions; it consists of adapting one's own decisions to the observed decisions of competitors, without, however,

anticipating their subsequent reactions. If all existing competitors adopt this kind of behaviour, a succession of mutual adaptations is observed, until stability is achieved. This kind of behaviour has been described by Cournot (1897), among others.

- *Leader behaviour* is a more sophisticated behaviour. It consists of anticipating competitors' reactions to the firm's own decisions, assuming they have the previous type of behaviour; here, the firm is assumed to know its rivals' reaction function and to incorporate it when elaborating its strategy. As strategic marketing develops, it is seen ever more frequently in oligopolistic markets, where competition laws are strictly enforced.

- *Aggressive or warfare behaviour* also consists of anticipating competitors' reactions to the firm's decisions. But in this case, rivals' behaviour is assumed to be such that they always adopt the strategy most harmful to the adversaries. This type of behaviour is mainly observed in oligopolistic markets where total demand is stagnant and any one firm's gains must be at the expense of the others. This kind of situation is analysed in game theory as a zero sum game, with optimal strategy being the one with the lowest risk of loss.

The most frequent behaviours in undifferentiated oligopoly are of the follower or leader kind. It is, however, not rare to observe aggressive behaviours of the kind described in game theory, especially as regards price decisions, with the risk of leading to price wars which are generally harmful to all.

Warfare marketing

In industrialized economies, oligopolistic situations are frequent. In many industrial sectors, firms face each other with weakly differentiated products, in stagnant and saturated markets, where one firm's gains are necessarily another's losses. A key factor of success is thwarting competitors' actions. This kind of competitive climate obviously breeds the adoption of *marketing warfare*, which puts the destruction of the adversary at the centre of preoccupations. Kotler and Singh (1981), Ries and Trout (1986), Durö and Sandström (1988) have taken the analogy with military strategy even further and proposed various typologies of competitive strategies directly inspired from von Clausewitz (1908). As put by Ries and Trout (1986):

> The true nature of marketing is not serving the customer, it is outwitting, outflanking and outfighting your competitors.

This point of view is in conflict with the market-driven orientation, which suggests that a balance should be maintained between customer and competitor orientations (see Figure 1.4). What is the

Table 8.1 Competitive reaction matrix (Lambin, 1976, p. 24)

Brand A actions	Competing brand B's reactions		
	Price (p)	Advertising (a)	Quality (x)
Price	$\varepsilon_{p,p}^{*}$	$\varepsilon_{p,a}$	$\varepsilon_{p,x}$
Advertising	$\varepsilon_{a,p}$	$\varepsilon_{a,a}$	$\varepsilon_{a,x}$
Quality	$\varepsilon_{x,p}$	$\varepsilon_{x,a}$	$\varepsilon_{x,x}$

* The first subscript is for the brand initiating the move; the second is for the rival's response

usefulness of beating competitors in products that the customer doesn't want?

Competitive reaction matrix

Firms compete with one another by emphasizing different elements of the marketing mix and by insisting differently on each component of the mix. The competitive reaction matrix presented in Table 8.1 is a useful instrument for analysing alternative action–reaction patterns among two competing companies (Lambin, 1976, pp. 22–7). The matrix might include two brands, the studied brand and its priority competitor, and three or four components of the marketing mix, such as price, media advertising, promotion or product quality.

In Table 8.1 the horizontal rows designate the actions initiated by our brand A. The alternative actions might be to cut price, increase advertising or improve quality. The responses of Brand B, the direct competitor, are represented by the vertical columns. The coefficients in the matrix are the reaction elasticities or the probabilities of brand B reacting to brand A's move.

On the diagonal we have the *direct reaction elasticities*, or the likelihood of brand B responding to a move of brand A with the same marketing instrument, i.e. meeting a price cut with a price cut. Off diagonal, we have the *indirect reaction elasticities*, or the probabilities of brand B responding to brand A with another marketing instrument, for example, meeting a price cut with increased advertising. These reaction elasticities can be estimated by reference to past behaviour or by seeking management's judgement concerning the strengths and weaknesses of competition. Once the matrix is developed, management can review each potential marketing action in the light of probable competitor reactions.

The entries of the matrix can also be probabilities. In this case, their horizontal sum must be equal to one.

For example, if management considers that there is a 70 per cent chance that competition will meet our price cut, but only a 20 per cent chance that it will meet a quality increase, it might consider that a quality increase programme will help more to develop a unique marketing approach than the price cut, since it is less likely to be imitated.

The competitive matrix is useful in helping to develop a distinctive marketing approach to the market and to anticipate competitors' reactions. More columns can be added representing other marketing instruments. Delayed responses can also be analysed. For an example of an application in the electric razor market, see Lambin *et al.* (1975).

Competitor analysis system

The attitude to be adopted towards competitors is central to any strategy. This attitude must be based on a refined analysis of competitors. Porter (1980, p. 47) describes the purpose of analysing competitors as follows:

> The objective of a competitor analysis is to develop a profile of the nature and success of the likely strategy changes each competitor might make, each competitor's probable response to the range of feasible strategic moves other firms could initiate, and each competitor's probable reaction to the array of industry changes and broader environmental shifts that might occur.

There are four areas of interest which constitute the structure to guide the collection and analysis of information about competitors. The relevant questions are the following:

- What are the competitors' major objectives?
- What is the current strategy being employed to achieve the objectives?
- What are the capabilities of rivals to implement their strategies?
- What are their likely future strategies?

The first three parts of the analysis are the background data needed to predict the future strategies. Together, these four areas of information collection and analysis compose a fairly complete picture of the competitors' activities.

Some companies have discovered the importance of competitor analysis. Some examples are:

- IBM has a commercial analysis department with thousands of branch office representatives responsible for reporting information about the competition.
- Texas Instruments has employees analyse government contracts won by competitors to discern their technological strengths.

- Citicorp has an executive with the title 'manager of competitive intelligence'.
- McDonalds distributes a Burger King and Wendy's competitive action package to its store managers.

Strong competitive interdependence in a product market is not very attractive, because it limits the firm's freedom of action. To escape it, the firm can either try to differentiate itself from rivals, or seek new product markets through creative market segmentation.

Imperfect or monopolistic competition

Monopolistic competition is halfway between competition and monopoly (Chamberlin, 1950). There are many competitors whose market powers are evenly distributed. But their products are differentiated, in the sense that, from the buyer's point of view, they possess significantly distinct characteristics and are perceived as such by the whole product market. Differentiation may take different forms: for example the taste of a drink, a particular technical characteristic, an innovative combination of features which provides the possibility of a variety of different uses, quality and extent of customer services, the distribution channel, power of brand image etc. Monopolistic competition is therefore founded on a *differentiation strategy* based on external competitive advantage.

Conditions for successful differentiation

For a differentiation strategy to be successful, a number of conditions need to be present:

- Differentiation of any kind must represent some *value* to buyers.
- This value can either represent a better *performance* (higher satisfaction), or reduced *cost*.
- The value to buyers must be high enough for them to be prepared to pay a *price premium* to benefit from it.
- The element of differentiation must be *sustainable*; in other words, other rivals should not be able to imitate it immediately.
- The price premium paid by buyers must exceed the *cost supplement* borne by the firm to produce and maintain the element of differentiation.
- Finally, in so far as the element of differentiation is not very apparent and is unknown by the market, the firm must produce *signals* to make it known.

The effect of differentiation is to give the firm some degree of *market power*, because it generates preferences, customer loyalty and weaker price sensitivity. The buyer's bargaining power is thus partially neutralized. Differentiation also protects the firm from rival attacks, given that as a result of the element of differentiation, substitution between products is reduced. The monopolistic firm is relatively independent in its actions *vis-à-vis* its rivals. Finally, it also helps the firm to defend itself better against suppliers and substitute products. *This is the typical competitive situation that strategic marketing seeks to create.*

In monopolistic competition, the firm offers a differentiated product and thus holds an external competitive advantage. This 'market power' places it in a protected position, and allows the firm to earn profits above the market average. Its strategic aim is therefore to exploit this preferential demand, while keeping an eye on the value and duration of the element of differentiation.

Measuring market power

The degree of market power is measured by the firm's ability to dictate a price above that of its priority competitors. One measure of this sensitivity is the price elasticity of the firm's or differentiated product's selective demand. The lower this demand elasticity, the less volatile or sensitive will market share be to a price increase.

If brand A has price elasticity equal to -1.5 and brand B an elasticity of -3.0, the same price increase of 5 per cent will lower demand for A by 7.5 per cent and demand for B by 15 per cent.

Therefore, a firm or brand with market power has a less elastic demand than a poorly differentiated product. As a result, it is in a position to make the group of buyers or consumers who are sensitive to the element of differentiation accept a higher price. In fact, economic theory shows that the less elastic (in absolute value) the demand for a product, the higher is the optimal price, that is the price that maximizes profits. If we know the elasticity, the optimal price can be calculated as follows:

$$P(\text{opt}) = C \times \varepsilon / (1 - \varepsilon)$$

or

$$\text{Optimal price} = \text{Unit direct cost} \times \text{Cost mark-up}$$

where

$$\text{Cost mark-up} = \text{Price elasticity} / (1 - \text{Price elasticity})$$

Thus, the optimal price is obtained by multiplying unit variable cost (marginal cost) by a percentage which depends on price elasticity and is independent of costs. The derivation of this optimization rule is presented in Appendix 8.1.

As Table 8.2 shows, the optimal cost mark-up is higher when price

Table 8.2 Optimal cost mark-up as a function of price elasticity

Price elasticity ε_{qp}	Optimal cost mark-up $\varepsilon_{qp}/(1-\varepsilon_{qp})$	Price elasticity ε_{qp}	Optimal cost mark-up $\varepsilon_{qp}/(1-\varepsilon_{qp})$
1.0	—	2.4	1.71
1.2	6.00	2.6	1.
1.4	3.50	...	...
1.6	2.67	3.0	1.50
1.8	2.22	4.0	1.33
2.0	2.00	5.0	1.25
2.2	1.83	...	...
...	...	15.0	1.07

Table 8.3 Measuring brand market power: the market for feminine hygiene products (Lambin, 1983)

Brands	Estimated price elasticity	Implied optimal cost mark-up	Indicator of market power
Brand A	−1.351	3.849	1.334
Brand B	−1.849	2.178	0.755
Brand C	−1.715	2.399	0.832
Brand D	−1.624	2.603	0.902
Brand E	−1.326	4.067	1.410
Brand F	−1.825	2.212	0.767
Average	−1.615	2.885	—

elasticity is lower in absolute value, i.e. closer to unity. When price elasticity is high, which is the case in highly competitive markets of undifferentiated products, mark-up is close to unity; the firm's market power is weak and the price accepted by the market is close to unit costs. Conversely, the closer elasticity is to unity, the higher is the price acceptable by the market.

To illustrate, Table 8.3 presents estimated price elasticities for six brands of a feminine hygiene product, as well as the mark-up on unit costs that each brand could adopt when calculating the optimal price. A measure of market power is obtained by calculating the ratio of the brand's mark-up to the average mark-up observed in the market.

Monopoly

This type of competitive structure is a limiting case, as for perfect competition. The market is dominated by a single producer facing a large number of buyers. Its product is therefore, for a limited period of time, without any direct competitor in its category.

This kind of situation is observed in the introductory stage of a product's life cycle, namely in emerging industries characterized by high technology innovations.

If monopoly exists, the firm has a market power which in principle is substantial. In reality, this power is rapidly threatened by new entrants who are attracted by the possibility of growth and profits. The foreseeable duration of monopoly then becomes an essential factor. It will depend on the innovation's power and the existence of sustainable barriers to entry. A monopoly situation is always temporary, due to the rapid diffusion of technological innovations. We saw in the previous chapter the strategic options and the risks that characterize innovation monopoly. A monopolist is also subject to competition coming from substitute products.

The logic of *state* or *government monopolies* is different from that of private firms. It is no longer the logic of profit, but that of public good and public service. Fulfilling these objectives in public services is hard because there is no incentive for adopting a market orientation. On the contrary, the public or state organization favours the adoption of a self-centred or internal orientation. This is one of the reasons in favour of the policy of deregulation adopted in many European countries.

This problem is dealt with in the field of social marketing, or marketing of non-profit organizations, which has developed quite substantially over the last few years (Kotler *et al.*, 1975; Bon and Louppe, 1980).

The dynamics of competition

Concluding the analysis of competitive forces, it is clear that market power and profit potential can vary widely from one market situation to another. We can thus put two limiting cases aside: one is the case where profit potential is almost zero; in the other case, it is very high. In the first case, the following situation will be observed:

- Entry into the product market is free.
- Existing firms have no bargaining power over their clients and suppliers.
- Competition is unrestrained because of the large number of rival firms.
- Products are all similar and there are many substitutes.

This is the model of perfect competition which is so dear to economists. The other limiting case is where profit potential is extremely high:

- There are powerful barriers that block entry to new competitors.
- The firm has either no competitors or a few weak competitors.
- Buyers cannot turn to substitute products.
- Buyers do not have enough bargaining power to make prices go down.
- Suppliers do not have enough bargaining power to make increased costs acceptable.

This is the ideal situation for the firm, which will have a very strong market power. Market reality is obviously somewhere in-between these two limits. It is the interplay of competitive forces that favours one or the other of these situations.

Achieving competitive advantage through cost domination

Gaining market power through successful product differentiation is one way to get a competitive advantage. Another way is to achieve cost domination *vis-à-vis* competition through better productivity and cost controls. Cost reductions can be achieved in many ways. In many industries, where the value added to the product accounts for a large percentage of the total cost, it has been observed that there is an opportunity to lower costs as a firm gains experience in producing a product. The observation that there exist 'experience effects' was made by Wright (1936) and the Boston Consulting Group (1968) who, towards the end of the 1960s, verified the existence of such an effect for more than 2000 different products, and deduced a law known as the *experience law*. This law, which has had great influence on the strategies adopted by some firms, translates and formalizes at the firm level what economists study at the aggregate level: improvements in productivity. We will first present the theoretical foundations of the experience law, and then discuss its strategic implications.

The experience law defined

The strategic importance of the experience law stems from the fact that it makes it possible not only to forecast one's own costs, but also to forecast competitors' costs. The law of experience stipulates that:

The unit cost of value added to a standard product, measured in constant currency, declines by a constant percentage each time the accumulated production doubles.

A certain number of points merit further comment:

- The word 'experience' has a very precise meaning: it designates the *cumulative number of units produced* and not the number of years since the firm began making the product.
- Thus the growth of production per period must not be confused with the growth of experience. Experience grows even if production stagnates or declines.
- The experience law is a *statistical law* and not a natural one; it is an observation which is statistically verified in some situations, but not always. Costs do not spontaneously go down; they go down if someone pushes them down through productivity improvements.
- Costs must be measured in *constant monetary units*, that is, they must be adjusted for inflation. Inflation can hide the experience effect.
- The experience effect is always stronger during the *launching and growth stages* of a new product's development cycle; later improvements are proportionally weaker and weaker as the product market reaches maturity.
- The experience law applies only to *value added costs*, that is costs over which the firm has some control, such as costs of transformation, assembly, distribution and service. Recall that valued added is equal to selling price minus input costs: the cost of value added is given by unit cost minus input costs.

In practice, total unit cost is often used as the basis of observation of experience effects, especially because it is more easily accessible than value added cost. The error introduced in this way is not too high when the cost of value added represents a large proportion of the total unit cost.

Causes of experience effects

Several factors contribute to drive unit costs down the experience curve (Figure 8.5). They are the improvements adopted by management in the production process as a result of learning from accumulated output. Abell and Hammond (1979, pp. 112–13) have identified seven sources of experience effects:

- *Labour efficiency*. As workers repeat a particular task, they become more dextrous and learn improvements and short-cuts which increase their efficiency.
- *Work specialization and methods improvements*. Specialization increases worker proficiency at a given task.
- *New production processes*. Process innovations and improvements can be an important source of cost reductions, such as the introduction of robotics or of computer-assisted systems.
- *Better performance from production equipment*. When first designed,

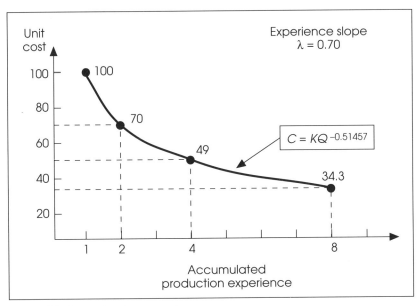

Figure 8.5 Example of an experience curve

a piece of production equipment may have a conservatively rated output. Experience may reveal innovative ways of increasing its output.

- *Changes in the resource mix.* As experience accumulates, a producer can often incorporate different or less expensive resources in the operation. For instance, less skilled workers can replace skilled workers, or automation can replace labour.
- *Product standardization.* Standardization allows the replication of tasks necessary for worker learning. Even when flexibility and/or a wider product line are important marketing factors, standardization can be achieved by modularization.
- *Product redesign.* Once the firm has a clear understanding of the performance requirements, a product can be redesigned to incorporate less costly materials and resources.

These factors are all under the control of the firm. They are part of the general policy of the firm of productivity improvements aiming at making an equivalent product for less cost or at making a better product for the same cost or a combination of the two. Thus experience *per se* does not generate cost reductions, but rather provides *opportunities for cost reductions*. It is up to management to exploit these opportunities.

To what extent are experience effects different from *scale effects*?

Scale effects are different from experience effects, even if in practice it is difficult to separate the two effects. Two major differences exist:

- Scale effects arise from the size of the operation, while experience effects accrue over time. The time dimension is what makes them different. Confusion between the two effects arises because size increases as experience accumulates.
- Another important difference exists. Cost advantages due to size always exist: fixed costs are divided by a larger number of units, thereby diminishing the unit cost. Cost advantages due to experience don't occur naturally: they are the result of concerted efforts to diminish costs.

Thus, scale effects can exist as a consequence of experience effects. For instance, the cost of capital (relative to that of its competitors) should decline as the firm gets bigger and gains access to more and cheaper sources of capital. But scale effects can also exist independently of experience effects and vice versa.

The mathematics of experience curves

The mathematical expression for the experience curve is as follows:

$$C_p = C_b \times (Q_p/Q_b)^{-\varepsilon}$$

where

C_p = projected unit cost
C_b = base unit cost
Q = experience: cumulative volume of production
ε = constant: unit cost elasticity

Thus we have

$$\text{Projected cost} = \text{Base cost} \left(\frac{\text{Projected experience}}{\text{Base experience}}\right)^{-\varepsilon}$$

The cost elasticity (ε) can be estimated as follows:

$$\frac{C_p}{C_b} = \left(\frac{Q_p}{Q_b}\right)^{-\varepsilon}$$

and hence

$$\varepsilon = \frac{\log C_p / \log C_b}{\log Q_p / \log Q_b}$$

In practice, it is convenient to refer to a doubling of experience. When the ratio of projected experience to base experience is equal to 2, i.e. $Q_p/Q_b = 2$, we obtain

$$\frac{C_p}{C_b} = 2^{-\varepsilon}$$

Table 8.4 Relationship between ε and λ

Slope of experience	1.00	0.95	0.90	0.85	0.80	0.75	0.70
Unit cost elasticity	0		0.074	0.152	0.234	0.322	0.450	0.515

where $2^{-\varepsilon}$ is defined as lambda (λ), the slope of the experience curve.

If, in the above equation, ε is 0.515, then λ is equal to 0.70 and C_p will be equal to 0.70 C_b. That is, the projected cost of the future unit of output C_p, when cumulative experience doubles, will be equal to 70 per cent of the base cost (C_b). Thus, the experience curve slope λ measures the percentage reduction in costs compared to the base value.

Table 8.4 show the relationship between ε, the unit cost elasticity, and λ, the experience curve slope, for values of λ ranging from 70 per cent to 100 per cent.

In Figure 8.5, we can see that the cost of the first unit is F100 and that of the second is F70. When the cumulative quantity has doubled from 1 to 2, unit cost has decreased by 30 per cent; the cost of the fourth unit will therefore be F49, the cost of the eighth unit F34.3, of the sixteenth F24.0 etc. In this example, the rate of cost decline is 30 per cent per doubling, and the experience slope is 70 per cent. This corresponds to a cost elasticity of -0.515.

Often, the coordinates of an experience curve are expressed on a logarithmic scale, so as to represent it as a straight line. The larger the slope of the curve, the steeper is the straight line. Experience slopes observed in practice lie between 0.70 (high degree of experience effect) and 1.00 (zero experience effect). The Boston Consulting Group observes that most experience curves have slopes between 70 per cent and 80 per cent.

For a given firm, the impact of experience effects depends not only on its experience slope, but also on the speed at which experience accumulates. The possibility of reducing costs will be higher in sectors which have rapidly growing markets; similarly, for a given firm the potential for cost reduction is high if its market share increases sharply, irrespective of whether or not the reference market is expanding. The figures in Table 8.5 give expected percentage reductions in annual costs for different experience slopes and different rates of sales growth.

Statistical estimation of experience curves

The statistical estimation of experience curves is made with historical data on unit costs (sometimes on the basis of unit prices) and on

Table 8.5 Annual percentage of cost reduction due to experience effects (Hax and Majluf, 1984, p. 112)

Experience curve slope	Annual market growth rate				
	2%	5%	10%	20%	30%
90%	0.3	0.7	1.4	2.7	3.9
80%	0.6	1.6	3.0	5.7	8.1
70%	1.0	2.5	4.8	9.0	12.6
60%	1.4	3.5	6.8	12.6	17.6

cumulative quantities, which should ideally cover several doublings of cumulated volume. Analysis of different cost components should in principle be carried out separately in order to pinpoint those that are behaving differently. For each group, unit costs are considered against cumulative volume, and after logarithmic transformations a line is fitted by the method of least squares. The estimated function is then used to forecast future costs for each of the components.

Two measurement problems occur regularly in estimating experience curves: the non-availability of competitors' cost data and the choice of the experience measurement units. To overcome the first problem, average prices for the industry as a whole are used. An alternative is to accept the assumption that all players in a particular product market are driving the same experience curve, an acceptable assumption if the same technology is prevalent. As to the experience measurement unit, the total number of units produced may not always be the most appropriate basis for measuring cumulative experience.

For instance, the experience curve phenomenon may not be readily discernible if a firm manufacturing refrigerators in various sizes ranging from 2 cubic feet to 26 cubic feet of storage space were to employ the number of units produced as a measure of cumulative experience. Cubic feet of refrigeration space may be a more appropriate measure when the experience phenomenon is examined at the aggregate product level (Kerin *et al.*, 1990, p. 117).

The estimated experience curves are only valid if the conditions that gave rise to past observations remain stable: the firm manufactures the same product according to the same process and technology. These conditions are in reality never fully satisfied. Like many management tools, the experience law is more a tool of analysis than an accurate forecasting instrument. Nevertheless, it is of great value in analysing disparities in competitive capacity and evaluating the significance of competitive cost advantage.

Strategic implications of the experience law

The experience law helps us to understand how a competitive advantage can exist based on a disparity in unit costs between rival firms operating in the same market and using the same means of production. The strategic implications of the experience law can be summarized as follows:

- The firm with the largest cumulated production will have the *lowest* costs, *if the experience effect is properly exploited.*
- The aggressive firm will try to drive down *as rapidly as possible* its experience curve, so as to build a cost advantage over its direct competitors.
- The goal is to grow faster than priority competitors, which implies *increased relative market share.*
- This growth objective is best achieved *right at the start*, when gains in experience are most significant.
- The most effective way of gaining market share is to adopt a *price penetration* strategy, whereby the firm fixes price at a level which anticipates future cost reductions.
- This strategy will give the firm *above normal profit* performance.

Thus, in an experience-based strategy, building market share and penetration pricing are the key success factors for achieving a competitive advantage based on cost domination.

Figure 8.6 illustrates the mechanism of a price penetration policy. The firm anticipates the movement of its unit cost in terms of

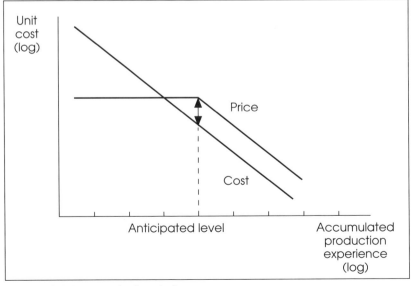

Figure 8.6 Price penetration strategy

Table 8.6 Evolution of unit cost as a function of experience effects

Cumulative production (× 1000)	Number of doublings	Slope of the experience curve		
		70%	80%	90%
1	—	100	100	100
2	1	70	80	90
4	2	49	64	81
8	3	34	51	73
16	4	24	41	66
32	5	17	33	59
64	6	12	26	48

cumulative production. It sets itself a target to reach which implies a faster sales growth than in the reference market and hence an increase in its relative market share. The selling price, when launching the product, is determined with respect to this anticipated volume. Once the level of experience has been reached, future cost decreases will be reflected in the price to maintain the advantage over priority competitors.

Assessing competitive cost disparities

If cumulative production does lead to the expected cost reduction, and if the dominant firm manages to protect the benefit of the experience it acquires, the experience effect creates an entry barrier to new entrants and a cost advantage for the leader. Firms with low market shares will inevitably have higher costs, and if they fix their prices at the same level as the dominant competitor they have to suffer heavy losses. Furthermore, the firm with the highest market share also enjoys larger cash flows. It can reinvest in new equipment or new processes and thus reinforce its leadership.

To illustrate, let us examine the data in Table 8.6. A comparison is made of movements in unit costs as a function of experience, for experience slopes equal to 70 per cent, 80 per cent and 90 per cent, respectively.

Let us consider the case of two firms, A and B, using the same technology and having the same initial conditions; they both have an experience slope of 70 per cent. Firm A is at its first doubling of cumulative production, while firm B is at its fourth. Their costs are 70 and 24, respectively. One can imagine that it might be quite hard for firm A to close this gap, given that it needs to increase its market share quite considerably to achieve cost parity.

Now let us assume that the two firms A and B have the same experience; they are both at their fourth doubling. However, firm A has better exploited cost reduction opportunities and is on an experience curve of 70 per cent, whereas firm B's experience curve has a slope of only 90 per cent; their unit costs are 24 against 66. Here too, it would be difficult to close the gap. Experience effects can therefore create large disparities in costs of firms which are of equal size, but have failed to incorporate this potential equally in productivity improvements.

Experience curves as an early warning system

As mentioned above, the main usefulness of the experience curve is to assess the dynamics of cost competition between two or more firms operating in the same reference market and to alert management as to the necessity of making timely strategic changes. The example of Figure 8.7, proposed by Sallenave (1985, p. 67), illustrates this last point. The chart shows the cost and experience curves of a polyester fibre manufacturer. Prices and costs are expressed in constant $/kg. Prices declined on a 75 per cent experience curve while the slope of the cost curve was only 86 per cent. In this example, the management of the plant could have predicted years before it was too late that the cost and price curves were converging rapidly.

In 1980, the plant made no profit. Its management immediately embarked on a cost reduction program, but at the same time demand slowed down. The plant was unable to operate at capacity level, which would have made the cost reduction programme effective. Unit costs remained unchanged. The plant closed down in 1983.

Had management read the early warning given by the experience curve analysis, it would have reacted early enough to decide between several possible remedial actions.

- Increase the capacity of the plant to accumulate faster and drive the unit cost down.
- Retool and/or improve the production process to operate on a 75 per cent cost slope, i.e. a slope compatible with the price slope.
- Specialize in special purpose fibres and sell them at a higher price than the normal price for regular polyester fibre.
- Sell the plant while it was profitable or convert it to another production line.

Thus, the experience curves can be used to anticipate future developments and to *simulate contemplated strategies*. The simulation exercise can be very instructive, as the following example shows.

Consider a firm with 6 per cent of a market that is growing at an 8 per cent real growth rate and whose leader has a 24 per cent share. To catch up with the leader's share, our firm would have to grow at a 26 per cent

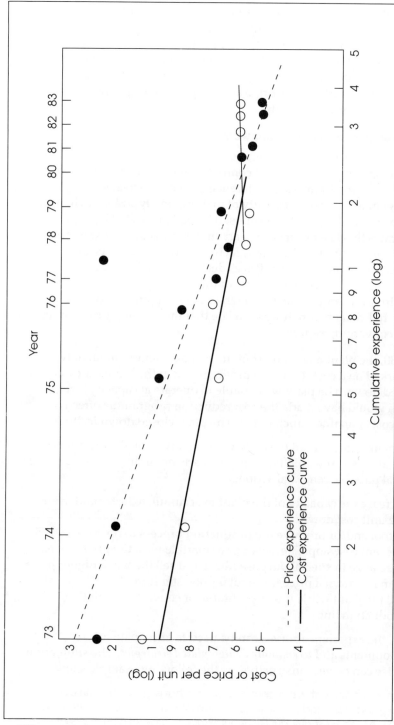

Figure 8.7 The experience curve as an early warning system (Sallenave, 1985. (Reprinted from *Long Range Planning*, **18**, Sallenave, J.P., 'The uses and abuses of experience curves', 64–72, 1985, with permission from Pergamon Press Ltd., Headington Hill Hall, Oxford OX3 0BW, UK.))

growth rate in nine years, if the leader held its share by growing at the 8 per cent industry rate. That means expanding at over three times the industry rate for nine years, and that sales and capacity have to expand by 640 per cent (Abell and Hammond, 1979, p. 118).

This is typically a 'mission impossible'. Before embarking on experience-based strategies, it is essential to calculate the time and the investment required to achieve the objective. Some companies, such as Texas Instruments, use experience curve simulations systematically before pricing a new product.

Limits of the experience law

The experience law is not universally applicable; it holds mainly in sectors where large scale brings economic advantage and in which the process of learning is important (Abernathy and Wayne, 1974). To be more specific, situations in which the experience law is of little relevance are the following:

- Learning potential is low or the part of value added cost in the total cost is not very significant.
- One competitor has access to a special source of supplies, thus having a cost advantage which bears no relation to its relative market share.
- Technology changes rapidly and neutralizes the experience-based cost advantage.
- The market is not price-sensitive.
- There is large potential for product differentiation.

Thus, if a firm is dominated by a competitor having a major cost advantage, two basic strategies can be adopted to circumvent the experience advantage:

- A *differentiation strategy* offering distinctive features valued by the buyer, who is ready to pay a premium price that would offset the cost handicap.
- A *technological innovation strategy* that would place the firm on a new and steeper experience curve, thereby neutralizing the cost advantage of the current market leader.

The experience law is not of general application. To avoid misuse of the experience curve theory, it is important to verify the validity of the assumptions on which the theory is based.

The competitive advantage matrix

A competitive advantage can be obtained in different ways, depending on the competitive structure and on the market characteristics. The Boston Consulting Group (Lochridge, 1981),

Table 8.7 The competitive advantage matrix (Lochridge, 1981)

Number of ways to achieve competitive advantage	Size of the competitive advantage	
	Small	Large
Many	Fragmented	Specialization
Few	Stalemate	Volume

which greatly contributed to spreading the law of experience, has proposed a classification of market situations which helps in identifying the type of competitive advantage to pursue. Two classification criteria are used:

- The size of the competitive advantage.
- The number of ways of achieving competitive advantage.

One then obtains a matrix, presented in Table 8.7. Horizontally, we have the size of the advantage, which can be small or large. Vertically, we have the number of ways to achieve advantage, which can be few or many. To each of the quadrants corresponds a particular market situation requiring a specific strategic approach. The four types of industry are: volume, specialization, fragmented and stalemate industries.

Volume industries are those where sources of competitive advantage are few and where cost advantage is the major opportunity. It is typically in this market situation that experience and/or scale effects manifest themselves, and where a large relative market share is a precious asset. Profitability is closely related to the size of market share as postulated by the experience curve theory.

Specialization industries are those with many ways of obtaining a sizeable competitive advantage. In these markets, the potential for differentiation is high, as is the case in situations of monopolistic competition, described earlier. Products have significant distinctive qualities from buyers' points of view, and they in turn are prepared to pay prices above those of direct competitors. In this kind of situation, the scale/experience effect brings no particular advantage. It is the value of differentiation or specialization that counts and determines profitability. Total market share has little value; it is market share in a specific segment or niche which is critical, even if the size of the niche is small.

In *fragmented industries,* sources of differentiation are many, but no firm can create a sustainable and decisive advantage over its rivals. Scale brings no significant economies and a dominant market share does not lead to lower costs. On the contrary, increased costs, linked to the complexity of the situation, limit the optimal size of the firm. Many service firms are good examples of the fragmented sector. Large and small firms can co-exist with very different profitability. Market share has no effect, irrespective of the way it has been calculated. In this category one can classify women's clothing, restaurants and car repair and maintenance services. In many cases, the best strategy is to transform a fragmented activity into a volume or specialized activity.

In *stalemate industries*, the ways of obtaining a competitive advantage are few, as in the case of volume industries. But unlike these, accumulated experience does not constitute a competitive advantage. On the contrary, it is sometimes the newcomers who have the most efficient tools of production, because they have the most recent investment. In situations where technology is easily available, as in the steel industry or basic chemicals, competitiveness is more dependent on the age of the investment rather than the size of the firm: the last firm to invest benefits from lowest operating costs.

We can therefore see that an experience-based strategy can in fact only be applied in commodity-based, volume-sensitive industries, in which low cost is one of the few potential sources of achieving competitive advantage.

Appendix 8.1: Derivation of the price optimization rule

We have the following demand function:

$$Q = Q\,(P/M, E)$$

where Q denotes quantity, P the selling price, M other marketing variables and E environmental factors. Assuming M and E are constant, the problem is to derive the optimum price.

The profit function is as follows:

$$\pi = (P - C)Q - F$$

where π is gross profit, C the direct unit cost and F the fixed costs specific to the activity considered.

To identify the optimum price, let us calculate the first derivative of π with respect to price and set the derivative equal to zero.

$$\frac{\delta\pi}{\delta P} = (P - C)\,\frac{\delta Q}{\delta P} + Q = 0$$

Multiplying each term by the ratio P/Q and rearranging terms we have

$$P(1 + \varepsilon_{qp}) = C\varepsilon_{qp}$$

which is the *marginal revenue–marginal cost equality rule* expressed by reference to price elasticity. Solving for P^*, the optimum price, we have

$$P^* = C \left(\frac{\varepsilon_{qp}}{1 - \varepsilon_{qp}}\right)$$

The *second order condition* stipulates that the price elasticity in absolute value should be larger than one.

By way of illustration, if $\varepsilon = -2.1$ and $C = 105$, the optimum price is

$$P^* = (105) \left(\frac{-2.1}{1 - (-2.1)}\right) = (105) (1.9) = F205$$

The optimal cost mark-up is therefore 1.9.

Formulating a marketing strategy

The objective of this chapter is to examine how a market-driven firm can select the appropriate competitive strategy to achieve an above-average profit performance in the different business units included in its product portfolio. Two sets of factors determine the performance of a particular business unit: first, the overall attractiveness of the reference market where it operates, and second, the strength of its competitive position relative to direct competition. The reference market's attractiveness is largely determined by forces outside the firm's control (see Chapter 7), while the business unit's competitiveness can be shaped by the firm's strategic choices (see Chapter 8). Product portfolio analysis relates attractiveness and competitiveness indicators to help guide strategic thinking by suggesting specific marketing strategies to achieve a balanced mix of products that will ensure growth and profit performance in the long run. In this chapter, we shall first define the conceptual bases of portfolio analysis and then describe the types of mission or objectives the firm should assign to each of its business units given their differentiated positions along the attractiveness–competitiveness dimensions. Finally, we shall discuss the strategic alternatives open to the firm in the field of international development.

Product portfolio analyses

The purpose of a product portfolio analysis is to help a multi-business firm decide how to allocate scarce resources among the product markets they compete in. In the general case, the procedure consists in cross-classifying each activity with respect to two independent dimensions: the attractiveness of the reference market where the firm operates, and the firm's capacity to take advantage of opportunities within the market. Various portfolio models have been developed, using matrix representations where different indicators are used to measure attractiveness and competitiveness. Here we shall concentrate on the two most representative methods: the Boston Consulting Group's method (BCG) called the 'growth–share' matrix (Boston Consulting Group, 1972; Henderson, 1970) and the 'multifactor portfolio' matrix attributed to General Electric and McKinsey (Hussey, 1978; Abell and Hammond, 1979). Although the two methods have the same objectives, their implicit assumptions are different and the two approaches will likely yield different insights (Wind *et al.*, 1983).

The BCG growth–share matrix

The BCG matrix is built around two criteria: the reference market's growth rate (corrected for inflation), acting as an indicator of attractiveness, and market share relative to the firm's largest competitor, measuring competitiveness.

As shown in Figure 9.1, we have a double entry table where a cut-off level on each axis creates a grid with four quadrants. Along the Market growth axis, the cut-off point distinguishing high-growth from low-growth markets corresponds to the growth rate of the GNP in real terms, or to the (weighted) average of the predicted growth

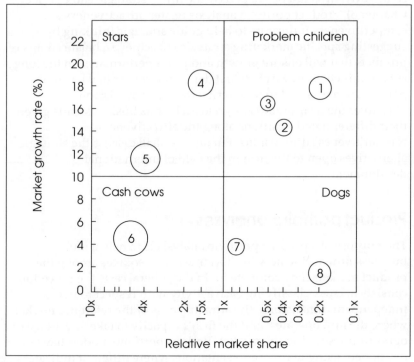

Figure 9.1 The BCG growth–share matrix

rates of the different markets in which the products compete. In practice, high-growth markets are often defined as those growing by more than 10 per cent per year. Markets growing by less than 10 per cent are deemed low-growth.

Similarly, on the Relative market share axis the dividing line is usually put at 1 or 1.5. Beyond this level, relative market share is high; below, it is low. Thus the matrix relies on the concept of relative market share to leading competitor (see p. 147–9), which calculates the ratio of unit sales for one firm with unit sales for the largest share firm.

If company A, for example, has a 10 per cent share of the market and the largest share belongs to company B, with 20 per cent, then company A has a relative market share of 0.5 (10 per cent/20 per cent). It has a low market share since the ratio is less than one. Similarly, company B has a relative market share of 2 (20 per cent/10 per cent). It has a high share of the market.

The use of relative market share is based on the assumption that market share is positively correlated with experience and therefore with profitability (see Chapter 8). Therefore the competitive implications of holding a 20 per cent market share are quite different if the largest competitor is holding 40 per cent or only 5 per cent.

We thus obtain four different quadrants, each of which defines four fundamentally different competitive situations in terms of cash flow requirements and which need to be dealt with by specific objectives and marketing strategies.

Basic assumptions of the growth-share matrix

There are two basic assumptions underlying the BCG analysis: one concerns the existence of experience effects, and the other the product life cycle (PLC) model. These two assumptions can be summarized as follows.

Higher relative market share implies cost advantage over direct competitors because of experience effects; where the *experience curve concept* applies, the largest competitor will be the most profitable at the prevailing price level. Conversely, lower relative market share implies cost disadvantages.

The implication of this first assumption is that the expected cash flow from products with high relative market share will be higher than those with smaller market shares.

Being in a fast growing market implies greater need for cash to finance growth, added production capacity, advertising expenditures etc. Conversely, cash can be generated by a product operating in a mature market. Thus, the *product life cycle model* is employed because it highlights the desirability of a balanced mix of products situated in the different phases of the PLC.

The implication of this second assumption is that the cash needs for products in rapidly growing markets are expected to be greater than they are for those in slower growing ones.

As discussed in Chapters 7 and 8, these assumptions are not always true. On this topic, see Abell and Hammond (1979, pp. 192–3).

Defining the type of business

Keeping in mind these two key assumptions, we can identify four groups of product markets having different characteristics in terms of their cash flow needs and/or contributions:

- *Low growth/high share* or *'Cash cow'* products
  These products usually generate more cash than is required to sustain their market position. As such, they are a source of funds for the firm to support diversification efforts and growth in other markets. The priority strategy is to 'harvest'.
- *Low growth/low share, 'dogs'* or *'Lame ducks'* products
  Dogs have a low market share in a low-growth market, the least desirable market position. They generally have a cost disadvantage and few opportunities to grow, since the war is over in the market. Maintaining these products generally turns into a financial drain without any hope of improvement. The priority strategy here is to 'divest' or in any case to adopt a low profile and to live modestly.
- *High growth/low share* or *'Problem children'* products
  In this category we find products with low relative market shares in a fast growing market. Despite their handicap *vis-à-vis* the leader, these products still have a chance of gaining market share, since the market has not yet settled down. However, supporting these products implies large financial means to finance share building strategies and to offset low profit margins. If the support is not given, these products will become dogs as market growth slows down. Thus, the alternatives here are to build market share or to divest.
- *High growth/high share* or *'Stars'* products
  Here we have the market leaders in a rapidly growing market. These activities also require a lot of cash to finance growth, but because of their leading position they generate significant amounts of profits to reinvest in order to maintain their market position. As the market matures, they will progressively take over as cash cows.

Every activity can be placed in a matrix similar to Figure 9.1. The

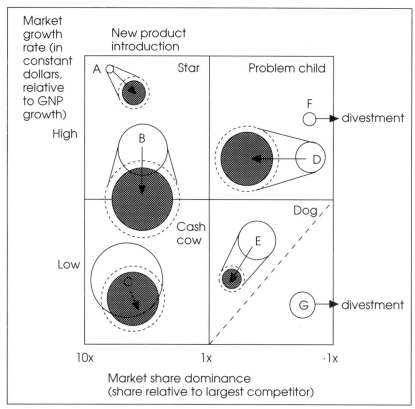

Figure 9.2 Product portfolio trajectory analysis (Day, 1977, p. 34)

significance of an activity can be represented by a circle of size proportional to sales volume, sales revenue or profit contribution. This analysis should be made in a dynamic way, i.e. by tracking the progression or movements of each business unit over a period of time, as illustrated in Figure 9.2.

Diagnosing the product portfolio

In this approach, it is important to properly define the reference market in which the activity is competing. Relative market share compares the strength of a firm relative to its competitors. If the market is defined too narrowly the firm appears as the segment leader; if it is too wide, the firm appears too weak. The following points arise from the analysis.

- The position in the matrix indicates the *credible strategy* for each product: maintain leadership for stars; abandon or low profile for dogs; selective investment and growth for problem children; maximum profitability for cash cows.

- The position in the matrix helps evaluate *cash requirements* and *profitability potential*. Profits are usually a function of competitiveness; cash requirements generally depend on the phase of the product's life cycle, that is, on the reference market's degree of development.
- Allocation of the firm's total sales revenue or profit contribution according to each quadrant allows *balancing of the product portfolio*. The ideal situation is to have products that generate cash and products in their introductory or growing stage that will ensure the firm's long-term viability. The needs of the second category will be financed by the first.

Based on this type of diagnostic, the firm can envisage various strategies either to maintain or to restore the balance of its product portfolio. To be more specific, it allows the firm:

- To develop *portfolio scenarios* for future years on the basis of projected growth rates and tentative decisions regarding the market share strategies for the various activities, assuming different competitive reaction strategies.
- To analyse the potential of the existing product portfolio, and to put a figure to the *total cash-flow* it can expect from each activity, every year, until the end of its planning horizon.
- To analyse the *strategic gap*, that is the observed difference between expected performance and desired performance.
- To identify the *means to be employed* to fill this gap, either by improving existing products' performances, or by abandoning products that absorb too much cash without any realistic hope of improvement, or finally by introducing new products that will rebalance the portfolio structure.

Too many ageing products indicate a danger of decline, even if current results appear very positive. Too many new products can lead to financial problems, even if activities are quite healthy, and this type of situation inevitably risks loss of independence.

Figure 9.3. describes two successful and two unsuccessful trajectories that can be observed for new or existing business units.

- The *'innovator' trajectory*, which uses the cash generated by the cash cows to invest in R&D and to enter the market with a product new to the world that will take over from existing stars.
- The *'follower' trajectory*, which uses the cash generated by the cash cows to enter as a problem child in a new market, dominated by a leader, with an aggressive market share build-up strategy.
- The *'disaster' trajectory*, whereby a star product evolves to the problem children quadrant as a consequence of insufficient investment in market share maintenance.

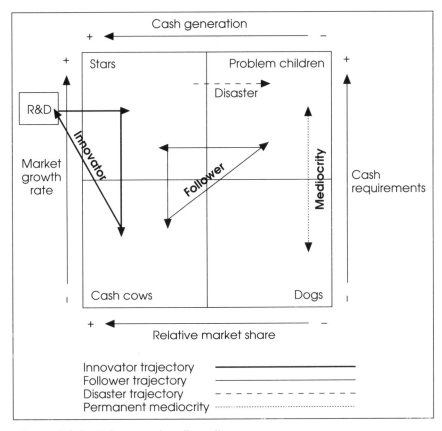

Figure 9.3 Portfolio scenarios alternative

- The *'permanent mediocrity' trajectory* involves a problem child product evolving to the dogs quadrant as a consequence of the failure to build market share for the product.

Let us remember that this type of diagnostic is only valid if the underlying assumptions mentioned earlier hold true. But, as already mentioned, the links between market share and profitability on the one hand and growth rate and financial requirements on the other are not always observed (see Abell and Hammond, 1979, pp. 192–3).

Limitations of the growth-share matrix

The most important merit of the BCG method is undoubtedly that it provides an appealing and elegant theoretical development which establishes a clear link between strategic positioning and financial performance. It is true that the initial assumptions are restrictive. But if they are true, they allow accurate analysis and valuable recommendations. General managers can thus concentrate on the major strategic problems and analyse the implications of alternative business strategies. Furthermore, the method is based on *objective indicators* of attractiveness and competitiveness, thus reducing the risk of subjectivity. Finally, it should also be added that the matrix provides a *visual, vivid and easy to comprehend synthesis* of the firm's activities, thus facilitating communication.

There are, however, a number of limitations and difficulties which need to be emphasized because they reduce the generality of the approach.

- The implicit hypothesis about the relation between relative market share and cash flows means that this technique can only be used when there is an experience effect, that is in *volume industries*, as we saw in the previous chapter (see Table 8.7). Thus the experience effect might be observed in only some product markets and not in all the product markets which are in the firm's portfolio.
- The method is based on the notion of 'internal' competitive advantage only and doesn't take into account any *'external' competitive advantage* enjoyed by the firm or the brand as a result of a successful differentiation strategy. Thus, a so-called 'dog' could very well generate cash despite its cost disadvantage if the market accepts the paying of a premium price for the product, given its distinctive qualities.
- Despite its simple appearance, some *measurement problems* can arise. Should the definitions of the product market be broad or narrow? What share of what market? How do we determine market growth rate? Wind *et al.* (1983) have shown that the analysis is very sensitive to the measures used. For a discussion of these questions see Day (1977, pp. 35–7).
- The recommendations of a portfolio analysis remain very vague and at most constitute *orientations* to be clarified. To say that in a given product market a strategy of 'harvest' or 'low profile' should be adopted is not very explicit. In any case, it is insufficient for an effective determination of policies regarding prices, distribution, communication etc. The main purpose of a portfolio analysis is to help guide, but not substitute for, strategic thinking.

These limitations are serious and restrict the scope of the growth-share matrix significantly, which is not equally useful in all corporate situations. Other methods based on less restrictive assumptions have been developed.

The multi-factor portfolio matrix

The BCG matrix is based on two single indicators. But there are many situations where factors other than market growth and share determine the attractiveness of a market and the strength of a competitive position.

Clearly, a market's attractiveness can depend also on factors such as market accessibility, size, existing distribution network, structure of competition, favourable legislation etc. The market for portable computers is in principle highly attractive if we judge it by its high growth rate. There are, however, many other factors, such as rapid change in demand, expected price changes, products' fast rate of obsolescence, intensity of competition etc., which make this a risky and therefore relatively less attractive market.

Similarly, a firm's competitive advantage may be the result of strong brand image or commercial organization, technological leadership, distinctive product qualities etc., even if its market share is low relative to the major competitor. When, in 1982, IBM introduced its personal computer, its competitiveness was very low according to the BCG matrix, since its market share was zero. Yet many analysts perceived IBM's competitive potential as very high because of its reputation in the computer market, its important technological know-how, its available resources and its will to succeed.

It is clear that several factors need to be taken into account to measure correctly the market's attractiveness and the firm's competitiveness potential. Instead of using a single indicator per dimension, multiple indicators can be used to assess attractiveness and competitiveness and to construct a composite index for each dimension. For an extensive list of possible factors, see Abell and Hammond (1979, p. 214). Thus, the BCG matrix described in the preceding section may be viewed as a special case of a more general theory relating market attractiveness and business competitiveness.

Development of a multi-factor portfolio grid

To illustrate, Table 9.1 presents a battery of indicators selected to measure the *attractiveness* of five product markets from the textile industry, as well as a series of indicators evaluating the competitiveness of the company Tissex, which operates in these five product markets.

Since each situation is different, the relevant list of factors has to be identified and a multi-factor portfolio grid is necessarily company-specific. The selection of the relevant factors is a delicate task and should involve several persons from the strategic marketing group and from other departments as well. Precise definition of each indicator must be given and the nature of the relationship should be clearly determined. Once the grid is developed, each product market is evaluated against each indicator.

Table 9.1 Multi-factor portfolio grid: selected indicators of attractiveness and competitiveness

Indicators	Weight (100)	Evaluation scale		
		Weak **1** **2**	**Moderate** **3** **4**	**Strong** **5**
Indicators of attractiveness				
Market accessibility	―――	Outside Europe & USA	Europe & USA	Europe
Market growth rate	―――	≤ 5%	5%–10%	≥ 10%
Length of the life cycle	―――	≤ 2 years	2–5 years	≥ 5 years
Gross profit potential	―――	≤ 15%	15%–25%	≥ 25%
Strength of competition	―――	Structured oligopoly	Unstructured competition	Weak competition
Potential for differentiation	―――	Very weak	Moderate	Strong
Concentration of customers	―――	Very dispersed	Moderately dispersed	Concentrated
Indicators of competitiveness				
Relative market share	―――	≤ ⅓ leader	≥ ⅓ leader	Leader
Unit cost	―――	Greater than direct competitors	Equal to direct competitors	Smaller than direct competitors
Distinctive qualities	―――	'Me too' product	Moderately differentiated	'Unique selling proposition'
Technological know-how	―――	Weak control	Moderate control	Strong control
Sales organization	―――	Independent distributors	Selective distribution	Direct sales
Image	―――	Very weak	Fuzzy	Strong

- A scale of 5 points is used, with 'low', 'average' and 'high' as reference points for scores equal to 1, 3 and 5, respectively.
- As far as indicators of competitiveness are concerned, ratings are not attributed 'in abstract', but relative to the most dangerous competitor in each product market or segment.
- If some indicators appear to be more important than others, weighting can be introduced, but the weights must remain the same for every activity considered.
- The ratings should reflect, as much as possible, future or expected values of the indicators and not so much their present values.

- A summary score can then be calculated for each product market's global attractiveness and the firm's potential competitiveness.

Contrary to the BCG approach, subjective evaluations enter into these measures of attractiveness and competitiveness. But the process may nevertheless gain in interpersonal objectivity, to the extent that many judges operate independently. Their evaluations are then compared in order to reconcile or to explain observed differences and disagreements. This process of reconciliation is always useful in itself.

Interpretation of the multi-factor grid

We then obtain a two-dimensional classification grid similar to the BCG matrix. It is current practice to subdivide each dimension into three levels (low, average, high), thus getting nine squares, each corresponding to a specific strategic position.

Each zone corresponds to a specific positioning. The firm's different activities can be represented by circles with an area proportional to their share in the total sales revenue or profit contribution. The four most clearly defined positionings are those corresponding to the four corners of the matrix in Figure 9.4.

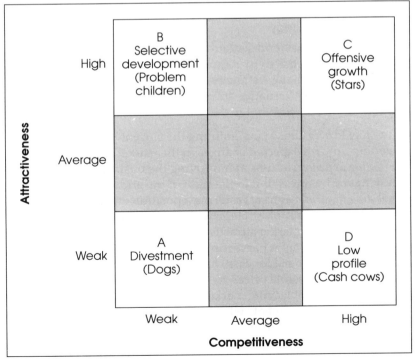

Figure 9.4 Multi-factor portfolio grid

- In quadrant C, both the product market's attractiveness and the firm's competitive potential are high; the strategic orientation to follow is *offensive growth*. The characteristics are similar to those of 'stars' in the BCG matrix.
- In quadrant A, both attractiveness and competitiveness are low; strategic orientation is *maintenance without investment* or *divestment*. We have the case of 'dogs' of Figure 9.1.
- Quadrant B depicts an intermediate situation: competitive advantage is low, but the reference market's attraction is high. This is typically the case of 'problem children'. The strategy to follow is *selective growth*.
- In quadrant D, we have the opposite situation. Competitive advantage is high but market attractiveness is low. A skimming and maintenance strategy without major new investment is called for. This is the equivalent of the 'cash cows' positioning in the BCG matrix.

The other intermediate zones correspond to strategic positions which are less clearly defined and often hard to interpret. The fuzzy value of the summary scores can reflect either very high marks on some indicators and very low marks on others, or simply an average evaluation on all the criteria. The latter case is often observed in practice and reflects imprecise information or simply lack of it.

Choice of future strategy

We thus have a visual representation of the firm's growth potential. By extrapolating each activity's expected growth under the assumption of 'no change' strategy, the firm is in a position to assess its future position. Alternative strategic options can also be explored, such as:

- *Investing to hold* aims at maintaining the current position and keeping up with expected changes in the market.
- *Investing to penetrate* aims at improving the business position by moving the business unit to the right of the grid.
- *Investing to rebuild* aims at restoring a position which has been lost. This revitalization strategy will be more difficult to implement if the market attractiveness is already medium or low.
- *Low investment* aims at harvesting the business, i.e. the business position is exchanged for cash, for example, by selling the activity at the highest possible price.
- *Divestment* aims at leaving markets or segments of low attractiveness or segments where the firm has not the capacity to acquire or to sustain a competitive advantage.

Figure 9.5 shows an example of multi-factor portfolio analysis. It represents the portfolio of a firm from the food industry. Note that

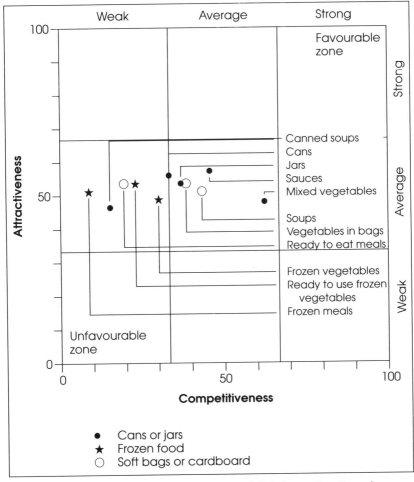

Figure 9.5 Example of a multi-factor portfolio (MDA Consulting Group)

product markets' attractiveness is very average and the firm's competitiveness is evaluated as low for almost all the products considered. The future of this firm is clearly very bleak.

Evaluation of the multi-factor portfolio grid

The multi-factor portfolio model leads to the same kind of analyses as the BCG matrix, with one major difference: the link between competitive and financial performance (i.e. cash flow) is lost. However, since this model is not based on any particular assumption, it does overcome many of the shortcomings of the BCG method and it is more widely applicable. Furthermore, it is much more flexible because the indicators used are company-specific.

The use of these types of matrix suffers nevertheless from certain limitations.

- Measurement problems are more delicate and the *risk of subjectivity* is much higher here. This shows up not only in the choice of indicators and their possible weighting, but especially when it comes to marking the criteria. The risk of subjectivity is greater for indicators of competitiveness, where there is necessarily self-evaluation.
- When the number of indicators and the number of activities to evaluate are high, the *procedure becomes heavy* and demanding, especially when information is scarce or imprecise.
- The *results are sensitive* to the ratings and to the weighting systems adopted. Manipulation of weights can produce a desired position in the matrix. It is therefore important to test the sensitivity of results to the use of alternative weighting systems.
- As for the BCG matrix, *recommendations remain very general* and need to be clarified. Furthermore, the link with financial performance is less clearly established.

The two approaches will very likely yield different insights. But as the main purpose of a product portfolio analysis is to help guide, but not substitute for, strategic thinking, the process of reconciliation will be useful. Thus it is desirable to employ both approaches and compare results (Day, 1977, p. 38).

Benefits of product portfolio analyses

Portfolio analysis is the outcome of the whole strategic marketing process described in the last four chapters of this book. A portfolio analysis rests on the following principles, irrespective of the method used:

- An accurate division of the firm's activities into product markets or segments.
- Measures of competitiveness and attractiveness allowing evaluation and comparison of different activities' strategic values.
- Links between strategic position and economic and financial performance, mainly in the BCG method.

Matrix representations help to synthesize the results of this strategic thinking exercise and to visualize them in a clear and expressive manner. Contrary to appearances, they are not simple to elaborate. They require complete and reliable information about the way markets function, about the firm and its rivals' strengths and weaknesses. More specifically, this analysis implies:

- Considerable effort to *segment the reference market*. This is particularly important, because the validity of the recommendations is conditioned by the initial choice of segmentation.

- Systematic and careful collection of *detailed information*, which does not normally exist as such and needs to be reconstituted by cross-checking and probing; the quality of results also depends on the reliability of this information.

This kind of analysis cannot be improved and it relies particularly on top management's complete support. Such a tool is obviously not a panacea, but it has the merit of emphasizing some important aspects of management:

- It moderates excessively short-term vision by insisting on keeping a balance between immediately profitable activities and those that prepare the future.
- It encourages the firm to keep both market attractiveness and competitive potential in mind.
- It establishes priorities in allocation of human as well as financial resources.
- It suggests differentiated development strategies per type of activity on a more data-orientated basis.
- It creates a common language throughout the organization and fixes clear objectives to reinforce motivation and facilitate control.

The main weakness of methods of portfolio analysis is that they can give an image of the present, or indeed of the recent past, and devote too little time assessing future changes and strategic options for dealing with these changes. There is also a risk of too mechanistic an application of these methods. As already underlined, different methods could lead to very different classifications. The tools described here must be viewed more as guides to informed reasoning than as prescriptive tools.

Portfolio models in practice

In a survey of the Fortune 1000 industrial firms, Haspeslagh (1982) studies the usefulness of portfolio analysis. Some of his findings follow:

- As of 1979, 36 per cent of the Fortune 1000 firms and 45 per cent of the Fortune 500 firms had introduced the portfolio model approach to some extent. About 14 per cent of the Fortune 1000 were engaged in the process of portfolio planning in which the portfolio became a central part of the management process.
- The decision as to which portfolio model to use was not regarded as critical. Considered fundamental to portfolio planning were (a) defining the business units; (b) classifying those business units according to their attractiveness and competitiveness; and (c) using this framework to assign financial objectives.

- As to the benefits of portfolio analysis, one third of the respondents felt that the most important benefit was achieving a better understanding of their businesses, which in turn led to better strategic decision-making. Another one-third felt that the key benefits were improved resource allocation, strategic reorientation and exit and entry decisions.

The survey also showed that firms using product portfolio models clearly had a longer time horizon than those not using portfolio planning. A more recent survey done by Hamermesch (1986) comes to the same conclusions.

A portfolio analysis leads to different strategic recommendations according to the positioning of activities in the portfolio. As we saw, such recommendations are mainly general guidelines, such as invest, maintain, harvest, abandon etc., which require clarification and need to be put in a more explicit operational perspective.

The choice of a generic strategy

The first step in elaborating a development strategy is to clarify the nature of the *sustainable competitive advantage* which will serve as the basis for later strategic actions and tactics. We saw in the previous chapter that competitive advantage can be described by reference to two aspects (see Figure 8.1): *productivity* (cost advantage) and *market power* (advantage in terms of maximum acceptable price). The question is to know which of these two aspects should be given priority, given the firm's characteristics, its strengths and weaknesses and those of its rivals. In other words, which advantage is 'sustainable' in a given product market?

Identifying this sustainable competitive advantage requires an analysis of the competitive structure, and, more specifically, answers to the following questions.

- What are the *key success factors* in a given product market or segment?
- What are the firms' *strengths and weaknesses* with regard to these factors?
- What are the strengths and weaknesses of the firms' *direct rival(s)* with regards to the same key success factors?

On the basis of this information, the firm can (a) assess the nature of the advantage for which it is best placed; (b) decide to create competitive advantage for itself in a particular domain; or finally, (c) attempt to neutralize rivals' competitive advantage.

Generic strategies will therefore be different according to the type of

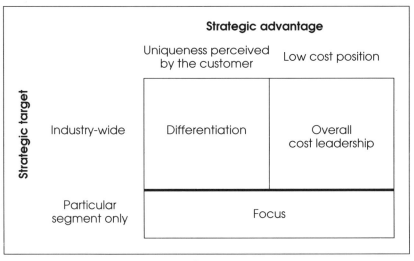

Figure 9.6 Three generic strategies (Porter, 1980)

competitive advantage sought, that is whether they are based on productivity and therefore cost advantage, or whether they rest on an element of differentiation and are therefore based on a price premium.

Porter (1980, p. 35) suggests that there exist three generic competitive strategies to outperforming other firms in an industry: overall cost leadership, differentiation or focus (Figure 9.6).

Overall cost leadership

This first generic strategy is based on *productivity* and is generally related to the existence of an experience effect. This strategy implies close scrutiny of overhead costs, of productivity investments intended to enhance the value of experience effects and of product design costs, and on cost minimization in service, selling, advertising and so on. Low cost relative to competitors is the major preoccupation of the entire strategy.

Having a cost advantage constitutes an effective protection against the five competitive forces (see Figure 8.2).

- Relative to its *direct competitors*, the firm is in a better position to resist a possible price war and still make a profit at its rivals' minimum price level.
- Powerful *buyers* can only drive down prices to the level of the most efficient competitor.
- Low cost provides a defence against powerful *suppliers* by providing more flexibility to cope with input cost increases.

- A low cost position provides substantial *entry barriers* in terms of scale economies or cost advantage.
- A low cost position usually places the firm in a favourable position *vis-à-vis substitutes* relative to competitors in the industry (Porter, 1980, p. 36).

Thus, cost leadership protects the firm against all five competitive forces, because the least efficient firms are the first ones to feel the effects of the competitive struggle.

Differentiation

The objective here is to give distinctive qualities to the product which are significant to the buyer and which create something that is perceived as being unique. What the firm tends to do is to create a situation of monopolistic competition in which it holds some *market power* because of the distinctive element (Chamberlin, 1950).

We saw before that differentiation can take many forms: design or brand image, technology, features, customer service, dealer network and so on (see Levitt, 1980). Differentiation, like cost domination, protects the firm from the five competitive forces, but in a very different way.

- Relative to its *direct rivals*, differentiation provides the firm with insulation against competitive rivalry because of brand loyalty and resulting lower price sensitivity. It also increases margins, which avoids the need for a low cost position.
- The resulting customer loyalty, and the need for a competitor to overcome uniqueness, provide *entry barriers*.
- Higher profitability increases the firm's ability to resist cost increases imposed by powerful *suppliers*.
- Finally, the firm that has differentiated itself to achieve customer loyalty should be better positioned *vis-à-vis substitutes* than its competitors (Porter, 1980, p. 37).

Successful differentiation enables the firm to realize higher profits than its rivals because of the higher price the market is willing to accept and despite the fact that costs are generally higher. This type of strategy is not always compatible with high market share, since most buyers are not necessarily prepared to pay a higher price, even though they recognize product superiority.

Differentiation strategies generally imply large investments in operational marketing, particularly in advertising expenditures to inform the market about the product's distinctive qualities.

Table 9.2 Risks associated with generic strategies
(Porter, 1980, pp. 45–6)

Risks of overall cost leadership
- Technological changes that nullify past investments or learning.
- Low cost learning by industry newcomers or followers, through imitation or through their ability to invest in state-of-the-art facilities.
- Inability to see required product or marketing change because of the attention placed on costs.
- Inflation in costs that narrows the firm's ability to maintain enough of a price differential to offset competitors' brand images or other approaches to differentiation.

Risks of differentiation
- The cost differential between low cost competitors and the differentiated firm becomes too great for differentiation to hold brand loyalty. Buyers sacrifice some of the features, services or image possessed by the differentiated firm for large cost savings.
- Buyers' needs for the differentiating factor fall. This can occur as buyers become more sophisticated.
- Imitations narrow perceived differentiation, a common occurrence as industries mature.

Risks of focus
- The cost differential between broad range competitors and the focused firm widens to eliminate the cost advantages of serving a narrow target or to offset the differentiation achieved by focus.
- The differences in desired products or services between the strategic target and the market as a whole narrows.
- Competitors find sub-markets within the strategic target and out-focus the focuser.

Focus

A third generic strategy is focusing on the needs of a particular segment, group of buyers or geographic market, without claiming to address the whole market. The objective is to take a restricted target and to serve its narrow strategic target more effectively than competitors who are serving the whole market. It implies either differentiation or cost domination, or both, but only *vis-à-vis* the particular target. For example, a paint manufacturer can decide to address professional painters only, excluding the public at large, car manufacturers and the naval industry. In the car industry, Mercedes (until recently) only addresses the high end of the market, but it covers that segment more effectively than other car manufacturers having a full line of models.

The focus strategy always implies some limitations on the overall market share achievable. A focus strategy can give the firm a large share of the market in the targeted segment, but it may be low relative to the whole market.

Risks associated with generic strategies

The choice of one strategy against another is not a neutral decision, in the sense that they involve differing types of risk and also different priority preoccupations in the organization. Table 9.2 summarizes the risks inherent in each generic strategy.

The implementation of these strategies implies different resources and different know-how:

- A cost domination strategy assumes sustained investment, a high degree of technological competence, close control of manufacturing and distribution costs and standardized products to facilitate production.
- A differentiation strategy assumes significant marketing know-how as well as technological advance. The ability to analyse and anticipate trends in market needs plays a fundamental role here. Interfunctional coordination between R&D, production and marketing is vital.

Finally, a *concentration* strategy also assumes the previous characteristics *vis-à-vis* the targeted segment.

Assessing growth opportunities

There are growth objectives in most strategies considered by firms, whether they are of sales growth, market share, profits or size. Growth is a factor that influences firm vitality, stimulates initiatives and increases motivation of personnel and management. Independent of this element of dynamism, growth is necessary in order to survive assaults from competitors, thanks to the economies of scale and experience effects it generates.

A firm can envisage growth objectives at three different levels:

- A growth objective within the reference market it operates; we shall refer to this as *intensive growth*.
- A growth objective within the industrial chain, lateral expansion of its generic activity, backwards or forwards; this is *integrative growth*.
- A growth objective based on opportunities outside its normal field of activity; this is *growth by diversification*.

To each of these growth objectives there correspond a number of possible strategies. It is interesting to examine them briefly.

Intensive growth

A strategy of *intensive growth* is called for when a firm has not yet fully exploited the opportunities offered by its products within its 'natural' reference market. Various strategies may be envisaged: market penetration, market and product development strategies.

Market penetration strategies

A market penetration strategy consists of trying to increase or maintain sales of current products in existing markets. Several options are open:

- *Primary demand development:* to increase size of total market by expanding primary demand, for example:
  —Broadening the customer base by converting non-users into users.
  —Increasing the frequency of purchase among present users.
  —Increasing the average quantity purchased per use occasion.
  —Identifying and promoting new uses.

  Note that this strategy can benefit all competitors since it influences primary demand more than selective demand.
- *Market share increase strategy*: to increase sales by attracting buyers from rival brands through significant spending on marketing mix variables. For example:
  —Improved product or service offering.
  —Repositioning the brands.
  —Aggressive pricing.
  —Significant reinforcement of the distribution and service network.
  —Major promotional efforts.

This more aggressive strategy will be mainly observed in market situations where primary demand is non-expansible, having reached the maturity phase of the product life cycle.
- *Market acquisition:* to increase market share substantially by acquisition or joint venture. For example:
  —Acquisition of a competitor to obtain its market share.
  —Joint venture to achieve control of a significant market share.
- *Market position defence:* to defend current market position (i.e. customer relationships, network, share, image etc.) by adjusting the marketing mix. For example:
  —Product or service minor modifications or repositioning.
  —Defensive pricing.

—Sales and distribution network reinforcement.
—Stepped-up or redirected promotional activities.
- *Market rationalization:* to modify significantly the markets served to reduce costs and/or increase marketing effectiveness. For example:
  —Concentration on the most profitable segments.
  —Use of the most effective distributors.
  —Limiting individual customers served via minimum volume requirements.
  —Selective abandonment of market segments.
- *Market organization:* to influence, using legally accepted practices, the level of competition within one's industry to enhance economic viability. For example:
  —Establishment of industry-wide competitive rules or guidelines, usually under government supervision.
  —Creation of joint marketing research organizations to improve informations systems.
  —Agreement on capacity stabilization or reduction.

These last three strategies are more defensive, aiming at maintaining the level of market penetration.

Market development strategies

A *market development strategy* refers to a firm's attempt to increase the sales of its present products by tapping new markets. This objective can be achieved using three alternative approaches.

- *New market segments:* to reach new groups of buyers within the same geographic market. For example:
  —Introducing an industrial product to the consumer market or vice versa.
  —Selling the product to another consumer age group (sweets to adults).
  —Selling the product to another industrial sector.
- *New distribution channels:* to distribute the product through another channel of distribution, complementary to the current ones. For example:
  —Adopting a direct marketing system for specific groups of buyers.
  —Distributing the products through vending machines.
  —Developing a franchise system parallel to the existing network.
- *Geographic expansion* towards other parts of the country or to other countries. For example:
  —Shipping existing products to foreign markets relying on local agents or on an independent worldwide trading company.
  —Creating an exclusive network of distributors to handle foreign business.

—Acquiring a foreign company in the same sector.

Market development strategies rely mainly on the distribution and marketing know-how of the firm.

Product development strategies

A *product development* strategy consists of increasing sales by developing improved or new products aimed at current markets. Several different possibilities exist.

- *Features addition strategy:* to add functions or features to existing products in order to expand the market. For example:
  —Increasing the versatility of a product by adding functions.
  —Adding an emotional or social value to an utilitarian product.
  —Improving the safety or convenience of the product.
- *Product line extensions strategy:* to increase the breadth of the product line by introducing new varieties to increase or maintain market share. For example:
  —Launching different packages of different sizes.
  —Increasing the number of flavours, scents, colours or composition.
  —Offering the same product in different forms or shapes.

  The strategy of line extension can lead to product proliferation and the question of cannibalization and synergistic effects should be addressed explicitly.
- *Product line rejuvenation strategy:* to restore the overall competitiveness of obsolete or inadequate products by replacing them with technologically or functionally superior products. For example:
  —Developing a new generation of more powerful products.
  —Launching environmentally friendly new models of existing products.
  —Improving the aesthetic aspects of the product.
- *Product quality improvement strategy:* to improve the way a product performs its functions as a package of benefits. For example:
  —Determining the package of benefits sought by each customer group.
  —Establishing quality standards on each dimension of the package of benefits.
  —Establishing a program of total quality control.
- *Product line acquisition:* to complete, improve or broaden the range of products through external means. For example:
  —Acquisition of a company with a complementary product line.
  —Contracting for the supply of a complementary product line to be sold under the company's name.
  —Joint venture for the development and production of a new product.

- *Product line rationalization:* to modify the product line to reduce production or distribution costs. For example:
  —Product line and packaging standardization.
  —Selective abandonment of unprofitable or marginal products.
  —Minor product redesign.

The lever used in product development strategies is essentially R&D. These strategies are generally more costly and risky than market development strategies.

Integrative growth

An integrative growth strategy is justified when a firm can improve profitability by controlling different activities of strategic importance within the industrial chain. It describes a variety of make-or-buy arrangements firms use to obtain a ready supply of strategic raw materials and a ready market for their outputs. Examples include ensuring stability of supplies, controlling a distribution network, or having access to information in a downstream activity to secure captive markets. There is a distinction between backward integration, forward integration and horizontal integration.

Backward integration

A *backward integration* strategy is driven by the concern to maintain or to protect a strategically important source of supplies, be it raw or semi-processed materials, components or services. In some cases, backward integration is necessary because suppliers do not have the resources or technological know-how to make components or materials which are indispensable to the firm.

Another objective may be to have access to a key technology which might be essential to the success of the activity. For example, many computer manufacturers have integrated backwards in the design and production of semiconductors in order to control this fundamental activity.

Forward integration

The basic motivation for a *forward integration* strategy is to control outlets without which the firm will choke. For a firm producing consumer goods, this involves controlling distribution through franchises or exclusive contracts, or even by creating its own chain stores, such as Yves Rocher or Bata. In industrial markets, the aim is mainly to ensure the development of downstream industries of transformation and incorporation that constitute natural outlets. This is how some basic industries actively participate in creating intermediary transformation activity.

In the steel industry, for example, Cockerill in Belgium has created Phoenix Works, specialized in coating and galvanizing sheet steel, Polypal, developing and manufacturing industrial storage systems, and Polytuile, manufacturing roof coverings with steel sheet.

In some cases, forward integration is done simply to have a better understanding of the needs of buyers of manufactured products. The firm creates in this case a subsidiary playing the role of a pilot unit: to understand problems of users in order to meet their needs more effectively.

Horizontal integration

A *horizontal integration* strategy has a totally different perspective. The objective is to reinforce competitive position by absorbing or controlling some competitors. There can be various arguments for this: neutralizing a dangerous rival, reaching the critical volume so as to benefit from scale effects, benefiting from complementarity of product lines and having access to distribution networks or to restricted market segments.

Growth by diversification

A strategy of *growth by diversification* is justified if the firm's industrial chain presents little or no prospect of growth or profitability. This may happen either because competitors occupy a powerful position, or because the reference market is in decline. Diversification implies entry into new product markets. This kind of growth strategy is as such more risky, since the jump into the unknown is more significant. It is usual to establish a distinction between concentric diversification and pure diversification.

Concentric diversification

In a *concentric diversification* strategy, the firm goes out of its industrial and commercial network and tries to add new activities which are related to its current activities technologically and/or commercially. The objective is therefore to benefit from synergy effects due to complementarity of activities, and thus to expand the firm's reference market.

For example, the Sports Division of Fabrique Nationale (FN) in Belgium, the leading European manufacturer of hunting weapons, has gradually diversified and added to its product line other sporting goods, such as golf clubs, fishing rods, tennis racquets and windsurfing boards. The aim was on the one hand to compensate for the decline in the hunting market, and on the other hand to take full advantage of a specialized distribution network of sporting goods controlled by FN, the Browning network in the USA in particular.

A concentric diversification strategy usually has the objectives of attracting new groups of buyers and expanding the reference market of the firm.

Pure diversification

In a pure diversification strategy, the firm enters into new activities which are unrelated to its traditional activities, either technologically or commercially. The aim is to turn towards entirely new fields so as to rejuvenate the product portfolio. At the end of 1978, for example, Volkswagen bought Triumph-Adler, which specializes in informatics and office equipment, for this very reason.

Diversification strategies are undoubtedly the most risky and complex strategies, because they lead the firm into unknown territory. To be successful, diversification requires important human as well as financial resources. Drucker (1981, p. 16) considers that a successful diversification requires a common core or unity represented by common markets, technology or production processes. He states that without such a unity core, diversification never works; financial ties alone are insufficient. Other organizational management specialists believe in the importance of a 'corporate culture' or a 'management style' which characterizes every organization and which may be effective in some fields and not others. The alternative growth strategies are summarized in Table 9.3.

The rationale of diversification

Calori and Harvatopoulos (1988) study the rationales of diversification in the French industry. They identify two dimensions. The first dimension relates to the *nature of the strategic objective:* diversification may be defensive (replacing a loss-making activity) or offensive (conquering new positions). The second dimension involves the *expected outcomes* of diversification: management may expect great economic value (growth, profitability) or first and foremost great coherence and complementarity with their current activities (exploitation of know-how).

Cross-classifying these two dimensions gives rise to four logics of diversification, as shown in Table 9.4.

- *Expansion,* whereby the firm tries to reinforce its activity (offensive aim) while taking full advantage of its know-how (coherence). This kind of diversification strategy has been followed by Salomon, for example, the world leader in ski bindings, which has gone into

Table 9.3 Alternative growth strategies

1 Intensive growth: to grow within the reference market
1.1 Penetration strategy
Increase sales of existing products in existing markets:
- Primary demand development.
- Market share increase.
- Market acquisition.
- Market position defence.
- Market rationalization.
- Market organization.

1.2 Market development strategy
Increase sales of existing products in new markets:
- Target new market segments.
- Adopt new distribution channels.
- Penetrate new geographic markets.

1.3 Product development strategy
Increase sales in existing markets with new or modified products:
- Features addition strategy.
- Product line extensions strategy.
- Product line rejuvenation strategy.
- Product quality improvement strategy.
- Product line acquisition.
- Product line rationalization.
- New product development strategy.

2 Integrative growth: to grow within the industrial chain
2.1 Backward integration.
2.2 Forward integration.
2.3 Horizontal integration.

3 Growth by diversification: to grow outside the industrial chain
3.1 Concentric diversification.
3.2 Pure diversification

Table 9.4 The rationales of diversification (Calori and Harvatopoulos, 1988)

Type of objective	Expected outcome	
	Coherence	Economic value
Offensive	Expansion (Salomon)	Deployment (Taittinger)
Defensive	Relay (Framatome)	Redeployment (Lafarge)

the market for ski boots, then the market for cross-country skiing and more recently in to manufacturing golf clubs and ski poles.

- *Relay*, which seeks to replace a declining activity (defensive objective), while using high quality staff (coherence). Framatome followed this strategy at the end of the 1970s, when the market for nuclear plants started to shrink.
- *Deployment* is an offensive strategy seeking high economic value. This was the case for Taittinger diversifying into the deluxe hotel business.
- *Redeployment* which is defensive in nature but seeks a new channel for growth. This strategy was followed by Lafarge which merged with Coppée and entered into biotechnology when faced with decline in the building industry.

Two more particular logics must be added to these basic ones: diversification driven by image improvement (the logic of image), and diversification driven by the will to watch the growth of a new promising technology (the logic of window).

It is important that management should define the logic of diversification from the outset and as clearly as possible. Upon this logic will depend the criteria for assessing and selecting potential activities.

Competitive strategies

An important element of a growth strategy is taking explicit account of competitors' positions and behaviours. Measuring business competitiveness (Chapter 8) helps to evaluate the importance of the firm's competitive advantage compared with its most dangerous rivals, and to identify their competitive behaviour. The next task is to set out a strategy based on a realistic assessment of the forces at work, and to determine the means to achieve defined objectives.

Kotler establishes a distinction between four types of competitive strategy; his typology is based on the level of market share held and comprises four different strategies: market leader, market challenger, market follower and market nicher (Kotler, 1991, p. 319).

Market leader strategies

In a product market, the market leader is the firm that holds a dominant position and is acknowledged as such by its rivals. The leader is often an orientation point for competitors, a reference that rival firms try to attack, to imitate or to avoid. The best-known market leaders are IBM, Procter & Gamble, Kodak, Benetton, Nestlé, L'Oréal etc. A market leader can envisage different strategies.

Primary demand development

The market leader is usually the firm that contributes most to the growth of the reference market. The most natural strategy that flows from the leader's responsibility is to *expand total demand* by looking for new users, new uses and more usage of its products. Acting in this way, the market leader contributes to expanding the total market size which, in the end, is beneficial to all competitors. This type of strategy is normally observed in the first stages of the product's life cycle, when total demand is expansible and tension between rivals is low due to high potential for growth of total demand.

Defensive strategies

A second strategy open to a firm with large market share is a *defensive strategy:* protecting market share by countering the actions of the most dangerous rivals. This kind of strategy is often adopted by the innovating firm which finds itself attacked by imitating firms once the market has been opened. This was the case for IBM in the mainframe computer market, for Danone in the fresh products market, for Coca Cola in the soft drink market etc. Many defensive strategies can be adopted:

- Innovation and technological advance which discourages competitors.
- Market consolidation through intensive distribution and a full line policy to cover all market segments.
- Direct confrontation, that is a direct show-down through price wars or advertising campaigns.

We have seen this type of strategy between firms such as Hertz and Avis, Coca Cola and Pepsi Cola, and Kodak and Polaroid.

Aggressive strategies

A third possibility available to a dominant firm is an *offensive strategy.* The objective here is to reap the benefits of experience effects to the maximum and thus improve profitability. This strategy is based on the assumption that market share and profitability are related. In the previous chapter, we saw that this relationship was mainly observed in volume industries, where competitive advantage is cost-based. Its existence has also been empirically established by works of PIMS (Buzzell *et al.*, 1975) and confirmed by Galbraith and Schendel (1983). Although increasing market share is beneficial to a firm, there exists a limit beyond which the cost of any further increase becomes prohibitive. Furthermore, an excessively dominant position also has the inconvenience that it attracts the attention of public authorities who are in charge of maintaining balanced competitive market conditions. This, for instance, is the task of the

Competition Commission within the European Community, and of anti-trust laws in the USA. Dominant firms are also more vulnerable to attacks by consumer organizations, who tend to choose the most visible targets, such as Nestlé in Switzerland and Fiat and Montedison in Italy.

Demarketing strategy

There is also a fourth strategy open to a dominant firm: *reduce its market share* to avoid accusations of monopoly or quasi-monopoly. Various possibilities exist. First, it can use *demarketing* to reduce the demand level in some segments by price increases, or reduce services as well as advertising and promotion campaigns.

Market challenger strategies

A firm that does not dominate a product market can choose either to attack the market leader and be its challenger, or to become a follower by falling into line with the leader's decisions. Market challenger strategies are therefore aggressive strategies with the declared objective of taking the leader's position.

The challenger faces two key questions: (a) the choice of the battleground from which to attack the market leader and (b) evaluation of the latter's reactive and defensive abilities.

In the choice of the battleground, the challenger has two possibilities: frontal attack or lateral attack. A *frontal attack* consists of opposing the competitor directly by using its own weapons, and without trying to use its weak points. To be successful, a frontal attack demands a balance of power heavily in favour of the attacker. In military strategy, this balance is normally put at 3 to 1.

For example, when in 1981 IBM attacked the microcomputer market with its PC, its marketing tools, advertising in particular, were very clearly superior to those of Apple, Commodore and Tandy, which dominated the market (*Business Week*, 25 March 1985). Two years later IBM had become the leader.

Lateral attacks aim to confront the leader over one or another strategic dimension for which it is weak or ill prepared. A lateral attack may, for example, address a region or a distribution network where the leader is not well represented, or a market segment where his or her product isn't well adapted. A classic market challenger strategy is to launch a price attack on the leader: offer the same product at a much lower price. Many Japanese firms adopt this strategy in electronics or cars (Kotler *et al.*, 1985, p. 91).

This strategy becomes even more effective when the leader holds a large market share. If the latter were to take up the lower price, it would have to bear important costs, whereas the challenger, especially if it is small, only loses over a low volume.

The major European steel producers severely suffered from price cuts offered by the Italian Bresciani mini-steelworks. The same phenomenon is observed in the oil market with 'cut-price firms' such as Seca in Belgium, Uno-X in Denmark and Conoco in Great Britain; dominant firms (BP, Exxon, Shell etc.) had more to lose in a price war.

Lateral or indirect attacks can take various forms. There is a direct analogy with military strategy and one can define strategies of outflanking, encircling, guerilla tactics, mobile defence etc. See on this topic Kotler and Singh (1981) and Ries and Trout (1986).

Before starting an offensive move, it is essential to assess correctly a dominant firm's *ability to react and defend*. Porter (1980, p. 68) suggests using the three following criteria:

- *Vulnerability:* to what strategic moves and governmental, macroeconomic or industry events would the competitor be most vulnerable?
- *Provocation:* what moves or events are such that they will provoke a retaliation from competitors, even though retaliation may be costly and lead to marginal financial performance?
- *Effectiveness of retaliation:* to what moves or events is the competitor impeded from reacting to quickly and/or effectively given its goals, strategy, existing capabilities and assumptions?

The ideal is to adopt a strategy against which the competitor cannot react because of its current situation or priority objectives.

As was underlined earlier, in saturated or stagnant markets the aggressiveness of the competitive struggle tends to intensify as the main objective becomes how to counter rivals' actions. The risk of a strategy based only on warfare marketing is that too much energy gets devoted to driving rivals away at the risk of losing sight of the objective of satisfying buyers' needs. A firm which is focusing entirely on its rivals tends to adopt a reactive behaviour which is more dependent on rivals' actions than the developments in market needs. A proper balance between the two orientations is therefore essential (Oxenfeld and Moore, 1978).

Market follower strategies

As we saw before, a follower is a competitor with modest market share who adopts an adaptive behaviour by falling into line with competitors' decisions. Instead of attacking the leader, these firms pursue a policy of 'peaceful coexistence' by adopting the same attitude as the market leader. This type of behaviour is mainly observed in oligopolistic markets where differentiation possibilities are minimal and cross price elasticities are very high, so that it is in no one's interest to start a competitive war that risks being harmful to all.

Adoption of a follower's behaviour does not permit the firm to have no competitive strategy; quite the contrary. The fact that the firm holds a modest market share reinforces the importance of having clearly defined strategic objectives which are adapted to its size and its strategic ambition. Hamermesch *et al.* (1978) analyse strategies of small firms and show that these firms can overcome the size handicap and achieve performances which are sometimes superior to dominant rivals. In other words, not all firms with low market share in low-growth markets are necessarily 'dogs' or 'lame ducks'.

Hamermesch *et al.* (1978, pp. 98–100) have uncovered four main features in the strategies implemented by companies with high performance and low market share:

- *Creative market segmentation.* To be successful, a low market share company must compete in a limited number of segments where its own strengths will be most highly valued and where large competitors will be most unlikely to compete.
- *Efficient use of R&D.* Small firms can't compete with large companies in fundamental research; R&D should be concentrated mainly on process improvements aimed at lowering costs.
- *Think small.* Successful low market share companies are content to remain small. Most of them emphasize profits rather than sales growth or market share, and specialization rather than diversification.
- *Ubiquitous chief executive.* The final characteristic of these companies is the pervasive influence of the chief executive.

A market follower strategy therefore does not imply passivity on the part of the chief executive of the firm, rather the concern to have a growth strategy which will not entail reprisals from the market leader.

Market nicher strategies

A nicher is interested in one or few market segments, but not in the whole market. The objective is to be a large fish in a small pond rather than being a small fish in a large pond. This competitive strategy is one of the generic strategies we discussed earlier, namely focus. The key to a focus strategy is specialization in a niche. For a niche to be profitable and sustainable, five characteristics are necessary (Kotler, 1991, p. 395):

- Sufficient profit potential.
- Growth potential.
- Unattractive to rivals.
- The market corresponds to the firm's distinctive competence.
- A sustainable entry barrier.

A firm seeking a niche must face the problem of finding the feature or criterion upon which to build its specialization. This criterion may relate to a technical aspect of the product, to a particular distinctive quality or to any element of the marketing mix.

International development strategies

We emphasized in the first chapter that internationalization of the economy means that a growing number of firms operate in markets where competition is global. As a result, international development strategies concern all firms, irrespective of whether they actively participate in foreign markets or not. We will examine here the stages of international development as well as the strategic reasoning of a firm that pursues an international marketing development strategy.

Objectives of international development

International development is no longer limited to large enterprises. Many small firms are forced to become international in order to grow, or simply to survive. Objectives in an international development strategy may be varied.

- Enlarge the *potential market*, thus being able to produce more and achieve better results thanks to economies of scale. For many activities, the critical volume is at such a level that it demands a large potential market.
- Diversify *commercial risk* by addressing buyers in different economic environments and enjoying more favourable competitive conditions.
- Extend the product's *life cycle* by entering markets which are not at the same development stage and still have expansible total demand, whereas in the domestic market of the exporting firm demand has reached the maturity phase.
- Protect from *competition* through diversification of positions on the one hand and surveillance of competitors' activities in other markets on the other.

- Reduce *costs of supplies and production* by exploiting different countries' comparative advantages.

The phenomenon of globalization of markets, already mentioned in Chapters 2 and 6, must also be added to these basic objectives.

Forms of international development

A firm's internationalization doesn't happen overnight, but results from a process that can be subdivided into six levels of growing internationalization (Leroy *et al.*, 1978).

Exporting is the most frequent form. Often, the first attempts to export result from a necessity to clear surplus production. Later, exports can become a regular activity, but one which is reconstituted every year without there being any kind of medium- or long-term commitment to foreign countries. Relations are purely commercial.

The second stage is the *contractual stage*. Here the firm seeks more long-term agreements so as to stabilize its outlets, especially if its production capacity has been adjusted in terms of the potential to export. It will then sign long-term contracts, either with an importer or with a franchised distributor, or with a licensed manufacturer if it is an industrial firm.

In order to control the foreign partner or to finance its expansion, the firm may directly invest its own capital; this is the *participatory stage* which leads to commercial companies or co-ownership production.

After a few years, involvement can become absolute, with the firm owning 100 per cent of the capital of the foreign subsidiary; this stage is *direct investment* in a subsidiary with controlled management.

Gradually, the foreign subsidiary looks for ways of autonomous development, using local finance, national managers and its own programme of R&D which is distinct from the parent company. This is the *autonomous subsidiary stage*. If the parent company has many subsidiaries of this kind, this subsidiary becomes a multi-national company. It would probably be more appropriate to use the term 'multidomestic', because it emphasizes the point that each of these companies is more concerned about its own internal market, and the group's various companies coexist independently of each other.

The final stage of development is the one which is taking shape at the moment. It is the stage of the *global enterprise* that addresses the international market as if it were a single market. This kind of firm bases itself on interdependence of markets, and the latter are therefore no longer administered autonomously.

Stages of international organization

To the various stages of international development there often correspond specific forms of organization at the international level which reflect different views of international marketing. Keegan (1989) suggests the following typology.

- *Domestic organization.* The firm is focused on its domestic market, and exporting is viewed as an opportunistic activity. This type of organization is frequent in the 'passive marketing' stage described in Chapter 1.
- *International organization.* Internationalization takes place more actively, but at this stage the firm's orientation is still focused on the home market, which is considered as the primary area of opportunity. The *ethnocentric* company, unconsciously, if not explicitly and consciously, operates on the assumption that home country methods, approaches, people, practices and values are superior to those found elsewhere in the world. Attention is mostly centred on similarities with the home country market. The product strategy at this stage is 'extension', i.e. products that have been designed for the home country market are 'extended' into markets around the world.
- *Multidomestic organization.* After a certain period of time, the company discovers that the difference in markets demands adaptation of its marketing in order to succeed. The focus of the firm is now multinational (as opposed to home country) and its orientation is *polycentric.* The polycentric orientation is based on the assumption that markets around the world are so different and unique that the only way to succeed is to adapt to the unique and different aspect of each national market. The product strategy is adaptation, i.e. to change or adapt products to meet local differences and practices. Each country is managed as if it were an independent entity.
- *Global organization.* A global market is one that can be reached with the same basic appeal and message and with the same basic product. Both the product and the advertising and promotion may require adaptation to local customs and practices, as illustrated in Table 6.10. The *geocentric* orientation of the global corporation is based on the assumption that markets around the world are both similar and different, and that it is possible to develop a global strategy that recognizes similarities which transcend national differences while adapting to local differences as well. The basic

notion of a world strategy can therefore be summarized as follows: 'think globally and act locally'.

This last stage is, at the moment, taking shape in the world and in particular in the European economy. It implies important changes in the logic of strategic marketing. On this topic see Hamel and Prahalad (1985).

10
New product decisions

The objective of this chapter is to analyse the concepts and procedures which allow a firm to implement new product development strategies. Redeployment, diversification and innovation are at the heart of all development strategies. In a constantly changing environment, a company must continuously reevaluate the structure of its portfolio of activities, meaning the decisions to abandon products, modify existing ones or launch new products. These decisions are of the utmost importance to the survival of the company and involve not only the marketing department, but all of the other functional areas as well. In this chapter, we shall examine the ways of establishing a dialogue between the various functional areas which play a role in the development of a new product. We do this in such a way as to minimize the risks in the strategy during the innovation process.

Assessing the risk of innovations

The expression 'new product' is used loosely to describe a whole spectrum of innovations ranging from very minor, such as a change in an existing product, to very major, such as perfecting a new medicine resulting from years of research and development. Clearly, the risk varies greatly in these two examples and the nature of the risk in each one is completely different. Therefore it is important to evaluate accurately the diversity of innovations and their specific risks. After having defined the elements which constitute innovation, we will examine the different classifications of innovations as well as the principal factors which explain the success or failure of new products.

Components of an innovation

In Chapter 2 we saw that there was a distinction between an invention and an innovation. The latter is defined as the original implementation of a concept, discovery or invention. According to

Table 10.1 Components of an innovation: two examples

The disengageable T-bar and downhill skiing
- The *need*: to avoid the long and tiresome process of climbing back up snow-covered slopes.
- The *concept*: traction by a disengageable cable with a seat.
- The *technology*: mechanics.

The problem of aeronautic vibrations
- The *need*: to eliminate the vibrations that affect electronic equipment in an aeroplane.
- The *concept*: a sort of mesh covering.
- The *technology*: a resilient steel weave.

Barreyre (1980, p. 10), an innovation may be subdivided into three elements:

- A *need* to be satisfied, or a function(s) to be fulfilled.
- The *concept* of an object or entity to satisfy the need, in other words, the 'new idea'.
- The *inputs*, comprised of a body of existing knowledge as well as materials and available technology, which allow the concept to become operational.

Examples are given in Table 10.1.

The degree of risk associated with an innovation will thus depend on two factors: the degree of originality and complexity of the concept, which will determine the reception by the market and transfer costs for the user (market risk), and the degree of technological innovation pertaining to the concept, which will determine the technical feasibility of the innovation (technology risk). Added to these two intrinsic risks is the degree of familiarity that the firm itself has with the market and technology (strategy risk).

Three possible criteria for classifying innovations emerge: (a) the degree of newness for the firm, (b) the intrinsic nature of the concept based on the innovation, and (c) the intensity of the innovation.

Degree of newness for the company

Assessing the degree of newness for the company is important because it is this newness which determines, at least in part, the company's competitiveness or competitive capacity. As Table 10.2 suggests, the more a company explores new territory, the greater the strategy risk becomes. Four distinguishable levels of risk for a new product are as follows:

Table 10.2 Assessing the newness of an innovation

Market	Product or technology	
	Known	**Unknown**
Known	*Increasing risks*	
New		⟶

- *Known market and technology*: the risk is doubly limited because the firm relies on its distinctive abilities.
- *New market, known technology*: the risk is essentially a commercial one and success relies heavily on the marketing know-how of the firm.
- *Known market, new technology*: the risk is technical in nature and success relies on the firm's technical know-how.
- *New market, new technology*: the risks increase and we find the characteristics for a strategy of diversification.

When considering product 'newness', it is important to distinguish between products 'new-to-the-world' and 'new-to-the-company'. Booz *et al.* (1982) established the following typology, based on a study of 700 companies and 13 000 new industrial and consumer products.

New-to-the-world products	10 per cent
New product lines	20 per cent
Additions to existing product lines	26 per cent
Improvements in/revisions to existing products	26 per cent
Repositionings	7 per cent
Cost reductions	11 per cent

Note that a small percentage of innovations is new-to-the-world (10 per cent), while the majority of innovations (70 per cent) essentially involve line extensions or modifications of existing products.

Choffray and Dorey (1983, p. 9) propose a classification based on the nature of the changes in the physical or perceptual characteristics. The proposed distinctions are as follows:

- *Original products*: products whose physical as well as perceptual characteristics are defined in new terms.
- *Reformulated products*: products whose physical characteristics have been redefined while leaving the basic perceptual characteristics unchanged.
- *Repositioned products*: the way in which the potential buyer

perceives the product is modified, thus only changing the perceptual dimensions.

The two preceding classifications are complementary. The latter one suggested by Choffray and Dorey describes more precisely the notions of reformulated versus repositioned products, recalling that a product is viewed by the potential buyer as a 'bundle of attributes', including both physical and perceptual dimensions. However, this typology does not clarify the extent of risk involved as well as the former.

Technological versus commercial innovations

A second classification of innovations deals with the intrinsic nature of the new idea. Based on this, we distinguish between commercial and technological innovations.

Technological innovation deals with the physical characteristics of the product, whether at the level of the manufacturing process (float glass), the use of a new ingredient (steel cord in radial tyres), the use of a new primary material (polyurethane foam), completely new products (composite materials), new finished products (compact disc), new physical conditioning of the product (instant coffee) or complex new systems (the TGV or high speed train).

The technological innovation results in the application of exact sciences for industrial practices. These innovations usually come from the laboratories or the R&D department. Some of these innovations require a lot of technology and capital (nuclear industry, space industry), while others require a lot of technology and very little capital (consumer electronic industry).

Commercial innovation deals mostly with the modes of organization, distribution and communication inherent in the commercialization process of a product or service. For example, the new presentation of a product (paperback books), a new means of distribution (cash and carry), a new advertising medium (posters at bus stops), a new combination of aesthetics and function (Swatch watches), a new application of an existing product, a new system of payment (credit card) or a new way of selling (telemarketing).

Thus commercial innovation deals with all that is linked to getting the product from the manufacturer to the end user. It also results in the application of the human sciences. In this sense, it is organizational in nature and does not concern itself specifically with scientific and technical progress. Commercial innovation examines matters of imagination, creativity and know-how more so than those of financial resources. Often these innovations require very little capital outlay and technology. However, some commercial innovations may require considerable financial resources, like the installation of a computerized banking network.

Admittedly, the boundary between these two types of innovation is blurred in the sense that technological innovations sometimes lead to commercial innovations. For example, the progress achieved in information technology has led to the development of credit cards which have revolutionized systems of payment and sales. The inverse is also true: certain organizational changes encourage technological innovations. For example, the generalization of self-service in distribution contributed to the development of scanning and computerized banking systems.

Technological innovations are generally considered 'heavier' i.e. they require greater financial means and are therefore more risky. Commercial innovations are generally 'lighter' and less risky, but also more easily copied.

Market-pull versus technology-push innovations

Concerning technological innovations, the degree of risk will vary according to the origin of the idea of the new product. A distinction can be made between a *market-pull* product, i.e. one that directly answers observed needs, or a *technology-push* product, i.e. one that results from research and technological opportunities.

A synthesis of American and European contributions in the area of innovations, notably in the industrial sectors, reveals that (Urban *et al.*, 1987, p. 23):

- About 60–80 per cent of successful products in many industries have been developed in response to market demand and needs.
- Consumer-based innovations often result in better sales growth.

These observations suggest that consumer needs and demand are a prime source of successful products. Thus, while a proactive strategy must include research and development, it must also have a strong marketing component that is critical to the successful development of new products.

> R&D isn't worth anything alone, it has to be coupled with the market. The innovative firms are not necessarily the ones that produce the best technological output, but the ones that know what is marketable (E. Mansfield, published in *Business Week*, June 8, 1976).

Fundamental versus applied research

On the other hand, an innovation strategy based on fundamental research, however risky it may be in the short term, may unleash the opportunity for a technological breakthrough. This could place the firm at a considerable advantage, with an advanced technology that the competition would have a difficult time catching up with. This brings up the argument that was touched on in Chapter 1, which dealt with the limitations of the marketing concept. A new product strategy which is based solely on the needs felt and expressed by the market inevitably leads to innovations which are less revolutionary, but also less risky, and which are therefore viewed as more attractive (Bennett and Cooper, 1979).

Therefore it is important to keep a balance between these two innovation strategies. An emphasis on applied research versus fundamental research can lead to a technological disadvantage from which it is difficult to recover. For example, the R&D strategy adopted by Japan (Mihaies, 1983) bears fruit, as is evidenced by the rapid improvement in Japan's high-technology industry.

Degree of newness to the market place

A third classification of innovations places emphasis on the degree of newness to the market place. A distinction is made between 'radical' or breakthrough innovations and 'relative' innovations. The originality of the concept results from the newness of the concept, as well as the technology used to produce the innovation (see Table 10.3). The concept or the technology can be classified as traditional, improved or brand new. Obviously, the closer one moves to the bottom right-hand corner of the table, the riskier the innovation.

Technology plays a key role in the competitive game. The acceleration of technological change has made it increasingly important to evaluate the strategic role that these technologies play. A study conducted by Arthur D. Little has suggested that there is a distinction between key technologies, basic technologies and emerging technologies (Ader, 1983).

- *Key technologies* are those put to use by a company and which have a major impact on the firm's competitive performance, expressed in terms of the quality of the product or productivity.
- *Basic technologies* are those which are readily available and no longer constitute the foundation for competition.
- *Emerging technologies* are those which are still in the experimental stage, but which could play a part in changing the basis of competition.

Note that these distinctions are not intrinsically linked to the relevant technologies, but rather to the way in which they are used in an industry. For example, computer-aided design (CAD) is now a key technology in the automobile industry, an emerging technology in the textile industry and a basic technology in aeronautics.

Table 10.3 Assessing the innovation intensity

Technology	Product concept		
	Traditional	Improved	New
Traditional			
Improved	_Increasing risks_		
Breakthrough			⟶

Taking the technological dimension into consideration in planning a strategy allows one to assign priorities with respect to technological choices. Ideally, competitive firms should always (a) aim to control all their key technologies, (b) be involved in at least one of the emerging technologies of the industry and (c) be ready to reduce and even to divest its basic technologies.

High-technology marketing

As emphasized in Chapter 2, the pace of technological change has considerably accelerated in recent years, and technology-push innovations have become the major source of competitive advantage in many fast growing markets. A question often raised is whether the marketing of high-technology innovations—or high-technology marketing—is different from traditional marketing?

High-technology industries have specific characteristics which differentiate them from more classic industrial sectors. They are science-intensive activities in continuous change, leading to unexpected applications often ahead of expressed market needs, striding across the boundaries of economic activity and upsetting the established balance of existing industrial sectors.

- *Shorter product life cycles.* Most industrial products have 10- to 15-year life cycles, while high-technology products rarely last more than three to five years. Moreover, copying and 'reverse engineering' from competition is common practice. Thus, speed in market development is a strategic issue.
- *Creative supply.* It is rarely clear where fundamental research will lead, and innovations are often impossible to predict. At the early stage of an emerging technology, it is not even apparent where the new technology will find applications. Once the technology is developed, the goal is to move quickly to the market and to apply the 'meta-technology' or 'technology platform' to as many products as possible. Thus the technology creates the market.
- *Blurred competitive environment.* The market boundaries are not well defined and competitive threats can come from very different

technological horizons. Technological uncertainties remain high and entry and exit of competitors is constant. The boundaries of existing sectors or market segments are modified and one observes either regrouping of segments into a new reference market—e.g. the office automation market—or upsetting of a traditional market into specialized segments.

These characteristics of high-technology industries have implications for the new product development process, namely speed and flexibility in product development (Stalk, 1988), close cooperation with customers and systematic monitoring of the technological environment.

The dimensions of new product success or failure

The available information on the success rate of new products is limited and sometimes contradictory. In 1971, the Nielsen Research Company observed a 47 per cent success ratio of new brands in a study based on a sample of 204 new products from the health and beauty aids (106), household (24) and grocery (74) markets. In a similar study done in 1962, but based on a smaller sample of 103 new brands, the observed success ratio was 54.4 per cent (*The Nielsen Researcher*, 1971, p. 6).

Urban *et al.* (1987, p. 41), summarizing the work of Mansfield and Wagner (1975) to determine the likelihood of a new product's success, showed that, given an identified opportunity, the probability of market success of new consumer products is 16 per cent. This compares with 27 per cent for industrial products. Their analysis also shows (for consumer goods) that there is a 16 per cent chance of a raw, untested idea succeeding in the market, but a 70 per cent chance of success if tested. This gain in confidence (54 per cent) is achieved at the expense of time and money. These authors do point out that success rates vary according to sectors.

From the study performed by Booz *et al.* (1982), one can deduce that the observed success rate in 1981 was 57 per cent, as compared with the 37 per cent figure observed in the same study done in 1968, a 54 per cent improvement (Booz *et al.*, 1982, p. 15).

Obviously, the estimations widely fluctuate. In the best cases, the probability of success is a little better than one in two. This implies that investing a large proportion of available funds in R&D and spending a great deal on commercialization are unproductive. (In other words, there is no correlation between large investments in R&D commercial spending and the success rate of a product.)

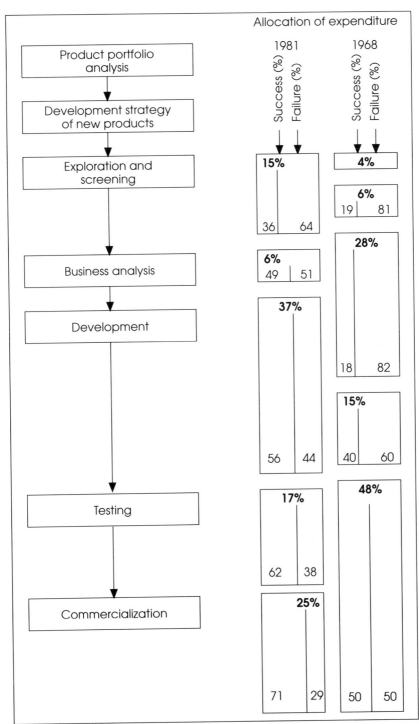

Figure 10.1 The new product development process (Booz *et al.*, 1982)

Effective management of an innovation

Booz *et al.* also analysed the success rate of innovations at different
stages of the new product development process. As seen in Figure
10.1, this process is composed of five stages. The observed success
and failure rates from both the 1968 and 1981 studies are represented.

On examining the data, one can observe that the success rate
increases continuously from 36 per cent in the first phase to 71 per
cent in the fifth phase. This implies that the evaluation process was
effective. It is also instructive to compare these data with the same
observations found in the 1968 study. It reveals that the selection
process has become more discriminating, as the probability for
success in the last phase rose from 50 per cent in 1968 to 70 per cent in
1981. This improvement in new product selection is probably due to
the change in spending distribution from 1968 to 1981. In other
words, a different proportion of money was spent during each phase.

Indeed, one can observe that a large proportion of resources was
spent during the first phases (21 per cent in phases 1 and 2 during
1981, as compared with 10 per cent in 1968). In contrast, 37 per cent of
resources were spent in phase 3 in 1981, compared with 28 per cent in
1968). On the other hand, 25 per cent of resources were allocated to
the commercial phase in 1981, as compared with 48 per cent in 1968.

These data suggest that the companies have increased upfront
strategic marketing analysis while reducing the share of the total
expended on commercialization efforts.

> Companies that have excellent records of successful new product
> introductions conduct more analyses early in the process and focus their
> idea and concept generation. And they conduct more rigorous screening
> and evaluation of the ideas generated (Booz *et al.*, 1982, p. 12).

This gain in new product management effectiveness is dramatically
represented in Figure 10.2, which compares the mortality rate of new
product ideas in 1968 and 1981. The data were taken from the 1982
study performed by Booz *et al.*

In 1968, on average, out of 58 new product ideas, 12 passed the initial
filtering test. Of these 12, seven remained after an extensive study of
their profitability potential. Only three of these went on to the
product development stage, two to market testing and only one was a
commercial success. It can therefore be concluded that 58 new
product ideas were considered for every successful new product.

In 1981, as a result of increased attention to the market and of
increased sophistication in segmenting the market, only seven ideas
were required to generate one successful new product.

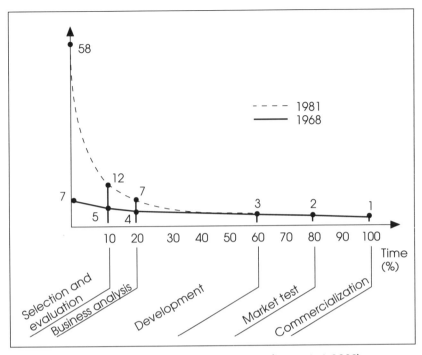

Figure 10.2 Mortality curve of new product ideas (Booz *et al.*, 1982)

Increased strategic marketing is therefore profitable for the company, since it improves the productivity of its investments in the conception and development phases. This allows the company to reduce its spending in operational marketing in the launching and commercialization.

Success factors of new products

Analysing the factors which explain the success or failure of innovations is particularly instructive and confirms the preceding conclusions. Several available studies, done in both the USA and Europe, have produced results which are remarkably similar.

Cooper's study

Cooper (1979) analysed the causes of success and failure of 195 industrial products. Of these products, 102 were considered successful by the company, while 93 were considered failures. The factors identified, along with their corresponding weights, are presented in Figure 10.3. Three success factors or dimensions appear to be the keys to success:

- *Product uniqueness and superiority to competing products*, i.e.

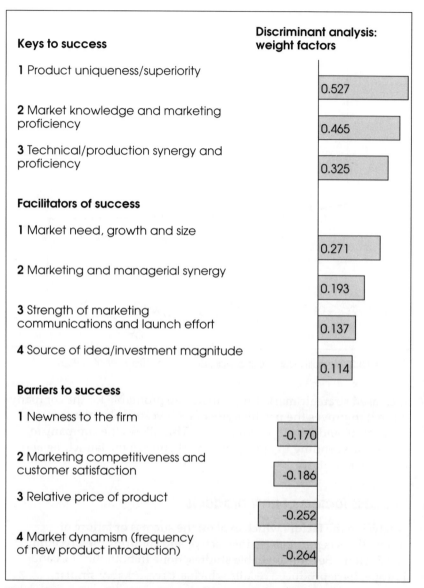

Figure 10.3 Determinants of new product success (Cooper, 1979)

existence of distinctive qualities allowing for the conception of superior products for the user.

● *Market knowledge and marketing proficiency:* detailed market potential study, well targeted sales force and distribution, test market and trial prior to launching and a market orientation.

● *Technical and production synergy and proficiency:* a good fit between the engineering and design skills of the firm and the requirements of the project.

Cooper's study shows that two out of three key factors directly relate to the quality of strategic marketing, which plays here a crucial role in the success of an innovation. The observed success rate for new products that perform well in one of the above three dimensions are 82 per cent, 79.5 per cent and 64 per cent, respectively. Moreover, if a new product is strong in all three dimensions, it has a success rate of 90 per cent; if it is weak in all three areas, the success rate is 7 per cent (Cooper, 1981, p. 75).

It is also important to emphasize that these three key success factors are all under the firm's control. Thus, success is directly determined by the quality of management and not just by chance, nor by the situation or by the environment the firm is facing. The message is clearly: 'It matters not what situation you face; it matters more what you do about it'.

The French CNME study

A French study done by the CNME (Caisse Nationale des Marches de l'Etat) analysed the principle reasons for the failure of new products and came to the same conclusions (Daudé, 1980, p. 44). The principal causes for failure that were identified, along with the frequency of occurrence, are presented in Table 10.4.

Table 10.4 The causes of new product failures (Daudé, 1980, pp. 38–48)

Causes for failure	Frequency of occurrence	
1 Superficial market analysis		50%
	(of which)	
• Underestimation of delays in distributing the product on the market	60%	
• Overestimation of the size or resources of the potential market	40%	
2 Production problems		38%
	(of which)	
• Difficulties in moving from the prototype to the test market	50%	
• Difficulties in final product development	50%	
3 Insufficient financial resources		7%
4 Commercialization problems		5%
	Total:	100%

Note here again that market knowledge is a much more basic factor than massive advertising, promotion and selling efforts behind the new product. The 'upfront' activities, i.e. those activities that precede the usual selling and launching efforts, have a vital role to play in a market-oriented new product process.

Davidson's study in the UK

The statistical study done by Davidson (1976) of a series of new products or new brands launched in the UK market largely confirms the results observed by Cooper. Analysing 100 new consumer products belonging to 38 categories which were launched between 1960 and 1970 in Great Britain, of these brands, 50 were successes and 50 were failures. Davidson (1976) identifies three factors of success:

- *Significant price or performance advantage.* Of the successes, 74 per cent offered the consumer better performance at the same or higher price, while only 20 per cent of the failures fitted this category.
- *Significant difference from existing brands.* The study revealed a close correlation between a brand's success and its distinctiveness. Out of the 50 successes, 68 per cent were dramatically or very different from existing products.
- *New, untried idea.* In 18 UK grocery categories largely developed since 1945, the pioneer company was still market leader in 12 cases.

The rules for developing a successful new brand are therefore simple and uncontroversial: (a) offer consumers better value for money than existing brands do, (b) ensure that your new brand has an important point of difference, and, if possible, (c) be there first with a new idea (Davidson, 1976, p. 120). For another view on new brand performance see Saunders (1990).

The Booz, Allen and Hamilton study in the USA

One last study, the previously mentioned Booz *et al.* study (1982) identified the following factors as contributing to the success of new products:

Product fit with market needs	85 per cent
Product fit with internal functional strengths	62 per cent
Technological superiority of product	52 per cent
Top management support	45 per cent
Use of new product process	33 per cent
Favourable competitive environment	31 per cent
Structure of new product organization	15 per cent

The two most important factors in successful new product

introductions are the fit of the product with market needs and with internal functional strengths. Having a technologically superior product, receiving support from top management and using a multiple step new product process are additional factors contributing to new product success. The relative importance of these factors, however, varies significantly by industry and by type of product being introduced.

Organization of the new product development process

The data presented in the previous section illustrate the high risk involved in launching a new activity. This risk may be reduced, however, by implementing a systematic evaluation and development procedure for new products. The key success factors are those which are controllable by the company. The purpose of this section is to examine the procedures and organizational methods which reduce the risk of failure throughout the innovation process. The objective is to organize a systematic and continuous dialogue between the relevant functions within an organization, i.e. R&D, marketing, operations and finance. In a market-driven company, developing a new product is a cross-functional effort which involves the entire organization.

A workable organizational structure

If it is true that top management bears the final say in decisions concerning new product launches, it remains that an organizational structure with specific responsibilities is essential in managing and coordinating the entire innovation process. Different organizational structures are possible. Large companies have created 'new product management' functions or 'new product departments', as Nestlé, Colgate Palmolive, Johnson & Johnson and General Foods have done.

Light organizational structures

A more flexible solution, which is available to all companies regardless of their size, is the 'new products committee' or 'venture team' in charge of a specific project.

A *new products committee* is a permanent group of persons which meets periodically, say, once a month. It is composed of individuals from different functions (e.g. R&D, operations, marketing, finance and human resources). Ideally, it is presided over by the Managing Director, whose responsibility is to organize and to manage the

development process of a new product from its conception to its
launching.

'Self-organizing project teams' or 'venture teams' are groups formed
for the development of a specific project (task force). This group is
composed of people from various departments, from which they are
temporarily separated, either completely or partially. This allows
better concentration on the creation of a new activity.

No matter which organizational structure is adopted, the most
important thing is a structure open to the ideas of new activities. The
objective is to institutionalize a new products' preoccupation within
the company and to do so in a way which is flexible and favours an
entrepreneurial approach to problems.

Sequential versus parallel development processes

Two processes are currently adopted by innovative companies, the
sequential or the parallel development process. The *sequential
development* process, evidenced by the Booz, Allen and Hamilton
study (1982), is where the project moves step by step from one phase
to the next: concept development and testing, feasibility analysis,
prototype development, market test and production. The whole
process is described in Figure 10.4.

The merits of the sequential approach have already been discussed.
But although it contributes to reducing the new product failure rate,
it also has some shortcomings. First, the sequential process in itself
leaves little room for integration since each functional specialist
passes the project to the next one. The move to the next phase is done
only after all the requirements of the preceding phase are satisfied. A
bottleneck in one phase can slow or even block the entire process.
Moreover, this product planning process is slow and requires long
lead times. It avoids errors, but at large cost in terms of time.
Changes in the market, entry of new competitors and risk of copying
often result in a product arriving too late in the market. Thus long
lead times can very well increase rather than reduce the risk of
failure. This will be particularly important for high-technology
products, where speed is a key success factor.

The *parallel development process* advocated by Takeuchi and Nonaka
(1986) speeds the process by relying on self-organizing project teams
whose members work together from start to finish. Under this
organizational scheme, the process development process emerges
from the constant interaction of a multidisciplinary team. Rather
than moving in defined, highly structured stages, the process is born
out of the team members' interplay. One of the potential benefits of
the parallel development process is the overlapping of the tasks

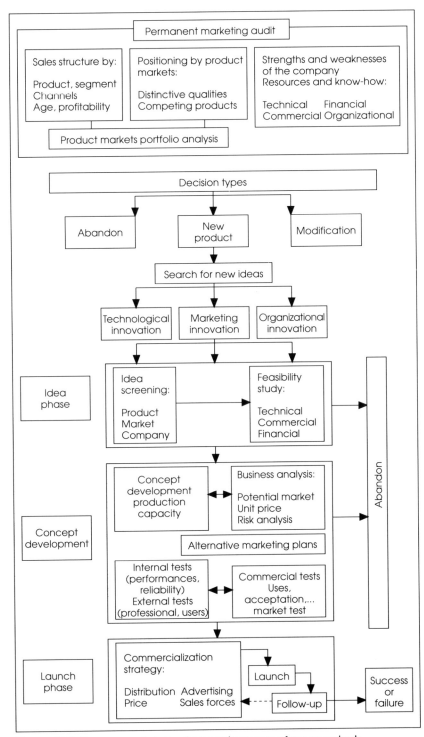

Figure 10.4 The sequential development process of new products

assumed by the different departments. While design engineers are still designing the product, production people can intervene to make sure that the design is compatible with production scale economies and marketing people can work on the positioning platform to communicate to the market. For a detailed discussion of the main characteristics of this approach, see Takeuchi and Nonaka (1986).

Idea generation

Naturally, the development process for innovation begins with researching new product ideas which are in line with the chosen development strategy. Some companies adopt an empirical approach to this problem, relying on a spontaneous stream of ideas originating from external and internal sources. However, the mortality rate of these ideas is very high; therefore, it is essential to feed on new ideas regularly. Generally, ideas, especially good ones, do not happen by themselves; organization and stimulation are needed to generate them. A company may use different methods for collecting ideas. These methods try to anticipate the change in needs and not simply respond to the demands expressed by the market. This is a 'proactive' versus a 'reactive' approach.

A creative idea is nothing but an unexpected combination of two or more concepts. Creativity can therefore be defined as 'the intellectual exercise of linking information in an unpredictable way so as to produce a new arrangement'.

Methods which are likely to stimulate creativity can be grouped into two categories: unstructured and structured methods. *Unstructured methods* are essentially based on imagination and intuition. These methods are usually implemented in the form of 'creativity groups', relying on the hypothesis that a group of individuals is usually more creative than a person working alone. This assumption is based on the synergy effect or the interaction between group members.

Creativity groups and brainstorming

Brainstorming is probably the most popular method, mostly because it is easy to organize. The only goal of a brainstorming session is to produce as many ideas as possible. Six to ten participants with diverse backgrounds and experience, from both within and outside the company, are gathered together and are given the objective of generating the greatest possible number of ideas on a particular theme in a spontaneous manner. The major rules governing a brainstorming session, according to Osborn (1963, p. 156), are the following:

- No evaluation of any kind is permitted, since criticism and judgement may cause people to defend their ideas rather than generate new and creative ones.

- Participants should be encouraged to think of the wildest ideas possible.
- Encourage a large number of ideas.
- Encourage participants to build upon or modify the ideas of others, as combinations or modifications of previously suggested ideas often lead to new ideas that are superior to those that sparked them.

This type of exercise is usually very effective; it is not out of the ordinary for a group to generate more than 100 ideas during a brainstorming session. Another somewhat more structured method is synectics (Gordon, 1965).

Psychologists do not unanimously agree with the hypothesis that a group of individuals is more creative than isolated individuals working alone (Taylor *et al.*, 1958). Structured 'expert-based' methods for idea generation use a systematic analysis of either product characteristics or product use.

Methods of functional analysis

The rationale behind functional analysis methods is that a product's users can provide useful information on how the product could be modified and improved.

Problem/opportunity analysis starts with the consumer. It is linked to the study of user behaviour in order to identify the kinds of problems a user may encounter during use of the product. Every problem or difficulty brought up could give rise to a new idea for improvement or modification. This modification is frequently used in industrial market studies with a panel of user clients.

The 'attribute listing' method has the same objectives as problem analysis, but instead of examining how the consumer uses the product, it examines the characteristics of the product itself. The method consists of establishing a list of the principal characteristics and then recombining them in such a way as to create some improvement. Osborn defined a list of questions intended to stimulate ideas for new products.

Can the product be used in any new way? What else is like the product and what can be learned from this comparison? How can the product be changed in meaning, function, structure, use pattern? What can be added to the product? To make it stronger, longer, thicker, etc.? What to delete? What to subtract, how to make it smaller, condensed, lower, shorter, lighter, etc.? (Osborn, 1963, pp. 286–7).

Morphological analysis consists of identifying the most important structural dimensions of a product and then examining the relationship between these dimensions in order to discover new and interesting combinations.

Suppose we are studying a cleaning product. The six key structural dimensions are as follows: product support (brush, rag, sponge etc.), ingredients (alcohol, ammonia, disinfectant etc.), things to be cleaned (glass, carpet, sinks, walls, cars etc.), substance to be got rid of (grease, dust, blood, paint, etc.), product texture (cream, powder, salt, liquid etc.), and packaging (box, bottle, aerosol, bag etc.). Paired combinations of these dimensions are evaluated and considered in terms of their potential value as new products.

A last method for idea generation must be added, one that is old but very effective: the 'suggestion box'. This can prove to be very helpful if certain rules are followed. Two rules are particularly important: follow up promptly on the proposed ideas and provide a complete recognition system to motivate employees.

There are other and varied methods for idea generation. Systematic analysis of competitive products through 'reverse engineering' is also widely used. For a more exhaustive description of these methods, see Wind (1982, Chapter 9). The most important objective for a firm is to keep a permanent portfolio of new product ideas which is sizeable enough to allow the firm to face the competition in an environment where innovation is omnipresent.

Idea screening

The objective of the second stage in the development process is to screen the ideas generated in order to eliminate the ones that are incompatible with the company's resources or objectives or simply unattractive to the firm. The purpose is to spot and drop unfeasible ideas as soon as possible. This is therefore an evaluation phase which presupposes the existence of criteria for choice. The goal of this screening is not to do an in-depth analysis, but rather to make a quick, inexpensive, internal evaluation about which projects merit further study and which should be abandoned. Therefore this is not yet a feasibility study, but simply a preliminary evaluation.

Typically, the new product committee is in the best position to do the screening. A single and effective method is the *evaluation grid* which has the following basic principles:

- An exhaustive inventory of all the key success factors (KSF) in each functional area: marketing, finance, production and R&D.
- Each factor or group of factors is weighted to reflect its relative importance.

Indicators	New product idea				Score
	Scores				**Not relevant**
Attractiveness	*Very good*	*Good*	*Weak*	*Very weak*	
1 Market trend		Growing	Stable	Declining	
2 Product life	10 years plus	5–10 years	3–5 years	2–3 years	
3 Spread of diffusion	Very fast	Fast	Slow	Very slow	
4 Market size (volume)	> 10000 T	5000–10000 T	1000–<5000 T	1000 T	
5 Market size (value)	1 billion	500 million–1 billion	100 million–500 million	> 100 million	
6 Buyer's needs	Net met	Poorly met	Well met	Very well met	
7 Receptivity of distribution	Enthusiastic	Positive	Reserved	Reluctant	
8 Advertising support required	Weak support	Moderate support	Important support	Very important support	
9 Market accessibility	Very easy	Easy	Difficult	Very difficult	
Competitiveness					
1 Product's appeal	Very high	High	Moderate	Weak	
2 Distinctive qualities	Exclusivity	Major distinctive quality	Weak distinctive quality		
3 Strength of competition	Very weak	Weak	High	Very high	
4 Duration of exclusivity	> 3 years	1–3 years	−1 year	−6 months	
5 Compatibility with current products	Very good	Good	Weak	Very weak	
6 Level of price	Lower price	Slightly lower	Equal price	Higher price	
7 Compatibility with distribution	Fully compatible	Easily compatible	Compatible but difficult	New demand	
8 Capacity of the sales force	Very good	Good	Weak	Very weak	
9 Level of quality	Clearly superior	Superior	Same	Inferior	

Figure 10.5 Example of a new product screening grid (MDA Consulting Group)

- Each new product idea is scored against each KSF by the judges of the new product committee.
- A desirability or performance index is calculated.

This procedure ensures that all the important factors have been systematically and equally considered and that the objectives and constraints of the company have been attended to.

When computing the performance index, it is preferable to adopt a 'conjunctive method' and not a simple weighted average procedure (compensatory approach). As seen in Chapter 5, the conjunctive method does not result in a global score, but aids in identifying ideas which are or are not compatible with the company's objectives or resources. The conjunctive approach presupposes that a maximum and minimum level of performance for each project has been specified. Only those ideas which satisfy each specified threshold are retained.

Several standard evaluation grids exist in the marketing literature, the most well known being that of O'Meara (1961). Such checklists provide a useful guideline for ideas evaluation. Ideally, an evaluation grid should be tailor-made and be adapted to the company's own needs. It is up to the new product committee to establish an appropriate structure which reflects the corporate objectives and the unique situational factors of the firm. Figure 10.5 shows an evaluation grid used in a consumer goods company to evaluate the marketing feasibility of new product ideas. Similar grids have been developed for the other functions: R&D, production and finance.

Concept development

At this phase of the development process, we move from 'product ideas' to 'product concepts'. The ideas, having survived to the screening phase, are now defined in more elaborated terms. A product concept can thus be defined as 'A written description of the *physical and perceptual characteristics* of the product and of the *'package of benefits'* (the promise) it represents for identified *target group(s)* of potential buyers'.

This is more than a simple technological description of the product, since the product's benefits to the potential user are emphasized. The product concept definition highlights the notion of a product as a bundle of characteristics or attributes. In defining the concept, a company is forced to be explicit in its strategic options and market objective.

A clear and precise definition of the product concept is important in many respects:

- The concept definition describes the *positioning sought* for the product and therefore defines the means required to achieve the expected positioning.
- The product concept is a kind of *specification manual* for R&D, whose job it is to examine the technical feasibility of the concept.
- The description of the product's promise serves as a *briefing* for the advertising agency who is in charge of communicating the new product's claims to the marketplace.

Thus, the product concept defines the *reference product market* in which the future product should be positioned. Four questions come to mind:

- Which attributes or product characteristics do potential buyers react favourably to?
- How are competitive products perceived with regard to these attributes?

- What niche could the new product occupy, considering the target segment and the positions held by competition?
- What are the most effective marketing means that will achieve the desired positioning?

Perceptual maps describing the positioning of competing brands in the reference market are useful here. The answers to these questions presuppose the existence of a fine-tuned market segmentation which is able to quantify the size of the potential market.

Concept testing

Concept testing represents the first investment (other than managerial time) a firm has to make in the development process. It consists of submitting a description of the new product concept to an appropriate group of targets users to measure the degree of acceptance.

The product concept description may be done in one of two ways: neutrally i.e. with no 'sell', or by a mock advertisement which presents the concept as if it were an existing product. The former is easier to do and avoids the pitfall of the inevitable and uncontrollable creative element inherent in an advertisement. The advantage of the advertisement, however, is that it more accurately reproduces the buying atmosphere of a future product and is therefore more realistic.

The following descriptions illustrate 'neutral' and 'advertising' forms of concept testing, respectively, for a new dessert topping.

> Here is a new dessert topping made of fruit and packaged in a spray can. It comes in four flavours: strawberry, cherry, apricot and redcurrant. It can be used in cakes, puddings and frozen desserts.

> Here is a new delicious fruit topping for desserts conveniently packaged in a spray can. These new toppings will enhance the desserts you serve your family. Your choice among four flavours—strawberry, cherry, apricot and redcurrant—will certainly embellish all your desserts including cakes, puddings, frozen desserts and more.

Twenty to fifty people with varying socio-demographic profiles are gathered to assess the degree of concept acceptance. They are shown slides or videos on the new concept and asked to react to it with questions similar to those presented in Table 10.5.

Obviously, the key question in Table 10.5 is the one dealing with intentions to buy (question 5). A score of positive intentions (i.e. 'would definitely buy' and 'would probably buy' responses grouped together) that adds up to less than 60 per cent is generally considered insufficient, at least in the field of consumer goods.

Table 10.5 Key questions in concept testing (Kotler, 1991, p. 325)

- Are the benefits clear to you and believable?
- Do you see this product as solving a problem or filling a need for you?
- Do other products currently meet this need and satisfy you?
- Is the price reasonable in relation to the value?
- Would you (definitely, probably, probably not, definitely not) buy the product?
- Who would use this product, and how often would it be used?

Predictive value of intentions

Results from concept testing should be interpreted with care, especially when the concept is very new. Consumers are asked to express their interest in a product which they have never seen or used. They are therefore often unable to judge whether or not they would like the new product. Numerous products which received mediocre scores during the concept testing phase actually turned out to be brilliant successes. Inversely, expensive failures were avoided using concept testing.

Measuring intention to buy is not always the best indication of the respondents' degree of conviction regarding a new product's ability to solve problems or to satisfy unmet needs. Yet, this is clearly a key success factor. In a test situation, respondents may express a willingness to purchase a new product out of simple curiosity or concern for keeping up with the latest innovation, or a need for variety. In light of this, scores for intention tend to overestimate the true rate of acceptance.

In order to deal with this problem, Tauber (1973) suggests using concept testing results based on measurements of perceived needs as well as of purchase interest. In an experiment on eight new product concepts, Tauber observed that virtually all the respondents who claimed that a product solved a problem or filled an unmet need had a positive intention to purchase the new product, while a considerable number of repondents who expressed purchase interest did not believe the product solved a problem or filled an unmet need. This observation suggests that overstatement of purchase intent may be simply those with curiosity to try but with little expectation of adopting. Thus, basing new product decisions on purchase intent data could be misleading in predicting the true rate of product adoption for regular use.

A more reliable way to estimate the adoption rate of a new product for regular use would be to base the decision on the percentage of

Table 10.6 Interpretation of intention-to-buy scores (Tauber, 1973)

	New product concepts							
	A	**B**	**C**	**D**	**E**	**F**	**G**	**H**
Gross intentions: Percentage of respondents with positive buying intention.	71	62	60	60	51	46	44	22
Adjusted intentions: Percentage of respondents with positive intentions and convinced of the novelty of the product.	45	37	18	19	27	37	10	19
Rate of conviction: Percentage of respondents convinced within the group with positive intentions.	63	59	30	31	53	79	26	86

people giving an affirmative answer to both questions, i.e. they do intend to buy and they are convinced that the new product solves a problem or fills an unmet need.

The adjusted purchase intent rates of Table 10.6 illustrate the argument. The ranking of the eight product concepts is significantly different from the ranking observed for the positive purchase intention.

Conjoint analysis

More elaborate approaches to concept testing may be used, including the 'conjoint analysis' which has been successfully used over the last few years (Green and Srinivasan, 1978). The distinctive value of conjoint analysis is to allow the impact of the product concept's key characteristics on product preferences, information which is not revealed by an overall reaction to the concept. The basic principles of this method were described in Chapter 4 (see p. 109–110) and an example was presented in Chapter 5 (pp. 142–145).

In concept testing, conjoint analysis helps in answering the following questions:

- What is the partial utility or *'value'* that a target group attaches to different characteristics of the product concept?
- What is the *'relative importance'* of each product characteristic?
- What kind of *'trade-offs'* are potential buyers ready to make between two or several product characteristics?
- What will be the *'share of preferences'* with regard to different

product concepts each representing a different bundle of characteristics?

The collected data are simple rankings of preference for the various concept combinations. Each concept constitutes a different assortment of characteristics. These preference data are submitted to one of the conjoint analysis algorithms and the output is partial utilities for each component of the product concept and for each individual respondent.

Conjoint analysis results provide the market analyst with four useful results:

- The identification of the *'best concept'*, i.e. the combination of concept components with the highest utilities, among all possible combinations.
- Information on what will be the *'utility or disutility of any change'* in the concept characteristics. This enables a selection of the most attractive trade-offs among concept components.
- Information on the *'relative importance'* of each component.
- Possibility of constructing *'segments'* based on the similarity of the respondents' reactions to the tested concepts.

On the basis of these results, alternative scenarios can developed and the expected share of preferences estimated in each case.

The problems raised by concept testing are usually less subtle in industrial markets, since industrial clients' needs are generally more clearly specified. Moreover, the respondent is a professional, and trade-off analysis is a more natural way of thinking. Conjoint analysis has many applications within industrial markets. For an interesting application see the Clarke Equipment case (Clarke, 1987).

To illustrate the contribution of conjoint analysis, let us examine the following example. The product studied is a hairspray, targeted to the Belgian market and defined in terms of the following five characteristics:

- *Design*: two designs are considered: the existing one and a new one.
- *Product's claim*: 'styling spray', 'extra strong hair spray' or 'fixing spray'.
- *Price*: three price levels are considered; 109, 129 and 149 Belgian francs.
- *Product range*: the product may be offered singly or included in a range comprising a gel, a mousse and a styling cream.
- *Brand*: the brand may be A, B or C.

These variables give a total of 108 possible combinations for new product concepts ($2 \times 3 \times 3 \times 2 \times 3$). Using a fractional factorial

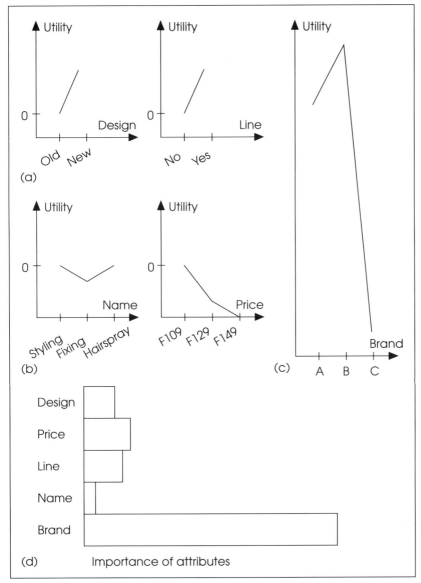

Figure 10.6 Example of conjoint analysis: hairspray products (Rochet, 1987)

design we can reduce the number of concepts to be tested to 18. All pertinent information on each of the characteristics is retained, but information on interactions of orders greater than 2 is lost. In order to estimate partial utilities, regression analysis is conducted, using binary variables (0,1) for describing the presence or absence of the product characteristics at each level. Figure 10.6 shows the average utility curves obtained from the sample examined.

The results show that consumers are very sensitive to the brand name and that they noticeably prefer brand B to the other brands. They also show the price elasticity to be -0.81. The new design is also clearly preferred over the old one. With regard to the product's claim, there appears to be very little sensitivity on the part of the respondents, who probably understand the claim poorly (Rochet, 1987).

Business analysis and marketing programming

Once the product concept has been developed and accepted by top management, it is up to the marketing department to quantify the market opportunity and to develop alternative marketing programmes. This implies sales forecasting and market penetration objectives under different marketing budgets. The economic viability of the new product within the chosen time horizon must be assessed and the risk of the new venture evaluated.

Estimating sales volume

Estimating the sales projection for the first three years is the first problem to examine, which will condition the rest of the analysis. Given estimates of total potential sales in the target segment, what will be the expected sales volume or market share of the new product under different assumptions regarding the size of the marketing efforts? Different methods to approach this question can be used: subjective methods, feasibility studies and methods based on a test market.

- *Subjective methods* rely on the marketing information system of the firm, but also on experience, judgement and on information accumulated more or less informally within the firm. This accumulated knowledge is based on sales history of similar products, on information from distributors, on the sales force, on comparison with competing products etc.
- *Feasibility studies* aim to gather the missing information in the field by interviewing directly potential users, distributors, retailers etc. Purchasing intention scores are collected and used to estimate sales volume.
- *Market tests* allow for observation of buyer behaviour in the real world. Trial and repeat purchase rates can be estimated and used for early projection of sales. Alternatives to market tests are in-home use tests, mini-test panels, laboratory experiments and regional introduction (see Wind, 1982, Chapter 14).

These three methods are not exclusive and may be used jointly where uncertainty and the degree of newness for the company are high. Regardless of the approach adopted, the marketing department needs to set a sales revenue objective and to estimate whether sales will be high enough to generate an acceptable profit to the firm.

Typical sales patterns

The new product sales pattern over time will differ according to whether it is a one-time purchase product, a durable good or a frequently purchased product.

For *one-time purchased products*, the expected sales curve increases steadily, peaks and then decreases progressively as the number of potential buyers diminishes. Thus, in this case, the occupation rate of the market is the key variable.

For *durable goods*, total demand can be subdivided into two parts: first equipment demand and replacement demand. First equipment demand is time dependent and determined by income variables, while replacement demand is determined by the product's obsolescence, be it technical, economic or style.

Purchases of *frequently purchased products* can be divided into two categories: first-time and repeat purchases. The number of first-time purchasers initially increases and then diminishes as the majority of potential buyers have tried the product. Repeat purchases will occur if the product meets the requirements of a group of buyers, who eventually will become loyal customers, and the total sales curve will eventually reach a plateau. In this product category, repeat purchases are the best indicator of market satisfaction.

The typical sales patterns for trial, repeat and total sales of a frequently purchased product are presented in Figure 10.7.

Panel data projection methods

In the case of frequently purchased products, the Parfitt and Collins theorem (1968) can be used to decompose market share, as shown in Chapter 5, and to generate market share projections. These measures are normally obtained from a consumer panel.

As seen before, market share can be divided into three distinct components.

- The *penetration rate* of a brand is defined as the cumulative trial, i.e. the percentage of buyers having made a trial purchase at time *t*; this rate first increases after launching and then tends to stabilize fairly rapidly as the stock of potential first-time buyers diminishes.

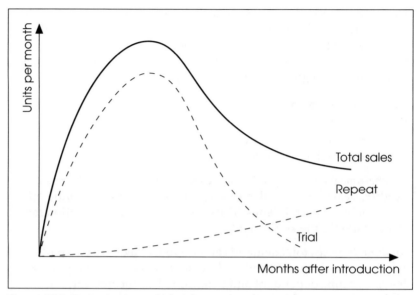

Figure 10.7 Typical sales pattern for trial and repeat sales

- The *repeat purchasing rate* is expressed as the proportion of total purchases in the product field by those buyers having tried the product. After a certain number of purchases, the repeat purchase rate will level off to some equilibrium state.
- The *intensity rate*, or buying level index, compares the rate of quantities purchased of the studied brand to the average quantities purchased within the product category. A distinction can be made here between heavy, light or average buyers (by volume) in the product field.

The expected market share is estimated by multiplying these three values, as shown on p. 150.

Suppose that the estimated rate for trial purchase is 34 per cent and that the repeat purchase rate is around 25 per cent. If the average quantities purchased are the same for the brand and the product category, the expected market share will be:

$$34\% \times 25\% \times 1.00 = 8.5\%$$

In cases of segmented markets, the expected market shares are calculated for each group. For example, the buying index level may vary according to the type of buyer. It may reach 1.20 for heavy buyers and 0.80 for light buyers. The expected market share in each of these cases will be around 10.2 per cent and 6.8 per cent, respectively.

This kind of market share projection can be quickly formulated after the first few months of launching a new product. This method also allows for measurement of the impact that advertising and promotional activities have on market share. For more on this topic, see Parfitt and Collins' seminal article (1968).

No method can estimate future sales with certainty. Therefore, it is useful to give a range of estimations, with minimum and maximum sales, in order to assess the extent of risk implied by the new product launch.

Determination of the base marketing mix

The expected level of sales for a new product will depend on the intensity and continuity of operational marketing support. The marketing programme should be described in precise terms and summarized in a projected profit and loss statement.

To illustrate this point, let us examine the case of a new, highly nutritional food product which has a variety of uses. This product can be used as a snack, a camping food or as a diet food. This illustration is based on the Newfood case developed by Eskin and Montgomery (1975, pp. 49–50). Early product and concept tests have been very encouraging, but the company has great difficulty in defining the market. It is now up to the product manager of the Newfood Corporation to analyse the economic data of the problem and to propose a marketing programme.

The product tests have led the product manager to believe that the product could easily sell 2 million cases (24 packages in a case) under the proposed marketing programme, involving a 24 cent package price and an advertising budget involving $3 million in expenditures per year. The distribution margin is 30 per cent and the direct cost for the product is $1 per case. Fixed manufacturing costs are $1 million. It is the company policy not to introduce new products with profit expectations of less than $0.5 million per year. A three-year planning horizon is usually considered.

Sales volume beyond the first year is mainly determined by the repeat purchase rate, which is difficult to estimate in this particular case. Historically, products in this category have had sales that decayed over time after the first year at a decay rate that varies with the size of marketing efforts. The average decay rate observed for similar products is 20 per cent. Third year sales would then be 80 per cent of second year sales, or equivalently, 64 per cent of first year sales. Thus total sales over all three years would be 2.44 times first year sales. This number (2.44) is called the sales multiplier or 'blow-up factor'.

Table 10.7 The Newfood case—Base Scenario: projected profit and loss statement

	Year 0	Year 1	Year 2	Year 3
1 Expected sales (cases)	—	1 925 000	1 540 000	1 232 000
2 Blow-up factor	—	1.00	0.80	0.64
3 Price	—	4.03	4.03	4.03
4 Unit cost	—	1.00	1.00	1.00
5 Gross margin	—	3.03	3.03	3.03
6 Sales revenue	—	7 757 750	6 206 200	4 964 960
7 Total gross margin	—	5 832 750	4 666 200	3 732 960
8 Marketing expenditure	—	3 000 000	3 000 000	3 000 000
9 Fixed cost	—	1 000 000	1 000 000	1 000 000
10 Gross contribution	—	1 832 750	666 200	−267 040
11 R&D expenditure	−500 000	—	—	—
12 Net cumulated contribution	−500 000	1 332 750	1 998 950	1 731 910
13 Break-even point (1st year)	—	1 485 148	—	—

A projected profit and loss statement over three years based on these assumptions and on the base marketing programme is presented in Table 10.7. On the whole, the project seems attractive and generates a $1.7 million net cumulative contribution. Note that the break-even point for the first year is around 1 500 000 cases.

Value of perfect information

The projected profit and loss statement of Table 10.7 is based on assumptions about the sales growth rate and the size of the marketing budget. Risk analysis consists in testing the sensitivity of these assumptions on expected sales and profit.

The product manager is satisfied with the sales estimate of 2 000 000 cases for the first year, although admitting that it contains some uncertainty. When pressed, however, the product manager will admit that sales could be as low as 1 million cases in the first year, but points out that sales might also exceed the estimate by as much as 1 million cases. The operational definition of these extremes is that each has no more than a 1 in 10 chance of occurring.

Using these estimates, one can derive a probability distribution for first year sales and calculate the expected value of sales. The objective is to assess the risk of having a sales volume inferior to the

Table 10.8 The Newfood case: expected value of sales and profit

Sales* Classes	Sales* Mid-point	Probability	Expected sales	Conditional payoffs*	Expected profit*
0.5–1.0	0.75	0.10	0.075	−6.455	−0.646
1.0–1.5	1.25	0.20	0.250	−2.759	−0.552
1.5–2.0	1.75	0.25	0.438	+0.938	+0.235
2.0–2.5	2.25	0.25	0.562	+4.635	+1.159
2.5–3.0	2.75	0.10	0.275	+8.331	+0.833
3.0–3.5	3.25	0.10	0.325	+12.028	+1.203
		1.00	$E(q) = 1.925$		$E(\pi) = 2.232$

* In million cases or dollars

break-even volume during the first year. The probability distribution is presented in Table 10.8.

The expected value of sales is 1 925 000 cases, which is very close to the deterministic estimation. There is, however, a 3 in 10 chance that the sales volume in the first year will fall below the break-even volume. This is a significant risk.

Risk can also be measured in financial terms by computing the value of perfect information or the cost of uncertainty. The expected value of the choice given perfect information (VPI) is obtained by computing the expected value of the best conditional payoffs of Table 10.8.

$$E(VPI) = 0.10(0) + 0.20(0) + 0.25(0.938) + 0.25(4.635) + 0.10(8.331)$$
$$+ 0.10(12.028)$$

That is,

$$E(VPI) = \$3.430 \text{ million}$$

Without perfect information, the optimal action is to go ahead, with an expected payoff of $2.232 million. Thus the expected gain from perfect information (or the uncertainty cost) is:

$$\$3.430 \text{ million} - \$2.232 \text{ million} = \$1.198 \text{ million}$$

In the Newfood case, there is the possibility of conducting a market test before proceeding with the launch. The cost will not exceed $75 000 and the test allows for a more precise estimation of the first year sales volume. The level of risk measured by the uncertainty cost suggests that postponing the decision to collect additional information should be considered by the product manager.

Comparing alternative marketing plans

There are also other marketing plans under consideration. Instead of trying to improve the precision of the first year sales forecast (often an illusive pursuit), would it not be better to try to develop a more aggressive and effective marketing programme? Several alternatives can be explored.

- Adopt a higher price, for example, 34 cents instead of 24 cents. This would support a bigger advertising budget, $6 million instead of $3 million for the first year. This strategy could induce a higher trial rate and therefore increase sales during the first year. There is a risk, however, that repeat sales will decline faster during the second year due to the higher price.
- Keep the same initial price of 24 cents, but increase the advertising budget during the second and third years so as to slow down the decline in sales after the first year.
- Try to combine the preceding two strategies by adopting a price of 29 cents and increasing the advertising budget by 50 per cent over the three years.

Each strategy has its implications for the shape of the response curve. The product manager feels that doubling the advertising will lead to 500 000 more cases sold in the first year and will increase repeat sales in the following two years. This will reduce the decay rate from 20 per cent to 15 per cent. The manager estimates, however, that a higher price of 34 cents would increase the decay rate of sales during the first year from 20 per cent to 30 per cent.

The profit and risk implications of these alternatives plans can be easily estimated by changing the price and advertising variables in the profit and loss statement. This simulation exercise is greatly facilitated through the use of spreadsheet software packages, such as *Lotus 1-2-3 Microsoft* or *Excel*.

Assessing the financial risk

For each strategy, it is important to determine as precisely as possible when the elimination of risk is supposed to occur. There are three levels of risk, identified in Figure 10.8.

- The *simple break-even point*, the moment where the new activity leaves the zone of losses and enters into the zone of profits.
- The *equilibrium break-even point*, when the present value of total receipts covers the present value of total expenses. The company has recouped its capital layout.
- The *capital acquisition point*, the point where the new activity generates a financial surplus allowing for reinvestments to prolong

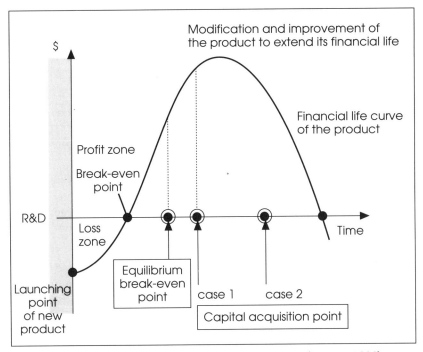

Figure 10.8 Assessing the financial risk of a new product (Daudé, 1980)

the economic life of the activity or for supporting the development of other businesses within the firm.

Ideally, the capital acquisition point should be reached before the maturity phase of the product's life cycle in order to allow the company timely redeployment, i.e. before competitive pressure begins to erode profit margins.

Total quality strategy

Quality control has traditionally been considered as a purely defensive measure whose objective was to prevent flaws in manufacturing and eliminate defective products. This function was normally included in the production department. Today, however, following the Japanese industry example, quality management is seen as a competitive weapon of great strategic importance, actively employed to gain market share. As such, quality strategy calls directly on marketing to define the expected excellence level for each of its manufactured products.

Quality from the buyer's point of view

For the buyer, a quality product does not necessarily mean a luxury good, but could simply mean a product that pleases, i.e. that fits the needs and expectations of a specific target group. Product quality can thus be defined as follows:

> The quality of a product is the degree of conformance of all of the relevant features and characteristics of the product to all of the aspects of a customer's need, limited by the price and delivery he or she will accept (Groocock, 1986, p. 27).

Comparisons in quality only make sense between products designed to meet the same needs and sold at the same price level. Buyer satisfaction is a function of the degree of conformance between the buyer's expectations of the product and the perception of the product's overall performance.

It is buyers who dictate to the company the level of excellence to be attained, as a function of their own needs. Quality management implies, above all, a knowledge of the expectations and motivations to buy of the target group. The person who buys a Renault 5 does not expect the same kind of performance from the car as does the person who purchases a Mercedes 190E. Both products, however, may be quality products in the sense that they both meet the excellence level expected by the buyers given the price paid.

Considering the diversity of needs, the level of excellence for each product must be defined for each target segment. This implies a different package of benefits or 'set of values' corresponding to the expected quality level and to the accepted price range. Thus, designing a quality strategy presupposes a market segmentation analysis.

The key dimensions of quality

We have seen that buyers perceive a product as a bundle of attributes likely to supply the core service sought as well as other added services or benefits. Quality management implies breaking down total quality into components so as to establish norms or performance standards for each component.

Garvin (1987) proposes eight dimensions or components of product quality:

- *Product or service performance*: the ability of a product to perform its basic function.
- *Proprietary features*: the range of other advantages a product offers in addition to its basic function .

- *Conformance*: adherence to norms or standards corresponding to a determined level of excellence (with a reduced tolerance margin).
- *Reliability*: the absence of failure or defective operation within a given time frame.
- *Durability*: the useful life span of a product or the frequency of product use before the product deteriorates.
- *Serviceability*: the extent, speed and efficiency of services offered before, during and after purchase.
- *Appearance or aesthetics*: the design, look, colour, taste etc. of a product (i.e. a much more subjective component).
- *Perceived quality*: the reputation or perceived image of a product or brand.

A quality control programme will consist of establishing norms for each of these components and monitoring conformance to these norms. Each of these components represents an opportunity to differentiate the product with respect to competition.

The same kind of process can be used in managing the *quality of services,* a much more complicated task because of its intangible nature (Lambin, 1987; Horowitz, 1987).

The empirical studies conducted in France (Eiglier and Langeard, 1987) and in the United States (Parasuraman *et al.*, 1985) identified ten factors which determine the perception of the quality of a service.

- *Competence* means the possession of the required skills and knowledge to perform the service.
- *Reliability* involves consistency of performance and dependability, and performing the service right the first time. It also means that the firm honours its promises.
- *Responsiveness* concerns the willingness or readiness of employees to provide service. It involves timeliness of service.
- *Accessibility* refers to both physical and psychological accessibility. Access involves approachability and ease of contact.
- *Understanding* or knowing the customer involves making the effort to understand the customer's needs.
- *Communication* means keeping customers informed in language they can understand and listening to them. It may mean that the company has to adjust its language for different customers.
- *Credibility* involves trustworthiness, believability and honesty. It involves having the customer's best interest at heart.
- *Security* is the freedom from danger, risk or doubt. It involves physical safety, financial and moral security.
- *Courtesy* involves politeness, respect, consideration and friendliness of contact personnel.
- *Tangibility* includes the physical evidence of the service: physical

facilities, appearance of personnel, physical representation of the service etc.

These ten components of service quality are somewhat redundant (Parasuraman *et al.*, 1985, Table 1, p. 47). Each organization must adapt them to its specific situation and establish quality norms which constitute commitments to customers. These norms must be measurable.

Lufthansa has just included in its service promise: 'Businessmen want to get there, not wait'. Translated into norms, this message means: 'a passenger should not wait more than thirty minutes'. This statement also induces norms for baggage checks, flight times, schedules and baggage claim (Horovitz, 1987, p. 99).

Once norms have been defined, they must be communicated and diffused throughout the company.

11
Distribution channel decisions

In most markets, the physical and psychological distance between producers and end-users is such that intermediaries are necessary to ensure an efficient matching between segments of demand and supply. Distributors and facilitating agencies are required because manufacturers are unable to assume by themselves, at a reasonable cost, all the tasks and activities implied by a free and competitive exchange process. The use of intermediaries means a loss of manufacturer control of certain distributive functions, since the firm sub-contracts activities that could, in principle, be assumed by marketing management. Thus, from the firm's point of view, channel decisions are critical decisions which involve developing a channel structure that fits the firm's strategy and the needs of the target segment. The design of a channel structure is a major strategic decision, neither frequently made nor easily changed. In this chapter, we shall first examine the channel design decisions from the manufacturer's point of view, and then analyse the type of positioning strategies available to retailers in consumer markets.

The economic role of distribution channels

A distribution channel is the structure formed by the interdependent partners participating in the process of making goods or services available for consumption or use by consumers or industrial users. These partners are the producers, intermediaries and end-users. Distribution channels are organized structures performing the tasks necessary to facilitate exchange transactions. Their role in a market economy is to bridge the gap between manufacturers and end-users by making goods available where and when they are needed and under the appropriate terms of trade. The functions of distribution channels are to create time, space and state utilities which constitute the added value of distribution (Figure 11.1).

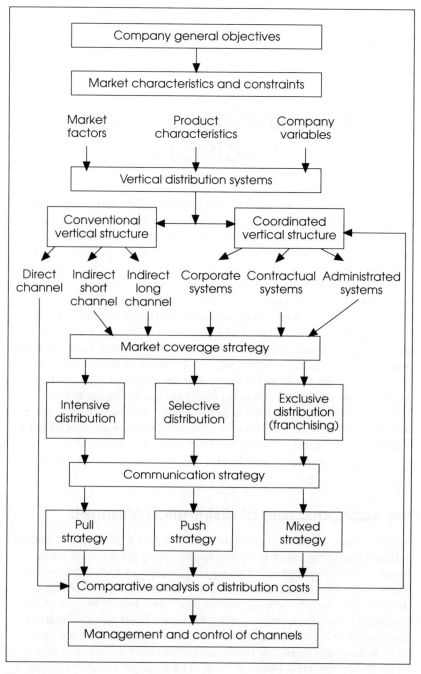

Figure 11.1 Overview of distribution channel decisions

The tasks of distribution

Many functions are provided by channels of distribution. These occur for the benefit of the producer or consumer or both. For producers, distribution channels perform seven different functions:

- *Transporting*: to make the goods available in places close to consumers or industrial users.
- *Storing*: to make the goods available at the time of consumption, thereby reducing the manufacturer's need to store its own products in company-owned warehouses.
- *Breaking of bulk*: to make the goods available in quantity or volume adapted to consumers' purchasing habits.
- *Assorting*: to constitute a selection of goods for use in association with each other and adapted to the buyer's use.
- *Contacting*: to establish personalized relationships with customers who are numerous and remote.
- *Informing*: to collect and disseminate information about market needs and about products and terms of trade.
- *Promoting*: to promote the products through advertising and promotions organized at the point of sales.

In addition to these basic functions, intermediaries also provide services such as financial credit, guarantees, delivery, repairs, maintenance, atmosphere etc. The main economic role of distribution channels is to overcome the existing disparities between demand and supply.

The distribution flows

These functions give rise to distribution flows between partners in the exchange process. Some of these flows are forward flows (ownership, physical and promotion), others are backward flows (ordering and payment), and still others move in both directions (information). The five main flows are the following:

- *Ownership flow*: the actual transfer of legal ownership from one organization to another.
- *Physical flow*: the successive movements of the physical product from the producer to the end-user.
- *Ordering flow*: the orders placed by intermediaries in the channel and forwarded to the manufacturer.
- *Payment flow*: successive buyers paying their bills through financial institutions to sellers.
- *Information flow*: the dissemination of information to the market and/or to the producer at the initiative of the producer and/or the intermediaries.

The key question in designing a channel of distribution is not whether these functions and flows need to be performed, but rather who is to perform them. These functions and the management of these distribution flows can be shifted among the channel's partners. The problem is to decide who could perform these economic functions most efficiently: the producer, the intermediary or the consumer.

The rationale for marketing channels

The distribution functions cannot be eliminated, but rather simply assumed by other more efficient channel members. Innovations in distribution channels largely reflect the discovery of more efficient ways to manage these economic functions or flows. Various sources of efficiency enable intermediaries to perform distribution functions at a lower cost than either the customer or the manufacturer could by themselves. This is particularly true for consumer goods, which are distributed to a large number of geographically dispersed customers.

Contactual efficiency

The complexity of the exchange process increases as the number of partners increases. As shown in Figure 11.2, the number of contacts required to maintain mutual interactions between all partners in the exchange process is much higher in a decentralized exchange system than in a centralized exchange system. Figure 11.2 shows that, given three manufacturers and five retailers who buy goods from each manufacturer, the number of contacts required amounts to 15. If the manufacturer sells to these retailers through one wholesaler, the number of necessary contacts is reduced to 8. Thus, a centralized system employing intermediaries is more efficient than a decentralized system of exchange, by reducing the number of transactions required for matching segments of demand and supply.

Economies of scale

By regrouping the products of several manufacturers, intermediaries can perform one or several distribution tasks more efficiently than manufacturers. For example, a wholesaler's sales representative can spread costs over several manufacturers and perform the selling function at a lower cost per manufacturer than if each firm paid its own company sales representative.

Reduction of functional discrepancies

By purchasing large volumes of goods from manufacturers, storing them and breaking them down into the volume customers prefer to purchase, wholesalers and retailers enable manufacturers and their

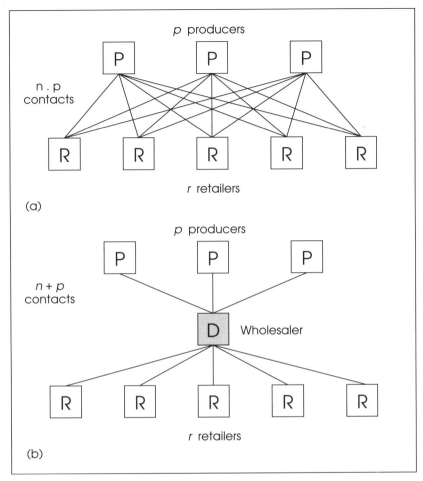

Figure 11.2 Contactual efficiency of distributors: (a) direct marketing system; (b) indirect marketing system

customers to operate at their more efficient scale. Rather than having to make small production runs to fill the orders of individual customers, manufacturers can achieve economies of scale. Similarly, their customers can buy small quantities without having their capital tied up in large inventories.

Better assortments

At the manufacturer's level, the assortment of goods produced is largely dictated by technological considerations, whereas the assortment of goods consumers usually desire is dictated by the use situation. Typically, consumers desire a limited quantity of a wide variety of goods. The role of intermediaries is to create wide assortments and to make it possible for consumers to acquire a large variety of products from a single source with one transaction. This reduces the time and effort that consumers must expend in finding the goods they need. The same economy of effort also exists on the manufacturer's side. For example, a manufacturer of a limited line of hardware items could open its own retail outlets only if it were willing to accumulate a large variety of items generally sold at this type of outlet. In general, hardware wholesalers can perform this assortment function more efficiently than individual manufacturers.

Better services

The intermediary is close to the end-users and therefore can have a better understanding of their needs and desires and adapt the assortment to local situations.

Channel design alternatives

The design of a channel structure implies decisions regarding the responsibilities to be assumed by the different participants in the exchange process. From the manufacturer's point of view, the first decision is whether or not to sub-contract certain distribution tasks and, if so, to what extent to sub-contract and under which trade conditions.

Types of intermediary

There are four broad categories of intermediary that a firm might include in the distributive network of its product: wholesalers, retailers, agents and facilitating agencies.

Wholesalers

These intermediaries sell primarily to other resellers, such as retailers or institutional or industrial customers, rather than to individual consumers. They take title of the goods they store and can provide quick delivery when the goods are ordered because they are usually located closer to customers than manufacturers. They purchase in large lots from manufacturers and resell in smaller lots to retailers. Wholesalers generally bring together an assortment of goods, usually of related items, by dealing with several sources of supply.

Retailers

Retailers sell goods and services directly to consumers for their personal, non-business use. Retailers take the ownership of the goods they carry, and their compensation is the margin between what they pay for the goods and the price they charge their customers. They can be classified in different ways; for example, according to the level of service they provide (self-service versus full service retailing) or according to their method of operation (low margin/high turnover or high margin/low turnover). Low margin/ high turnover retailers compete primarily on a price basis, while high margin/low turnover retailers focus on unique assortments, speciality goods and prestigious store image. For other classifications of retail establishments, see Rosenbloom (1978, p. 33) and Dupuis (1991).

Agents

These are functional intermediaries who do not take title of the goods with which they deal but who negotiate sales or purchases for clients or principals. They are compensated in the form of a commission on sales or purchases. They are independent business persons or freelance sales people who represent client organizations. Common types of agent include import or export agents, traders, brokers and manufacturers' representatives. Manufacturers representatives usually work for several firms and carry non-competitive, complementary goods in an exclusive territory or foreign country.

Facilitating agencies

Facilitating agencies are business firms that assist in the performance of distribution tasks other than buying, selling and transferring title. From the firm's standpoint, they are sub-contractors carrying out certain distribution tasks because of their specialization or special expertise. Common types of facilitating agencies are: transportation agencies, storage agencies, advertising agencies, market research firms, financial agencies, insurance companies etc. These agencies are involved in a marketing channel on an as-needed basis and they are compensated by commissions or fees paid for their services.

Many different types of institutions participate in a distribution channel. The channel structure will be determined by the manner in which the different distribution tasks have been allocated among the channel participants.

Configurations of a distribution channel

Distribution channels can be characterized by the number of intermediary levels that separate the manufacturer from the end-user. Figure 11.3 shows the different channel designs commonly used to distribute industrial or consumer goods. A distinction can be made between direct and indirect distribution systems.

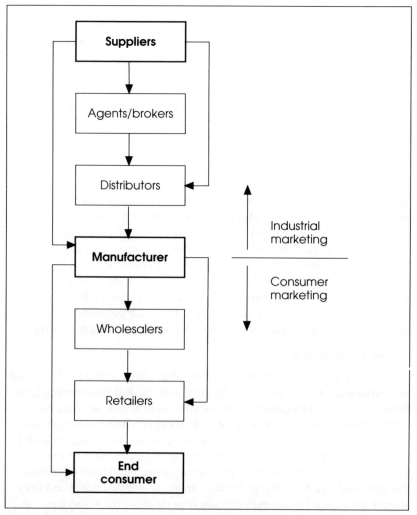

Figure 11.3 Structure of a conventional vertical marketing system

- In a *direct distribution system*, the manufacturer sells directly to the end-user and there is no intermediary in the channel. This structure is also called a direct marketing system.
- In an *indirect distribution system*, one or several intermediaries participate and bring the product closer to the final buyer. An indirect system is said to be 'short' or 'long' depending on the number of intermediary levels.

In the field of consumer goods, distribution channels tend to be long and involve several intermediaries, typically wholesalers and retailers. In industrial markets, channels are generally shorter,

Table 11.1 Factors affecting channel structure (adapted from Rosenbloom (1978, pp. 119–27))

Influencing factors	Channel structure		
	Direct	Indirect short	Indirect long
Market factors			
Large number of buyers		**	***
High geographical dispersion		**	***
Purchases in large quantity	***		
Buying highly seasonal		**	***
Product characteristics			
Perishable products	***		
Complex products	***		
Newness of the product	***	**	
Heavy and bulky products	***		
Standardized products		**	***
Low unit value		**	***
Company variables			
Large financial capacity	***	**	
Complete assortment	***	**	
High control sought	***	**	

particularly when buyers are large and well identified. From the producer's point of view, the longer the channel, the more difficult becomes the problem of control.

In most market situations, companies use *multiple channels* to reach their target segments, either to create emulation among distributors or to reach separate target segments having different purchasing habits. For example, many industrial companies use distributors to sell and service small accounts and their own sales force to handle large accounts.

Factors affecting the channel structure

The selection of a particular channel design is largely determined by a set of constraints related to market and buyer behaviour factors and to product and company characteristics. These factors and their implications for the channel configuration are described in Table 11.1.

Market factors

The number of potential buyers determines the *size of the market*. A very general heuristic rule about market size relative to channel structure is: if the market is large, the use of intermediaries is more likely to be needed. Conversely, if the market is small, a firm is more likely to avoid the use of intermediaries and to assume most of the distribution tasks. Also, the more *geographically dispersed* the market, the more difficult and expensive distribution is. The more geographically dispersed the market, the more likely it is that intermediaries will be used because of the high costs involved in providing adequate services to many dispersed customers.

Patterns of buying behaviour also influence the channel structure. If customers typically buy in very *small quantities* and if demand is highly *seasonal* a long distribution channel involving several intermediaries will be more appropriate.

Product variables

Characteristics of the product also determine the channel structure. Channels should be as short as possible for highly *perishable products*. Heavy and *bulky products* have very high handling and shipping costs and the firm should try to minimize these costs by shipping the goods only in truck-load quantities to a limited number of places; the channel structure should also be short.

Short structures are also desirable for *complex and technical products* requiring extensive after-sales service and assistance in use. Similarly, for *innovative products* requiring aggressive promotion in the introductory stage of the PLC, a shorter channel will facilitate the development and control of promotion activities aiming at creating product acceptance by the market. Long channel structures will be more adequate, on the other hand, when products are highly standardized and when they have *low unit value*. In this latter case, the costs of distribution can be shared by many other products handled by the intermediaries.

For example, it would be difficult to imagine the sales of packages of crisps by the Smiths Company to the consumer. Only by spreading the costs of distribution over the wide variety of products handled by wholesale and retail intermediaries is it possible to buy a packet of crisps at retail for BF50.

A manufacturer's channel choice is also influenced by the *extent of its product line*. The manufacturer with only one item may have to use wholesaling intermediaries, whereas it could go directly to retailers if it made several products which could be combined on a large scale. A retailer ordinarily cannot buy a truck-load of washing machines alone, but it might buy a truck-load of mixed appliances.

Company variables

The key variables here are the size and the financial capability of the producer. Large firms in general have large financial resources and therefore the capacity to assume several distribution tasks directly, thereby reducing their dependence on intermediaries. Several distribution activities, such as transportation and storage, imply fixed costs. Large companies are better able to bear these costs. On the other hand, the use of intermediaries implies a cost which is proportional to the volume of activity, since their compensation takes the form of commissions on actual sales revenue. Therefore, small firms will be inclined to have extensive recourse to intermediaries. In some cases, the entire output is sold under the retailer's brand. The disadvantage of this arrangement is that the producer is completely at the mercy of its own large retailer.

Other considerations are also important. For example, the lack of marketing expertise necessary to perform the distribution tasks may force the firm to use the services of intermediaries. This happens frequently when the firm is penetrating new or foreign markets. Also, high-technology companies built upon the engineering abilities of management often rely heavily on distributors to do the marketing job. A manufacturer may establish as short a channel as possible simply because it wants to *control the distribution* of its product, even though the cost of a more direct channel is higher.

Vertical marketing systems

If the adopted channel structure is indirect, some degree of cooperation and coordination must be achieved among the participants in the channel. Two forms of vertical organization can exist: conventional vertical structures and coordinated vertical structures, called vertical marketing systems.

- In a *conventional vertical structure* each level of the channel behaves independently as a separate business entity seeking to maximize its own profit, even if it is at the expense of the overall performance of the distribution channel. This is the traditional way in which a distribution network works, where no channel member has control over the other members.
- In a *coordinated vertical structure*, the participants in the exchange process behave like partners and coordinate their activities in order to increase their bargaining power and to achieve operating economies and maximum market impact. In this type of vertical organization, a channel member takes the initiative of coordination, be it the manufacturer, the wholesaler or the retailer (McCammon, 1970).

Several forms of vertical marketing system have emerged. A distinction is usually made between corporate, contractual and administered vertical marketing systems.

Corporate vertical marketing systems

In corporate vertically integrated marketing systems a particular firm achieves coordination and control through corporate ownership. The firm owning and operating the other units of the channel may be a manufacturer, wholesaler or retailer. Firms such as Bata in shoes and Rodier in clothing own their own retail outlets. However, it is not always the manufacturer that controls the channel system through forward integration. Backward integration occurs when a retailer or a wholesaler assumes ownership of institutions that normally precede them in the channel. Sears in the USA, for example, and Marks & Spencer in the UK have ownership interest in several manufacturing firms that are important suppliers of their private brands.

Contractual vertical marketing systems

In a contractual vertical marketing system, independent firms operating at different levels of the channel coordinate their activities through legal contracts that spell out the rights and duties of each partner. The three basic types of contractual system are retail cooperatives, wholesale-sponsored voluntary chains and franchise systems. Franchise systems have expanded the most in recent years. Their organization is discussed in more detail in the next section.

Administered vertical marketing systems

In this third system, firms participating in the channel coordinate their activities through the informal guidance or influence of one of the channel members (and not through ownership or contractual agreements). The leading firm, usually the manufacturer, bases its influence on the brand or company reputation or managerial expertise. Companies like L'Oréal in cosmetics and Procter & Gamble in detergents are examples of firms having successfully achieved this form of cooperation.

Vertical marketing systems have become the dominant mode of distribution in the field of consumer marketing over the last twenty years. They can be viewed as a new form of competition, *channel system competition*, setting complete channels against other complete channels, as opposed to traditional vertical competition, opposing channel members at different levels of the same channel, i.e. retailers versus wholesalers, manufacturer versus wholesaler etc. Vertical marketing systems help eliminate the sources of conflicts that exist in conventional vertical structures, and increase the market impact of their activities.

Market coverage strategies

If the decision made by the producer is to use intermediaries to organize the distribution of its products, the firm must then decide on the number of intermediaries to use at each channel level to achieve the market penetration objective. Three basic market coverage strategies are possible:

- Hollywood distributes its chewing gums wherever possible: in food stores, tobacconists, drug stores, through vending machines etc.
- Pierre Cardin distributes his dresses and women's suits in carefully selected clothing stores and tries to be present in the most elegant shops.
- VAG distributes its cars through exclusive dealership; each dealer has an exclusive territory and no other dealer is authorized to carry the VAG makes.

Hollywood is adopting an intensive distribution strategy, Cardin a selective strategy and VAG an exclusive strategy. The best strategy for a given product depends on the nature of the product itself, on the objective being pursued and on the competitive situation.

Consumer goods classifications

In the field of consumer goods, the choice of a particular market coverage strategy is largely determined by the shopping habits associated with the consumers of the distributed product. Consumer goods fall into four sub-groups: convenience goods, shopping goods, speciality goods and unsought goods. The purchasing behaviour associated with these products varies primarily in the amount and type of effort consumers exert in buying these products.

Convenience goods

Convenience products are purchased with as little effort as possible, frequently and in small quantities. We have here a routine buying behaviour. Convenience goods can be further subdivided into staple goods, impulse goods and emergency goods.

- *Staple goods* are purchased on a regular basis and include most food items. Brand loyalty facilitates routine purchase and the goods must be pre-sold, namely through repetitive advertising.
- *Impulse goods* are purchased without any planning (crisps, magazines, sweets etc.). These goods must be available in many places; the packaging and the in-store displays in supermarkets are important in the sale of these products.
- *Emergency goods* are those needed to fill an unexpected and urgent

need. These goods are purchased immediately as the need emerges and therefore they must be available in many outlets.

For these product categories, the firm has practically no alternative. These products require an intensive market coverage. If the brand is not found at the point of sale, consumers will buy another brand and the sales occasion will be lost.

Shopping goods

Shopping goods are high perceived-risk products. For these products, consumers are willing to spend time and effort to shop around and to compare product alternatives on criteria such as quality, price, style, features etc. Examples include major appliances, furniture and clothing, i.e. expensive and infrequently bought products. Prospective buyers visit several stores before making a decision and sales personnel have an important role to play by providing information and advice. For shopping goods maximal market coverage is not required and a selective distribution system will be more appropriate, more especially as the cooperation of the retailer is necessary.

Speciality goods

Speciality goods are products with unique characteristics and sufficiently important to consumers that they make a special effort to discover them. Examples would include specific brands, fancy goods, exotic foods, deluxe clothings, sophisticated photographic equipment, etc. For those products prospective buyers do not proceed to comparisons; they search for the outlet carrying the wanted product. Brand loyalty or the distinctive features of the product are the determining factors. For speciality goods, retailers are especially important; thus the firms of such goods will tend to limit their distribution to obtain strong support from the retailers. A selective or exclusive distribution system is the best option for the producer.

Unsought products

Unsought goods are products that consumers do not know about or know about but do not consider buying. Examples are heat pumps, smoke detectors, encyclopaedias and life insurance. Substantial selling efforts are required for those products. The cooperation of intermediaries is indispensable, or the firm must adopt a direct marketing system.

Intensive distribution

In an intensive distribution system, the firm seeks the maximum possible number of retailers to distribute its product, the largest number of storage points to ensure maximum market coverage and the highest brand exposure. This strategy is appropriate for convenience goods, common raw materials and low-involvement services. The advantages of intensive distribution are to maximize product availability and to generate a large market share due to the brand's broad exposure to potential buyers. There are, however, significant disadvantages or risks associated with this strategy.

- The sales revenue generated by the different retailers varies greatly, while the contact cost is the same for each intermediary. If the firm receives many small orders from an intensive network of small retailers, distribution costs (order processing and shipping) can become extremely high and undermine the overall profitability.
- When the product has an intensive distribution in multiple and very diversified sales points, it becomes difficult for the firm to control its marketing strategy: discount pricing, poor customer service and lack of cooperation from retailers are practices difficult to prevent.
- Intensive distribution is hard to reconcile with a brand image building strategy and with a specific product positioning strategy due to the lack of control of the distributive network.

For these reasons, market-driven companies are induced to adopt a more selective distributive system once the brand awareness objectives have been achieved.

Selective distribution

In a selective distribution system, the producer uses fewer distributors than the total number of available distributors in a specific geographic area. It is an appropriate strategy for shopping goods that customers buy infrequently and compare for differences in price and product features.

To have a selective distribution, the firm must decide the criteria upon which to select its intermediaries. Several criteria are commonly used.

- The *size of the distributor*, measured by its sales revenue, is the most popular criterion. In the majority of markets, a small number of distributors achieve a significant share of total sales revenue. In the food sector, for instance, the concentration ratio is very high in Switzerland, the UK and Belgium, where the first 5 distributors in the food sectors account for 82, 53 and 52 per cent respectively of the total turnover (Nielsen, 1990). In these conditions, it is obviously unprofitable to contact all distributors.

- The *quality of the service* provided is also an important criterion.
  Intermediaries are paid to perform a certain number of well-
  defined functions and some dealers or retailers are more efficient
  than others.
- The technical competence of the dealer and the availability of
  up-to-date facilities, mainly for complex products where after-
  sales service is important, is a third important criterion.

In adopting a selective distribution system, the firm voluntarily
agrees to limit the availability of its product in order to reduce its
distribution costs and to gain better cooperation from the
intermediaries. This cooperation can take various forms.

- Participating in the advertising and promotion budget.
- Accepting new products or unsought products requiring more
  selling efforts.
- Maintaining a minimum level of inventory.
- Transferring information to the producer.
- Providing better services to customers.

The main risk of a selective distribution system is to have insufficient
market coverage. The producer must verify whether the market
knows the distributors handling the brand or the product. If not, the
reduced availability of the product could generate significant losses
of sales opportunities.

It may happen that the firm has in fact no alternative and is forced to
maintain a certain degree of selectivity in its distributive network.
For example:

- A new product which is not yet a proven success will be accepted
  by a retailer only if it receives an exclusive right to carry the
  product in its territory.
- If the assortment is large because the consumer must be able to
  choose among several product forms (design, colour, size),
  selectivity will be necessary, otherwise the expected sales revenue
  will be too low to motivate the retailer.
- If the after-sales service implies long and costly training of the
  dealers, selectivity will be necessary to reduce the costs.

If the firm decides to adopt a selective distribution system, it is
important to realize that this decision implies the adoption of a
'short' indirect distribution channel. It is very unlikely, indeed, that
wholesalers will agree to voluntarily limit their field of operation
simply to meet the strategic objectives of the producer.

Exclusive distribution and franchise systems

In an exclusive distribution system, the manufacturer relies on only one retailer or dealer to distribute its product in a given geographic territory. In turn, the exclusive dealer agrees not to sell any competing brand within the same product category. Exclusive distribution is useful when a company wants to differentiate its product on the basis of high quality, prestige or excellent customer service. The close cooperation with exclusive dealers facilitates the implementation of the producer's customer service programmes. The advantages and disadvantages of exclusive distribution are the same as in selective distribution, but amplified. A particular form of exclusive distribution is franchising.

Franchising is a contractual, vertically integrated marketing system which refers to a comprehensive method of distributing goods and services. It involves a continuous and contractual relationship in which a *franchisor* provides a licensed privilege to do business and assistance in organizing, training, merchandising, management and other areas in return for a specific consideration from the *franchisee*. Thus, the franchisee agrees to pay an initial fee, plus royalties calculated on the sales revenue, for the right to use a well-known trademarked product or service and to receive continual assistance and services from the franchisor. In fact, the franchisee is buying a proven success from the franchisor.

Types of franchise systems

The franchisor may occupy any position within the channel; therefore there are four basic types of franchise system:

- The *manufacturer–retailer* franchise is exemplified by franchised automobile dealers and franchised service stations. Singer in the USA and Pingouin and Yves Rocher in France are good examples.
- The *manufacturer–wholesaler* franchise is exemplified by soft drink companies like Coca Cola and 7-Up who sell the soft drink syrups they manufacture to franchised wholesalers who, in turn, carbonate, bottle, sell and distribute to retailers.
- The *wholesaler–retailer* franchise is exemplified by Rexall Drug Stores, by Christianssens in toys and Unic and Disco in food.
- The *service sponsor–retailer* franchise is exemplified by Avis, Hertz, McDonald's, Midas and Holiday Inn.

The faster growing franchises include business and professional services, fast food, restaurants, car and truck rentals, and home and cleaning maintenance (Sanghavi, 1991).

Characteristics of a good franchise

A good franchise must be above all a *transferable proven success*, which can be replicated in another territory or environment. According to Sallenave (1979, p. 11), a good franchise must:

- Be related to the distribution of a *high quality* product or service.
- Meet a *universal need* or want which is not country- or region-specific.
- Be a *proven success* in franchisor-owned and -operated pilot units which serve as models for the other franchisees.
- Ensure the full transfer of *know-how* and provide the training of the franchisee in the methods of doing business and modes of operation.
- Offer to the franchisees *initial and continuing service* to gain immediate market acceptance and to improve modes of operation.
- Have a regular *reporting and information system* which permits effective monitoring of the performance and collection of market information.
- Specify initial franchise *fees* and the royalty fees based on the gross value of a franchisee's sales volume (generally 5 per cent).
- Involve the franchisee in the *management* and development of the franchise system.
- Specify *legal provisions* for termination, cancellation and renewal of the franchise agreement, as well as for the repurchase of the franchise.

Franchise systems constitute a viable alternative to completely integrated corporate vertical marketing systems. In a franchise system, funds are provided by the franchisees, who invest in the stores and in the facilities. From the franchisor's point of view, the establishment of franchised dealers is an ideal means to achieve rapid national or international distribution for its products or services without committing large funds and while keeping the control of the system through contractual agreements.

John Y. Brown, President of Kentucky Fried Chicken Corporation, has stated that it would have required $450 million for his firm to have established its first 2700 stores if they would have been company-owned. This sum was simply not available to his firm during the initial stages of its proposed expansion. The use of capital made available from franchisees, however, made the proposed expansion possible, (McGuire, 1971, p. 7).

Thus a franchise system is an integrated marketing system controlled by the franchisor but financed by the franchisees. A successful franchise is a partnership in which the mutual interests of both franchisor and franchisees are closely inter-dependent.

Benefits to the franchisor

The motivations of the franchisor for creating and developing a franchise system are the following:

- To acquire funds without diluting control of the marketing system.
- To keep high flexibility in the use of the capital collected for developing the system.
- To avoid the fixed overhead expenses associated with distribution through company-owned branch units or stores.
- To cooperate with independent business people, the franchisees, who are more likely to work hard at developing their markets than salaried employees.
- To cooperate with local business people well accepted and integrated in the local community or in the foreign country.
- To develop new sources of income based on existing know-how and marketing expertise.
- To achieve faster sales development thanks to the snowball effect generated by the franchising of a successful idea.
- To benefit from economies of scale with the development of the franchise system.

Franchisors provide both initial and continuous services to their franchisees (McGuire, 1971). *Initial services* include market survey and site selection; facility design and layout; lease negotiation advice; financing advice; operating manuals; management training programmes and franchisee employee training.

Continuous services include field supervision; merchandising and promotional materials; management and employee retraining; quality inspection; national advertising; centralized purchasing; market data and guidance; auditing and record keeping; management reports; and group insurance plans.

The franchise system is present in almost all business fields, and total franchise system sales have grown dramatically during the last decade. The number of franchise companies and franchisees active in each of the major markets of the EC is summarized in Table 11.2.

Benefits to franchisees

From the perspective of the potential franchisee, franchising has several strong appeals which explain the success of this distribution arrangement.

- Franchising enables an individual to enter a business which would be prohibitively expensive if the individual tried to go it alone.

Table 11.2 Number of franchise companies in the EC (Sanghanvi, 1991)

Country	Number of franchisors	Number of franchised units
Belgium	82	4100
Denmark	10	30
France	700	30 300
Italy	210	12 500
Holland	255	8800
Spain	100	9000
UK	295	16 600
West Germany	190	9100

- The amount of uncertainty is reduced, since the business idea has been successfully tested.
- The extensive services provided by the franchisor, both initial and continuous, reduce the risks of the operation.
- Franchising offers better purchasing power, the access to better sites and the support of national advertising.
- The introduction of new products and the constant rejuvenation of the product portfolio are made possible.
- Managerial assistance in marketing and finance is provided.
- The opportunity is provided for individuals to operate as independent business people within a large organization.

Franchising is a very flexible organization and many variants exist. Three basic rules must be met to have a successful arrangement:

- The will to work as partners.
- The right to mutual control.
- The value of the business idea.

This last condition is vital. Franchising will work only if the business idea is a proven success.

Communication strategies in the channel

Gaining support and cooperation from independent intermediaries is a key success factor for the implementation of the firm's marketing objectives. To get this cooperation, two very distinct communication strategies can be adopted by the firm: a push strategy or a pull strategy. A third alternative is a combination of the two.

Table 11.3 Incentives for motivating channel members (Boyd and Walker, 1990)

Functional performance	Examples of channel incentives
Increased purchases or carry large inventories	Large margins, exclusive territories, buy-in promotions, quantity discounts, buy-back allowances, free goods, shelf-stocking programmes
Increased personal selling effort	Sales training, instructional materials, incentive programmes for channel members' sales people
Increased local promotional effort	
• Local advertising	Cooperative advertising, advertising allowance; print, radio, TV ads for use by local retailers
• Increased display space	Promotion allowances tied to shelf space
• In-store promotions	Display racks and signs, in-store demonstrations, in-store sampling
Improved customer service	Service training programmes, instructional materials, high margins on replacement parts, liberal labour cost allowances for warranty service

Push strategies

In a push communication strategy, the bulk of the marketing effort is devoted to incentives directed at wholesalers and retailers to induce them to cooperate with the firm, to carry the brands in their assortments, to keep a minimum level of inventory, to display the products and to give them enough visibility on their shelf spaces. The objective is to win *voluntary cooperation* by offering attractive terms of trade, i.e. larger margins, quantity discounts, local or in-store advertising, promotional allowances, in-store sampling etc.

Personal selling and personal communication are the key marketing instruments here. The role of the sales representatives and of the merchandisers will be particularly important. Table 11.3 lists a variety of incentives the firm can use to increase the number of channel members.

A programme of incentives is indispensable to get the support of intermediaries. The larger their negotiation power, the more difficult it will be for the firm to obtain the support of distributors. In markets where distribution is highly concentrated, it is the intermediary who specifies the conditions for carrying the brand. The risk of an exclusive push strategy is the absence of countervailing power and the dependence of the firm on the intermediary who controls the access to the market.

The only alternative for the firm is the adoption of a direct marketing system which completely bypasses intermediaries. This is a costly operation, however, since all distribution tasks must then be assumed by the firm. Recent developments in communication technologies present new opportunities, however. The potential of direct or interactive marketing will be discussed in the final section of this chapter.

Pull strategies

When adopting a pull strategy, the manufacturer focuses its communication efforts on the end-user, bypassing intermediaries and trying to build company demand directly among potential customers in the target segment. The communication objective is to create strong customer demand and brand loyalty among consumers in order to pull the brand through the distribution channel, forcing the intermediaries to carry the brand to meet consumers' demand.

To achieve these objectives, the manufacturer will spend the largest proportion of its communication budget on media advertising, consumer promotions and direct marketing efforts aimed at winning end-customer preferences. If this branding policy is successful, the manufacturer has the power to influence channel participants and to induce them to carry the brand, since a substantial sales volume will be achieved. The strategic objective is to neutralize the bargaining power of the intermediary who could block the access to the market.

Pull strategies imply in general large financial resources to cover the costs of brand image advertising campaigns. These costs are fixed overhead expenses, while the costs of a push strategy are proportional to volume and therefore easier to bear, particularly for a small firm.

In fact, a pull strategy must be viewed as long-term investment. The goal of the firm is to create a capital of goodwill, a *brand equity*, around the company name or around the brand. A strong brand image is an asset for the firm and is the best argument for obtaining support and cooperation from intermediaries.

In practice, these two communication strategies are used in combination, and it is hard to imagine a market situation where no incentives would be used to motivate intermediaries. With the development of marketing expertise and the increased cost of personal selling, the trend among market-driven companies is to reinforce branding policies and pull communication strategies.

Distribution cost analysis

The distribution cost is measured by the difference between the unit sales price paid by the end-user and the unit cost paid to the producer by the first buyer. Thus, the distribution margin measures the *added value* brought by the distribution channel. If several intermediaries participate in the distribution process, the distribution margin is equal to the sum of the different distributors' margins. The margin of a particular distributor is equal to the difference between its selling price and its purchase cost. The two definitions coincide when there is only one intermediary in the channel.

Trade margins

A trade margin is often expressed as a percentage. This is sometimes confusing, since the margin percentage can be computed on the basis of purchase cost (C) or on the basis of selling price (P). The trade margin (D) is then referred to as a 'mark-up' or as a 'discount'. The conversion rules are presented in Table 11.4

Suppose a retailer purchases an item for £10 and sells it at a price of £20, that is, at a £10 margin. What is the retailer's margin percentage? As a percentage of the selling price, it is

$$£10/£20 \times 100 = 50 \text{ per cent}$$

As a percentage of cost, it is

$$£10/£10 \times 100 = 100 \text{ per cent}$$

Trade margins are usually determined on the basis of selling price, but practices do vary between firms and industries.

Trade margins are based on a distributor's place in the channel and represent payment for performing certain distribution tasks. In some cases, several margins are quoted to distributors, as illustrated in Table 11.5. The manufacturer's problem of suggesting a list price, i.e.

Table 11.4 Definitions of trade margins

Trade margins

Trade margin   = Selling price − Purchase cost

$$D = P - C$$

Trade margin as percentage

'of selling price' (discount)   'of purchase cost' (mark-up)

$$D^* = \frac{P - C}{P} \qquad\qquad D^\circ = \frac{P - C}{C}$$

Conversion rules

$$D^* = \frac{D^\circ}{1 + D^\circ} \qquad\qquad D^\circ = \frac{D^*}{1 - D^*}$$

the final suggested price of the product, is more complex, as the number of intermediaries between the producer and the final consumer increases.

Comparison of distribution costs

The distribution margin compensates the distribution functions and tasks assumed by the intermediaries in the channel. If some of these distribution tasks are assumed directly by the producer, it will have to support the organization and the costs implied. By way of illustration, Table 11.6 shows a costs comparison of two indirect distribution channels: a 'long' indirect channel involving two intermediaries, wholesalers and retailers, and a 'short' indirect channel involving only retailers, the wholesaling function being assumed by the manufacturer.

In the *indirect long channel,* most of the physical distribution tasks (storage and transportation) are taken on by wholesalers and the distribution costs are largely proportional to the rate of activity and covered by the wholesalers' distributor's margin. The manufacturer has to maintain a minimum sales administration unit and the overhead costs are minimized. In this type of conventional vertical marketing organization, however, the producer is dependent on the goodwill of the distributors and has only limited control of the sales organization. To offset this handicap, the producer can create its own sales force (merchandisers) to stimulate sales at the retailers' level and also to use mass media advertising to create brand awareness and brand preference among end-users through a 'pull communication' strategy.

Table 11.5 Developing a price structure (adapted from Monroe (1979, p. 169))

Trade margins are based on a distributor's place in the channel and represent payment for performing certain distribution tasks.

Prices are usually quoted to distributors as a series of numbers depending on the number of functions performed. In the case of large retail chains, we would have the following quotation:

'30, 10, 5 and 2/10, net 30'

The first three numbers represent successive discounts from the list price:

30 per cent: as functional discount for the position the retailer occupies in the channel

10 per cent: as compensation for performing the storage function, usually performed by the wholesaler

5 per cent: as an allowance for the retailer's efforts to promote the product through local advertising

2/10: as cash discount, 2 per cent, as reward for payment of an invoice within 10 days.

Net 30: the length of the credit period; if the payment is not made within 10 days, the entire invoice must be paid in full within 30 days.

Examining now the cost structure of the *indirect short channel*, one observes that overheads or fixed costs represent the largest share of total distribution costs. It means that the manufacturer has to support the costs of the physical distribution functions and organize a network of warehouses plus a much more extensive sales administration unit. The financial costs involved by the inventory management and by the customers' accounts receivables are also completely assumed by the producer, as well as the selling function.

By adopting a selective distribution strategy, the firm has to contact at least once a month 2500 retailers. One sales representative can perform on average 4.8 calls per day during 250 working days per year. The required sales force is therefore 25 sales representatives to achieve the market coverage objective.

Thus, adopting an indirect short distribution channel implies for the producer a major financial risk. The benefits of this strategy, however, are better control of the commercial organization and closer contact with the end users.

The two cost equations are compared in Figure 11.4. One sees that the costs of distribution are the same at a certain level—the break-

Table 11.6 Distribution cost analysis of two distribution channels (adapted from Brown *et al.* (1968))

Distribution tasks	Indirect long channel		Indirect short channel	
	Cost	Comments	Cost	Comments
Transport	—	• M → W: in charge of M—more expensive W → R: in charge of M—cheaper	—	• M → warehouses: in charge of M—cheaper warehouses → R: in charge of M—more expensive
Assortment	Covered by the wholesaler margin: 16% of the manufacturer's sales revenue	• in charge of M and R: complete assortment	—	• in charge of R: risk of incomplete assortment
Contact		• warehouses: in charge of W • stocks: in charge of W • customer: in charge of W	$750 000 2.5% of sales revenue 1.25% of sales revenue $500 000	• 7 warehouses (fewer) • 4 rotations/year (rate 10%) • payment at 45 days (rate 10%) • 25 sales people at $20 000 more dynamic (push strategy)

Information	2.5% of sales revenue	• push strategy on W and R	1.5% of sales revenue	• pull strategy
Sales administration	$30 000	• principally in charge of W; small team	$200 000	• principally in charge of M; large team
Total cost	$30 000 + 0.185 (sales revenue)	• cost proportional to the activity rate	$1 450 000 + 0.0525 (sales revenue)	• largest part of cost is fixed

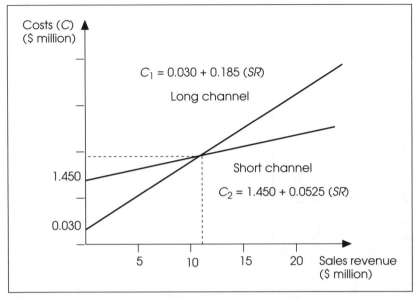

Figure 11.4 Comparing the cost structures of two distribution channels

even level—of the total sales revenue. If the expected sales revenues are the same in both cases, the 'longer' channel will be preferred for any turnover inferior to the break-even level and conversely for any higher turnover. This observation is in line with the common observation that small companies tend to favour long distribution channels, their financial capacities being in general too weak to support the costs of a short distribution channel.

In general, the sales revenue expectations are not the same for each distribution channel. The profitability rate of each channel will be determined as follows:

$$R = \frac{\text{Sales revenue} - \text{Distribution costs}}{\text{Distribution costs}}$$

where R is an estimate of the expected rate of return when all the costs are taken into account for each channel. This quantitative indicator must of course be interpreted with care and with due consideration of the more 'qualitative' factors discussed above.

The retailer's strategic marketing

Significant changes have occurred during the 1990s in the way retailers, and in particular large retailers, perceive their roles in the exchange process. Traditionally, retailers have limited their role to intermediaries, acting rather passively between the producer and the consumer by simply performing the physical tasks of distribution and by making the goods available to consumers in the condition, place and time required by them. From this rather passive role, intermediaries are increasingly adopting an innovative and active role, thereby modifying the balance of power between manufacturers and retailers.

This evolution has coincided with significant sociocultural changes in affluent economies which have induced retailers to redefine their roles as economic agents and to adopt a more market-driven perspective. From a traditional 'shop' or 'in-house' orientation, retailers are now discovering strategic marketing and are moving away from a business philosophy where the marketing function is confined to the physical distribution tasks and to the purchasing function.

Major changes in the distribution sector

The major changes in the macro-environment have been described in Chapter 2. In addition to these structural changes, significant evolutions in government regulations, purchasing habits and in retailing have also influenced the development of the distribution sector.

Legislation regulating business

Because the distribution sector has an important social and economic role in the economy, government authorities have regulated distributive activities in different fields in most Western European countries. The forms of regulation include:

- Controls of prices and distribution margins in order to reduce inflation either through authoritarian *price freezes and controls* or through sectoral agreements.
- Consumer protection against unfair business practices through *consumerist legislation* on labelling, product safety, deceptive advertising, unit pricing, promotions etc.
- Legislation aiming at the protection of *small businesses* by limiting further expansion of large retail chains.
- Laws to define and prevent *unfair competition* based on the Treaty of Rome and enforced by the European Commission's general directorate for competition.

Within the European Community, substantial efforts are being made to standardize these regulations to meet the objective of the single European market which came into force in 1993.

Changing socio-cultural environment

These changes are demographic, social, economic and cultural. They have occurred at a different rate within each west European country.

- Although the world population is showing explosive growth, in Western Europe one observes a slow-down in the birth rate, smaller families and ageing populations.
- The number of single-adult households is growing as well as the number of working wives; the rate of equipment in household appliances is very high and the number of better educated people continues to rise.
- In terms of values, radical changes are emerging; more attention is given to the quality of life, to high-touch products and services, to more personalized services, and to the value of time, change and stimulations.
- Regarding the economic situation, in 1993 the recession was still present, with a modest 2 per cent growth of real GNP, persistent unemployment and a slow-down in consumption expenditure.

The new consumers are better educated and informed and more professional in their buying behaviour. They seek gratifying experiences and are strongly differentiated in their preferences and expectations. In this context, mass marketing techniques become ineffective and retailers are confronted with highly *fragmented markets* and *smarter shoppers* searching for the best value for money. Clearly, these changes constitute important challenges for the distribution sector, and in particular for the retailer.

Changes in the retailing industry

In many west European countries, retailing has become a mature industry, and several indicators confirm this observation.

- Keeping pace with the growth of the economy, the retailing industry has experienced *zero* or *minimal growth* for several years, particularly in the food sector. The share of large retail chains has reached a plateau and is even declining in some markets.
- The *proliferation of retailers* has created over-capacity, and today a retailer must compete against a crowd of tough competitors, not only in the food sector, but also in sectors like clothing, household appliances and even in the newest product categories like home computers.
- *Competition* is intensive and based almost exclusively on price for all the branded products. In most product categories, consumers can buy exactly the same product or brand at a discount store at bargain prices as they could at a department store at its full price.
- In several European countries, a *high level of concentration* is observed among large distributors. Table 11.7 displays the

Table 11.7 Concentration of the distribution industry in Europe: the food sector (Nielsen, 1990)

Countries	Market share of the first 5 distributors	Market share of the first 10 distributors
Belgium	52	68
Spain	19	22
France	42	65
Italy	29	43
Norway	10	15
Holland	59	79
Portugal	15	18
Germany	27	33
UK	53	66
Switzerland	82	91

concentration ratios of the top five and top ten distributors in the food sector. These distributors have substantial purchasing power (and bargaining power), reinforced recently by the creation of joint purchasing units at the European level (Dupuis, 1991; Ducrocq, 1991).

All these characteristics—maturity, overcapacity, concentration and price competition—are typical of commodity markets, suggest that the retailing industry has become 'commoditized'. This conclusion must be qualified, however, by country and by product category. As suggested by Wortzel (1987, p. 46), several factors explain this evolution.

- During the 1960s, *manufacturers' brand names* became prominent in a broadening range of product categories, and more and more retailers began featuring these brands. Thus, the presence of the brand in the retailer's assortment became the determining choice criterion in choosing a particular store. In the process, retailers abdicated much of their stores' marketing and positioning responsibilities to the manufacturers.
- This situation has stimulated the development of *hard discounters*, who sell well-known brands exclusively on bargain pricing with minimum services.
- The proliferation of slightly differentiated brands and the adoption of *intensive distribution strategies* by manufacturers have also contributed to reducing store differentiation, most stores carrying the same assortments of brands.
- Retailers once had the major responsibility for *after-sales service*, and choosing a retailer was important when one bought products like appliances and consumer electronics. Now consumers can get

after-sales service for most products independently of the retailer,
and this type of store differentiation is also waning.
- Finally, the tremendous growth in *bank credit cards* also
  contributes to undermining store loyalty. Consumers no longer
  choose a store because they have established credit there: bank
  cards entitle customers to buy items almost anywhere they please.

These factors have all contributed to reducing store differentiation
and store loyalty and to modifing consumer's buying behaviour.

Changes in consumer's retail buying behaviour

Retail consumers today behave differently, not only because of the
social and demographic changes described above, but also because
they are more educated and professional in their purchase decisions.
As suggested by Wortzel (1987, p. 47), one of the biggest changes is
the rise of the *'smart shopper'*. Being a smart shopper implies several
capabilities:

- Being informed about the products one wants to buy and being
  able to compare and choose independently of brand, advertising,
  store and sales person's recommendations. It means finding the
  best value for money.
- Being able to separate the product features and the benefits and
  services provided by a store to augment the product value. Smart
  shoppers distinguish between what is inherent in the product and
  can therefore be obtained anywhere they buy it, and what a
  specific store adds to the purchase. They routinely compare stores
  as well as brands on this basis.
- Being able to recognize that brands have become increasingly
  similar. They will not necessarily choose a well-known brand over
  a less well-known brand simply because it is familiar or because of
  its image. The product must also be viewed as offering superior
  value.

In addition, for many consumers, and for a broadening range of
goods, shopping is no longer viewed as fun or recreational, but
rather as a tedious task to be performed as economically and
efficiently as possible. In their search for value, an expanding group
of consumers seek not only good merchandise but savings of time
and effort as well.

The product concept of a store

Confronted with these changes, the retailer has to review its
traditional strategic positioning by redefining its *'store concept'* and
by adopting a positioning which provides unique value to
consumers. The adoption of a store differentiation strategy becomes

a necessity in a market place where retailing has become commoditized. Thus the concepts of strategic marketing developed for product marketing can be directly applied to retail marketing.

From the consumer standpoint, the store concept can be viewed as a package of benefits and the *multi-attribute product concept* described in Chapter 4 is useful here to help design the store concept. Six different characteristics or attributes can be identified in a store, which constitute as many action variables for the retailer:

- *Location*. This defines the territorial coverage or trading area within which to develop business relations. The alternatives are downtown location, community, suburban or regional shopping centres.
- *Assortment*. The number of product lines that will be sold, which implies decisions on the product assortment breadth (narrow or wide) and product assortment depth (shallow or deep) for each product line.
- *Pricing*. The general level of prices (high or low gross margins) and the use of loss-leaders, discount pricing and price promotions.
- *Services*. The extent of the service mix. A distinction can be made between pre-purchase services (telephone orders, shopping hours, fitting rooms etc.), post-purchase services (delivery, alterations, wrapping etc.) and ancillary services (credit, restaurants, baby sitting, travel agencies etc.); see de Maricourt (1988).
- *Time*. The time required for a shopping trip. Proximity is the key factor, but also opening and closing hours, accessibility, ease of selection, fast completion of transaction and queueing time at checkout counters.
- *Atmosphere*. The lay-out of the store, but also the light, the space the musical ambience, the look and the interior decoration etc.

These store attributes are used by consumers when they compare retail stores. It is up to the retailer to define a store concept based on some innovative combination of these attributes and which constitutes a package of benefits differentiated from the competition.

Store positioning strategies

Three basic store positioning strategies can be adopted by the retailer: product differentiation, service and personality augmentation, and price leadership.

- A *product differentiation* strategy is based on offering products that are intrinsically different, e.g. different brands or different styles from those in the same product category offered by other stores.

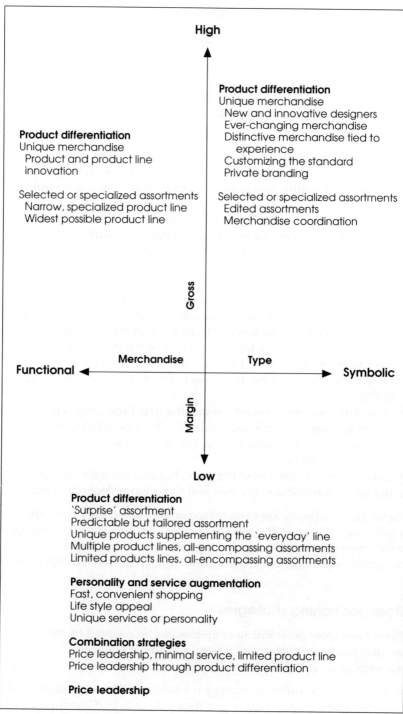

Figure 11.5 Retail positioning strategies (Wortzel, 1987)

- In a *service and personality augmentation* strategy, a retailer offers products that are intrinsically similar to those offered by competitors, but adds specific services and personality to differentiate the store.
- A *price leadership* strategy means offering the same products as the competition at lower prices.

Each strategy is implemented using certains tools, which are summarized in Figure 11.5. Wortzel (1987) suggests the following store differentiation strategies for high margin goods.

- Feature new and innovative designers.
- Offer ever-changing merchandise.
- Offer distinctive merchandise that ties in with consumers' desires.
- Customize the standardized.
- Feature private branding.
- Be the first to introduce product or product line innovations.
- Edit the assortment for specific target segments.
- Coordinate merchandise for a particular function from a wide array of products.

For a discussion of differentiation strategies for low margin goods see Wortzel (1987).

Interactive or direct marketing

Direct marketing (i.e. a zero intermediary level channel) is current practice in industrial markets when potential buyers are few and products are sophisticated or custom made and of high unit value. The surprising fact in recent years is the development of this selling system in the field of consumer goods, largely as a result of the development of new communication media, such as telemarketing, direct response radio and television, electronic shopping (Minitel) etc.

Direct marketing is defined by the Direct Marketing Association as 'an interactive system which uses one or more advertising media to effect a measurable response and/or transaction at any location'. Thus, according to this definition, direct marketing does not necessarily imply non-store marketing, i.e. a marketing system without using intermediaries. To clarify the field, a distinction must be made between 'direct-order' marketing and 'direct-relationship' marketing.

- In *direct-order marketing*, purchases are made from the home and delivered to the home, and the firm distributes directly without using intermediaries. This is non-store marketing, and the techniques used are mail order catalogues, direct mail, telemarketing, electronic shopping etc.

- In *direct-relationship marketing*, the objective is to stimulate sales by establishing direct contacts with prospects and customers to create or maintain a continuing relationship.

Thus, direct-relationship marketing can very well co-exist with a conventional vertical indirect marketing system. For this reason, the expression 'interactive marketing' seems more appropriate than 'direct marketing', which refers essentially to non-store marketing practices.

The development of interactive marketing is indicative of a significant change in the exchange and communication process between producers and consumers in affluent economies. It suggests that the marketing monologue which prevails in most market situations tends to be replaced by a marketing dialogue, *customized marketing* being substituted for mass or segment marketing.

Rationale of direct-order marketing

Several factors explain the development of more direct marketing and communication systems.

- First, the considerable *cost increase of personal communication*. According to a study by Forsyth (1988), the average cost of a business sales call rose to $251.63 in 1987, i.e. 160 per cent of the 1977 cost of $96.79.
- Simultaneously, one observes a *weakening of mass media advertising's effectiveness*, caused by the proliferation of advertising messages and changing viewing habits in TV (zapping, VCR) combined with the rising cost of brand image advertising campaigns.
- Shopping is no longer associated with fun and excitement, and is perceived as a bore and as time-consuming by educated consumers who tend to give their time higher value. For consumers, catalogue shopping is a convenient shopping alternative.
- For the manufacturers, direct marketing presents several potential advantages. It allows *greater selectivity* in communicating with the market, personalization of messages and the maintenance of a continuous relationship. From a strategic point of view, interactive marketing gives to the producer a way to bypass intermediaries and to reduce the firm's dependence on the goodwill of too-powerful retailers.
- Finally, the formidable development of *low-cost computers*, with their immense storage and processing capabilities, has greatly

facilitated the use of databases to record and keep track of commercial contacts with customers. This information is then used to reach them individually with highly personalized messages.

The economic incentive of increasing the productivity of marketing expenditure is very appealing.

Organization of direct-order marketing systems

Direct-order marketing supposes the development of a marketing database system. The essence of the system is to communicate directly with customers and ask them to respond in a tangible way. A database system can be defined as follows:

> A marketing database is an organized collection of data about individual customers, prospects or suspects that is accessible and actionable for such marketing purposes as lead generation, lead qualification, sale of a product or of a service, or maintenance of customer relationships (Kotler, 1991, p. 627).

The development of a direct marketing campaign implies the creation of personalized messages containing an offer and an invitation to respond. The database is then used to record the response of customers and to adapt the next message.

- *The message content.* The end objective is of course to achieve a sale, but the immediate objective is to create a dialogue and to maintain a relationship. The intermediate objective may be to obtain prospect leads, to reactivate former customers, to acknowledge receipt of an order, to welcome new customers, to inform customers and to prepare them for later purchase, to generate requests for catalogues or leaflets, to propose a visit to a showroom etc.
- *Personalized messages.* This is the main superiority of direct marketing over mass media advertising. Instead of using standardized advertising messages and a 'shotgun' approach, a marketing database makes possible a 'rifle' approach and, at the limit, a truly personalized message by including details relevant to the target customer and not to others.
- *The offer.* To obtain a positive behavioural response from the prospect, the message must include an offer or a proposition sufficiently attractive to induce prospects to respond. In the simplest case, it is an offer to purchase the product. It could also be the proposal to inspect the product, a free sample or free credit, participation in a contest or in a club etc. The attractiveness of the offer is a key success factor.

Table 11.8 Growth of direct marketing in Europe (1989 expenditure in million ECUs) (European Direct Marketing Association (1991))

Country	Mailings	Direct advertising	Telemarketing and others	Total	ECU per head	Percentage of total
Germany	3650	2340	810	6800	109	33
UK	1370	1330	160	2860	51	14
Italy	2210	460	70	2750	48	11
France	880	1170	230	2280	36	10
Holland	970	250	920	2140	144	11
Spain	380	940	30	1350	35	7
Denmark	600	190	90	880	162	4
Belgium/Luxembourg	190	190	50	430	43	2
Portugal	10	50	10	70	6	—
Greece	10	50	10	70	6	1
Ireland	10	50	10	60	14	—
Total	10 280	7020	2390	16 690	60	100
Percentage	52	36	12	100		

- *Measurable response*. In an interactive marketing system, the key objective is to engage in a dialogue with individual customers, and it is therefore essential to obtain some kind of response. The ideal response is placing an order, but other forms of response are sought, such as agreeing to a sales appointment, returning a reply coupon, confirming receipt of information, agreeing to attend an exhibition, providing more information about needs and wants etc. In an interactive marketing system, potential customers are self-selected since only potentially interested customers will respond.
- *Communication mix*. The communication media used are mainly the personalized media like direct mail, catalogue marketing and telemarketing. Then come radio, magazine and television direct-response marketing and electronic shopping. Direct mail remains the most important medium.

One of the greatest advantages of direct marketing is that responses to campaigns are measured, enabling marketing management to identify the effectiveness of different approaches. It is testable and it permits privacy in that the marketing offer is not visible to the competition (Roscitt and Parket, 1988).

Limits of direct-order marketing

Convenience is the major benefit for the consumer, but many consumers can be less interested in convenience than in product quality, reliable delivery and in being able to touch, feel and smell the merchandise. In addition, as direct marketing becomes more and more popular, many consumers view the techniques of direct marketing—the unsolicited telephone calls, the junk mail and the trading and renting of mailing lists—as an *invasion of privacy*.

Quelch and Takeuchi (1981, p. 84) questioned the future of non-store marketing by raising the following questions.

- What if postal rates double?
- What if privacy laws prevent direct marketers from selling or buying mailing lists?
- What if a freeze is placed on credit card usage?
- What if consumers mount a revolt against catalogue clutter?

These questions are more relevant than ever with the spectacular development of direct marketing, and the European Commission is currently examining proposals for regulating this ever increasing field (see Table 11.8). Direct marketing is probably less controversial in the field of business-to-business marketing than in the field of consumer marketing, as suggested by the data of Table 11.9.

Table 11.9 Success of telemarketing in industrial sales (based on 249 respondents) (Marshall and Vredenburg (1988, p. 18))

Overall level of success	Percentage of respondents ($n=249$)
Very successful	37.3
Moderately successful	41.0
Not very successful	21.7
Change in the use of telemarketing since adoption	
Increased	39.7
Stayed about the same	38.2
Decreased	22.1
Change in the number of telemarketing sales representatives since adoption by the firm	
Increased	42.3
Stayed the same	38.1
Decreased	20.6

Relationship marketing

Interactive marketing does not necessarily imply direct-order marketing. *Relationship marketing* is a marketing system oriented towards a strong, lasting relationship with individual customers, in contrast with *transaction marketing*, where the firm has a more short-term orientation and is mostly interested in immediate sales achievement (see Dwyer *et al.*, 1987).

In a relationship marketing system, the profit centre is the customer and not the product, and attracting new customers is viewed as an intermediate objective. Maintaining and cultivating the existing customer base is the key objective, in order to create a long-term mutually profitable relationship. Relationship marketing is particularly useful in industrial marketing, where buyers' and sellers' relationships are frequently close, long-lasting and important for both parties.

Jackson (1985) establishes a distinction between two types of customer behaviour: the 'lost-for-good' model and the 'always-a-share' model of behaviour.

- The *'lost-for-good'* model assumes that if a customer does decide to leave a supplier, the account is lost forever, or, alternatively, that it is at least as difficult and costly for the vendor to win back such an account as it was to win the customer in the first place. Because of high switching costs, the customer changes suppliers very reluctantly.

- The 'always-a-share' model assumes that buyers can maintain less intense commitments than they do in the 'lost-for-good' model and that they can have commitments to more than one vendor at the same time. The account can easily switch part or all of its purchases from one vendor to another, and therefore it can share its patronage, perhaps over time, among multiple vendors.

These two models provide the end-points of a spectrum of behaviour of industrial customers. Relationship marketing is sensible for customers behaving as in the 'lost-for-good' model; transaction marketing is appropriate for customers behaving as suggested by the 'always-a-share' model (Jackson, 1985, p. 16).

Strategic pricing decisions

Each product has a price, but each firm is not necessarily in a position to determine the price at which it sells its product. When products are undifferentiated and competitors numerous, the firm has no market power and must take the price level imposed by the market. But when the firm has developed strategic marketing and thus has gained some degree of market power, setting the price is a key decision which conditions the success of its strategy, to a large extent. Until recently, pricing decisions were still considered from a purely financial viewpoint, and largely determined by costs and profitability constraints. This approach changed because of the upheavals in the economic and competitive situation during the crisis years: double digit inflation, increased costs of raw materials, high interest rates, price controls, increased competition, lower purchasing power, consumerism etc. All these factors play an important part in making pricing decisions of strategic importance. After describing the strategic role of price in marketing, we will analyse pricing decisions that emphasize costs, competition and demand successively. Figure 12.1 describes the general problem of price setting in a competitive environment.

Pricing and the marketing mix

From the firm's point of view, the question of price has two aspects: the price is an instrument to stimulate demand, much like advertising for example, and at the same time price is a determinant factor of the firm's long-term profitability. Therefore the choice of a pricing strategy must respect two types of coherence: an internal coherence, i.e. setting a product price respecting constraints of costs and profitability, and an external coherence, i.e. setting the price level keeping in mind the market's purchasing power and the price of competing goods. Furthermore, pricing decisions must remain coherent with decisions regarding product positioning and distribution strategy.

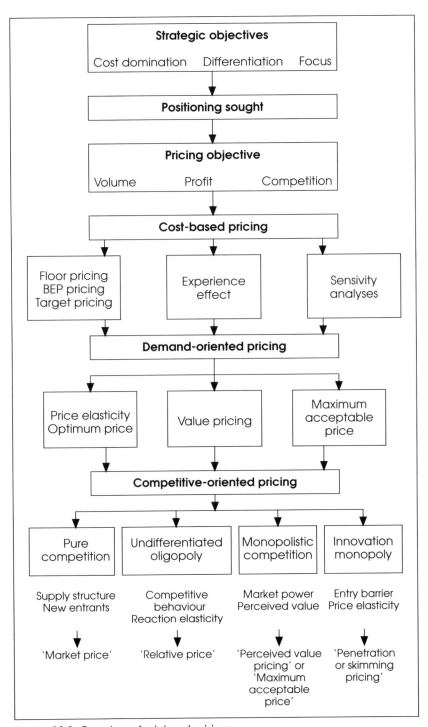

Figure 12.1 Overview of pricing decisions

The buyer's perception of price

Price is the *monetary expression of value* and as such occupies a central role in competitive exchange. Purchasing behaviour can be seen as a system of exchange in which searching for satisfaction and monetary sacrifices compensate each other. This behaviour results from forces that balance a need, characterized by the buyer's attitude towards the product and the product's price. From the buyer's point of view, the price he or she is willing to pay measures the intensity of the need and the quantity and nature of satisfaction that is expected; from the seller's point of view, the price at which he or she is willing to sell measures the value of inputs incorporated in the product, to which the seller adds the profit that is hoped to be achieved.

Formally, monetary price can be defined as a ratio indicating the amount of money necessary for acquiring a given quantity of a good or service:

$$\text{Price} = \frac{\text{Amount of money provided by the buyer}}{\text{Quantity of good provided by the seller}}$$

In fact, the notion of price is wider and goes beyond the simple coincidence of purely objective and quantitative factors. The amount of money paid measures incompletely the sacrifice made, and, in the same way, the quantity of good obtained measures actual satisfaction imperfectly.

The total value of a product

We saw in Chapter 4 that, as far as the buyer is concerned, a product is a *package of benefits*, and the services that are derived from the product are many. The latter not only result from the product's core service, but also from all the objective and perceptual secondary utilities that characterize the product. Therefore the price must reflect the value of all such satisfaction to the buyer.

Let us compare two watches having the same objective technical quality. Brand A is a prestigious one, with an elegant design, sold exclusively by watchmakers; it carries a five-year guarantee and is advertised using sport and theatre personalities. Brand B is little known, soberly designed, sold in department stores with a 6-month guarantee and advertised as being reliable.

Although these two watches provide the same core or functional service (time measurement), we can see that they are two distinct products and their *value as perceived by potential buyers* will be very different. Therefore, seen from the demand point of view, price must be conceived as the compensation for all services rendered and set according to the total value of total utility perceived by the buyer.

Hence the importance of a well-defined positioning before setting the selling price.

The total cost of acquiring a product

Just as the obtained quantity of a good measures actual satisfaction imperfectly, the amount of money paid measures the importance of actual sacrifice imperfectly. In fact, the actual cost borne by the buyer not only covers the price paid, but also the *terms of exchange*. These refer to all the concrete practical procedures that lead to transfer of ownership, such as conditions of payment, delivery terms and times, after-sale service etc. In some cases, the buyer may have to bear important costs to compare prices, transact and negotiate. This can happen if, for example, the buyer is located in isolated regions. Similarly, the buyer may face high *transfer costs* if he or she changes suppliers after having set the product specifications in relation to a given supplier. The main sources of transfer costs are as follows:

- Costs of modifying products so as to fit a new supplier's product.
- Changes in habits of consuming or using the product.
- Expenditures on training and reorientation of users.
- Investments to acquire new equipment necessary for the use of new products.
- Psychological costs related to change.

All these costs may be higher for some clients than others. When transfer costs exist, the real cost to the buyer is much higher than the product's monetary price.

Therefore, from the buyer's point of view, the notion of price goes well beyond that of monetary price. It involves all the benefits provided by the product and all the costs borne by the buyer. Hence measures of price sensitivity must take into account all these benefits and costs as well as the product's nominal price. To illustrate the complexity of pricing, seven different ways of changing the above price ratio are presented in Table 12.1.

Table 12.1 How to change price? (Monroe, 1979, pp. 5–6)

- Change the quantity of money or goods and services given up by the buyer.
- Change the quantity of goods and services provided by the seller.
- Change the quality of goods and services provided.
- Change the premiums or discounts to be applied for quantity variations.
- Change the time and place of transfer of ownership.
- Change the place and time of payment.
- Change the acceptable form of payment.

Importance of pricing decisions

The following points highlight the importance of pricing strategies in the current macro-marketing environment.

- The chosen price directly influences *demand level* and determines the level of activity. A price set too high or too low can endanger the product's development. Therefore, measuring price elasticity is of crucial importance, and it is difficult to achieve.
- The selling price directly determines the *profitability of the operation*, not only by the profit margin allowed, but also through quantities sold by fixing the conditions under which fixed costs can be recovered over the appropriate time horizon. Thus, a small price difference may have a major impact on profitability.
- The price set by the firm influences the product or the brand's general perception and contributes to the *brand's positioning* within potential buyers' evoked sets. Buyers perceive the price as a signal, especially in consumer goods markets. The price quoted invariably creates a notion of quality, and therefore is a component of the brand image.
- More than any other marketing variable, the price is an easy means of *comparison between competing products or brands*. The slightest change in price is quickly perceived by the market, and because it is so visible it can suddenly overturn the balance of forces. The price is a forced point of contact between competitors.
- Pricing strategy must be compatible with the *other components of strategic marketing*. The price must allow for financing of promotional and advertising strategy. Product packaging must reinforce high quality and high price positioning; pricing strategy must respect distribution strategy and allow the granting of necessary distribution margins to ensure that the objectives of covering the market can be achieved.

Recent developments in the economic and competitive environment, which were discussed in Chapter 2, have played their part in increasing the importance and complexity of pricing strategies significantly.

- Acceleration of technological progress and *shortening of product life cycles* means that a new activity must be made to pay over a much shorter time span than previously. Given that correction is so much more difficult, a mistake in setting the initial price is that much more serious.
- *Proliferation of brands* or products which are weakly differentiated, the regular appearance of new products and the range of products all reinforce the importance of correct price positioning; yet small differences can sometimes modify the market's perception of a brand quite significantly.

- Increased prices of some raw materials, inflationary pressures, wage rigidities and price controls call for more rigorous *economic management*.
- *Legal constraints*, as well as regulatory and social constraints, such as price controls, setting maximum margins, authorization for increases etc., limit the firm's autonomy in determining prices.
- *Reduced purchasing power* in most Western economies makes buyers more aware of price differences, and this increased price sensitivity reinforces the role of price as an instrument for stimulating sales and market share.

Given the importance and complexity of these decisions, pricing strategies are often elaborated by the firm's general management.

Alternative pricing objectives

All firms aim to make their activities profitable and to generate the possible economic surplus. This broad objective can in practice take different forms and it is in the firm's interest to clarify from the outset its strategic priorities in setting prices. Generally speaking, possible objectives can be classified in three categories, according to whether they are centred on profits, volumes or competition.

Profit-oriented objectives are either profit maximization or achievement of a sufficient return on invested capital. *Profit maximization* is the model put forward by economists. In practice it is difficult to apply this model. Not only does it assume precise knowledge of cost and demand functions for each product, it also assumes a stability which is seldom enjoyed by environmental and competitive factors. In Chapter 8 (see Appendix 8.1), we described the problem of calculating optimal price. The objective of *target return rate on investment* (ROI) is widespread. In practice it takes the form of calculating a target price, or a sufficient price; that is, a price which, for a given level of activity, ensures a fair return on invested capital. This approach, often adopted by large enterprises, has the merit of simplicity, but is incorrect. It ignores the fact that it is the price level that ultimately determines demand level.

Volume-oriented objectives aim to maximize current revenue or market share, or simply to ensure sufficient sales growth. Maximizing market share implies adopting a *penetration price*, i.e. a relatively low price, which is lower than competitors' prices, in order to increase volume and consequently market share as fast as possible. Once a dominant position is reached, the objective changes to one of sufficient or 'satisfactory' rate of return. As we saw in Chapter 8, this is a strategy often used by firms having accumulated a high production volume and who expect reduced costs due to learning effects. A totally different strategy is that of *skimming pricing*. The goal here is to achieve high sales revenue, given that some buyers or market segments are prepared to pay a high price because of the product's distinctive (real or perceived) qualities. The objective here is to achieve the highest possible turnover with a high price rather than high volume.

Competition-oriented objectives either aim for price stability or to be in line with competitors. In a number of industries dominated by a leading firm, the objective is to establish a stable relationship between prices of various competing products and to avoid wide fluctuations in prices that would undermine buyers' confidence. The objective of keeping in line with other firms reveals that the firm is aware of its inability to exercise any influence on the market, especially when there is one dominant firm and products are standardized, as in undifferentiated oligopolies. In this case, the firm prefers to concentrate its efforts on competing over features other than price. Forms of non-price competition will prevail in the market.

To elaborate a pricing strategy, three groups of factors must be taken into consideration: costs, demand and competition. We will now examine successively each of these factors and their implications for price determination.

Cost-based pricing procedures

Starting with costs analysis is certainly the most natural way to approach the pricing problem, and it is also the one most familiar to firms. Given that the manufacturer has undergone costs in order to produce and commercialize a product, it is natural that its main preoccupation would be to determine various price levels compatible with constraints such as covering direct costs and fixed costs and generating a fair profit. Figure 12.2 shows a typical cost structure in which the definitions of the main cost concepts are given.

Cost-based price concepts

Prices which are based on costs and make no explicit reference to market factors are called 'cost-based prices'. Cost analysis identifies four types of cost-based prices, each responding to specific cost and profit requirements.

The *floor price*, or the minimum price, corresponds to direct variable costs (C), also known as 'out-of-pocket costs'. It is the price that only

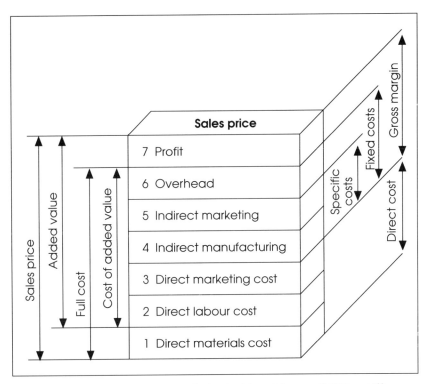

Figure 12.2 The elements of price (adapted from Monroe (1979, p. 61))

covers the product's replacement value, and therefore implies zero gross profit margin.

$$\text{Floor price} = \text{Direct variable costs}$$

This price concept is useful for negotiating exceptional orders or for second market discounting, when the firm has unused capacity and has the possibility to sell in a new market such that there will be a negligible loss of sales in its main market. Floor price, also called 'marginal price', is the absolute minimum selling price the firm should accept. Any price above the floor price can allow a firm to use its production capacity to a maximum and still generate extra funds to cover overheads or improve profits. Exceptional orders, generics for large retail chain and foreign markets, provide opportunities for this form of discriminatory pricing strategy.

The *break-even price* (BEP) corresponds to the price where fixed costs and direct costs are recovered, given the sales volume assumed. It ensures that both the product's replacement value as well as fixed costs (F) are recovered.

$$\text{Break-even price} = C + F / E(Q)$$

where $E(Q)$ denotes expected sales volume. The BEP corresponds to the full cost concept, where the level of activity is used as criterion for allocating the fixed costs.

Break-even prices are usually calculated for different volume levels, as shown in the example of Table 12.2. This defines a range of minimum prices. Note that the break-even price depends on the volume of activity and only coincides with the full cost at that level.

Table 12.2 Cost-based pricing: an example of application

Basic data

Production capacity	180 000 units
Capital invested (K)	BF240 000 000
Expected rate of return (r)	10 %
Unit direct cost (C)	BF1050 per unit
Fixed costs (F)	BF90 000 000 per year
Expected sales volume $E(Q)$	120 000 units
Pessimistic estimate	90 000 units
Optimistic estimate	150 000 units

Cost-based prices

Floor price: $\qquad P = C = $ BF1050 per unit

BEP price: $\qquad P = C + \dfrac{F}{E(Q)} = 1050 + \dfrac{90\,000\,000}{E(Q)}$

$$P_1 = \text{BF2050} \quad P_2 = \text{BF1800} \quad P_3 = \text{BF1650}$$

Target price: $\qquad P = C + \dfrac{F}{E(Q)} + \dfrac{r_,K}{E(Q)}$

$$P = 1050 + \dfrac{90\,000\,000}{E(Q)} + \dfrac{0.10 \times 240\,000\,000}{E(Q)}$$

$$P_1 = \text{BF2317} \quad P_2 = \text{BF2000} \quad P_3 = \text{BF1810}$$

Break-even (be) thresholds

Sales price: $\qquad P = $ BF1950 per unit

BEV (in volume):

$$Q = \dfrac{F}{P - C} = \dfrac{90\,000\,000}{1950 - 1050} = 100\,000 \text{ units}$$

BES (in sales revenue):

$$R = \dfrac{F}{(P - C)/P} = \dfrac{90\,000\,000}{0.46} = \text{BF195 652 174}$$

The *mark-up price* is set by adding a standard mark-up to the break-even price. Assuming that the firm wants to earn a 20 per cent mark-up on sales, the mark-up price is given by

$$\text{Mark-up price} = \text{BEP} / (1 - \text{desired mark-up})$$

This pricing method, popular for its simplicity, ignores demand and competition. It will work only if the expected sales level is achieved.

The *target price*, or sufficient price, includes, apart from direct costs and fixed costs, a profit constraint, which is normally determined by reference to a 'normal' rate of return (r) on invested capital (K). This cost-based price is also calculated with reference to an assumed level of activity.

$$\text{Target price} = C + F / E(Q) + r K / E(Q)$$

where K denotes invested capital and r the rate of return considered as sufficient or normal. Like the break-even price, target price depends on the activity volume being considered.

The same criticism must be formulated here. This pricing method will work only if the expected sales volume is achieved.

The risk of circular logic

Target and mark-up prices are used widely, because of their simplicity and the apparent security arising from the illusory certainty of a margin, since mark-up and target pricing procedures promise to ensure a given return on cost. Their most important shortcoming is the lack of any relationship between price and volume. In fact, they implicitly contain a built-in circular logic: volume determines costs, which determine price, which in turn determines the level of demand.

Indeed, there is no guarantee that the adopted target price or mark-up will generate the activity volume on the basis of which it was calculated. Table 12.2 shows what happens to the target price if the firm's sales volume is below the assumed level.

In the example, the expected activity level is 120 000 units and the corresponding target price is F2000. If demand is only 90 000 units, to maintain the desired profitability level the price would have to be increased and the product sold at F2317.

Is raising price the appropriate response in the face of declining demand? Similarly, if the firm's sales exceed expectations, fixed costs are spread over a larger volume and the target price declines. Should management respond to excess demand by cutting prices?

This pricing behaviour runs counter to economic logic and leads to inappropriate recommendations. The firm that sets price from the sole perspective of its own internal needs generally forgoes the profit it seeks.

> During the recession of 1974–75, the automobile industry faced such a dilemma. During 1974–75, car prices rose on average $1000 while sales fell by 25 per cent. Yet, the automobile industry could not reduce price because of its inflexible, formularized method of pricing (*Business Week*, 1975).

If all firms within a given industry adopt the same mark-up or target rate of return, the prices tend to be similar and price competition is minimized. In practice, cost-based prices are used only as a convenient starting point, because, in general, firms have more reliable information about costs than about demand factors.

Usefulness of cost-based pricing

Cost-orientated prices constitute a starting point for setting a price. They cannot be the only basis for determining prices because these pricing procedures ignore demand, product perceived value and competition. However, they do have a real usefulness, because they provide answers to the following types of questions:

- What is the sales volume or sales revenue required to cover all costs?
- How does the target price or the mark-up price compare with prices of direct competition?
- To what level of market share does the level of sales at the break-even point correspond?
- What is the expected sales increase required to cover a fixed cost increase, such as an advertising campaign, assuming constant price?
- In the case of a price change, what is the necessary volume change to maintain the present level of profitability?
- If prices go down, what is the minimum volume increase required to offset the price decrease?
- If prices go up, what is the permissible volume decrease to offset the price increase?
- What is the implied price elasticity necessary to enhance or maintain profitability?
- What is the rate of return on invested capital for different price levels?

Cost analysis is a first necessary step which helps to identify the problem by focusing attention on the financial implications of various pricing strategies. Armed with this information, the firm is better placed to approach the more qualitative aspects of the problem, namely market sensitivity to prices and competitive reactions.

Demand-oriented pricing procedures

Pricing based exclusively on the firm's own financial needs is inappropriate. In a market economy, it is the buyer who ultimately decides which products will sell. Consequently, in a market-driven organization an effective pricing procedure *starts with the price the market is most likely to accept*, which in turn determines the target cost. An important concept in demand analysis is the *notion of elasticity*, defined in Chapter 5 (see Appendix 5.1). We will first examine the main factors affecting price sensitivity, and then describe various approaches that can be adopted to measure it.

Factors affecting price sensitivity

Every buyer is sensitive to prices, but this sensitivity can vary tremendously from one situation to another, according to the importance of the satisfaction provided by the product, or conversely depending on the sacrifices, other than price, imposed by obtaining the product. Nagle (1987) has identified nine factors affecting buyers' price sensitivity:

- *Unique-value effect*: buyers are less price-sensitive when the product is more unique.
- *Substitute awareness effect*: buyers are less price-sensitive when they are less aware of substitutes.
- *Difficult comparison effect*: buyers are less price-sensitive when they cannot easily compare the quality of substitutes.
- *Total expenditure effect*: buyers are less price-sensitive the lower the expenditure is to a ratio of their income.
- *End benefit effect*: buyers are less price-sensitive the lower the expenditure is compared with the total cost of the end product.
- *Shared cost effect*: buyers are less price-sensitive when part of the cost is borne by another party.
- *Sunk investment effect*: buyers are less price-sensitive when the product is used in conjunction with assets previously bought.
- *Price—quality effect*: buyers are less price-sensitive when the product is assumed to have more quality, prestige or exclusiveness.
- *Inventory effect*: buyers are less price-sensitive when they cannot store the product.

The questions to examine for assessing buyers' price sensitivity are presented in Table 12.3.

Tables 12.3 Factors affecting price sensitivity (Nagle, 1987, pp. 73–6)

1 **The unique value effect**
- Does the product have any (tangible or intangible) attributes that differentiate it from competing products?
- How much do buyers value those unique, differentiating attributes?

2 **The substitute awareness effect**
- What alternatives do buyers have (considering both competing brands and competing products)?
- Are buyers aware of alternative suppliers or substitute products?

3 **The difficult comparison effect**
- How difficult is it for buyers to compare the offers of different suppliers? Can the attributes of a product be determined by observation, or must the product be purchased and consumed to learn what it offers?
- Is the product highly complex, requiring costly specialists to evaluate its differentiating attributes?
- Are the prices of different suppliers easily comparable, or are they stated for different sizes and combinations that make comparisons difficult?

4 **The total expenditure effect**
- How significant are buyers' expenditures of the product in cash terms and (for a consumer product) as a portion of their incomes?

5 **The end benefit effect**
- What benefit do buyers seek from the product?
- How price-sensitive are buyers to the cost of the end benefit?
- What portion of the benefit does the product's price account for?

6 **The shared cost effect**
- Do the buyers pay the full cost of the product?
- If not, what portion of the cost do they pay?

7 **The sunk investment effect**
- Must buyers of the product make complementary expenditures in anticipation of its continued use?
- For how long are buyers locked in by those expenditures?

8 **The price–quality effect**
- Is a prestige image an important attribute for the product?
- Is the product enhanced in value when its price excludes some consumers?
- Is the product of unknown quality, and are there few reliable cues for ascertaining quality before purchase? If so, how great would the loss to buyers be of low quality relative to the price of the product?

9 **The inventory effect**
- Do buyers hold inventories of the product?
- Do they expect the current price to be temporary?

Note that these determinants of price sensitivity apply equally to the decision of buying a particular product category (market demand price sensitivity) and that of buying a particular brand within a product category (interbrand price sensitivity). In the first case, the question would, for example, be to choose between a laptop computer or a hi-fi; in the second case, the alternatives would be, for example, to buy a Toshiba or an IBM laptop computer. Both kinds of decision are affected by the price level of the alternatives.

Price sensitivity of the organizational buyer

We saw in Chapter 3 that in industrial markets buyers' needs are generally well defined and the functions performed by products clearly specified. In these conditions, it is sometimes easier to determine the importance of price to the organizational customer. Porter (1980, pp. 115–18) observed that buyers who are *not price sensitive* tend to have the following behavioural characteristics or motivations:

- The cost of the product is a small part of the cost of the buyer's product cost and/or purchasing budget.
- The penalty for product failure is high relative to its cost.
- Effectiveness of the product (or service) can yield major savings or improvement in performance.
- The buyer competes with a high quality strategy to which the purchased product is perceived to contribute.
- The buyer seeks a custom designed or differentiated variety.
- The buyer is very profitable and/or can readily pass on the cost of inputs.
- The buyer is poorly informed about the product and/or does not purchase from well-defined specifications.
- The motivation of the actual decision-maker is not narrowly defined as minimizing the cost of inputs.

Industrial market research studies can help in identifying these behavioural characteristics or requirements. These are useful to know in order to direct pricing policy.

To summarize, price sensitivity of demand is determined by a variety of factors closely related to the benefits or values that the product represents to the buyer. This price sensitivity is measured quantitatively by price elasticity.

Measuring price elasticity

Elasticity directly measures buyers' price sensitivity, and ideally allows the calculation of quantities demanded at various price levels.

Table 12.4 Comparing average elasticity of marketing variables

Published sources	Number of observations	Average value of estimated elasticities			
		Advertising	Price	Quality	Distribution
Lambin (1976; 1988)	127	0.081	−1.735	0.521	1.395
Leone and Schultz (1980)	25	0.003–0.230	—	—	—
Assmus et al.(1984)	22	0.221 (0.264)	—	—	—
Hagerty et al. (1988)	203	0.003 (0.105)	−0.985 (1.969)	0.344 (0.528)	0.304 (0.255)
Neslin and Shoemaker (1983)	25	—	−1.800	—	—
Tellis (1988)	220	—	−1.760	—	—

Recall the definition of price elasticity: it is the percentage change in a product's unit sales resulting from a 1 per cent change in its price:

$$\varepsilon = \frac{\text{Percentage change in unit sales}}{\text{Percentage change in price}}$$

Price elasticity is negative, since a price increase generally produces sales decline, whereas a price cut generally produces a sales increase.

The economic and marketing literature contains many econometric studies on measuring price elasticities, as shown in Table 12.4. For a summary of elasticity studies, see Hanssens *et al.* (1990). Tellis (1988) found a mean price of elasticity of -2.5. Broadbent (1980) reported an average price elasticity of -1.6 for major British brands. Lambin, covering a sample of 137 brands, reported an average price elasticity of -1.74 (Lambin, 1976; 1988).

Furthermore, if the firm is pursuing profit maximization, it is also possible to determine the optimal selling price using a price elasticity estimate (see Table 8.2). In the case of a monopolistic situation, the price optimization rule is

$$P^* = C(\varepsilon/1 + \varepsilon)$$

where C is the direct cost and ε the brand price elasticity. As explained in Chapter 8, the optimal cost mark-up ($\varepsilon/1 + \varepsilon$) is large if the brand price elasticity is close to one in absolute value, thereby denoting the existence of a strong market preference for the brand.

Price optimization rules originally developed for the case of a monopoly (Dorfman and Steiner, 1954), have been extended to oligopolies (Lambin *et al.*, 1975) and to the dynamic case where market response is spread over time (Nerlove and Arrow, 1962; Jacquemin, 1973).

Limitations of price elasticity measures

Despite the relevance of these works, there have been very few practical applications of this highly quantitative approach to the problem of pricing, except maybe in some large enterprises. The reason is that the notion of elasticity presents a number of conceptual and operational difficulties which reduce its practical usefulness.

- Elasticity measures a relationship based on buying behaviour and is therefore only observable *after the fact*; its predictive value depends on the stability of the conditions that gave rise to the observation; it cannot for example, be used to determine the price of new products.
- In many situations, the problem is not so much to know how to

Table 12.5 Impact of price elasticity on quantity and on sales revenue

| | Elastic demand curve: $\varepsilon = -3.7$ | | Inelastic demand curve: $\varepsilon = -0.19$ | | |
Price	Quantity (× 1000)	Sales revenue (× F1000)	Price	Quantity (× 1000)	Sales revenue (× F1000)
12 000	80	960 000	8.00	300	2 400
9 000	400	3 600 000	6.00	320	1 920
7 000	1 200	8 400 000	4.00	340	1 360

adapt prices to present market sensitivities, but to know how to change and *act upon this sensitivity* in the direction sought by the firm. From this viewpoint, it is more interesting to know the product's perceived value by the targeted group of buyers.

- Elasticity measures the impact of price on quantity bought, but does not measure the effect of price on the propensity to try the product, on repeat purchases, exclusivity rate etc. But these are all important notions for understanding consumers' response mechanisms with respect to prices. Therefore, *other measures*, which are less aggregate, need to be developed for marketing management.

Furthermore, in practice it is often very hard to get sufficiently stable and reliable estimates of price elasticities which could be used to calculate an optimal selling price. In an econometric study, an estimate having a Student t-value of 4 (rarely obtained) is very satisfactory, because it implies a statistical significance level of 1 per cent for degrees of freedom above 30 (rarely observed). However, at this level of precision, the coefficient of variation, which is the ratio of the standard deviation to the mean, is 25 per cent; this implies that it is highly likely that the true value of the estimated price elasticity falls in an interval of plus or minus 25 per cent, which is operationally a totally unacceptable level of imprecision.

These limitations are inherent in the economic model, which is developed more to help understand economic behaviour than as a decision-making tool. This does not imply, however, that the economic theory of price determination has no relevance to the study of the problem of price determination. Even if imprecise, the order of magnitude of an estimated price elasticity helps to determine the direction of price changes and its impact on sales revenue. Table 12.5 shows the comparison of the 'price–quantity–sales revenue' relationship in two demand functions, with one price elastic and the other inelastic.

Usefulness of elasticity measures

Knowledge of the order of magnitude of an elasticity is on the whole useful in many ways:

- Elasticities provide information about the direction in which prices should change in order to stimulate demand and increase turnover.
- Comparing elasticities of competing brands identifies those which can withstand a price increase better, thus revealing their market power.
- Comparing elasticities of products in the same category helps to adjust prices within the category.

Table 12.6 Price elasticity estimates: two examples from the US market (automobile data from Carlson (1978); air transport data from Oum and Gillen (1981)

Demand for automobiles		Demand for air transport	
Sub-compact	−0.83	First class	−0.75
Compact	−1.20	Economy	−1.40
Intermediate	−1.30	Discount	−2.10
Full-size	−1.54		
Luxury	−2.07		

• Cross elasticities help to predict demand shifts from one brand to another.

To illustrate, Table 12.6 shows estimated price elasticities in the car market and in the market for air transport in the USA. Although the estimates have insufficient precision for the exact calculation of prices, the results are nevertheless very enlightening as far as pricing policy orientation for each product category is concerned.

Value pricing

Value pricing is a customer-based pricing procedure which is an outgrowth of the multi-attribute product concept. From the customer's viewpoint, a product is the total package of benefits that is received when using the product. Therefore, the customer-oriented company should set its price according to customers' perceptions of product benefits and costs. To determine the price, the marketer needs to understand the customers' perceptions of benefits as well as their perceptions of the costs other than price. Customers balance the benefits of a purchase against its costs. When the product under consideration has the best relationship of benefit to cost, the customer is inclined to buy the product (Shapiro and Jackson, 1978). This customer-based pricing procedure can be implemented in different ways.

The maximum acceptable price

This approach is particularly useful for setting the price of industrial products, whose core benefit to the buyer is a cost reduction. To evaluate what the customer is prepared to pay, the procedure followed is to identify and evaluate the different satisfactions or services provided by the product as well as all the costs (other than price) it implies. Thus the procedure is the following:

• Understand the total use of the product from the buyer's point of view.

- Analyse the benefits generated by the product.
- Analyse the costs implied by the acquisition and the use of the product.
- Make cost–benefit trade-offs and determine the maximum acceptable price.

The highest price that the customer will be willing to pay for the product is given by

$$\text{Benefits} - \begin{array}{c} \text{Costs other} \\ \text{than price} \end{array} = \begin{array}{c} \text{Maximum Acceptable} \\ \text{Price (MAP)} \end{array}$$

The benefits to consider can be functional (the core service), operational, financial or personal. Similarly, the costs implied other than price are just as diverse: acquisition costs, installation, risk of failure, custom modification etc.

If the target market is segmented, this analysis should be done for different groups of buyers with non-identical behaviours.

Comparing the maximum acceptable price with competitors' prices helps evaluate the firm's margin for manoeuvre. Table 12.7 presents an example of the application of this method. See also Ross (1984).

The product's perceived value

The basic idea behind this method is the same: it is the product or the brand's perceived value which should determine the price level. By analysing and measuring the buyers' perception and its determinants, a score of total perceived value can be derived and used to set the price. The notion of perceived value is a direct extension of the multi-attribute attitude model described in Chapter 5.

To illustrate, let us reconsider the information of Table 5.3 already discussed in Chapter 5. We have here evaluations given by a group of potential buyers on six competing brands of laptop computers over five attributes. Respondents were asked to allocate 100 points to the five attributes in order to determine their relative importance and to rate the degree of perceived presence of each attribute on each brand on a 10-point scale. The overall perceived value of each brand is then measured by multiplying the points given to each attribute by their determinance. Finally, the measures are expressed as an index based on the average. In the example, we have respectively

$$A=1.07 \quad B=1.05 \quad C=1.09 \quad D=1.10 \quad E=0.98 \quad F=0.70$$

We notice that brands C and D have perceived values well above the average. In so far as these results can be assumed to be representative, and assuming that marketing pressure on the other

Table 12.7 Calculating the maximum acceptable price: the Hudson Chemical case (Leighton *et al.*, 1972, pp. 407–12)

Product description

A chemical compound to be used in conjunction with the regular water-softening chemicals.

Uses of the product

- To disperse the water softening compounds, thus lengthening their economic life.
- To reduce rust formation in the boiler system.

Benefits of the product

- Core benefit: reduce the amount of softening chemicals used by 35 per cent.
- Prevent rust formation.
- Reduction in time and effort required to regenerate the softeners.

Costs other than price

- Installation of a dispenser and of a storage tank in the plant.
- Service of the installation and technical assistance.
- Risk of breakdown.
- Lack of reference of the supplier.
- Custom modification.

Cost–benefit trade-off analysis

- Average use: 40 000 gallons of softenings per year.
- Cost per gallon: 50 cents.
- Average cost saving: 14 000 gallons (35 per cent), or $7000.
- Volume of Aqua-Pur: ratio:1/7, or 3715 gallons (26 000/7).
- Cost of installation: $450, or $50 per year over 5 years.
- Cost of maintenance: $320 per year.
- Total maximum acceptable cost: $7000 − ($50 + $320) = $6590.
- Maximum acceptable unit price: $6590/3714 gallons = $1.77 per gallon.
- Price of direct competitor: $1.36.

factors is equal, these two brands could set their prices above the average price offered by existing competitors.

Suppose that average price is FF33 000. Prices proportional to perceived values would therefore be

A=35 146   B=34 700   C=35 991   D=36 418   E=32 406   F=23 216

If brand D adopts a price which is below the price corresponding to its perceived value, it can hope to achieve a higher market share, because it would thus be increasing its relative marketing pressure.

This method, based on the *compositional approach*, is particularly appropriate when price sensitivity is determined by the presence of qualitative factors, such as perceived image effects.

Contributions of conjoint analysis

The same kind of result can be obtained with a *decompositional approach*, described in Chapter 5. Let us look again at the results obtained for the price variable in the cigarette study reported in Table 5.4.

For respondent 17, the following utilities were obtained:

$$(F\ 62;\ U = -2.5),\ (F\ 67;\ U = -3.5)\ \text{and}\ (F\ 72;\ U = -5.0)$$

We thus have three observations and using ordinary least squares (OLS) average price elasticity was calculated as: $\varepsilon = -3.59$ ($R^2 = 0.958$).

For respondent 86, we obtained the following pairs of values:

$$(F\ 62:\ U = -0.25),\ (F\ 67:\ U = -1.25),\ (F\ 72:\ U = 1.50)$$

The calculated elasticity here is : $\varepsilon = -1.11$ ($R^2 = 0.914$)

Note that the difference in price sensitivity between the two respondents is quite high. Now, suppose that we have similar information for a representative sample of 200 buyers. An average price elasticity could be estimated for the whole sample as well as for sub-groups of buyers of high or low price-sensitivity.

This kind of elasticity coefficient measures price sensitivity in terms of utility rather than in terms of quantity. Although more vague, it is nevertheless useful for comparison of different buyers' relative price sensitivities.

Flexible pricing strategies

Firms do not have a single price, but a variety of prices adapted to different market situations. Flexible pricing strategies occur in market situations where the same product is sold to different customers at different prices. Flexible pricing strategies arise primarily because of customers' heterogeneity, showing different price sensitivities. Price flexibility can be achieved in different ways: by region, period, product form or from one segment to another. We shall examine four different ways of achieving price flexibility. In the economic literature, the term 'price discrimination' has been used to designate the pricing strategies discussed here. In what follows, we shall adopt the classification of pricing strategies suggested by Tellis (1986).

Second market discounting

This situation occurs when a firm has excess production capacity and has the opportunity to sell in a new market such that there will be a negligible increase in fixed or variable costs and no loss of sales in its first market. The minimum acceptable selling price the firm should accept is the floor price, i.e. the unit direct cost. Opportunities for this pricing strategy exist in foreign trade, private label brands or special demographic groups, like students, children or senior citizens. The essential requirement for this strategy is that customers of the lower price market cannot resell the product in the higher price market because of the high transaction costs implied.

Periodic discounting

The pricing problem is different here: how to price a product confronted with different price sensitivity among potential buyers at the beginning and at the end of the seasonal period? Some buyers want to buy only at the beginning of the period and are not very price-sensitive, while others want to buy the product at any time, but are price-sensitive. To exploit the consumers' heterogeneity of demand, the firm will sell at the high price at the beginning of the period and systematically discount the product at the end of the period. This is the principle often involved in the temporal mark-downs and periodic discounting of off-season fashion goods, off-season travel fares, matinée tickets and happy hour drinks. An essential principle underlying this strategy of periodic discounting is the manner of discounting, which is predictable over time and generally known to consumers, who will, therefore, behave accordingly (Tellis, 1986, p. 150).

Random discounting

Which pricing strategy should be adopted in a market where the same product is sold at a low price by some firms and at a high price by others, knowing that some buyers are ready to spend time searching for the low price while others are not ready to do so? In this case, we have heterogeneity of demand with respect to perceived search costs among consumers. The objective of the firm is twofold here: (a) to sell at a high price to the maximum number of 'uninformed' consumers and at the same time (b) to prevent 'informed' consumers from buying at the low price of the competition. The recommended strategy here is 'random discounting', which involves maintaining a high price and discounting the product periodically 'at random'. The manner of discounting is crucial: it should be undiscernible or random so that uninformed buyers will buy randomly, usually at the high price, and the 'informed' will look around or wait until they can buy at the low price (Tellis, 1986, p. 150).

Price administration

Price administration deals with price adjustments for sales made under different conditions, in different quantities, to different types of intermediary in different geographic locations, with different conditions of payment etc. These price adjustments or discounts are designed for rewarding customers whose buying behaviour contributes to cost reductions for the firm. This is the case for quantity discounts, cash payment discounts, seasonal discounts, functional discounts etc. For more on this topic, see Monroe (1979, Chapter 11). (See also Table 11.5 of this book, p. 373.)

Competition-oriented pricing procedures

As far as competition is concerned, two kinds of factors greatly influence the firm's autonomy in its pricing strategy: the sector's competitive structure, characterized by the number of competing firms, and the importance of the product's perceived value.

- *Competitive structures* were described in Chapter 8. Clearly, when the firm is a monopoly, autonomy is great in setting its price; it tends to diminish as the number of competitors increases; we have monopoly and perfect competition at the extremes, and differentiated oligopoly and monopolistic situations as the intermediate positions.
- The *product's perceived value* results from the firm's efforts to differentiate in order to achieve an external competitive advantage; where an element of differentiation exists and is perceived by the buyer as a value, the buyer is usually prepared to pay a price above that of competing products. In this case, the firm has some degree of autonomy over prices.

Table 12.8 presents these two factors, each at two levels of intensity (low or high). We can thus identify four distinct situations, in each of which the question of price determination takes on a different form.

Table 12.8 Competitive environments of pricing decisions

Market power: perceived value of the product	Number of competitors	
	Low	High
High	Monopoly or differentiated oligopoly	Monopolistic competition
Weak	Undifferentiated oligopoly	Pure or perfect competition

Reality is, of course, more complex, and there is a continuum of situations. Nevertheless, it is helpful to place a product in one of these quadrants to understand the problem of price determination.

- When the number of competitors is low and the product's perceived value is high, we are in structures close to *monopoly or differentiated oligopoly*. Price is a tool for the firm which has a margin for manoeuvre varying with the buyer's perceived value of the differentiating attribute.
- At the other extreme, where there are many competitors and products are perceived as a commodity, we are close to the *perfect competition* structure where prices are largely determined by the interplay of supply and demand. The firm has practically no autonomy in its pricing strategy.
- The lower left quadrant, with low number of competitors and low perceived value, corresponds to an *undifferentiated oligopolistic* structure in which interdependence between competitors is often high, thus limiting their autonomy. Here prices will tend to be aligned with those of the market leader.
- Finally, in the upper right quadrant we have highly differentiated products offered by a large number of competitors; this corresponds to imperfect or *monopolistic competition* where there is some degree of autonomy, this being limited by the intensity of competition.

These market structures are very different and they can be observed at various stages of a product market's life cycle.

Anticipating competitors' behaviour

In many market situations, competitors' interdependence is high and there is a 'market price' which serves as a reference to all. This is usually the case when there is *undifferentiated oligopoly*, where total demand is no longer expanding and the offerings of existing competitors are hardly differentiated. This type of competitive structure tends to prevail during the maturity stage of a product's life cycle.

In these markets, the firm can align itself with competitors' prices or those of the industry leader. It can fix its price at a higher level, thus taking the risk of losing some market share. Alternatively, it can fix its price below the market level, thus seeking a competitive advantage that it cannot find from other sources, but also taking the risk of launching a price war. The problem therefore is to determine *relative price*. The outcome of these strategies largely depends on the reactions of competitors.

The objective of analysing competition in pricing strategies is to evaluate competitors' capabilities to act and react. In particular, one needs to estimate the reaction elasticity of the most dangerous competitor(s) if prices were to go up or down. We discussed the notion of reaction elasticity in Chapter 8 (see p. 252). A complete outline of analysing competitors' behaviour is presented in Porter (1980, Chapter 3).

The direction and intensity of competitors' reactions varies when prices move upwards or downwards. As shown in the box below, the firm faces a kinked demand curve. Elasticity is different on either side of the market price because of different competitive reactions. Some conditions are more favourable to price decreases and some to price increases. These are the conditions that need to be identified.

Price elasticity in an oligopolistic market situation

In an undifferentiated oligopoly, when total demand is non-expansible, the firm's demand function can be written as

$$Q = F(P_i, P_r(_i)/M, \ldots)$$

where

P = sales price
M = other marketing factors
i = the firm
r = direct competitors of i

Firm i's price sensitivity is given by

$$\frac{dq_i}{dp_i} = \frac{\delta q_i}{\delta p_i} + \frac{\delta q_i}{\delta p_r} \times \frac{dp_r}{dp_i}$$

Multiplying by the ratio q/p, one gets the price elasticity:

$$\varepsilon(q_i,p_i) = \varepsilon(q_i,p_i) + \varepsilon(q_i,p_r) \times r(p_r, p_i)$$

The net price elasticity is the combined result of two effects:
- A direct price effect of i's price on i's sales volume.
- An indirect price effect of r's price on i's sales volume, the importance of which depends on the strength of firm r's reaction.

In an undifferentiated oligopoly, the strength of competitors' reactions will, in general, be larger in the case of a price cut than in the case of a price increase.

Thus, the price elasticity will be higher at the upper end of the demand curve, and less price elastic at the lower end. The demand curve is said to be a 'kinked' demand curve.

Initiating price cuts

Initiating a *price cut* with a view to stimulating demand is relevant only when total demand for the product can grow. Otherwise, if the firm reduces its price and if all the competitors react immediately and follow suit, the profits of each will drop and their respective market shares will remain exactly as before in a market which remains of the same size, although average price has decreased.

There are, however, some situations which might be favourable to a price cut in a non-expansible market, without entailing rapid reactions from competitors:

- When competitors' costs are higher and they cannot lower their prices without endangering profitability; not following the price cut implies a loss of market share unless factors of differentiation neutralize the price difference.
- Smaller firms can use a price cut more easily. This represents a lighter investment for them as opposed to larger enterprises which hold a higher market share, because the cost of promoting a product via price is proportional to sales volume. Larger competitors may indeed prefer to maintain their prices and react on a different front, for example by increasing advertising, which represents a fixed cost.

A firm may therefore choose not to follow a price cut, particularly when its product's perceived value is above that of its immediate competitors. It will then be protected from the effects of a price cut by differentiation factors, such as brand image, range of services or customer relations. Changing suppliers implies transfer costs which are not always compensated by the price difference. In industrial markets, for example, it is frequently observed that customers accept price differentials of up to 10 per cent without much difficulty if relationships with the usual supplier are well-established.

Determining the cost of a price cut

It is important to realize that the cost of a *price cut* is often very high, especially for a firm with a high proportion of variable costs. The data in Table 12.9 define the necessary increases in sales revenue and in volume required to retain the same gross margin (25 per cent in this case) at different levels of price cut.

In this particular case, where the gross margin of 25 per cent before the price cut is to be held, the number of units sold must more than double to compensate for a price cut of 15 per cent. One can imagine that the necessary increase in sales can rapidly be above the impact that can reasonably be expected from a price cut.

Table 12.9 Minimum volume and sales revenue increase required to offset a price decrease (assuming a gross profit margin of 25 per cent) (Monroe, 1979, pp. 70–3)

Price decrease	Percentage minimum sales revenue increase required	Percentage minimum volume increase required
5%	18	25
10%	50	66
15%	112	150
20%	300	400

Furthermore, it can be shown that a price cut is less favourable to a firm with high variable costs, because the necessary increase in sales to keep the same margin will be higher, the higher the proportion of variable costs (Monroe, 1979, p. 73). In general, for a price decrease, the necessary volume increase to maintain the same level of profitability is given by

$$\text{Volume increase (\%)} = \left(\frac{x}{M^* - x}\right) \times 100$$

where x is the percentage price decrease expressed as a decimal and M^* is the gross profit margin as a percentage of selling price before the price cut.

To illustrate, if a price cut of 9 per cent is envisaged and the gross profit margin is 30 per cent, the required sales volume increase is

$$\text{Volume increase (\%)} = \left(\frac{0.09}{0.30 - 0.09}\right) \times 100 = 42.86 \text{ per cent}$$

If the gross profit margin were to decrease to 25 per cent or 20 per cent the same price cut of 9 per cent would require sales increases of 56.25 per cent and 81.82 per cent, respectively. For the derivation of the break-even formula, see Nagle (1987, pp. 44–6).

Therefore the firm having the lowest variable costs will be induced to initiate a significant price cut, in the knowledge that other firms could not follow suit.

Computing implied price elasticity

It is also possible to derive an *implied price elasticity* from these figures. This is the price elasticity that should prevail within the targeted group of buyers before profits could be increased.

In the previous example, the price cut of 9 per cent ought to give rise to a 42.86 per cent increase in sales volume in order to retain the gross profit margin at 30 per cent. Therefore, the implied price elasticity is

$$\varepsilon = \frac{+\,42.86}{-9} = -4.76$$

A price elasticity of -4.8 per cent is very high and assumes a very price-sensitive demand. If it is considered that the product market's demand is less elastic, and if profit is the only choice criterion, then the price cut is not economically justified.

The risk of a *price war* is always present in an oligopolistic market, which explains why firms are reluctant to initiate price cuts. There are, however, situations where a price cut can improve the competitive position of the firm. As discussed in Chapter 8, reducing the profit margin with price cuts may be compensated for by market share gains, which in the long run mean higher profitability because of cost reductions due to experience effects. Another reason for a price war might be to eliminate a potentially dangerous competitor.

Experience curve pricing

As discussed in Chapter 8, in sectors where the cost of value added represents a large proportion of total unit cost, substantial cost reductions can be obtained as accumulated production increases. If consumers in this market are price sensitive, a good strategy for the firm having the largest experience is to price aggressively, even below current cost, as illustrated in Figure 12.3(a). This strategy presents several advantages. First, competing firms will have to leave the market and the leading company will be confronted with fewer rivals. Second, the firm can benefit from the sales of the other firms and gain experience more rapidly. Also, because of the lower

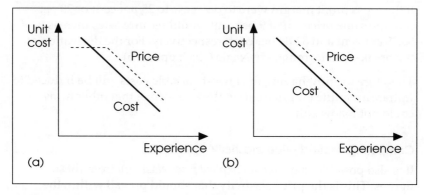

Figure 12.3 Experience curve pricing strategies (logarithmic axes)

prevailing market price, new buyers will be encouraged to enter the market. However, pricing below cost cannot be maintained for extended periods of time. A less aggressive pricing strategy is the one depicted in Figure 12.3(b) where a parallel is maintained between cost and price reductions.

Initiating price increases

Initiating a *price increase* is also a difficult decision. The firm initiating the increase must be certain that competitors are willing to follow suit. Generally speaking, this willingness depends on the prevailing market conditions at the time, and in particular when production capacity is fully used and demand is growing. As in the case of a price cut, before starting any initiative, it is in the firm's interest to evaluate its margin for manoeuvre.

If price is increased, the permissible volume decrease, i.e. leaving the previous level of profit unchanged, is determined as follows:

$$\text{Permissible volume decrease (\%)} = \frac{x}{M^* + x} \times 100$$

where x is the percentage price increase expressed as a decimal. If a 9 per cent price increase is contemplated and if the gross profit margin is 30 per cent, the percentage sales volume decrease is

$$\text{Volume decrease (\%)} = \left(\frac{0.09}{0.30 + 0.09}\right) \times 100 = 23.08 \text{ per cent}$$

and the implied price elasticity is -2.56.

For the price increase to enhance profit, market demand must have a price elasticity below the implied price elasticity of -2.6.

Pricing in an inflationary economy

During inflation, all costs tend to go up, and to maintain profits at an acceptable level price increases are very often a necessity. The general objective is that price should be increased to such a level that the profits before and after inflation are approximately equal. Decline in sales revenue caused by the price increase should be explicitly taken into account and the market reaction evaluated.

It should be noted that it is not always necessary for a company to increase prices to offset inflationary effects. Non-price measures can be taken as well to reduce the impact of inflationary pressures, namely by improving productivity to offset the rise in costs. Also price increases well above inflationary pressures can be justified to the market if the brand has a competitive advantage over competing brands.

Prices may also be increased to segment the market. This pricing strategy will be discussed in the final section of this chapter.

Price leadership

Price leadership strategy prevails in oligopolistic markets. One member of the industry, because of its size or command over the market, emerges as the leader of the industry. The leading company then makes pricing moves which are duly acknowledged by other members of the reference market.

Initiating a price increase is typically the role of the *industry leader*. The presence of a leader helps to regulate the market and avoid too many price changes. Oligopolistic markets, in which the number of competitors is relatively low, favour the presence of a market leader who adopts an anticipative behaviour and periodically determines prices. Other firms then recognize the leader's role and become followers by accepting prices. The leadership strategy is designed to stave off price wars and 'predatory' competition, which tends to force down prices and hurt all competing firms. There are different types of leadership.

- *Leadership of the dominant firm*, that is the firm with the highest market share. The dominant firm establishes a price and the other producers sell their products at this price. The leader must be powerful and undisputed and must accept maintaining a high price.
- *Barometric leadership* which consists of initiating desirable price cuts or price increases, taking into account changes in production costs or demand growth. In this case the leader must have access to an effective information system providing him or her with reliable information on supply and demand, competition and technological change.
- *Leadership by common accord*, where one firm is tacitly recognized as leader, without there being a formal understanding or accord. The latter would in fact be illegal. Such a leader could be the most visible firm in the sector, for example the firm that leads in technology. It should also have a sensitivity to the price and profit needs of the rest of the industry.

According to Corey (1991, p. 267), the effective exercise of leadership depends on several factors:

- The leader must have a superior market information system for understanding what is going on in the market and reacting in a timely way.
- It should have a clear sense of strategy.
- The price leader should use long-term measures to assess managerial performance.
- It should want to lead and to act responsibly.
- It should have a broad concern for the health of the industry.
- It will tend to behave in a way that preserves short-run market share stability.

On the whole, the presence of a leader acts as a market stabilizer and reduces the risk of a price war.

Pricing new products

The more a new product is unique and brings an innovative solution to the satisfaction of a need, the more delicate it is to price. This price is a fundamental choice upon which depends the commercial and financial success of the operation. Once the firm has analysed costs, demand and competition, it must then choose between two very contradictory strategies: (a) a high initial price strategy to skim the high end of the market, and (b) a strategy of low price from the beginning in order to achieve fast and powerful market penetration.

Skimming pricing strategy

This strategy consists of selling the new product at a high price and thus limiting oneself to the upper end of the demand curve. This would ensure significant financial returns soon after the launch. Many considerations support this strategy; furthermore, a number of conditions need to be met for this strategy to prove successful (Dean, 1950).

- When there are reasons to believe that the new *product life cycle* will be short, or when competition is expected to copy and to market a similar product in the near future, a skimming price strategy may be recommended because a low price strategy would make the innovation unprofitable.
- When a product is so innovative that the market is expected to mature slowly and the buyer has no elements on which to compare it with other products, *demand is inelastic*. It is tempting to exploit this situation by setting a high price and then readjusting it progressively as the market matures.
- Launching a new product at a high price is one way of *segmenting*

the market. The segments have different price elasticities. The launching price skims the customers who are insensitive to price. Later price cuts then allow the firm to reach successively more elastic segments. This is a form of time discriminatory pricing.

- When demand is hard to evaluate, it is *risky to anticipate* what kind of demand growth or cost reduction can result from a low price. This is particularly true when the manufacturing process is not yet stabilized and costs are likely to be underestimated.
- To be effective, the introduction of a new product requires heavy expenditure on advertising and promotion. When the firm does not have the *financial means* necessary for a successful introduction, charging high prices is one way of generating the resources.

Price skimming strategy is definitely a cautious strategy which is more financial than commercial. Its main advantage is that it leaves the door open for a progressive price adjustment, depending on how the market and competition develop. From a commercial point of view, it is always easier to cut a price than to increase it. The importance of the strategy lies mainly in its financial aspect: the fact that some capital which can be used for alternative activity is freed early on.

Penetration price strategy

Penetration strategy, on the other hand, consists of setting low prices in order to capture a larger share of the market right from the start. It assumes the adoption of an intensive distribution system, the use of mass advertising to develop market receptivity, and especially an adequate production capacity from the beginning. In this case the outlook is more commercial than financial. The following general conditions must prevail to justify its use.

- Demand must be *price elastic* over the entire demand curve; there are no upper segments to be given priority and the only strategy is to address the whole market at a price low enough to satisfy the greatest number.
- It is possible to achieve *lower unit costs* by increasing volumes significantly, either because of economies of scale or because of potential experience effects.
- Soon after its introduction, the new product is threatened by *strong competition*. This threat of new entrants is a powerful reason for adopting low prices. The penetration strategy is used here to discourage competitors from entering the market. Low prices act as very efficient barriers to entry, as discussed in Chapter 8.
- The top range of the market is *already satisfied*; in this case, penetration policy is the only valid policy to develop the market.

- Potential buyers can easily integrate the new product in their consumption or production; the *transfer costs* of adopting the product other than its price are relatively low and, therefore, a mass market can be developed rapidly.

A penetration price strategy is therefore more risky than a skimming price strategy. If the firm plans to make the new product profitable over a long period, it may face the situation that new entrants might later use new production techniques which will give them a cost advantage over the innovating firm.

Product line pricing

Strategic marketing has led firms to adopt segmentation and diversification strategies which have resulted in the multiplication of the number of products sold by the same firm or under the same brand. Generally a firm has several product lines, and within each product line there are usually some products that are functional substitutes for each other and some that are functionally complementary. This strategy of product development brings about an interdependency between products, which is reflected either by a *substitution effect* (or cannibalism) or by a *complementarity effect*. Since the objective of the firm is to optimize the overall outcome of its activities, it is clearly necessary to take this interdependence into account when determining prices (Oxenfeld, 1966).

The risk of a cannibalism effect

Figure 12.4 illustrates the possible scenarios of 'cannibalization' between two brands of the same firm, the old and the new. The circles represent buyers, with the intersections representing switchers. The total market is defined by the outer boundaries of all circles combined. Brand X denotes the competing brands (Traylor, 1986).

- The first case is the worst: the new brand brings no advantage whatsoever and simply shares sales with the firm's current brand. This situation might still be tolerated if the new brand's gross margin is well above that of the old brand.
- The second case is better, because the new brand has increased the size of the market and also its market share, but without going over the competitor's position. The operation will be globally profitable if the margin obtained on sales to new buyers is greater than that lost on sales of the old brand.
- In the third scenario, the new brand overlaps with the old brand's market as well as with the competing brand's, while extending the

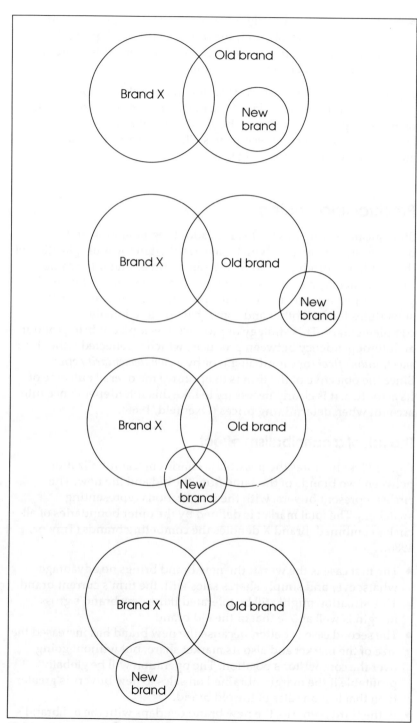

Figure 12.4 Cannibalism in multi-brand firms (Traylor, 1986)

size of the market by attracting new customers. As in the previous case, one needs to compare the margins lost and gained to evaluate whether there is a net positive gain.

- The fourth case is the ideal situation, with no cannibalization. The new brand cuts into competitors' sales and reaches new buyers. Total market share increases and the new brand is bringing in a net cash flow increment (Traylor, 1986, p. 72).

How can a multi-brand firm eliminate cannibalism? As firms look for finer and more subtle definitions of new market segments, the risk of cannibalism goes up. The main objective to pursue is to position the firm's brands against each other as well as against competitors' brands. In addition, some form of cannibalism should be tolerated if the net effect of the multi-brand strategy is in the best strategic interest of the firm as a whole.

Coca-Cola is a good example of a company that has flipped from a very conservative protectionism to an almost reckless use of the Coke name. The intended (Diet Coke, Cherry Coke) and unintended (Coke Classic) brand extensions represent radical departures from the company's traditional reluctance to extend the Coke name (Traylor, 1986, p. 73).

A firm concerned about market power may accept short-term profit losses resulting from cannibalism if it stands to increase its market power overall.

The concept of cross elasticity

A cross elasticity measures the degree of interdependence between products sold by the same firm or under the same brand, and identifies the nature of this dependence when it exists: complementarity or substitution.

In the case of two products A and B, their cross elasticity is defined as follows:

$$\text{Cross elasticity} = \frac{\text{Percentage change of product A's sales}}{\text{Percentage change of product B's price}}$$

If cross elasticity is positive, the products are substitutes; if elasticity is negative, then they are complementary. If elasticity is zero or very close to it, then the products are independent.

Contribution analysis in product line pricing

The complexity of product mix pricing is due to the fact that, apart from demand interaction, there is often cost interaction as well. For example, this is true when a change in the manufacturing process of one product affects the cost of other products. In this case, to study the implications of changing the price of one product in a range of products it is important to take into account the effect of such a change on the overall result.

To illustrate, let us examine the data of an example presented in Table 12.10. A firm is selling three interdependent products and has a marketing programme which it is planning to modify as follows.

By increasing advertising by F350 000, it is expected that sales of product B will increase by 6000 units at a price increased by F20, and increased packaging cost by F5. Sales of product A are expected to decrease by 1000 units because of product interdependence, and sales of product C are expected to decrease by 3000 units because of production capacity constraint. Should this change in the marketing programme for product B be adopted? (Blondé, 1964).

What would be the impact of such a change on the overall result? A convenient way to proceed is to reason in terms of variations (V). The variation in the gross margin (M) of product B is

$$V(M) = V(P) - V(C)$$

which in this case gives

$$V(M) = (+20) - (+5) = +15$$

To determine the effect on the overall result, let us use the following expression:

$$V(R) = \sum_{n} [V(Q) \times M + Q \times V(M) + V(Q) \times V(M)]$$

The summation is over the n products made. In the case of this example, for the three products A, B and C we have

$R = (0) \times 20\,000 + 50 \times (-1000) + (0) \times (-1000) - 0 + (+15)$
$\times 15\,000 + 40 \times (+6000) + (+15) \times (+6000) - (+350\,000)$
$+ (0) \times 10\,000 + 20 \times (-3000) + (0) \times (-3000) - (0)$

or

$R = + F95\,000$

that is, an increased profit of 19 per cent.

The new marketing programme is therefore profitable. Total gross margin obtained from the new sales volume for product B with its new unit gross margin is higher than the loss of gross margins on products A and C, due to their lower sales volume and increased fixed costs.

Table 12.10 Product line pricing: an example

	Product A	Product B	Product C
Selling price (F)	200	220	100
Direct cost (F)	150	180	80
Unit profit margin (F)	50	40	20
Volume (units)	20 000	15 000	10 000
Total profit margin (F)	1 000 000	600 000	200 000
Fixed costs (F)	700 000	500 000	100 000
Net profit (F)	300 000	100 000	100 000
Total net profit (F)		500 000	

Product line pricing strategies

When a firm is selling a set of related products, the price of each product must be set in such a way as to maximize the profit of the entire product line rather than the profit of a single product. The pricing strategy adopted will be different according to whether the related products are complementary to or competitive with each other.

Price bundling

When the products are related but are non-substitutes, i.e. complementary or independent, one strategic option for the firm is optional price bundling, where the products can be bought separately, but also as a package offered at a much lower price than the sum of the parts. Because the products are not substitutes, it is possible to get consumers to buy the package instead of only one product of the line. This pricing strategy is common practice, for instance, in the automobile and audiovisual markets, where packages of options are offered with the purchase of a car or of stereo equipment. A simple example will illustrate the profit implication of this pricing strategy (Tellis, 1986, p. 155).

Assume a market situation where two related products are offered to two customers, who could buy one product or both. The maximum prices they are ready to pay are as follows:

	Customer 1	Customer 2
Product A	12	18
Product B	25	10

What is the best pricing strategy to adopt if tying contracts are excluded? Charging each customer the maximum price would yield a total revenue of $65. But this strategy, if not illegal, is difficult to implement if the buyers are sufficiently informed. Selling product A at $12 and product B at $10 could induce buyers to buy the two products but the total revenue will be only $44. On the other hand, pricing the first product at $18 and the second at $25 will generate even lower total revenue of only $43, since the customers will not be able to buy the two products.

> The best solution is to price product A at $18 and product B at $25 and offer both at $28 for a total revenue of $56. Both customers will accept the package for $28 since this price is compatible with their maximum budget ($37 for customer 1 and $28 for customer 2). (Tellis, 1986.)

This strategy of 'optional bundling', in contrast with 'indivisible bundling', leaves the option to the customer to buy only one product or the total package.

Several computer companies have adopted the indivisible bundling strategy. Under this pricing system, not only are costs of hardware and profits covered, but also included are the anticipated expenses for extra technical assistance, design and engineering of the system concept, software and applications to be used on the system, training of personnel and maintenance.

For the customer, this strategy is very attractive because the manufacturing firm is selling a 'solution' and not simply a product. To be able to sell a solution, however, the manufacturer has to cover the anticipated expenses for providing services and assistance in use and for keeping the system in working condition. Such a bundling strategy also permits an ongoing relationship with the customer and first-hand knowledge of the customer's needs. In recent years, however, with the inflationary pressures on costs of services, many companies have begun unbundling their services and charging separately for them.

Premium pricing

This pricing strategy applies to different versions of the same product, a superior version and a basic or standard model. Potential buyers for the standard model are very price sensitive, while buyers of the superior model are not. If economies of scale exist, it is unprofitable for the firm to limit its activity to one of the two market segments. The best solution is to exploit jointly economies of scale and heterogeneity of demand by covering the two segments, the lower end of the market with a low price and the high end with a premium price. The following example illustrates this.

Consider a firm having the following target prices: $50 at 20 units and $35 at 40 units. The cost of producing a superior version of the same product is $10. Forty consumers per period are on the market for the product. Half of them are price-insensitive and are ready to pay $50 for the superior version. The other half are price-sensitive and will not pay more than $30. In what version and at what price should the firm sell the product? (Tellis, 1986, p. 156).

> Costs and profit constraints seem to exceed prices if the firm decides to sell to only one segment or at only one price. A premium price strategy can solve the problem. The firm should sell the basic product for $30 and the superior version for $50, half of which will be of the superior version, for an average target price of $40. The firm takes a premium on its higher priced version and a loss on its lower priced version, but can profitably produce and sell the product to both segments (Tellis, 1986, p. 156).

This pricing strategy is common practice in many markets, typically durable goods for which several versions differing in price and features cater to different consumer segments.

The same pricing strategy can be applied in the service sector by modifying the service package. For example, airlines have used this pricing strategy very successfully. Their market consists of both a price-insensitive business traveller and a very price-sensitive holiday traveller. Business people place a high value on flexible scheduling. In contrast, holiday makers generally plan their trips far in advance. Capitalizing on these differences, airlines set regular ticket prices high and offer discounts only to buyers who purchase their tickets well before departure. By offering lower fares only with inflexible schedules, airlines have been able to price low enough to attract price-sensitive buyers without making unnecessary concessions to those who are less price sensitive (Nagle, 1987, p. 169).

Image pricing

A variant of premium pricing is 'image pricing'. The objective is the same: to signal quality to uninformed buyers and use the profit made on the higher priced version to subsidise the price on the lower priced version. The difference is that there is no real difference between products or brands, it is only in image or perceptual positioning. This is common practice in markets like cosmetics, dresses, snacks etc., where the emotional and/or social value of a product or a brand is important for the consumer.

Complementary pricing

The problem here is to determine the prices of complementary products, such as durable goods and accessories or supplies necessary for the use of the basic product. Examples of complementary products are razors and blades, cars and spare parts, computers and software etc. To the extent that buyers are source loyal and want to buy supplies or accessories from the original manufacturer, low prices can be charged for the main product and high prices for the supplies.

> For example, Kodak prices its cameras low because it makes its money on selling film. Those camera makers who do not sell film have to price their cameras higher in order to make the same overall profit (Kotler, 1991, p. 495).

In evaluating the effect of a price change of complementary products, management must examine the changes in sales revenue and costs not only for the product being priced, but also for the other products affected by the price change. By way of illustration, let us examine the pricing problem of a company selling personal computers and software.

In this company, the typical buyer of a personal computer also purchases on average three software packages. The gross profit margin on a computer is $1000 or 40 per cent on selling price, while the profit margin on software is $250. If management treated sales of computers and software as independent, the break-even sales quantity for a 10 per cent price cut would be 33.3 per cent $(-10\%/40\% - 10\% = 0.333)$. Thus sales should increase by 33.3 per cent to justify the 10 per cent price cut.

How likely is this sales increase? In fact, the profit contribution for a computer sale is much higher than 40 per cent, since each buyer of a computer also purchases on average three software packages. Thus, the relevant gross profit margin here is $1750 ($1000 + (3 \times $250))$, or 70 per cent of the selling price. The adjusted break-even sales change is 16.7 per cent $(-10\%/70\% - 10\% = 0.167\%)$. Thus, the company could cut its price even if it expects a percentage increase in sales much less than 33.3 per cent.

In retailing, the corresponding strategy is called 'loss leadership'. It involves dropping the price on a well-known brand to generate store traffic (Tellis, 1986, p. 157).

13

Strategic communication decisions

We saw in Chapter 1 that marketing is an action-oriented process as well as a business philosophy. To be effectively implemented, the firm's strategic choices must be supported by dynamic action programmes, without which there is very little hope for commercial success. To sell, it is not enough to have a competitively priced product made available to target potential buyers through a well-structured distribution network. It is also necessary to advertise the product's distinctive features to the target segment, and to stimulate the demand through selling and promotional activities. An effective marketing strategy requires the development of a communication programme having the two interrelated objectives of *informing* potential buyers about products and services and *persuading* them to buy. Such a programme is based on various means of communication, the most important of which are personal selling, advertising, promotion and public relations. The objective of this chapter is to examine the major strategic decisions facing a firm when developing its communication programme (see Figure 13.1).

The role and nature of marketing communication

As underlined in Chapter 1, to ensure an efficient matching of segments of demand and supply, communication flows must be organized between the trading partners to facilitate the exchange process. It is therefore up to the producer to initiate and control these communication flows to create a brand or a corporate image consistent with the firm's strategic objectives.

The marketing communication mix

Marketing communication refers to all the *signals or messages* made by the firm to its various publics, i.e. customers, distributors, suppliers, shareholders and public authorities, and also its own

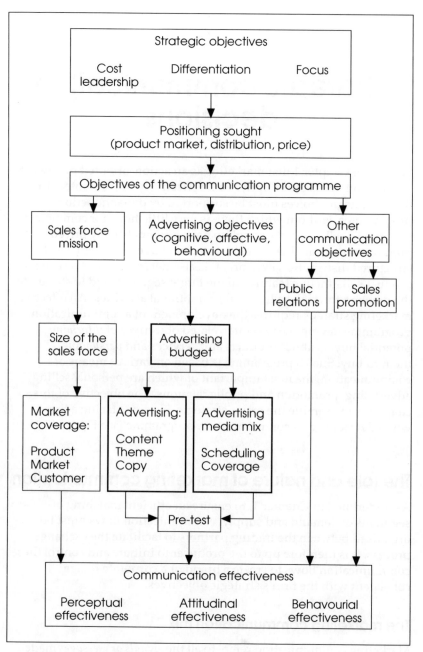

Figure 13.1 Overview of communication decisions

personnel. The four major communication tools, called the
communication mix, are advertising, personal selling, promotion and
public relations. Each of these communication tools has its own
characteristics.

- *Advertising* is a unilateral and paid form of non-personal mass
  communication, designed to create a favourable attitude toward
  the advertised product and coming from a clearly identified
  sponsor.
- *Promotion* includes all short-term incentives, generally organized
  on a temporary and/or local basis, and designed to stimulate
  immediate purchase and to move sales forward more rapidly than
  would otherwise occur.
- *Public relations* involve a variety of actions aimed at establishing a
  positive corporate image and a climate of understanding and
  mutual trust between a firm and its various publics. Here, the
  communication objective is less to sell and more to gain moral
  support from public opinion for the firm's economic activities.
- *Personal selling* has the objective of organizing a verbal dialogue
  with potential and current customers and to deliver a tailor-made
  message with the short-term objective of making a sale. Its role is
  also to gather information for the firm.

In addition to these traditional communication tools, one must
also add direct mail, catalogue selling, fairs and exhibitions,
telemarketing etc. Although these means of communication are very
different, they are also highly complementary. The problem is
therefore not whether advertising and promotion are necessary, but
rather how to allocate the total communication budget to these
various communication tools, given the product's characteristics and
the chosen communication objectives.

The communication process

Any communication involves an *exchange of signals* between a sender
and a receiver, and the use of a system of encoding and decoding
which allows the creation and the interpretation of the message.
Figure 13.2 describes the communication process in terms of nine
elements (Kotler, 1991, p. 568):

- *Sender*: the party sending the message to another party.
- *Encoding*: the process of transforming the intended message into
  images, language, signs, symbols etc.
- *Message*: the information or the claim to be communicated to the
  receiver by the sender.
- *Media*: the communication channel through which the message
  moves from the sender to the receiver.

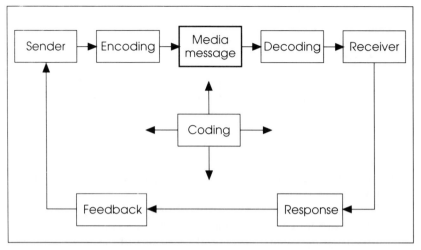

Figure 13.2 The communication process (Kotler, 1991, p. 589)

- *Decoding*: the process through which the receiver assigns meaning to the symbols transmitted.
- *Receiver*: the target audience.
- *Response*: the set of reactions that the receiver has after exposure to the message.
- *Feedback*: the part of the target audience's response that the receiver communicates to the sender.
- *Noise*: the distortions that occur during the communication process.

Figure 13.2 describes the relationship between these nine factors and helps to determine the *conditions for effective communication*. Four conditions can be identified:

- *Communication objectives*. Senders must know what audiences they want to reach and what type of response they want. This implies the choice of a target audience and the determination of specific communication objectives. These tasks are typically the responsibilities of strategic marketing people.
- *Message execution*. Communicators must be skilful in encoding messages and able to understand how the target audience tends to process messages. This involves designing advertisements and ensuring, through testing, that they are processed by the target group in the intended manner to produce the desired communication effect.
- *Media planning*. Two decisions are involved here. First, media selection, i.e. 'where' to reach the target audience most efficiently; second, media scheduling, i.e. 'how often' the target audience

needs to be reached to produce the intended communication objective.

These last two tasks are in general assumed by advertising agencies and/or by agencies specializing in media planning.

- *Communication effectiveness.* The advertiser must identify the audience's response to the message and verify to what extent the communication objectives have been achieved. This is again the task of marketing management.

Applying the concept of marketing to advertising implies developing messages that relate to buyers' experiences, namely by adopting a language they can decode. These four conditions for efficient communication determine the various decisions to be taken in any marketing communication programme.

Personal versus impersonal communication

The two most important tools of marketing communication are personal communication, assumed by the sales force, and impersonal communication, achieved through media advertising. The problem is to know when direct intervention by a sales representative is more effective than advertising. A comparison of the main features of each of these two means of communication is shown in Table 13.1.

This comparison suggests the following:

- Personal selling is by far the most efficient and powerful communication tool. But it costs almost a hundred times more to contact a prospect with a salesperson's visit than with an advertising message.
- Media advertising, however, has the advantage over personal selling in that it can reach a large number of people in a short period of time, while a sales representative can only visit a limited number of customers within a day.
- When a product is complex and difficult to use and is targeted to a limited number of people, a sales representative is clearly much more effective than an advertising message, which is necessarily too general and too simplistic.
- A salesperson acts directly and can obtain an immediate order from the customer, whereas advertising works through brand awareness and through attitude formation. These are often long-term effects.

Consequently, whenever the personal factor is not essential to communication, advertising is more economical both in terms of costs and of time. Recent developments in the field of advertising

Table 13.1 Comparing personal and impersonal communication (adapted from Darmon *et al.* (1982, p. 398))

Elements of the communication process	Personal communication	Impersonal communication
Target	Very well identified target.	Average profile of the target.
Message	Tailor-made message. Many arguments. Weak control of form and content.	Standard message. Few arguments. Strong control of form and content.
Media	Personalized and human contact. Few contacts.	Unpersonalized contact. Several contacts.
Receiver	Continued attention. Weak consequence of encoding error.	Volatile attention. Strong effect of encoding error.
Response	Immediate behavioural response possible.	Immediate behavioural response difficult.

tend to reconcile the advantages of these two communication means, which is indeed the objective of interactive or response advertising.

It is therefore not surprising to observe that firms selling industrial goods devote a larger proportion of their communication budget to personal selling than firms operating in the field of consumer goods.

Costs of communication activities

It is difficult to evaluate the *costs of communication activities* because available information is sketchy. Furthermore, orders of magnitude vary tremendously with the field of activity. It is nevertheless generally accepted that personal communication expenses devoted to the sales force are greater by far than advertising expenditure; they are also more significant in industrial markets as compared to consumer goods markets. The following figures are quite revealing.

In France, in 1986, total media advertising amounted to FF30.6 billion and, in 1982, to more than FF100 billion for personal selling. In the USA, in 1986, total advertising outlays amounted to $66 billion and, in 1982, to $100 billion in personal selling (Xardel, 1982; Waterson, 1988).

Table 13.2 International comparison of advertising intensities (1989) (Waterson, 1992)

Country	Expenditure (ECUs) (× 1 000 000)	In percentage of the GDP (local currency)	Expenditure per head (ECU)
USA	65 725.2	1.41	264.2
Europe (EC)	42 458.5	—	143.3
Japan	22 969.3	0.9	186.6
UK	9 841.6	1.29	171.9
Germany	9 284.1	0.86	149.8
France	6 636.7	0.76	118.2
Spain	6 490.2	1.88	166.9
Italy	4 845.6	0.62	84.2
Netherlands	1 992.5	0.98	134.2
Switzerland	1 743.2	1.08	259.3
Denmark	1 514.4	1.57	295.1
Sweden	1 469.7	0.85	173.0
Finland	1 055.2	1.01	212.6
Austria	1 045.4	0.91	137.1
Belgium	847.1	0.61	85.2
Norway	631.9	0.77	149.5
Greece	383.4	0.78	38.2
Ireland	314.8	1.02	89.6
Portugal	308.1	0.75	29.8

Note: these data include agency commission and press classified advertising, but exclude production costs.

Using the data in Table 13.2 we can evaluate the relative importance of advertising expenditure in the gross domestic product (GDP) of various economies and also compare advertising intensities in the main industrialized countries.

The cost of a sales person is constantly increasing, especially in industrial markets, while the cost of an advertising contact tends to decrease because of better selectivity by the medias.

According to a study by Forsyth (1987), the average cost of a well-targeted contact through a printed industrial advertising medium is 17 cents. This cost must be compared with the average cost of an industrial sales call, which was $252 in 1987, against $97 in 1977.

This trend in communication costs calls for a reassessment of the respective roles of advertising and personal selling. It is even more urgent because of the development of new communication means.

Electronic communication

As a result of the impetus from developments in telematics, cable television, pay-TV, satellite communication, interactive videotext terminals, personal computers etc., electronic communication is at present in full development. These new possibilities influence our way of life as well as the communication strategies of firms. As put by Daniel Bell (1979):

> ... telecommunications constitute for humanity as big a revolution as did the advent of printing, writing and language.

The development of electronic communication not only modifies the respective roles of personal selling and of advertising, but also changes the objectives and the content of advertising communication. Many significant changes are already observable in our society.

- To begin with, the new means of communication tend to be more *interactive*, i.e. two-way rather than one-way as in the past. Today, the general public has the possibility of asking for, choosing and sending back information rather than simply being passively subjected to a bombardment of irrelevant messages. We are moving in fact towards demanded advertising.
- Furthermore, it is now possible to have access to huge data banks, in the most varied fields, on available products, their comparative performance, their prices etc. The firm will therefore face a more and better informed public. Such facts will further reinforce the *informative and factual character* of communication, which will increasingly be set up as an aid to the buyer rather than as a sales instrument.
- Another consequence of the development of electronic communication is its *greater selectivity*. The combination of possibilities offered by the telephone, the computer and the television means that very well-defined targets can be reached with personalized messages. We are therefore moving towards personalized electronic mail systems which improve communication effectiveness and favour the development of interactive marketing.

Some sectors, such as the car industry, already use personalized mail. Access to the central file of the Road Traffic Bureau helps identify and reach, by direct mail for example, owners of a particular brand of car who purchased their vehicle more than five years ago and might thus be likely to replace it in the near future.

- *Regionalization* of radio and television programmes also favours selectivity of communication. The introduction of local channels will allow local firms and local advertisers to have access to radio and television. Media plans could allocate different degrees of pressure from region to region and thus better adapt the brand situation from one region to another.

- Finally, a last consequence is that the considerable increase in geographic zones covered by a transmitting station, thanks to the use of satellites and cable, will *reinforce the internationalization* of brands and advertising campaigns.

Thanks to these developments in the means of communication, a whole series of tasks once exercised by sales persons could henceforth be achieved by impersonal means of communication at a lower cost. Well-addressed direct mail, the telephone, a catalogue that can be consulted on a TV screen or a computer can all bring more extensive and more precise information faster than a sales person's sales speech. This is why we now observe a spectacular development of direct marketing systems, as shown in Table 11.8 (see p. 386).

> What we observe is a basic transformation of the selling function, which becomes more a sedentary activity. The contact with the prospect is not any more the exclusive privilege of the sales person but the role of the entire organization. The number of persons engaged in sales forces may decrease, but the number of contacts with the customer will nevertheless increase. Hence, the importance of having a market-driven orientation within the organization (Xardel, 1982).

Note that the growth of these new communication means doesn't imply elimination of the sales person. A personal contact will always be necessary. Electronic communication completes the action, prepares it and makes it more productive.

Personal communication

Personal selling is the most effective means of communication at certain stages of the buying process, especially when preferences need to be developed and the decision to buy spurred on. Due to the developments in communication technology, the role of sales persons is now undergoing a major transformation. Their role in strategic marketing is on the increase and the more routine tasks are increasingly being assumed by cheaper impersonal means of communication.

Sales force tasks and objectives

The first step in developing a personal communication strategy is to define the role of the sales force in the overall marketing strategy. This can only be done by clearly defining the kind of relationship the firm wants to establish with its customers in each product market.

One can define three types of activity that any sales force exercises:

- *Selling*, which implies prospecting and approaching potential buyers, negotiating sales conditions and closing sales.
- *Servicing*, which implies delivery, technical assistance, after-sale service, merchandising etc.
- *Information gathering*, which involves market research, business intelligence, monitoring of competitors' activities, needs analysis etc.

Thus, the sales person is not only the firm's commercial arm, but also an important element in its marketing information system.

Mission of the sales force

In practice, the terms 'sales person' and 'sales representative' can cover very different missions, depending on the emphasis placed on one or other of the three functions above. The following categories of sales person can be identified.

- *The delivery person's* function is to ensure the physical delivery of the product.
- *The sales clerk's* role is to assist customers in their choice and to take orders. Sales clerks operate at the point of sale or stand behind the counter.
- *The travelling sales person* visits the retailers or the distributors, takes their orders and performs non-selling activities such as checking inventory, handling retailers' complaints etc.
- *The merchandiser's* role is not to sell but rather to organize promotional activities at the sales point and to arrange point-of-purchase displays.
- *The missionary delegate* is not permitted to take an order, but has a role to inform and educate potential users. This is typically the role played by the medical representatives in the pharmaceutical industry.
- *The sales engineer* has a technical competence and operates as a consultant *vis-à-vis* the customer, providing assistance and advice. It is the role played by IBM sales engineers.
- *The sales representative* is an independent sales person selling durable goods like cars and vacuum cleaners, or services like insurance, where creative selling is very important.
- *The negotiator* is in charge of the financial engineering of vast industrial projects and responsible for negotiations with government authorities and industrial partners.

Once the type of mission assigned to the sales person is defined, the problem is to know how to organize commercial relations and which tasks to assign to the sales force, to the distribution network and to advertising.

Personal selling in the marketing mix

Generally speaking, the true role of a sales person remains first and foremost tied to satisfying the need for two-way communication felt by well-informed customers who have demands about how the product can be adapted to their own needs. From the firm's viewpoint, the sales force's new effectiveness is mainly linked to their ability in collecting and transmitting information so as to increase the speed of adjustment to market changes. This is how a Japanese firm conceives the role of the sales force.

> Salesmen are irreplaceable canvassers of information; they must be trained:
> - to listen to the customer, much more than to know seductive sales speech of the kind: 'the ten secrets of selling';
> - to be humble when criticized, much more than display militant pride of the kind: 'the products of firm X are the best';
> - to be in solidarity with other salesmen and with his firm to facilitate cross-checking and return of information, much more than pursue the superficial solitude of the salesman who only tries to reach his quota in order to improve his own performance (Xardel, 1982, p. 59–75).

This evolution in the notion of the role of the sales force therefore tends to increase its direct participation in strategic marketing. In addition to operational marketing functions, various strategic functions are now exercised by the sales force. The typical *functions of the sales force* are:

- Winning acceptance for new products.
- Developing new customers.
- Maintaining customer loyalty.
- Providing technical service to facilitate sales.
- Communicating product information.
- Gathering information.

Several of these selling objectives, such as winning acceptance for new products, developing new customers and gathering information, are typically related to strategic marketing. The sales person can therefore play an important role in strategic marketing, in so far as he or she participates in elaborating product policy through the information they supply regarding buyers' needs.

The sales force organization

A firm can organize its sales force in different ways. The organization can be by territory, by product, by customer or even a combination of these.

- *Territory-based organization.* This is the most common structure and also the simplest organization. The sales person is the firm's exclusive representative for its full product line for all current and potential customers. This structure has several advantages: first, it defines clearly the sales representative's responsibilities; second, it motivates the sales person, who has the full exclusivity on the territory; and finally, it minimizes costs and travel expenses.

This structure is only appropriate when products are few in number or similar and when customers have the same kind of needs. A firm producing paints and varnishes, whose customers are wholesalers, retailers and industrial users (building painters, car bodies etc.) clearly cannot use the same sales person to cultivate these different customer groups.

- *Product-based organization.* This second structure is preferable when products are very different, technically complex and require appropriate technical competence. In this case, the sales person is more specialized and better equipped to meet clients' needs and also to counter rivals.

The problem with this structure is that costs may increase manyfold, since several sales persons from the same firm may visit the same customer. For example, Rank Xerox uses different sales persons for photocopying machines and for word-processing units.

- *Customer-based organization.* Organization by customer categories is adopted when clients' needs are very different and require specific abilities. Customers may be classified by industrial sector, by size or by their method of buying. We find here the same criteria as those of segmentation presented in Chapter 6.

The advantage of a customer-based structure is that each sales force is specialized and becomes very knowledgeable about specific customer needs. But if customers are dispersed geographically, this organization can be very costly. Most computer firms organize their sales force by customer groups: banks and insurance, industrial customers, retailers etc.

Other more complex forms of organization combining pairs of criteria also exist. Sales persons can be specialized by product-territory, customer-territory or even by territory-customer-product. This normally happens in very large enterprises with many products and varied clients.

Advertising communication

Advertising is a means of communication by which a firm can deliver a message to potential buyers with whom it is not in direct contact. When a firm resorts to advertising, it is effectively following a *pull communication strategy*. Its main objective is to create a brand image and brand equity, and to ensure cooperation from distributors. Just as the sales force is the best tool for a push strategy, advertising is the best means for a pull strategy.

Setting the role of media advertising

In Chapter 4, we described what advertising represents for the advertiser and its utility to the buyer. Recall briefly that:

- For the *firm*, the function of advertising is to produce knowledge for consumers and to generate interest among them in order to create demand for its product.
- For *consumers*, advertising allows them to learn about the distinctive characteristics claimed by the manufacturer. Advertising also helps them to save personal time, since the information reaches them directly without their having to collect it.

Since the advent of the early form of advertising, advertising communication objectives have diversified considerably, and different forms of advertising can be identified while using the same media.

Concept advertising

This is a media advertising message with a mainly 'attitudinal' communication objective: to influence the buyer's attitude towards the brand. Its role can be defined as follows:

> The creative efforts of many national advertisers are designed, not to induce immediate action, but to build favourable attitudes that will lead to eventual purchase (Dhalla, 1978).

This definition implies that the effectiveness of this type of advertising can only be viewed from a long-term perspective. The notion of attitude holds a central position here. The objective is mainly to create an image based on communicating a concept.

Promotional advertising

This is a media advertising message with a mainly 'behavioural' communication objective: to influence buyers' purchasing behaviour rather than their attitudes. The objective is to trigger the act of purchase. Its effectiveness is evaluated directly in terms of actual sales.

This is the most aggressive type of communication, although it is not incompatible with image creation. However, its immediate purpose is to achieve short-term results.

Response advertising

This is a personalized message of an offer, having the objective of generating a 'relationship' with the prospect by encouraging a response from the latter on the basis of which a commercial relation can be built.

This type of advertising tries to reconcile the characteristics of the two previous ones: building an image, but also encouraging a measurable response allowing an immediate appraisal of the effectiveness of the communication. This type of media advertising is expanding rapidly now, and is directly linked to interactive marketing, discussed in chapter 11 (see pp. 383–89).

Institutional advertising

In the first three styles of communication, the product or brand is at the heart of the advertising message. Institutional advertising does not talk about the product, but aims to create or reinforce a positive attitude towards the firm.

The objective is therefore to create an image, but that of the firm: to describe the firm's profile and stress its personality in order to create a climate of confidence and understanding. The purpose is to *communicate differently* in a saturated advertising world and to fight against the fatigue of product advertising with a softer approach, by drawing attention to the firm itself, its merits, its values and talents. Clearly, the effectiveness of this kind of advertising can only be evaluated in the long-term and can essentially work on attitudes.

Sponsoring and patronage

These are two specific ways of institutional advertising. The latter runs the risk of tiring the public, which can become irritated and view these campaigns as attempts at self-satisfaction. Hence new forms of communication have developed, based on the idea that '. . . there is more splendour in being virtuous than taking credit for it' (VanHecke, 1988).

A typical example of one of these media stunts is the financing by American Express of the restoration of Van Eyck's masterpiece 'L'agneau mystique', which considerably increased its prestige in a way that no other campaign could have done.

The objective is to increase awareness of the firm's brand and to improve its image by association with positive values. The event being supported, which often unfolds in an unpredictable manner, thus reinforcing the credibility of the message, must have a testimony value, in the sense that a link should exist between the sponsored event and the sponsoring organization, even if the link is indirect.

Whether the firm is sponsoring an expedition in the Himalayas or a transatlantic race, it is emphasizing its adherence to moral values such as team spirit and courage. On the one hand it proves its open-mindedness and its harmonious integration in society, and on the other hand, with regards to internal communication, it increases support from its personnel and develops a favourable climate within the firm (VanHecke, 1988).

It should be noted that sponsorship is a commercial operation, implying a two-way relation of rights and obligations: on the one hand material or financial support for the sponsored event, and on the other hand direct and methodical exploitation of the event by the firm. Thus sponsorship is distinct from patronage, in which generosity and lack of interest in profit is dominant.

It is clear that forms of advertising, pursued objectives and the means used to achieve them are very different. Before launching the advertising, it is therefore important to have a clear view of the role that advertising is to play in the marketing programme.

Prerequisites of concept advertising

There are still too many firms that tend to assimilate advertising with marketing and to approach marketing by advertising. In fact, advertising is only a complement, which is sometimes but not always indispensable, to a more fundamental process of strategic marketing. For advertising to be effective, a number of prerequisites should ideally prevail:

- Advertising is one element of the *marketing mix* and its role cannot be separated from the roles of the other marketing instruments. As a general rule, advertising will be effective only when the other marketing factors have been chosen: a differentiated and clearly positioned product sold at a competitive price through a well-adapted distribution network.
- Advertising is useful to the consumer mainly for complex products having *internal qualities* that cannot be discovered by inspection. For experience goods, such as motor oil and hair conditioner, consumers have lots to gain from truthful advertising (Nelson, 1974).
- To be effective, advertising should promote a *distinctive characteristic* to clearly position the brand in the minds of consumers as being different from competing brands. The distinctive characteristic can be the promise of the brand, but also its personality, its look or its symbolic value.
- Advertising is particularly effective in markets or segments where *primary demand is expansible*. Its role is then to stimulate the need for the product category as a whole. In non-expansible markets,

the main role of advertising is to stimulate selective demand and to create communication effects at the brand level.

- The size of the reference market must be large enough to absorb the cost of an advertising campaign, and the firm must have enough financial resources to reach the *threshold levels* of the advertising response function.

Thus, the advertising communication platform is the complement of a strategic marketing programme. The advertising positioning sought must be in line with the marketing positioning adopted and based on a sound strategic thinking, without which advertising cannot be effective.

Alternative advertising objectives

To determine the objectives of advertising communication, it is useful to refer back to the three levels of market response analysed in Chapter 5.

- *Cognitive response*, which relates to awareness and to knowledge of the product characteristics. At this level, the advertiser can set objectives of information, recall, recognition or familiarity.
- *Affective response*, which relates to the overall evaluation of the brand in terms of feelings, favourable or unfavourable judgements and preferences. The objectives will be to influence attitude and to create purchase intention.
- *Behavioural response*, which refers to buying behaviour and to post-purchase behaviour, but also to all other forms of behavioural response observed as the result of a communication, such as visiting a showroom, requesting a catalogue, sending a reply coupon.

It is common practice to consider these three levels as a sequence, as potential buyers pass successively through the three stages: cognitive, affective and behavioural (Lavidge and Steiner, 1961). This sequence of reactions is known as the *learning model*. As noted in Chapter 5, this model needs to be adjusted in terms of the buyer's degree of involvement (see Figure 5.1). Although not generally applicable, the learning response model nevertheless remains a useful tool for defining the priority objectives of communication.

Keeping this hierarchy of objectives in mind, Rossiter and Percy (1987, p. 132) have identified *five different communication effects* that can be caused, in whole or in part, by advertising (Table 13.3). These effects reconstitute the process followed by the buyer when confronted with a purchasing decision; there can therefore be as many possible objectives for communication.

Table 13.3 The five basic communication effects (adapted from Rossiter and Percy (1987, p. 132))

- Development of primary demand or category need.
- Creating brand awareness or cognitive response.
- Creating a favourable attitude, or affective response.
- Stimulating brand purchase intention.
- Purchase facilitation.

Development of primary demand

Existence of need is a prerequisite that determines the effectiveness of any act of communication. Every product satisfies a product category need. Perception of this need by potential buyers can be stimulated by advertising. Advertising thus helps develop total demand in the market. Three distinct situations can exist:

- The category need is *present and well perceived* by potential buyers. In this case, generic advertising is not justified. This is the case for many low-involvement, frequently purchased products, where purchasing is done on a routine basis.
- The category need is *perceived but neglected or forgotten* and the role of generic advertising is to remind the prospective buyer of previously established need. This is the case for infrequently purchased or infrequently used products like pain remedies.
- The perception of the category need is *weak or not established* in the target group of potential users. In this case, generic advertising can sell the benefits of the product category. The typical example is the campaign in favour of the use of condoms to fight against the spread of AIDS. Selling category need is a communication objective for all new products, and in particular for new-to-the-world products.

In generic advertising campaigns, the advertising content places the emphasis on the core service of the product and/or on the product benefits. This type of communication message will benefit the advertiser but also the competing firms as well.

Creating brand awareness

This is the first level of cognitive response. In Chapter 5, we defined brand awareness as the buyer's ability to identify a brand in sufficient detail to propose, choose or use a brand. Three kinds of advertising objective, based on awareness, can be identified:

- To create or maintain *brand recognition* so that buyers identify the brand at the point of sale and are induced to check the existence of a category need.

- To create or maintain *brand recall* to induce buyers to select the brand once the category need has been experienced.
- To emphasize both *brand recognition and brand recall.*

These communication objectives imply different advertising contents. For brand recognition, the advertising content will emphasize the visual elements (logo, colours, packaging), while for brand recall the advertising will seek to repeat the brand name in audio and visual media and in headlines and to associate the brand name with the core service.

Creating a favourable brand attitude

The objective is to create, improve, maintain and modify buyers' attitudes towards the brand. It is therefore affective response which intervenes here. Chapter 5 describes the components of attitude (see pp. 134–45). The following communication strategies are open to the advertiser:

- To convince the target audience to give *more importance* to a particular product attribute on which the brand is well placed in comparison to rival brands.
- To convince the target audience of the firm's *technological superiority* in the product category.
- To *reinforce beliefs* and the conviction of the target audience on the presence of a determining attribute in the brand.
- To *reposition the brand* by associating its use with another set of needs or purchase motivations.
- To eliminate a *negative attitude* by associating the brand with a set of positive values.
- To call attention to *neglected attributes* by consumers in their decision-making process.
- To alter the beliefs of the target audience about *competing brands.*

The last strategy can only be adopted in countries where comparative advertising is authorized, as in the UK, but which is not yet the case in Belgium or in France.

It is important to identify clearly the implicit assumptions of a communication strategy based on brand attitude. They can be summarized as follows.

- The advertiser must emphasize the features of characteristics in which it has the strongest competitive advantage.
- It is useless to try to modify buyers' perceptions when the brand does not really have the claimed characteristic.
- The major criticism directed against advertising is the adoption of arguments or themes which are totally unrelated to product attributes important to the buyer.

In other words, a *market-driven communication strategy* is based on the idea that advertising is mainly designed to help the buyer buy and not simply to praise the advertiser. This vision of a communication strategy falls well in line with the marketing concept.

Stimulate brand purchase intention

Purchase intention is halfway between the affective and the behavioural response. Two kinds of situation may arise:

- The buyer is weakly or not at all involved in the purchasing decision and there is *no conscious, prior intention to buy* until the last minute at the point of purchase. This is the case for low perceived-risk products and also for routinely purchased products. In this type of situation, stimulating brand purchase intention is not an advertising objective.
- The buyer has a *conscious purchase intention* during advertising exposure.

In the latter case, promotional advertising can play a role by using incentives (price reductions, special offers etc.) that precipitate the buying decision or encourage re-purchase.

Recall that the intention to buy is only expressed when there is also a *state of shortage*, that is *when the category need is felt*. Thus, the two states, need and intention, are closely associated. Yet intention to buy is not a frequently recurring event in any particular consumer.

> Markets that are huge in their annual volume are made up of buying decisions made by very small numbers of people in a given period of time. For example, in a typical week in 1982, American retailers sold over $365 million worth of shoes. But during that week (as shown in our study that year) only six persons in 100 bought shoes for themselves or their children. Similarly, only 28 adults in 1,000 bought any kinds of women's slacks, jeans, or shorts in the course of a week, and only 21 bought a dress. Fourteen in 1,000 bought a small appliance; 18 in 1,000 bought furniture; 3 in 1,000 bought an article of luggage (Bogart, 1989, p. 267).

Hence, many markets with very high turnovers, like the ones mentioned in the examples above, depend each week on the buying decisions of a small number of people. It is not surprising to find that advertising messages give rise to relatively few immediate purchase intentions, since in most cases the prerequisite is not there: namely the existence of a state of need.

Purchase facilitation

This last objective of advertising communication deals with the *'other marketing factors'* (the four Ps), without which there can be no purchase: a product that keeps its promise, retail availability of the

product, acceptable price, and competence and availability of the
sales force. When these conditions are not all met, advertising can
sometimes help to reduce or minimize problems by, for example,
defending the market price, or by working as a substitute to
distribution through direct marketing.

Creativity in concept advertising

Advertisers can adopt various creative approaches in their choice of
the communication platform. The most conventional approach,
called *'copy strategy'* in the advertising jargon, is based on four
components:

- *Target*: What is the target group to reach?
- *Promise*: What is the distinctive proposal made to the target?
- *Argument*: What is the support of the promise?
- *Tone*: What style or format should be adopted for executing the
  message?

The *copy strategy statement* is a blueprint for creative people: it
defines what must be communicated by advertising. Its strength lies
in the fact that it forces marketing managers to choose an axis of
communication which will be maintained over many years. As a
result, the brand becomes endowed with a specific image and a
positioning.

Kapferer (1985) underlines in particular the effectiveness of this
strategy in the case of predominantly functional products for which
there exist elements of differentiation based on technical features.

> For example, during the 1960s, when Ariel was being launched,
> housewives in large families (target) were promised unparalleled washing
> (promise) thanks to the biological agents in the powder (argument); The
> communication had a resolutely serious style (tone) so as to give the
> message credibility (Kapferer, 1985, p. 102).

Yet in many fields brands have proliferated, and it is difficult to find
specific promises which are not already 'occupied' by competing
brands. To differentiate at any price, the manufacturer might run the
risk of putting out details which might be significant to it, but
derisory to the buyer.

Star strategy

This trend has led advertisers, in France in particular, to adopt
another creative approach called *'star strategy'*, developed by Séguéla
(1982), which emphasizes the 'tone' of the communication and its
personality, the brand's character.

No properly respected copy strategy would have allowed TBWA to launch the pen Pentel in France with its campaign based on the three following slogans referring to the green colour of the Pentel pens:

'Mettez-vous au *vert*' (reference to ecology)
'Allez les *verts*' (reference to a football team wearing green shirts)
'En*vers* et contre tout' (reference to the word 'vert')

Here, there is no promise. But what does Pentel exactly promise? Nothing, or nothing distinctive. On the other hand, the advertising has managed to create an attractive brand personality which drives people to try Pentel. Its actual properties will only be discovered once the pen is in the hand (Kapferer, 1985, p. 103).

Star strategy determines the axis of communication on the basis of three elements: the brand's physical characteristics (its function), its character or personality, and the style of expression. This kind of creative approach is particularly effective when the product has no significant factor of differentiation.

Other creative notions have also been proposed. Variot (1985) extends Séguéla's approach and suggests that a brand's identity can be decomposed into six facets: its physique and its personality, but also the uses to which it is associated, its cultural facet, its buyers' image (others' viewpoint) and its self-image. For example, the identity of the brand Porsche in France can be described as follows (example quoted in Kapferer (1985, p. 104)):

- *Physical*: Performance.
- *Personality*: Perfectionist.
- *Use*: Personal rather than family oriented.
- *Cultural*: German technology.
- *Buyers' image*: Winners' car.
- *Self-image*: Surpassing oneself.

This advertising approach is very demanding because it requires great coherence of expression. The reason is that form, style and tone are more important than substance in constructing the image.

The Maloney grid

In the USA, Maloney (1961) has developed a model which continues to be relevant today, and which helps to generate ideas for advertising themes. Table 13.4 classifies on the one hand the kinds of rewards buyers seek in a product, and on the other hand the source of those rewards in the use of the product. This classification identifies 12 possible axes of advertising communication and creative people can put forward a theme for each.

As underlined above, the choice of the advertising message (theme,

Table 13.4 Searching for advertising appeal (Maloney, 1961, pp. 595–618)

Type of potentially rewarding experience	Potential type of reward			
	Rational	Sensory	Social	Ego satisfaction
Results of use experience	(1)	(2)	(3)	(4)
Product-in-use experience	(5)	(6)	(7)	(8)
Incidental-to-use experience	(9)	(10)	(11)	(12)

appeal, copy) is part of the product positioning decision, since it expresses the major benefits that the brand offers to the buyer. Yet within this concept there are several possible messages, and creative people have latitude to change the message without changing the product positioning concept. Consistency in advertising communication is important for building brand image and brand equity.

The dilemma: quality versus quantity

Which is more important in an advertising campaign: the creativity factor or the amount of money spent? At least one thing is clear. Only after gaining attention can an advertising message help to generate sales. Gross (1972) has shown the economic value of creative advertising and several empirical studies have confirmed his observations.

An interesting argument has been put forward in the USA by Nelson (1974) and recently confirmed in the UK by Davis *et al.* (1992). For experience goods, i.e. for goods that consumers cannot discover the quality or usefulness of without buying them repeatedly over a long time period (e.g. motor oil or shampoo), the mere fact of advertising heavily is more important than the advertising content. For this type of goods, the advertiser should not simply tell consumers that its product is better than its rivals; everyone says that. Rather, it should signal that it believes the product will be around for a long time by spending more than its rivals on advertising. Consumers will decode the message in this sense and therefore the cost or volume of advertising can be just as important as any direct or creative message the advertising contains. For good discussions of this question, see Nelson (1974) and Davis *et al.* (1992).

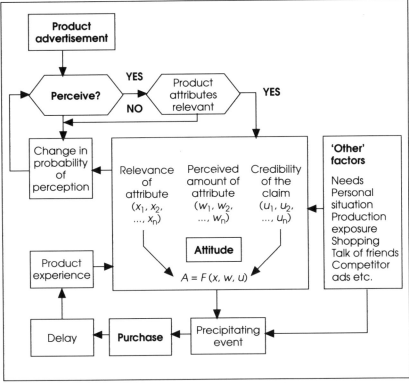

Figure 13.3 The advertising communication process (Dalrymple and Parsons, 1976, p. 462)

Measuring advertising effectiveness

Once the objectives of advertising communication have been clearly defined and translated into messages, it is already much simpler to measure advertising effectiveness. Figure 13.3 describes the process of advertising communication. Three key stages can be distinguished, defining three distinct levels of advertising effectiveness: perceptual, attitudinal and behavioural, corresponding to the three levels of market response mentioned earlier (cognitive, affective and behavioural).

Perceptual effectiveness

Effectiveness at this stage means the ability to overcome potential buyers' indifference or perceptual defences and to be seen, read, heard and memorized by the target group. Clearly, the first quality of an advertisement is to be noticed. Without it, nothing can happen to attitudes or behaviours. One can thus better understand advertisers' preoccupation—sometimes irritating to the outside observer—with 'getting across' and their willingness to achieve it using means such as humour, dreams, the unseemly, stars etc. Also, the *proliferation of advertising messages* aggravates their worry, because it leads inevitably to reduced levels of attention from a public that rejects boring or undesirable elements. In the USA, the number of advertising messages had doubled between 1967 and 1982. Most experts believe that the number of messages will double again before 1997 (Bogart, 1986, p. 220).

> The consequence for communication effectiveness can easily be imagined. In 1965, 18 per cent of TV viewers were able to remember one of the last advertising spots to which they had been exposed the previous day. In 1987, this percentage had fallen to 7 per cent (Bogart, 1986, p. 240).

This first level of 'advertising quality'—the perceptual effectiveness —determines the *productivity of advertising communication*. Important differences between advertising campaigns of the same intensity are observed in practice. Indicators of effectiveness used are tests of brand recognition, of unaided awareness, brand recall (Beta factor) etc., described in Chapter 5.

Overemphasizing the perceptual stage, however, runs the risk of leading to unbridled advertising creations which lose sight of the fact that advertising is only to complement and support a marketing position. Some advertising critics even go as far as suggest that advertising is too important to be left in the hands of creative or agency people, who are often tempted to emphasize the communicational impact of advertising at the expense of the marketing positioning objective.

The copy strategy approach has precisely the merit of refraining from creative outbursts, as opposed to the star strategy where the risk is less well contained.

Attitudinal effectiveness

The second level of effectiveness concerns the psycho-sociological aspect, which calls into question the affective response and the impact of the perceived message on attitudes towards the product or brand. The fact that a message has been properly perceived by the targeted group of buyers doesn't imply effectiveness in terms of attitude change. A message which is perfectly received, understood and digested, may be totally inoperative because of being maladapted, not credible or simply irrelevant. This is why knowledge of the target group's components of attitude is required to define the advertising appeal.

Twedt (1969) suggests that the proposition or promise made must have the following characteristics:

- *Desirability*: the message must first say something desirable or interesting about the product.
- *Exclusiveness*: the message must say something exclusive that does not apply to every brand in the product category.
- *Believability*: the message must be believable or provable; at stake here is the credibility of the message sender.

There is no recipe in the field of creative advertising, even if there are many advertisers who claim to have one (see, in particular, Reeves (1970) and Ogilvy (1964)). In addition to the criteria already suggested, the following questions can also be addressed regarding the quality of effective advertising.

- Is the advertising positioning in line with the *marketing positioning* sought for the brand?
- Is the *benefit* brought to the buyer clearly evidenced, simple to understand and, if possible, provable?
- To what extent is the promise *unique* as compared to the promises made by competing brands?
- To what extent is there *consistency and continuity* in the adopted advertising theme across media and over time?
- Is the message based on a *creative* idea easy to memorize for the target audience?
- Does the advertisement succeed in gaining *attention* from the reader or the viewer?
- Is there a clear and simple *link* between the product, the benefit, the advertising appeal and the advertisement's execution?

Generally speaking, one should beware of too original ideas in advertising. They run the risk of obscuring the message to be put across, and the public remembering the advertisement but not the brand name. Some agencies tend to make the advertisement the centrepiece, forgetting that the centrepiece is the product.

If these conditions are met, advertising has achieved its objectives regarding attitudes and the target group is in a state of positive receptiveness towards the product or brand. This state of receptiveness will either be reinforced by repeated exposure to the message, or, on the contrary, modified by competing messages.

Table 13.5 shows one example of measuring the effectiveness of the attitudinal stage of a concept advertising campaign. The same kind of results can be obtained for institutional advertising, as shown in Table 13.6. This table compares scores of public attitude towards two types of company: those using institutional advertising and those who do not (de Jaham, 1979).

Table 13.5 Example of attitudinal measure of advertising effectiveness: Texasgulf phosporic acids and fertilizer manufacturers (Bryk and Davis, 1973)

Advertising objective
To increase by 10% within 1 year the knowledge and conviction about the product's distinctive characteristics among fertilizer manufacturers.

Advertising theme
To gain conviction about the product's superiority. It contains fewer impurities and has a distinctive green colour: 'clean and green'.

Results of the advertising effectiveness study

	Before advertising	After advertising
Identification of the message	3.6%	16.3%
Knowledge of the claimed distinctive characteristics	15.3%	35.1%
Conviction of product superiority over competing products	9.4%	24.3%

Table 13.6 Attitudinal impact of institutional advertising (de Jaham, 1979)

Indicators of attitude	Categories of advertiser	
	Do not use institutional advertising	Use institutional advertising regularly
Knowledge of the firm's existence	82%	93%
Familiar with the firm's activities	63%	77%
Positive impression of the firm	38%	51%

Behavioural effectiveness

The third level of the process is the *effectiveness of the behavioural stage*, that is purchasing behaviour directly caused by advertising, which is the ultimate objective being pursued. Indicators used are then trial purchases, sales or market share, decomposed into penetration intensity, exclusivity or loyalty rates as shown in Chapter 5 (see pp. 149–50).

The growth in the use of response advertising and direct marketing means a greater use of *intermediate measures of the behavioural response*, such as reply coupons, requests for catalogues and brochures, visits to showrooms etc., which all reflect active interest caused by advertising and thus can be used to measure its effectiveness. In fact, these indicators also reveal communicational effectiveness, since it would be difficult to identify from the replies those which are motivated by the attractiveness of the offer and those who are showing real interest in the product. The only way to tell is to convert expressions of interest into actual purchases.

As underlined before, advertising can only give rise to purchasing behaviour if the other (non-advertising) determinants of the purchasing behaviour are also manifest, such as for example the need for the product, seeing the product at a point of sale, a reduction in the price, users' favourable opinions etc. A favourable attitude created by advertising is only a *predisposition which increases the probability of purchase* of the brand. Once bought, it is mostly the buyer's degree of satisfaction or dissatisfaction and the price–quality relation which become significant and will act upon the attitude and the propensity to remain loyal.

It is therefore not possible to measure directly how much advertising contributes to increasing sales. To measure its effect on sales, one would have to take into account all the relevant factors and estimate their respective weights in a dynamic context. For example, an econometric model can be used to find quantitative measures of demand elasticity with respect to each of the relevant factors, as shown in Table 5.6. Other methods are also available, as shown convincingly by Simon (1983). An interesting survey of empirical work in this domain is given by Assmus *et al.* (1984).

As for any kind of investment, it is essential to measure the effectiveness of advertising (Colley, 1961; Aaker and Carman, 1982). Yet one hears frequently in advertising circles that it is impossible to really measure advertising effectiveness. Negative attitudes in this respect are often due to the fact that the world of advertising is often dominated by creative people, who, more or less consciously, refuse to be judged by anyone other than their peers. Furthermore, there is often great confusion about the level of effectiveness one is referring to. While it is undoubtedly difficult (but not impossible) to measure sales or market share advertising effectiveness, intermediate measures of effectiveness are easier to use and they often help to improve the productivity of advertising investments.

Advertising–sales effectiveness research

Two methods can be used to estimate the sales or market share effect of advertising: the econometric approach based on historical data

and the experimental design approach. One study undertaken by
Lambin (1969) illustrates the profit maximization approach applied
to advertising.

The product concerns a well-established, frequently purchased
consumer good sold on the Belgian market. The objective of the
study was to examine the profitability of the advertising investment.
The demand function parameters were estimated by regression
analysis. The resulting equation is presented in Figure 13.4. Since
advertising spending is the object of the study, other decision
variables (price, visit frequency and packaging) have already been
decided upon and uncontrollable variables have been predicted or
fixed. Substituting the values of these variables, the demand
equation reduces to

$$q_t = 2.024 \times q_{t-1}^{0.565} \times s_t^{0.190}$$

For a one-period forecast q_{t-1} is known and we thus have the
advertising sales response curve presented in Figure 13.4. This
response function can be used to assess the profitability of the
advertising investment (see Lambin, 1969) and to determine the
advertising budget.

If the issue is to find out if current advertising expenditure is too
high, too low or about right, the model will produce a specific figure
which should be used as a guideline rather than as something
absolute.

Media planning

Having defined the target, message content and the expected
response, the advertiser must choose the best combination of media
support that will allow it to achieve the desired number of exposures
to the target within the limits imposed by the advertising budget.
Table 13.7 shows the definition of the important terms used in the
field of media planning. Different strategies of how to use the media
can be envisaged.

The *first alternative* opposes the two objectives of 'reach' and
'frequency': adopting an *extensive campaign* with a view to reaching
the greatest number of people through maximum reach, or, on the
contrary, adopting an *intensive campaign* to reach, as emphatically as
possible, a restricted target through maximum frequency or
repetition.

Generally, a high degree of reach is necessary when launching a new
product or starting an ambitious programme of promotion. On the
other hand, a high degree of frequency is required when the message

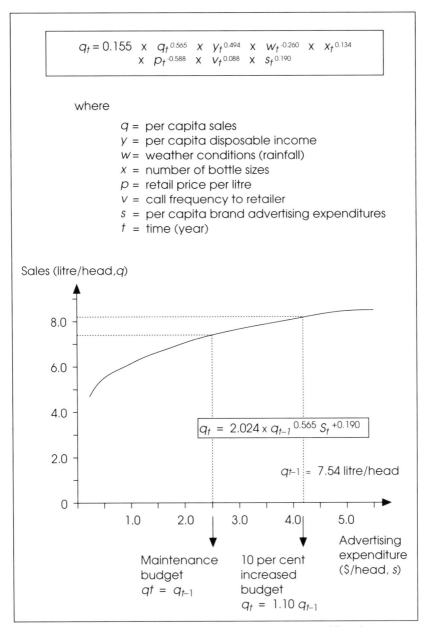

Figure 13.4 The estimated demand function for brand X and the advertising–sales relationship (Lambin, 1969)

is complex, the product frequently bought and brand loyalty low. However, too much repetition is useless, as it may cause boredom or irritation. Krugman (1975, p. 98), for example, considers that three 'perceived' exposures are often sufficient.

Table 13.7 Definition of the parameters used in media planning

Target: the specific group of prospects to be reached.
Circulation: the number of physical units through which advertising is distributed.
Audience: the number of people who are exposed to a particular vehicle.
Effective audience: the number of people with the target's characteristics who are exposed to the vehicle.
Exposure: the 'opportunity to see' (OTS) or opportunity to hear (OTH) the message, which does not imply that the person actually sees or hears the advertisement.
Reach: the number of different persons or households exposed to a particular medium vehicle at least once during a specified period of time.
Frequency: the number of times within a specified period of time that a prospect is exposed to the message.
Gross rating point (GRP): equal to reach multiplied by frequency and measures the total number of exposures (weight).
Impact: the qualitative value of an exposure through a given medium.

The *second strategic option* is between 'continuity' as opposed to 'intermittence' in advertising: seeking *continuity* of advertising efforts over time to overcome the forgetting rate, stimulate repeated purchases, oppose rivals' efforts etc., or, on the contrary, seeking *intermittence* (pulsing) so as to optimize consumer learning or reinforcement, or to 'stretch budgets' to coincide with consumption patterns.

The problem is to decide how to schedule advertising. But there is no clear answer to the dilemma. It is important to take into account the nature of the product. Its purchase frequency, seasonality in sales, rivals' strategies and the distribution of memory over time. The fact that the life of a message is a function of its communication quality renders the problem even more complicated.

Finally, the *third strategic choice* is between media 'concentration' or media 'diversification': seeking *diversification* in various types of media so as to enjoy complementarity between them, obtain a better net reach, a better geographical allocation etc., or, on the contrary, *concentration* on a single medium, so as to dominate the medium best suited to the target, to personalize the campaign and the product and to benefit from economies of scale and discounts.

All depends on the adopted segmentation strategy. Diversification is desirable if the firm follows undifferentiated marketing; if, on the contrary, it follows a market nicher strategy, then it is probably more effective to concentrate on a single medium.

Criteria for media selection

Media selection is guided by quantitative and qualitative criteria which are listed below. Among *quantitative criteria*, the following are important:

- *Target audience* media habits, i.e. the proportion of the target group that can be reached through the medium.
- The *stability* of the reach over time, for instance from one week to another or from one season to another.
- The possibility of having *frequent exposures* to the message.
- The medium *selectivity* in terms of socio-demographic or life style profiles.
- The *cost per thousand* persons reached, which is a function of the vehicle audience and of the medium cost.

Qualitative criteria of media selection must complement the quantitative ones. The following can be noted in particular:

- *Audience attention* probability, which is, for instance, very high for cinemas and very low for outdoor advertising.
- The duration of the *message's life*, i.e. the period during which the message can be perceived.
- The *editorial quality* of the vehicle, i.e. its prestige and credibility.
- The *technical quality* of the medium, for instance, the use of colour, the quality of sound or of images etc.
- The degree of *advertising saturation* of the vehicle and the presence of competitive advertising.

The final choice is concretized in a *media plan* describing budget allocation between the different media. Once one has chosen the media, the next decision is to select the *specific vehicles* to advertise in within the media. Although the choices are complex and numerous, a number of paid research services in media and vehicles selection provide data to help the decision-maker. The latter choice is now increasingly made using computer models of vehicle selection.

Advertising budget decisions

Conceptually, advertising budget decisions can be analysed using marginal rules of economic theory. Expenditure on each method of communication is increased until any further increase reduces profits. Similarly, the allocation of total budget between different

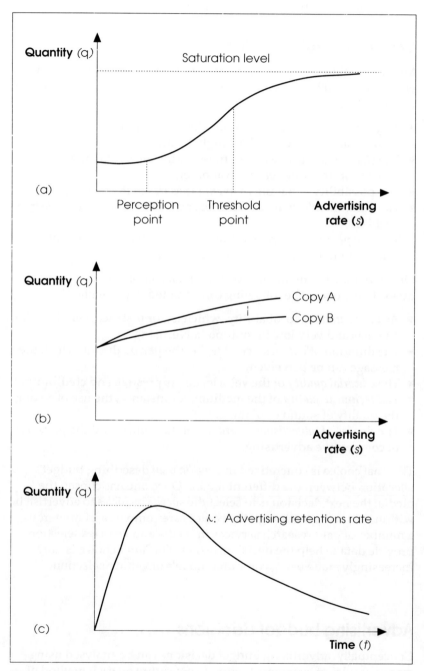

Figure 13.5 Characteristics of advertising response functions

methods is such that each instrument is used to the level where all marginal revenues are equal. Economists have developed optimization rules based on elasticities (Dorfman and Steiner, 1954), also extended to situations of oligopoly (Lambin *et al.*, 1975), as well as dynamic models to allow for lagged response to advertising (Palda, 1963; Jacquemin, 1973). The derivation of the optimization rule for the advertising budget is illustrated on p. 468.

As for the selling price, this approach is rarely operational in practice because of all the problems of estimating response functions already mentioned on p. 405 in Chapter 12. It is therefore necessary to use other more general methods, and to only use marginal rules as guidelines. When available, the analysis of elasticities can be useful *a posteriori* to evaluate the effectiveness of advertising and of the sales force. In this section we will examine different methods of determining the advertising budget.

Characteristics of advertising response functions

Advertising response curves have important characteristics which must be taken into account in advertising budget decisions.

- Advertising response functions are typically *non-linear* and subject to the law of diminishing returns, as illustrated in Figure 13.5(a). Thresholds exist reflecting inertia, perceptual resistance or fatigue effects.
- The slope of the response curve is determined by the *communication quality of the message*. For an identical level of advertising expenditure, very different response curves can be observed as a function of the medium used, the relevance of the message, the creativity of the advertisement etc.
- The advertising response is *dynamic* and its effects are distributed over time. The structure of the lagged effects also varies with media, products and advertising themes. In a way, advertising can be viewed as an investment which creates for the brand a lasting demand over time.
- Last, but not least, the advertising effect does not exist independently of the *other marketing factors*, such as distribution and price. The interaction effect between these factors is multiplicative, which means that the sum of their isolated effects is different from their joint effects.

The presence of such characteristics simply reflects the complexity of buyers' behaviours. But it also seriously complicates the problem of quantitative estimation both for advertising and the sales force. For a fuller discussion of the characteristics of sales and market share response functions, see Hanssens *et al.* (1990, Chapters 6 and 7).

Cost-oriented advertising budgets

As for cost-oriented prices, discussed in the previous chapter, cost-oriented budgets are calculated on the basis of cost considerations, without explicitly taking demand reactions into account. There are three types of cost-oriented budget: affordable, break-even and percentage of sales budgeting methods.

Affordable budget

The budget is directly linked to the short-term financial possibilities of the company. Advertising will be appropriated after all other unavoidable investments and expenses have been allocated. As soon as things go badly, this budget can be eliminated, and if cash is abundant then it can be spent. The fiscal system also encourages this type of practice, since increased advertising expenditure reduces taxable profit. This is not a method as such, but rather a state of mind reflecting an absence of definite advertising objectives.

Break-even budget

The break-even budget method is based on the analysis of advertising's profitability threshold. The absolute increase in unit sales and in turnover necessary to recoup the incremental increase in advertising expenditures is simply obtained by dividing advertising expenditures (S) by the absolute gross profit margin or by the percentage of gross profit margin:

$$\text{Break-even volume} = S/P - C$$

and

$$\text{Break-even turnover} = S/(P - C/P)$$

For instance, if the gross profit margin is £60, or 30 per cent of the unit price, the absolute increase in unit sales to recoup a £1.5 million advertising budget will be

$$1\ 500\ 000/60 = 25\ 000 \text{ units}$$

and the break-even turnover

$$1\ 500\ 000/0.30 = £5\ 000\ 000$$

To determine the percentage increase of sales volume or turnover necessary to maintain the previous level of profit, one can use the following expression:

$$\text{Percentage sales increase} = \delta Q/Q = 100 \times \delta S/(F + S + \text{Profit})$$

where δS is the proposed change in budget. The advertiser can determine by how much sales must increase to retain the same level of profit, and also calculate the implicit demand elasticity of advertising, by comparing expected sales levels 'with advertising' to expected volume 'without advertising'.

Using these data, the advertiser can verify whether the proposed budget implies an unrealistic increase in market share given the state of the market, competitors' power etc. The weakness of the method is that it is strictly an accounting exercise. But clearly some advertising objectives are not necessarily reflected in higher sales in the short-run, even if they have been reached completely. Nevertheless, this type of analysis is useful because the advertiser is encouraged to view advertising as an investment rather than overhead costs.

The percentage of sales budget

The percentage of sales budget method is used frequently and treats advertising as a cost. In its simplest form the method is based on a fixed percentage of the previous year's sales. One advantage of this procedure is that expenditures are directly related to funds available. Another advantage is its relative simplicity.

Although this method is quite popular, it can easily be criticized from a logical point of view, because it inverts the direction of causality between advertising and sales. Relating advertising appropriation to *anticipated sales* makes more sense, because it recognizes that advertising precedes rather than follows sales. Nevertheless, this approach can lead to absurd situations: reducing the advertising budget when a downturn in sales is predicted, and increasing it when turnover is growing, with the risk of overshooting the saturation threshold.

In practice, however, it seems that this method is mainly used by managements with the objective of controlling total advertising expenditure at the consolidated level of turnover, in order to keep an eye on total marketing expenditures or to compare with competitors. More refined methods are used when deciding on advertising at the brand level.

Cost-oriented advertising budgets are only the first stage of the process of determining the advertising budget. They enable the firm to define the problem in terms of financial resources, production capacity and profitability. As for the determination of prices, these methods must be completed with an analysis of market attitudinal and behavioural responses.

Communication-oriented advertising budgets

This approach, also called the 'task and objective' method, is the one most widely used. It emphasizes communication objectives and the means necessary to reach them. Two methods can be adopted: one based on 'contact', defined in terms of reach and frequency, and one based on 'perception'.

Task and objective budgeting

The method starts either with an objective of reach and frequency for which a budget is calculated, or with a budget constraint for which the best combination of reach and frequency is sought to maximize total exposure. By trying to maximize exposure, this approach places the emphasis on the first level of advertising effectiveness, i.e. communication effectiveness, while clearly linking the communication objectives to costs.

As defined in Table 13.7, the term 'exposure' here has a very precise meaning, because it only refers to opportunity to see (OTS) or to hear (OTH), which does not imply perception. Newspapers only sell OTS to advertisers: a certain number of readers (maybe) will have the paper in their hands, but this does not imply that they will see the advertisement, or that they will familiarize themselves with it or assimilate it. The method ensures the productivity of the budget by searching for the best way to spend the money in the media given the target audience and given an expected creative level of the campaign. This is why the task and objective method is widely used by advertising agency people.

Perceptual impact budgeting

Perceptual impact budgeting is based on psycho-sociological communication objectives. To achieve these objectives, conditions are defined in terms of the means used (media, reach, repetitions, perceptions etc.). Next, the cost of the various activities is calculated and the total determines the necessary budget. What is sought here is an impact on one of the three components of attitude (cognitive, affective or behavioural).

This is a much more fundamental approach, based on the learning process (Lavidge and Steiner, 1961) and the resulting hypothesis about the hierarchy of advertising effects (Colley, 1961). The difficulty with it is that the advertiser must be able to link the communication impact to the perceptual impact and the perceptual impact to the attitudinal impact and finally to the behavioural response. Typically, the budgeting problem is stated in the following terms:

'How many OTS or exposures to the message in a given medium are necessary to achieve, among 60 per cent of the potential buyers within the target group, the cognitive objective of "knowing product characteristics", the attitudinal objective "being convinced of product superiority" and the behavioural objective "intention-to-buy"?'

This method is very demanding, but it has the advantage of requiring management and advertising people to spell out their assumptions about the relationships between money spent, exposure, perceptions, trial and repeat purchase.

Communication-oriented advertising budgets constitute the second stage of the process of determining the advertising budget. They are in fact an initial way of explicitly taking into account market response. Because it is mainly based on intermediary objectives of communication, the advantage of the method is the emphasis it places on results directly attributable to advertising, and the fact that it allows the advertiser to control the advertising agency's effectiveness.

The limitations of these methods are that there is not necessarily any link between achieving the intermediate communicational objective and the final goal of improving sales. One cannot therefore view measures of communicational effectiveness as substitutes for direct measures linking advertising to sales or market share.

Sales-oriented advertising budgets

Determining a sales or market share-oriented advertising budget requires knowledge of the parameters of the response function. In some market situations, in particular where advertising is the most active marketing variable, it is possible to establish this relationship and then use it to analyse the effects of various levels of expenditure on market share and profits.

Various models of determination of advertising budget exist in the literature. The most operational among them are the model by Vidale and Wolfe (1957) and the model ADBUDG by Little (1970). Both models have some strong and some weak points which we shall consider briefly. The contribution of economic analysis will also be reviewed.

Budgeting to maximize profit

The advertising optimization rules are presented in the box on p. 468. These rules can be used to verify whether the current level of advertising spending is about right or whether the firm is over-advertising. To illustrate, let us use the example presented in Figure 13.4.

The advertising–sales elasticity is 0.190. The product currently sells for BF6 and the gross profit margin is BF3.30 (55 per cent). Average

---

Derivation of the advertising optimizing rule

In a monopolistic market, where primary demand is non-expansible, the brand demand function can be written as

$$Q(S) = K_S \, S_\varepsilon$$

and the profit function

$$\pi = (P - C) \, Q(S) - S - F$$

where S denotes advertising expenditures, ε advertising–sales elasticity, C variable cost and F fixed costs. The optimum is reached when

$$\frac{\delta\pi}{\delta S} = (P - C) \, \frac{\delta Q}{\delta S} - 1 = 0$$

Multiplying by S/PQ, we obtain the advertising optimization rule expressed by reference to advertising–sales elasticity,

$$\frac{P - C}{P} \, \frac{\delta Q}{\delta S} \, \frac{S}{Q} - \frac{S}{PQ} = 0$$

Rearranging terms, we obtain the following decision rules:

$$\text{Optimal advertising sales ratio} = \frac{S}{PQ} = (\varepsilon_{q,s}) \, (P - C/P)$$

and the optimal advertising budget is given by

$$\text{Optimum budget} = S^* = (\varepsilon_{q,s} \, (P - C) \, K)^{1/1 - \varepsilon}$$

The second-order condition stipulates that $0 \leqslant \varepsilon \leqslant 1$.

---

advertising per 1000 inhabitants is BF3440 with corresponding sales of 4060 units. The current advertising ratio is therefore

Current advertising–sales ratio =
$$\alpha = \frac{S}{PQ} = \frac{3440}{(6)\,(4060)} = 14.1 \text{ per cent}$$

At optimality, we should have (see box above)

$$\alpha_{opt} = (\varepsilon_{q,s}) \, (P - C/P) = (0.190) \, (0.55) = 10.4 \text{ per cent}$$

Thus, when only short-term advertising effects are considered, it would appear that the firm is overspending on advertising. The optimal advertising budget would be

$$S_{opt} = \left((0.190)\,(3.30) \, \frac{4060}{(3440)^{0.190}} \right)^{1/1 \,-\, 0.190} = \text{BF2372}$$

Thus, current advertising expenditures exceed the optimal level by 45 per cent. At this level of advertising spending, sales would be 3783 units (−6.8 per cent) and the profit BF10 112 per 1000 inhabitants instead of BF9958 with the current budget, a 1.55 per cent increase. Thus, the firm should make here a trade-off between profit gain and market share loss.

The advertising–sales elasticity estimate is not a sure thing. Adopting a plus or minus 20 per cent margin of error for ε, the optimal advertising budget is included in the interval BF1854–2949 per 1000 inhabitants. Note that the upper limit of the budget interval is significantly inferior to the current budget.

Only short-term advertising effects were considered so far, whereas the presence of advertising lagged effects is suggested in the demand function presented in the box on p. 459. If the retention rate of advertising (L) is estimated by the coefficient of lagged sales Q_{t-1} (0.565) and assuming a discount rate $r = 10$ per cent, then the present value of cumulative advertising elasticity is equal to

Cumulative advertising elasticity =

$$\varepsilon_{q,s} \left(\frac{1}{(1 - L)/(1 + r)} \right) = 0.190 \left(\frac{1}{(1 - 0.565)/(1 + 0.10)} \right) = 0.391$$

If the firm takes a long view, the optimal budget is then BF4877, 42 per cent above the current advertising budget. Here again, it is up to the firm to decide which perspective is the most relevant, given its strategic objectives. For the derivation of the dynamic optimization rule, see Lambin and Peeters (1977, Chapter 13).

The optimization rules used in this example are adapted to a situation of monopolistic competition where competitive advertising and reactions can be safely neglected in the analysis. For an extension of these optimization rules to oligopolies, see Lambin *et al.* (1975).

The normative value of this type of economic analysis is reduced, not only because of the always present uncertainty about the true value of the response coefficients, but also because the advertiser faces multiple objectives other than profit maximization. Also, the advertising quality (copy and media) is taken here at its average value, while large differences may exist from one campaign to another. For these reasons, the output of economic analysis should be used as a guideline for advertising budget decisions and be complemented by other approaches.

The Vidale and Wolfe advertising model

The model developed by Vidale and Wolfe expresses the following relationship between sales (in units or value) and advertising expenditure:

$$\frac{dq}{dt} = \left[(\beta) \ (s) \ \left(\frac{Q-q}{Q} \right) \right] - (1-L) \ (q)$$

where

$\dfrac{dq}{dt}$ = rate of increase of sales at any time t

β = sales response constant when $q = 0$

s = rate of advertising

q = company or brand sales

Q = product category saturation level

L = sales retention rate

In words, within a given period, the increase in sales (dq/dt) due to advertising is equal to

- The product of the sales response constant per dollar of advertising when sales are zero and of the rate of advertising during the period (response effect) . . .
- . . . adjusted by the proportion of the untapped market potential (saturation effect) . . .
- . . . reduced by the fraction of current sales that will decrease in the absence of advertising because of product obsolescence, competing advertising etc. (depreciation effect).

This is an interesting model because it takes into account the main features of advertising response functions while explicitly setting out the key parameters to be estimated. It does however have some weak points:

- The model does not allow explicit consideration of marketing variables other than advertising, such as price, distribution etc.
- The model does not integrate competitive advertising and is therefore implementable only in monopolistic situations.
- The model assumes that advertising merely obtains new customers and increased customer usage is neglected.
- The model does not explicitly consider possible variations in advertising quality, unless one could assume different sales constants per medium or per advertising theme.
- In some markets, it is difficult to estimate the absolute market potential.

Vidale and Wolfe's model has an interesting conceptual structure, but its range of application is limited.

The ADBUDG model

The ADBUDG model, developed by Little (1970), can be applied to a market where primary demand is non-expansible and where advertising is a determinant factor in sales and market share development. The model establishes a relationship between market share and advertising and assumes that managers are able to provide answers to the following five questions:

- What is the current level of advertising expenditure for the brand?
- What would market share be if advertising were cut to zero?
- What would maximum market share be if advertising were increased a great deal, say to saturation (saturation advertising)?
- What would market share be if the current level of advertising were halved?
- What would market share be if the current level of advertising were increased half as much?

The market share level estimates in response to these five questions can be represented as five points on a market share response to advertising curve, as illustrated in Figure 13.6. The ADBUDG model has the following mathematical expression:

$$MS(t) = MS(\min) + [MS(\max) - MS(\min)] \frac{Adv^{\varepsilon}}{\delta + Adv^{\varepsilon}}$$

where

$$
\begin{aligned}
MS(t) &= \text{initial market share} \\
MS(\min) &= \text{minimum market share with zero advertising} \\
MS(\max) &= \text{maximum market share with saturation advertising} \\
Adv &= \text{effective advertising (adjusted for media and copy} \\
&\quad\ \text{effectiveness)} \\
\varepsilon &= \text{advertising sensitivity coefficient} \\
\delta &= \text{constant}
\end{aligned}
$$

In words, the expected market share in any given period is then equal to:

- The minimum market share (min) expected at the end of the period if advertising is cut to zero (depreciation effect) . . .
- . . . plus a fraction of the maximum market share change due to advertising; this maximum change is equal to the difference between the maximum share expected with saturation advertising and the minimum share expected with zero advertising.
- The intensity of the response is determined by an 'advertising intensity coefficient' characterized by two parameters: ε, which influences the shape of the response function and δ, which is a moderator factor. Both parameters are determined by input data.

Effective advertising is given by the following expression:

$$Adv(t) = [\text{medium efficiency}(t)] \, [\text{copy effectiveness}(t)] \, (Adv) \text{ dollars}$$

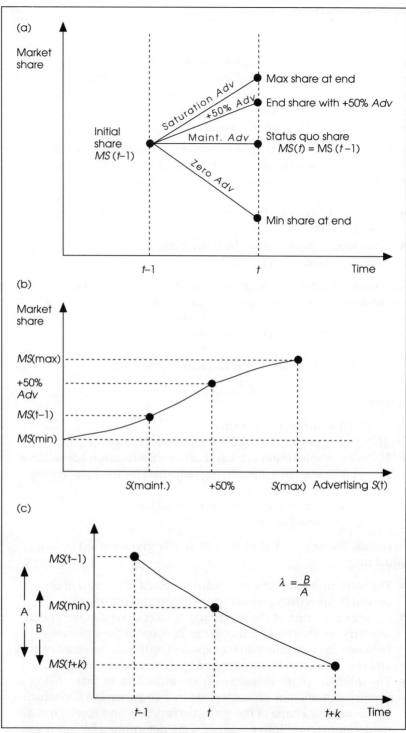

Figure 13.6 The ADBUDG model (Little, 1970). (a) Static advertising–sales response curve: input data. (b) Static advertising–sales response curve: graphic representation. (c) Dynamic advertising–sales response curve: graphic deduction of retention rate.

Both indices will be assumed to have a reference value of 1.0. These indices can be determined on the basis of copy testing and media exposure data.

This is an interesting model in many respects, and it has most of the features of advertising response functions. Furthermore, it can be easily estimated on microcomputers in interactive mode. Thus, users can test the model themselves without any help from outside experts. These are the model's strong points:

- The model parameters can be estimated either on the basis of management judgements using the five questions procedure outlined above, or through econometric analysis of historical or experimental data.
- The dependent variable can be sales, market share or measures of cognitive response, like awareness.
- The advertising input data can be adjusted for advertising quality using indices of media efficiency and of copy effectiveness.

The ADBUDG model was initially made essentially for interactive use relying on the decision-maker's subjective judgements. However, experience has shown that this approach is elusive because most decision-makers hold only a small fraction of the necessary information. On the other hand, it forms a useful framework for integrating objective information coming from various sources and for simulating the implications of different advertising strategies on market share and profits (for a similar approach, see Lambin (1972)).

Deciding on the size of the sales force

Determining the number of sales people is a problem logically similar to the advertising budget. In practice, however, it can be resolved more simply because market response is easier to measure. Different approaches are possible. The simplest no doubt is the one based on the sales person's 'work load'. An example of its application was shown in Chapter 11 (see p. 373). The procedure is as follows.

The underlying philosophy in the call-load approach is that large customers should be serviced differently from medium-sized customers, and medium-sized customers differently from small customers. Thus, the first step is to have a *breakdown of customer by class*.

The next step is to develop a theoretical *call frequency for each class*. Experience shows that as a customer grows larger, the number of sales calls does not grow in direct proportion to the increase in sales. Talley (1961, p.8) suggested that the relationship between customer size and sales calls can be clearly seen when these two factors are plotted on semi-log paper, which reflects the presence of diminishing returns. For every customer class, a specific call frequency is provided and the total work load is obtained by multiplying the call frequency times the number of account in any class.

In the third step, the *number of calls* made by an average sales person during one year must be determined. The factors to consider here are: number of working days after deducting holidays, weekends, vacations etc.; percentage of non-selling time devoted to sales meetings, sick leave, laboratory training etc.; number of calls made per day by sales person and by territory; and variation in call capacity between urban and rural territories.

Given the number of visits that a sales person can make in a given customer class, it is then possible to determine the size of the necessary sales force from the following expression:

Size of sales force =

$$\frac{\text{(Number of customers per class) (Call frequency)}}{\text{Average number of calls per salesperson}}$$

The calculation is repeated for each customer class. This approach is valid for current customers and must be extended to prospective customers as well. For other methods of setting the size of the sales force, see Semlow (1959) and Lambert (1968).

14

The strategic marketing plan

Sound strategic thinking about the future must be spelled out in a written document which describes the ends and means required to implement the chosen development strategy. In the short term, the firm's success is directly dependent on the financial performance of its ongoing activities. In the longer run, however, its survival and growth imply the ability to anticipate market changes and to adapt the structure of its product portfolio accordingly. To be effective, this strategic and proactive thinking must be organized in a systematic and formal way. The role of strategic marketing planning is the design of a desired future and of effective ways of making things happen. Its role is also to communicate these choices to those responsible for their implementation. This planning task is of course particularly hard when great uncertainties prevail in the firm's environment. Anticipating the unexpected is also part of the strategic planning process. In this chapter, we shall build on the concepts and procedures described in previous chapters and examine the steps needed to make strategic marketing happen in the firm.

Overview of strategic planning

The *raison d'être* of a strategic plan is to formulate the main strategic options taken by the firm, in a clear and concise way, in order to ensure its long-term development. These strategic options must be translated into decisions and action programmes. We shall briefly examine the overall structure of a plan and the benefits expected from strategic planning.

Overall structure of the strategic marketing plan

As shown in this book, the strategic marketing process can be summarized around six key questions. The answers provided to these questions constitute the backbone of the plan and also the objectives for the firm.

1 What business are we in and what is the *firm's mission* in the chosen reference market?
2 Within the defined reference market, what are the targeted product markets or segments and what is the *positioning strategy* likely to be adopted within each segment?
3 What are the key business *attractiveness factors* in each segment and what are the opportunities and threats presented by the environment?
4 Within each segment, what are the firm's distinctive qualities, strengths and weaknesses and *competitive advantages*?
5 Which *development strategy* and strategic ambition should be adopted for each activity in the firm's product portfolio?
6 How do these strategic options translate into *operational marketing programmes* defined in terms of product, distribution, pricing and communications decisions?

Once the answers to these questions are obtained as the result of a strategic marketing audit, the task remains to summarize the options taken, to define the means required to achieve the stated objectives, to design the specific action programmes and, last but not least, to prepare projected profit and loss statements for each activity and for the company as a whole.

In fact, a strategic marketing plan is nothing more than a financial plan, but with much more information on the origins and destinations of the financial flows. As discussed in Chapter 1 (see Figure 1.2.), the strategic marketing plan has direct implications for all the other functions of the firm and vice versa.

- *Research and development*: market needs must be met through new, improved or adapted products and services.
- *Finance*: the marketing programme is subject to financial constraints and to availability of resources.
- *Operations*: sales objectives are subject to production capacity and to physical delivery constraints.
- *Human resources*: the implementation of the plan implies the availability of qualified and well-trained personnel.

Thus strategic planning will result in a better integration of all the company's functions and contribute to maximization of efforts in reaching corporate goals. In a market-driven organization, the mission of strategic marketing is to identify prospects for growth and profit given the company resources and *savoir faire*. As already emphasized in this book, this role is much broader than the traditional domain of marketing management, and implies interfunctional coordination.

Importance of strategic planning

Every company, even those resistant to the idea of formal planning, has to formulate forecasts in a minimum of three areas:

- The calibration of the *investment programme* required to meet the level of market demand or to penetrate a new product market.
- The *production programme* organization needed, given the seasonality of sales and the periodicity of orders.
- The *financial liquidity*, based on income and expenses forecasts, which is required to meet the financial liabilities.

These managerial problems are common to all companies and they imply that reliable sales forecasts be handled properly.

In addition to this argument of necessity, other arguments in favour of formal strategic planning exist.

- The plan expresses the value system, philosophies and views of top management. This information gives people a *sense of direction* and a sense of how to behave.
- The plan presents the facts on 'where the business has come from and where it stands'. The situation analysis helps to understand the *reasons* for the strategic options taken by top management.
- The plan *facilitates coordination* among the different functions, maintains consistency in the objectives, and facilitates trade-offs among conflicting goals.
- The plan is a *monitoring instrument* which provides the opportunity to review the progress made in implementing the plan and to redirect parts of the action programme that are off target.
- The plan minimizes the degree to which the company is taken by surprise to the extent that 'best case–worst case' scenarios have been explored.
- The plan encourages a more *rigorous management* of scarce resources by using standards, budgets, schedules etc., thereby reducing the risk of improvization.

Most strategic plans are complemented by some form of contingency plan to be activated if certain events occur. Contingency plans are developed for factors which are key to the survival of the company.

Objections to formal planning

Although strategic planning is a widely adopted practice, a certain number of firms avoid using formal written strategic plans. Their objections to formal planning are as follows.

Lack of needed information

Ideally the planner would have at hand all the pertinent information required on industry and market trends, competitive intentions, market share, technological innovations and so forth. The most common complaint concerns lack of adequate information for the purpose of planning. On deeper investigation, however, it nearly always turns out to be a case of too much information rather than too little. The real problem is much more the lack of in-depth analysis. Thus, a marketing information and business intelligence system must exist in any case, and this is a costly operation with or without formal planning.

Futility of forecasting

In a turbulent environment, what good are strategic plans which will be contradicted by future events? This attitude results from a misunderstanding as to the nature of forecasting, which is erroneously likened to a crystal ball. As emphasized in Chapter 7, a forecast is a quantitative or qualitative estimate of what one expects, given a set of assumptions on the environment. A forecast is not an end in itself, but a forward thinking exercise, a tool used to increase the company's responsiveness and adaptability to the unexpected. This objective can be achieved even if the predicted outcome is not attained.

Bureaucratic ridigity

Formal planning would commit the firm to a given direction, whereas adaptability and flexible response are required in a fast-changing environment. This objection questions more the authoritarian planning style than planning itself. A plan should be designed to enhance creativity and quick reaction to changes. The mere fact of having analysed possible changes in the market in advance will help to revise programmes and objectives faster whenever it is desirable to do so.

In practice, strategic planning is widely used, as evidenced by various surveys conducted in Europe and in the USA (Haspeslagh, 1982; Hamermesch, 1987; Greenley, 1987; Caeldris and Van Dierdonck, 1988). For an analysis of the main barriers to the development of marketing plans, see McDonald (1991).

Content of a strategic marketing plan

A strategic marketing plan typically sets out to answer the six key questions presented at the beginning of this chapter. In this section, we shall describe the basic elements of a strategic marketing plan and the type of information required on which to base recommendations.

The mission statement

Sometimes called a *creed statement* or a statement of business principles, a *mission statement* reveals the company's long-term vision in terms of what it wants to be and who it wants to serve. It defines the organization's value system and its economic and non-economic objectives. The mission statement is important from both an internal and external point of view.

- Inside the company, it serves as a focal point for individuals to identify with the organization's direction and to ensure unanimity of purpose within the firm, thereby facilitating the emergence of a *corporate culture*.
- From an external point of view, the mission statement contributes to the creation of *corporate identity*, i.e. how the company wants to be perceived in the market place by its customers, competitors, employees, owners and shareholders, and by the general public.

A mission statement should include at least the four following components.

History of the company

Knowledge of the past history of the company, its origin and successive transformations is always useful to understand its present situation and the weight given to some economic or non-economic goals and objectives.

Materne-Confilux celebrated its 100th anniversary in 1987. This company has accumulated a broad experience in the field of purchase and transformation of fruits and has succeeded in maintaining a family managerial structure. This strong foothold in the fruit sector is a key factor to consider when exploring alternative diversification strategies.

In searching for a new purpose, a company must remain consistent with its past achievements and fields of competence.

Business definition

This is a key component in the mission statement. As emphasized in Chapter 4, what customers buy and consider valuable is never the product, but rather its utility, i.e. what a product or a service does for them. Thus, the market definition should be written in terms of the benefit provided to the buyer. As discussed in Chapter 6, the three relevant questions to examine here are:

- What business(es) are we in?
- What business(es) should we be in?
- What business(es) should we not be in?

These are not easy questions to answer, particularly when the environment is changing very quickly. Examples of business definitions were presented in Chapter 6, on pp. 159.

Ideally, the mission statement should be stated in terms narrow enough to provide practical guidance, yet broad enough to stimulate imaginative thinking, such as openings for product line extensions, or for diversification into adjacent product areas. At the Grumman Corporation, the guidelines for the mission statement advise:

> We should be careful not to confine the market boundaries by our existing or traditional product participation. The market definition analysis is purposely meant to create an outward awareness of the total surrounding market, and of its needs and trends that may offer opportunity for, or on the other hand challenges to, our current or contemplated position (Hopkins, 1981, p. 119).

Every organization has a unique purpose and reason for being. This uniqueness should be reflected in the market definition. In a market-driven organization, the market definition will express the degree of customer orientation of the firm.

Corporate goals and restraints

Goals set the direction for both long- and short-term development and therefore determine limitations and priorities to comply with. These general goals, usually defined at the corporate level, are constraints within which the strategic plan must be developed. They should be clearly defined in advance to avoid proposals that contradict objectives of general management or corporate shareholders.

These goals may be economic but also non-economic. Examples are : a minimum rate of return on investment, a growth objective, the conservation of the family ownership of the company, the refusal to enter particular fields of activity, or a minimum level of employment etc.

The description of *available company resources* (capacity, equipment, human resources, capital etc.), also forms part of the restraints and should be made explicit in order to avoid the adoption of a 'mission impossible' given the resources needed. *Codes of conduct and corporate ethics* for dealing with others (customers, distributors, competitors, suppliers etc.) should also be formulated.

Basic strategic choices

Independent of the general goals imposed at the corporate level by general management, basic strategic options can be defined for each strategic business unit. For example, the extent of the strategic

Table 14.1 What components are included in company mission statements? (David, 1989)

1 Customers	Who are the company's customers?
2 Products or services	What are the firm's major products or services?
3 Location	Where does the firm compete?
4 Technology	What is the firm's basic technology?
5 Concern for survival	What is the firm's commitment to economic objectives?
6 Philosophy	What are the basic beliefs, values, aspirations and philosophical priorities of the firm?
7 Self-concept	What are the firm's major strengths and competitive advantages?
8 Public image	What are the firm's public responsibilities and what image is desired?
9 Concern for employees	What is the firm's attitude towards its employees?

ambition and the role played by the firm in the target segment, i.e. leader, follower, challenger or nicher, may be defined. Reference could be made here also to the three basic positioning strategies suggested by Porter (1980) and discussed in Chapter 9 (see pp. 290–94): cost advantage, differentiation or focus.

At this stage of the strategic plan, only broad orientations are given. They will be redefined in quantitative terms in the action programmes developed for each business unit.

In a survey conducted in the USA, out of a total of 181 responses received, 75 organizations provided a formal description of their mission statements. The main components included are summarized in Table 14.1.

External audit—market attractiveness analysis

This external audit—also called opportunities and threats analysis— is the first part of the situation analysis. As explained in Chapter 7, an attractiveness analysis examines the major external factors, i.e. the factors which are out of the control of the firm, but that may have an impact on the marketing plan.

The following areas should be reviewed:

- Market trends.

- Buyer behaviour.
- Distribution structure.
- Competitive environment.
- Macro-environmental trends.
- International environment.

These external factors may constitute *opportunities or threats* that the firm must try to anticipate and monitor through its marketing information system and through business intelligence. In what follows, we shall simply list the critical questions to raise in each of these areas. The precise type of information required will of course differ by product category: consumer durable or non-durable goods, services or industrial goods.

Market trends analysis

The objective is to describe, segment by segment, the total demand's general trends within a three- to five-year horizon. The task is to position each product market in its life cycle and to quantify the market size. Both unit volume and monetary values should be identified. The key demand concepts to examine have been reviewed in Chapter 7.

Questionnaire 1: Total market trends

- What is the size of the total market, in volume and in value?
- What are the trends: growth, stagnation, decline?
- What is the average per capita consumption?
- How far are we from the saturation level?
- What is the rate of equipment per household or per company?
- What is the average lifetime of the product?
- What is the share of replacement demand in total demand?
- What is the seasonal pattern of total sales?
- What are the main substitute products performing the same service?
- What are the major innovations in the sector?
- What is the structure of the distributive system?
- How will supply–demand relationships affect price levels?
- What is the level of total advertising intensity?
- What are the most popular advertising media?

This list is certainly incomplete. It simply illustrates the type of information required. If the product studied is an industrial good, several information items should pertain not only to the direct customers' demand, but also to the demand expressed further down the line in the industrial chain by the customers of the direct customers.

Buyer behaviour analysis

The task here is to examine buyer behaviour in terms of purchasing, use and possession. Table 5.5 presents the type of information sought. In addition to this buyers' purchasing habits description, it is also useful to know the buying process and to identify the influencing factors.

Questionnaire 2: Buyer behaviour analysis

- Per segment, what is the buyers' socio-demographic profile?
- What is the composition of the buying centre?
- Who is the buyer, the user, the decider, the influencer?
- What is the decision process adopted by the buyer?
- What is the level of involvement of the buyer?
- What are the main motivations of the buying decision?
- What is the package of benefits sought by the buyer?
- What are the different uses of the product?
- What changing customer demands and needs do we anticipate?
- What are the purchasing frequency and periodicity?
- To which marketing factors are customers most responsive?
- What is the rate of customer satisfaction or dissatisfaction?

These descriptive data must be complemented with measures of the cognitive and affective response (recall, attitudes, preferences, intentions etc.), as well as with brand or company image analyses.

Distribution structure analysis

This part of the external audit is probably more relevant in the field of consumer goods than in the sector of industrial goods, where direct distribution is common practice. The objective is to assess the future development of distribution channels and to understand the motivations and expectations of the company's trading partners.

Questionnaire 3: Structure and motivation of distribution

- What are industry sales by type of outlet?
- What are product type sales by type of outlet?
- What are product type sales by method of distribution?
- What is the concentration ratio of distribution?
- Is distribution intensive, selective or exclusive?
- What is the share of advertising assumed by distributors?
- What change does one observe in the assortments?
- What is the market share held by private brands?
- Which market segments are covered by the different channels?
- What are the total distribution costs?
- What is the distribution margin for each channel of distribution?
- What kind of distributor support is currently provided?
- What is the potential of direct distribution?

The distributor, as a business partner, has strong negotiation powers *vis-à-vis* the firm. One of the roles of a distribution analysis is to assess the degree of autonomy or dependence of the firm in the distributive system.

Competitive environment

The competitive structure of a market sets the framework within which the firm will operate. As Porter (1980) has said: 'The essence of strategy formulation is coping with competition'. The basic attractiveness of a market segment is largely determined by the strength of competitors' capabilities. Assessment of what is driving competition is of vital importance to the firm.

Questionnaire 4: Competition analysis

- What is the market's competitive structure?
- What is the market share held by the top three to five rivals?
- What type of competitive behaviour is dominant?
- What is the strength of competing brands' images?
- What is the nature of the competitive advantage of direct competitors?
- To what extent are these competitive advantages well protected?
- What are the competitors' major objectives?
- What is the current strategy being used to achieve the objectives?
- What are the strengths and weaknesses of competitors?
- What are their likely future strategies?
- Are there entry barriers in this market?
- Which are the main substitute products?
- What is the bargaining power of customers and suppliers?

The gathering of this type of information implies the development of a *competitor intelligence system*. For a more detailed framework of competitor analysis, see Porter (1980, Chapter 3).

Macro-environmental trends

This section describes the macro-environmental trends— demographic, economic, political/legal and sociocultural—that bear on the studied market's future development. These external factors can provide productive opportunities or severe limitations for the company's products.

Questionnaire 5(a) Economic macro-environment

- What is the expected GNP rate of growth?
- What major economic changes could affect our business?
- What is the expected level of employment?
- What is the expected rate of inflation?
- Do these trends affect our business and how?

Questionnaire 5(b) Political and legal macro-environment

- Are there any specific changes in the law that affect our company?
- Are there legal or political areas that affect our customers?
- Which regulations could affect our advertising or selling strategy?
- Is our industry subject to criticisms from consumer organizations?
- Are there political or legal trends that could be used to our advantage?

Questionnaire 5(c) Socio-demographic and cultural macro-environment

- What are the major demographic trends that affect our business?
- What is the cultural climate within which our business operates?
- Are present and future life styles favourable to our business?
- Is society's attitude towards our business changing?
- Are there changes in society's values that could affect our business?

Questionnaire 5(d) Technological environment

- What major changes are occurring in product technology?
- How can we adjust our activities to cope with these changes?
- What major generic substitutes might replace our product?
- Do we have the required R&D capabilities?
- Do we need to update our equipment and at what cost?

Questionnaire 5(e) Ecological environment

- Are our products environmentally friendly?
- Do we use processes or raw materials which threaten the environment?
- Is green marketing a potential strategy for our company?
- Is our industry a potential target for environmentalists?
- How can we improve the ecological quality of our products?

Questionnaire 5(f) International environment

- To what extent are we dependent on imports for key components?
- What is the economic and political stability of the supplier country?
- What alternatives do we have should our imports be interrupted?
- What is the economic and political stability of the customer countries?
- What opportunities does the European Single Market represent?
- Are there emerging global segments in our business?
- Is our business affected by changing world trade patterns?

Questionnaire 5(g) Industry and corporate ethics

- Does our company or industry have a stated code of ethics?

- What is the ethical level of our industry?
- Are industry values in alignment with those expected by society?
- How could our industry improve its ethical practice?

This information, dealing with the macro-environment of the firm, is indispensable for exploring alternative scenarios of market development. The sources of information are numerous and varied, but often very scattered. Professional organizations and local chambers of commerce have economic data available for their members to use in planning. In addition to national statistics and foreign trade institutes, international financial institutions like the Bank for International Settlements (BIS), the International Monetary Funds (IMF), the World Bank (WB), the Office for Economic and Cooperation Development (OECD), the United Nations (UN) etc. are the major public sources, with periodic publications readily available. University research centres and large international consulting firms, like Business International, McKinsey, the Economist Intelligence Unit etc., also publish newsletters, articles and monographs which are very useful for planning purposes.

Internal audit—company competitiveness analysis

The objective of the internal audit, also called the company strengths and weaknesses analysis, is to assess company resources and to identify the type of sustainable competitive advantage on which to base the development strategy. *Strengths and weaknesses* are internal factors, in contrast with opportunities and threats, which are external factors. Company strengths (or distinctive qualities) point to certain strategies the company might be successful in adopting, while company weaknesses point to certain things the company needs to correct.

A competitiveness analysis should not be abstract. Reference to competition in general is too vague. Therefore, competition should be referred to in terms of the most dangerous competitors, called priority competitors.

To illustrate, distinctive qualities for a brand of laptop computer, as compared to those of the priority competitor, might be:

- An excellent brand awareness and an image of high quality.
- Dealers who are knowledgeable and well trained in selling.
- An excellent service network and customers who know they will get quick repair service.

The weaknesses of the same brand could be,

- The screen quality of the brand is not demonstrably better than

the quality of competing machines, yet screen quality can make a big difference in brand choice.
- The brand is budgeting only 5 per cent of its sales revenue for advertising and promotion while major competitors are spending twice that level.
- The brand is priced higher relative to other brands without being supported by a real perceived difference in quality.

The strengths of the company or of the brand constitute potential *competitive advantages* on which to base the positioning and the communication strategy. The weaknesses determine the *vulnerability* of the brand and require remedial action. Some weaknesses may be structural, i.e. linked to the size of the firm and therefore difficult to correct. Examples of structural weaknesses are:

- National market share leadership, if not accompanied by international distribution, creates a home country vulnerability to the extent that the local company has little freedom for retaliation in the country of foreign competitors.
- If total sales volume is generated by a single powerful distributor, the company has weak bargaining power.
- A small or medium-sized company does not have the financial capability to use the most powerful media, like television advertising.

So a distinction must be made between the weaknesses that the company can correct and therefore which become priority issues that must be addressed in the plan, and the high risk structural weaknesses which are beyond the control of the firm and which require a high degree of surveillance.

Competitiveness analysis is organized much like attractiveness analysis. The major difference comes from the fact that the company, and not the market, is the central subject of the analysis.

Company current marketing situation

Data on the served markets for each of the products of the company's portfolio, in volume and market shares for several years and by geographical areas, are presented, as well as data on the current marketing mix.

Questionnare 6: Product portfolio analysis

- What is the rate of current sales per product, segment, distributive channel, region and country etc. in volume and value?
- What is the current market share per product category, segment, distributive channel, region, country etc.?
- How strong is the company's product brand image?

Table 14.2 Priority competitors analysis form. Each factor must be evaluated on a 10-point scale

Marketing variables	Our product	Competitor 1	Competitor 2	Competitor 3
Product				
Quality:	_____	_____	_____	_____
Company price:	_____	_____	_____	_____
Product line:	_____	_____	_____	_____
Packaging:	_____	_____	_____	_____
Evaluation on				
attribute: _____ :	_____	_____	_____	_____
attribute: _____ :	_____	_____	_____	_____
attribute: _____ :	_____	_____	_____	_____
Distribution				
Dist. number :	_____	_____	_____	_____
Dist. value :	_____	_____	_____	_____
channel 1:_____ :	_____	_____	_____	_____
channel 2:_____ :	_____	_____	_____	_____
channel 3:_____ :	_____	_____	_____	_____
Facing:	_____	_____	_____	_____
Margin:	_____	_____	_____	_____
Discounts:	_____	_____	_____	_____
Promotion:	_____	_____	_____	_____
Sales force				
Size of sales force:	_____	_____	_____	_____
Quality:	_____	_____	_____	_____
Call frequency:	_____	_____	_____	_____
Training:	_____	_____	_____	_____
Advertising				
Size of budget:	_____	_____	_____	_____
Media mix:				
medium 1:_____ :	_____	_____	_____	_____
medium 2:_____ :	_____	_____	_____	_____
medium 3:_____ :	_____	_____	_____	_____
Advertising copy:	_____	_____	_____	_____
Advertisment quality:_____	_____	_____	_____
Promotion				
Size of budget:	_____	_____	_____	_____
Type of promotion:	_____	_____	_____	_____
Consumer price:	_____	_____	_____	_____
Distribution margin:	_____	_____	_____	_____
Other promotions:	_____	_____	_____	_____

Table 14.2 *cont.*

Marketing variables	Our product	Competitor 1	Competitor 2	Competitor 3
Services				
Range of services:	——	——	——	——
Delivery terms:	——	——	——	——
After-sales service:	——	——	——	——
Research and development				
Size of budget:	——	——	——	——
Staff:	——	——	——	——
Performance in R&D	——	——	——	——
Marketing research				
Quality of MIS:	——	——	——	——
Data banks:	——	——	——	——
Performance:	——	——	——	——

- Does the firm have a complete product line?
- How does the quality of our products compare with that of competition?
- What is the structure of our portfolio of customers?
- How concentrated is our total turnover?
- What is the age profile of our product portfolio?
- What is the contribution margin per product, segment, channel etc.

This analysis is to be repeated for each product of the company's portfolio. Profit and loss statements for the last three years should be presented along with the current budget. A typical profit and loss statement is shown in Table 14.6 on p. 496.

Priority competitor analysis

Priority competitor(s) should be identified for each product market. For each of these competitors, the same data collected for the company products will be gathered and compared as shown in Table 14.2. Other information is required to assess the strength of priority competition.

Questionnaire 7: Priority competition analysis

- What is the relative market share?
- Does competition have a cost advantage?
- What is the relative price?
- What is the competitive behaviour of rivals?
- How strong is the image of competing products?

- On what basis are competing products differentiated?
- What is their retaliation capacity in case of frontal attack?
- Which are their major sources of vulnerability?
- What type of aggressive actions could they take?
- What changes could modify the present balance of power?
- Is competition able to destroy our competitive advantage?

With the information provided by questionnaires 6 and 7, a product portfolio analysis can be conducted using one of the procedures described in Chapter 9.

Distribution penetration analysis

Distributors, a company's partners in the marketing process, control the access to the end-users' market and play an important role in ensuring the success of the contemplated marketing programme. In addition, if they are powerful buyers they have a strong bargaining power *vis-à-vis* their suppliers. In fact, distributors must be viewed as intermediate customers just like end-user customers. The role of 'trade marketing' is to analyse the needs and requirements of these intermediate customers in order to develop a mutually satisfactory exchange relationship.

Questionnaire 8: Distribution analysis

- How many distributors do we have in each channel?
- What is our penetration rate in number and value in each channel?
- What are the growth potentials of the different channels?
- What are the efficiency levels of the different distributors?
- Should the firm consider changing its distribution channels?
- What is the potential of direct marketing in our business?
- Are the present trade terms motivating for distributors?
- What changes could modify relationships with our dealer network?
- Are there new forms of distribution emerging in the market?

The objectives pursued by the firm and by its distributors are not exactly the same and conflicts can arise in the channels. Distributors are no longer passive intermediaries in most markets. The role of 'trade marketing' is to ensure that distributors are viewed by the firm as partners and as intermediate customers.

Communication programme analysis

Mass media advertising, interactive advertising, personal selling, publicity etc. are powerful competitive weapons if properly used, i.e. when the target markets are well chosen and when the content of the communication programme is well in line with the product positioning, pricing and distribution strategies.

Questionnaire 9: Communication programme analysis

- What is the advertising intensity compared to direct competition?
- What is the advertising cost per thousand target buyers per medium?
- What is the communication effectiveness of media advertising?
- What are the consumers' opinions on the advertisement content?
- What is the number of reply coupons stimulated by direct advertising?
- How well are the advertising objectives defined?
- What is the sales or market share effectiveness of advertising?
- What is the impact of advertising on awareness, attitude and intentions?
- What is the average number of sales call per sales representative per week?
- What is the number of new customers per period?
- What is the sales force cost as a percentage of total sales?

These questionnaires should be used as guidelines for periodically reviewing the company's marketing situation within the framework of a marketing audit. For a guide to marketing auditing, see Barnoux (1990).

Objectives and action programmes

At this point, management knows the major issues and has to make some basic decisions about the objectives. Using the information provided by the strategic marketing audit and by the positioning statement, the firm's identified priority objectives must then be translated into operational action programmes.

Definition of objectives

Every firm has several objectives which can be regrouped into two broad categories: marketing and non-marketing objectives. *Non-marketing objectives* have been described in the firm's mission statement. They describe the overall value system of the company and as such they apply for all market targets. *Marketing objectives* are of three types: sales, profit and customers. They should be defined for each product market or segment.

Sales objectives

It is a quantitative measure of the impact the firm 'wants' to achieve in the future within a particular product market. It is not simply a forecast of what one 'expects' may occur in the future. It is an active, not a passive, statement about the future.

Table 14.3 Examples of sales-oriented objectives

1 Achieve total sales revenue of $2 150 000 by the end of 1992.
2 Attain a 20 per cent market share of the management distance learning market.
3 Reach a sales volume of 150 000 units per year.

Sales objectives can be stated in currency, in volume or in market share. Examples of sales-oriented objectives are presented in Table 14.3.

- *Sales revenue* objectives are the most convenient way to express a sales objective because they are easily integrated in the accounting and financial system. Sales revenue may be misleading, however, if not adjusted for inflation and also for modifications in the sales mix if, for example, the share of high-priced products has changed from one period to another.
- *Unit sales* represent the best indicator provided there is no change in the volume definition. In the soft drink sector, for example, it is current practice to think in terms of cases sales. What about cases of 12 or 18 bottles? Conversion to 'litres equivalent cases' must be made. In many markets a meaningful unit definition simply does not exist. For example, in life insurance the number of contracts subscribed is not a good indicator of sales performance.
- *Market share*, as discussed in Chapter 5, is the best indicator of competitive performance. Also, in volume industries where experience effects occur, high market share implies a cost competitive advantage over direct competition.

Sales data are a key element in the projected income statement. They must be translated into financial terms.

Profit objectives

Marketing, as for all other functions within the firm, must be accountable for profits. The inclusion of formal profit objectives forces marketing people to estimate the cost implications of the stated sales objectives. Examples of profit objectives are presented in Table 14.4.

The definition of profit objectives implies a close interfunctional coordination within the firm. A statement of profitability cannot be made without a close look at the cost–volume relationship and capacity constraints. For new products, the investment in fixed costs and working capital, in addition to manufacturing and marketing costs, should be analysed before launching. Similarly, the marketing expenses involved in implementing the proposed marketing strategy

Table 14.4 Examples of profit objectives

1 Produce net profits of $150 000 before tax by December 1993.
2 Earn an average 15 per cent return on investment during the next 5 years.
3 Produce a dollar contribution of $350 000 at the end of the fiscal year.

Table 14.5 Examples of customer objectives

1 Create at least a 60 per cent awareness for brand A within the 15–25 age group by the end of 1992.
2 To increase by 20 per cent the repeat purchase rate of brand A within the 15–25 age group by the end of 1993.
3 To position brand A at the high end of the market in the minds of consumers belonging to the upper income bracket.

must be carefully evaluated and their expected contribution to sales and/or market share development assessed. Go back to Figure 1.2 for a description of the interrelationships among the key managerial functions.

Customer objectives

Customer objectives are deduced from the positioning statement. They describe the type of behaviour or attitude the firm would want customers to have towards its brands or services. Examples of customer objectives are presented in Table 14.5. These customer objectives are important because they provide directions to advertising people for the development of communication strategies and for supporting the positioning theme adopted.

Integration of objectives

Kotler (1991, p. 77) suggests starting with the profit objectives and deducing the required sales and customer objectives.

For example, if the company wants to earn $1 800 000 profit, and its target profit margin is 10 per cent on sales, then it must set a goal of $18 million in sales revenue. If the company set an average price of $260, it must sell 69 230 units. If it expects total industry sales to reach 2.3 million units, that is a 3 per cent market share. To maintain this market share, the company will have to set certain goals for consumer awareness, distribution coverage, and so on.

This logical and apparently simple procedure is difficult to implement in the real world because it implies complete knowledge of the functional relationships between market share and price, market share and distribution, market share and awareness etc. The merit of this approach is to identify clearly the required information for sound marketing planning.

Characteristics of good objectives

Sound marketing objectives should have the following characteristics. They must be (a) clear and concise, avoiding long statements and phrases; they should (b) be presented in a written form to facilitate communication and to avoid altering objectives over time; they should (c) be stated within a specific time period and (d) in measurable terms; they must (e) be consistent with overall company objectives and purpose; they must (f) be attainable but of sufficient challenge to stimulate effort; and they should (g) name specific results in key areas, such as sales, profits and consumer behaviour or attitudes (Stevens, 1982, pp. 80–2).

Selection of the strategic path

To define an objective is one thing. To know how to reach that objective is another story, since the very same objective can be achieved in different ways. A 10 per cent revenue increase can be obtained, for instance, by increasing the average selling price, or by expanding total demand through a price decrease, or by increasing market share without a price change but through intensive advertising or promotional actions.

Clearly these alternative actions are not substitutes and their efficiency will vary according to market and competitive situations. Thus, beyond the general directions given by the basic strategic options discussed in Chapter 9, it is necessary to specify the action programmes segment by segment.

If the strategic option is to defend current market position with existing products in an existing segment, the alternative actions to consider in a *market position defence strategy* could be:

- Product or service modifications, e.g. new features or packaging, or product repositioning through concept advertising.
- Sales, distribution and service network reinforcement.
- Stepped-up or redirected promotional activities.
- Defensive pricing through bundling or premium pricing.

If the objective is to complete, improve or broaden the range of products, the alternative of a *product line extension strategy* could be:

- Filling gaps in the existing product line.
- Introduction of new products to serve untapped segments in related business areas.

- Systematic brands proliferation to blanket the market.
- Acquisition of a company with a complementary product line.
- Contracting for the supply of a complementary product line to be sold under the company's name.
- Joint venture for the development and production of a new product line.

If the objective is *international development* by shipping existing products to foreign markets, the alternatives could be:

- Use of an independent, worldwide trading company.
- Use of a network of export agents to handle all foreign business.
- Setting up of a network of distributors or import agents in target markets.
- Acquisition of a foreign company in the same industrial sector.
- A joint venture to enter a restricted foreign market.

These alternative strategy paths may have very different implications in terms of resources, both financial and human, and their feasibility must be carefully assessed.

The strategy statement

The strategy statement requires making basic choices among the strategy alternatives. It is a summary overview designed to state 'how' the objectives for the business unit will be met. The strategy statement will govern not only marketing planning, but the manufacturing, financial and R&D functions. It is the mainstream guidance from which all subsequent planning functions flow. The strategy statement should address the following:

- Market segments selected and targeted.
- Positioning relative to direct competition.
- Product line requirements, mix, extensions etc.
- Channels of distribution, direct, indirect etc.
- Pricing and price structure.
- Personal selling.
- Advertising and promotion.
- After-sale, warranty, services etc.
- Marketing research.

The strategy statement should not exceed two or three pages of text. At this point, general management should review and approve the objectives.

Criteria for selecting a strategic option

A certain number of simple rules, inspired by military strategy, should be followed in selecting a strategy.

- *Feasibility*: assess skills and resources constraints.
- *Strength*: always try to have a strength advantage.
- *Concentration*: avoid scattering of efforts.
- *Synergy*: ensure coordination and consistency in efforts.
- *Adaptability*: be ready to respond to the unexpected.
- *Parsimony*: avoid waste of scarce resources.

In the 1990s environment, forward thinking is a dynamic exercise which requires adaptability and flexibility (Gilbreath, 1987).

The marketing budget

Once the course of action is identified, a detailed description of the means required will be made for each component of the marketing mix. The strategy statement allows the product manager to prepare a supporting budget, which is basically a projected profit and loss statement. A standard structure of a projected profit and loss statement is presented in Table 14.6.

Table 14.6 Projected profit and loss statements form

Variables	$t-3$	$t-2$	$t-1$	Current	$t+1$	$t+2$	$t+3$
1 Total demand in units							
2 Company market share							
3 Average selling price							
4 Unit direct cost							
5 Unit gross profit margin $(3-4)$							
6 Company sales in units (1×2)							
7 Company sales revenue (3×6)							
8 Total gross profit margin (5×6)							
9 Overhead							
10 Net profit margin $(5-6)$							
11 Advertising and promotion							
12 Sales force							
13 Market research							
14 Operating profit $10-(11-12-13)$							

In addition to financial considerations, the budget should also specify the timing of the action programmes and the responsibilities, i.e. who is in charge of what.

Gap analysis

In summarizing the objectives of each business unit, it is instructive to project the current performance trends to verify whether the projected performance is satisfactory. If gaps appear between the current and the desired performances, then strategic changes will need to be considered. The graph presented in Figure 14.1 illustrates the contribution of growth opportunities under two growth scenarios:

- An 'all things being equal performance', where growth is achieved through a penetration strategy based on existing products and existing markets, assuming no change in the current strategy.
- A 'desired performance', where growth is the outcome of the proposed marketing programme and of different growth opportunities.

As shown in Figure 14.1 the gap between these two performance levels can be subdivided into two parts:

- An *'operational gap'*, which reveals the improvement potential of existing businesses that could be achieved through a market and product rationalization strategy, i.e. reducing costs and/or improving marketing effectiveness, while keeping the structure of the product portfolio unchanged.

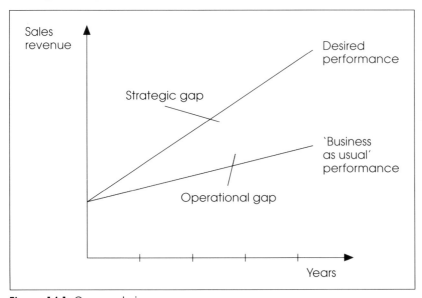

Figure 14.1 Gap analysis

- A *'strategic gap'*, which requires new growth opportunities, i.e. new products, new markets, international development, diversification or integration.

These growth opportunities should be listed in order of priority and their potential financial contribution to the desired performance evaluated.

Vulnerability analysis and contingency planning

The value of strategic planning is a continuing topic for debate. Not long ago, planning departments enjoyed a high status within the corporate organization. Today, most corporate planners downplay their formal planning roles. Experience with such largely unforeseen upheavals as the two oil crises of the 1970s, the stock market crash of 1987, the Gulf War, the East European revolutions etc. has revealed the shortcomings and the limitations of rigid planning procedures. Under fairly static conditions, planning works well, but when faced with uncertainties, turbulences, unanticipated market and competitive changes, general management becomes suspicious of the forecasts of revenue and profit performance that come from the business units.

Testing the robustness of a strategic plan

Just because a strategy must be developed and implemented under turbulent and uncertain conditions is no reason to abandon the discipline of structured planning. Planning is necessary for the functioning of the firm. To improve strategic planning performance, it is therefore important to test the robustness of the proposed strategy. Gilbreath (1987) suggests applying a 'shake test' to the proposed strategy.

> When structural or mechanical engineers wish to determine the reaction of a proposed design to mechanical vibrations, they either model it mathematically and calculate its response to input vibrations or, if feasible, build a prototype, put it on a special 'shaking table' and actually witness the outcome. This is called a 'shake test'. . . . It is proposed that a similar exercise be applied to strategic plans—giving them the shake test before the unforgiving test our markets and competitors will surely apply (Gilbreath, 1987, p. 47).

Day (1986) proposed testing the robustness of a proposed strategy through the following seven 'tough questions' to be examined by corporate management and operating managers.

- *Suitability*: is there a sustainable advantage given the potential threats to and opportunities for the business and in light of the capabilities of the firm?

- *Validity*: are the assumptions realistic? What is the quality of the information on which these assumptions rely?
- *Feasibility*: do we have the skills, resources and commitment?
- *Consistency*: does the strategy hang together? Are all elements of the strategy pointing in the same direction?
- *Vulnerability*: what are the risks and contingencies?
- *Adaptability*: can we retain our flexibility? How could the strategy be reversed in the future?
- *Financial desirability*: how much economic value is created? What is the attractiveness of the forecast performance relative to the probable risk? (adapted from Day, 1986, p. 63–8).

Strategies that do not meet these criteria are unlikely to succeed. A good way to proceed is to apply this shake test with the assistance of outside persons to avoid the risk of myopia and wishful thinking. Also, given the rapidity of environmental change, the test should be applied periodically to facilitate adaptability and revision.

Vulnerability and risk analysis

The vulnerability of a strategic plan is determined by two factors: the strategic importance of risk and the degree of control the firm has over the risk factor. The risk factor is a combination of (a) the impact of extreme but plausible values on overall performance, and (b) the likelihood that these extreme values could occur during the planning period.

The vulnerability grid presented in Figure 14.2 can be used to position the different risk factors and to isolate those few that could cause the most damage. To each quadrant there corresponds a specific risk situation which requires appropriate action.

- In the *strategy quadrant*, i.e. where both risk and degree of control are high, the risk factors are subject to company control, need to be understood very well, are the focus of major strategic actions and should be tightly monitored.
- In the *vulnerability quadrant*, the risks are high but the degree of control is weak. The factors positioned here are critical and must be continuously monitored. Contingency plans should be developed.
- In the *fine-tuning quadrant*, the risks are low but the degree of control high. These factors are controlled and managed by operational management.
- In the *non-strategy quadrant*, both risk and degree of control are low and the factors positioned here will be included in the base scenario.

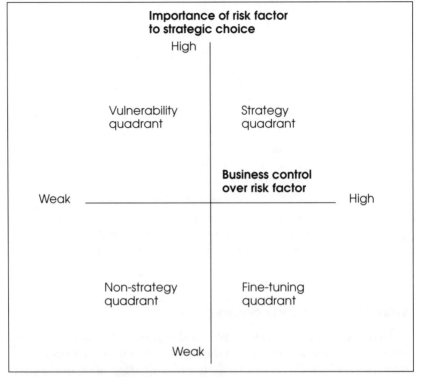

Figure 14.2 Vulnerability grid (Day, 1986).

The vulnerability quadrant deserves particular attention, since major and unanticipated crises could come from these risk factors. Examples of vulnerability factors are presented in Table 14.7.

Strategic surprise management

In spite of the best planning efforts, some issues or unexpected changes will slip by the environmental monitoring system and become 'crises', or 'strategic surprises' in Ansoff's terminology (1984). A crisis is characterized by four elements:

- The issue arrives suddenly, unanticipated.
- It poses novel problems in which the firm has little prior experience.
- Failure to respond implies either a major financial reversal or loss of a major opportunity.
- The response is urgent and cannot be handled promptly enough by the normal systems and procedures (Ansoff, 1984, p. 24).

Table 14.7 Identifying vulnerability factors (adapted from Gilbreath (1987))

Vulnerability factors	Stability factors
Reliance on fads	Projection of lasting symbols
Single use	Multiple use of products
Technology dependence	Technology transcendence
Single distribution network	Multiple distribution network
Heavy capital investment	Leasing, renting and joint ownership
Prescriptive identities	Non-restrictive identities
Building with products outside our control	Building with unchanging needs

The combination of these four elements creates major problems for the firm. A crisis or disaster can be any emergency that happens suddenly, that disrupts the routine of the organization and that demands immediate attention. Examples of crises are numerous: the 'Nestlé kills babies' affair, the Tylenol incident, the Union Carbide disaster in Bhopal, the Société Générale of Belgium's takeover bid, the Pan Am Boeing 747 crash at Lockerbie, the Chernobyl and Three Mile Island nuclear accidents, the change in the Coke formula etc.

The suddenness and the prospects of a major loss create a danger of widespread panic, and 'business as usual' managerial systems are inefficient to deal with a crisis. The firm needs to invest in a *crisis recovery plan*, because disaster recovery planning is more conducive to a rational perspective and more cost-effective if the process is begun before a crisis, rather than pulled together in the heat of battle (Phelps, 1986, p. 6).

According to Ansoff (1984) and Lagadec (1991), a crisis recovery plan should have the following characteristics:

- An emergency communication network which crosses normal organizational boundaries, filters the information and rapidly communicates with the entire organization.
- A repartition of top management responsibilities between three groups: one in charge of the organization's morale control and maintenance; one in charge of 'business as usual'; and one in charge of the response to the surprise.
- A strategic task force to deal with the surprise whose members cross normal organizational lines.
- The task force and communication networks are pre-designed and trained under non-crisis conditions before they are put to the actual test.

To go further on this topic, see the excellent book by Lagadec (1991).

The new roles of global strategic planning

Business International (1991) conducted a survey with 18 of the world's leading global companies on three continents for gaining insights into their approaches to global planning. The 10 most frequently mentioned functions of corporate planners are the following:

- Compiling of information for top management.
- Competitor research.
- Forecasting.
- Consulting services.
- Creating a common language.
- Communicating corporate culture.
- Establishing and communicating corporate objectives.
- Group facilitation and team leadership.
- Guardianship of the planning system.
- Developing planning methods.

Most corporate planners downplay their formal planning roles and instead emphasize their functions as 'facilitators', 'communicators' or 'consultants'. They see their role less as representatives of corporate authority than as consultants charged with assisting the divisions in developing their own plan and strategies.

Bibliography

Chapter 1

Ames, B.C. and Hlavacek, J.D. (1989). *Market Driven Management*, Homewood, ILL: Dow Jones-Irwin.

Bennett, R.C. and Cooper, R.G. (1979). 'The misuse of marketing: an American tragedy', *Business Horizons*, Nov–Dec, 51–60.

Booz, Allen and Hamilton (1982). *New product Management for the 1980s*, New York.

Cooper, R.G. (1979). 'The dimension of industrial product success and failure', *Journal of Marketing*, **43**, 93–103.

Drucker, P. (1973). *Management, tasks, responsibilities and practices*. New York: Harper & Row.

Friedman R. and M. (1980). *Free to choose*. New York, Avon Books.

Kotler, P. (1988). *Marketing management: analysis, planning, implementation and control*. Englewood Cliffs, NJ: Prentice-Hall.

Kuehn, A.A. and Day, R.L. (1962). 'Strategy of product quality', *Harvard Business Review*, **40**, Nov–Dec, 100–10.

Ladrière, J. (1984). *Les enjeux de la rationalité*. Paris: Editions Aubier Montaigne.

Levitt, Th. (1960). 'Marketing Myopia', *Harvard Business Review*, **38**, July–Aug, 24–47.

de Maricourt, R. (1987). 'Les principes et les techniques du marketing sont-ils applicables aux pays en voie de développement?', *Revue Française du Marketing*, March–April, 5–17.

Miller, R.B. and Heiman, S.E. (1987). *Conceptual selling*. Berkeley, CA: Heiman-Miller.

Narver, J.C. and Slater, S.F. (1989). *The effects of market orientation on business profitability*. Cambridge, MA: Marketing Science Institute. (Report No. 89–120.)

Schumpeles, J.A. (1949). *The Theory of Economic Development*, Cambridge, MA: Harvard University Press.

Searles, P.D. (1980). 'Marketing principles and the arts', in *Marketing the arts* (ed. M.D. Mokwa *et al.*). New York: Praeger.

Smith, A. (1776). *The wealth of nations*. London: Methuen.

Urban, G.L., Hauser, J.R. and Dholakia, N. (1987). *Essentials of new product management*. Englewood Cliffs, NJ: Prentice-Hall.

Chapter 2

Aaker, D.A. and Day, G.S. (1982). *Consumerism: search for the consumer interest*, 4th edn. New York: Free Press.

Ansoff, I.H. (1984). *Implanting strategic management*. Englewood Cliffs, NJ: Prentice-Hall.

Bennett, R.C. and Cooper, R.G. (1981). 'The misuse of marketing: an American tragedy', *Business Horizons*, Nov–Dec, 51–60.

Bossier, F. and Hugé, P. (1981). 'Une vérification empirique de l'existence de cycles longs à partie de données Belges'. *Cahier économiques de Bruxelles*, **9**, second trimester.

Buzzell, R.D. (1968). Can you standardize multinational marketing? *Harvard Business Review*, Nov–Dec, **46**, 102–13.

Catinat, M. and Jacquemin, A. (1990). Europe et marché unique, in *Encyclopédie économique* (eds X. Gresse, J. Mairesse and L.L. Reiffers). Paris: Economica.

Cecchini, P., Catinat, M. and Jacquemin, A. (1988). *1992, the benefits of a single market*. Aldershot: Wildwood House.

Drucker, P.F. (1980). *Managing in Turbulent Times*, New York: Harper & Row.

Drucker, P.F. (1973). *Management, Tasks, Responsibilities, Practices*. New York: Harper & Row.

Forrester, J.W. (1961). *Industrial Dynamics*. New York: J. Wiley and Sons.

Kondratiev, N.D. (1935). The long waves in economic life. *The Review of Economics and Statistics*, **27**, November, 105–15.

Kotler, P. (1979). Axioms for societal marketing, in *Future Directions for Marketing* (eds G. Fisk, J. Arndt and K. Gronharg). Boston: Marketing Science Institute.

Kotler, P. (1988). *Marketing management*, 7th edn. Englewood Cliffs, NJ: Prentice-Hall.

Kotler, P., Fahey, L. and Jatusripitak, S. (1985). *The new competition*. Englewood Cliffs, NJ: Prentice-Hall.

Levitt, Th. (1983). 'The globalization of markets', *Harvard Business Review*, May–June, **61**, 92–102.

Maïsseu, A. (1984). 'Une issue à la crise: le redéploiement des entreprises', *Futuribles*, November, 44–54.

Marchetti, C. (1982). 'Invention et innovation: les cycles revisités', *Futuribles*, **53**, March, 43–58.

OECD (1991). *OECD economic outlook*. Paris: OECD.

Ohmae, K. (1987). 'The triad world view', *The Journal of Business Strategy*, **7**, 4.

Picardi, M. (1987). 'Globalization: théorie et pratique', *Revue Française du Marketing*, **114**, 83–88.

Pitt-Watson, D. and Frazer, S. (1991). 'Eastern Europe: commercial opportunity or illusion?', *Long Range Planning* **24** (5), 17–22.

Porter, M.E. (1982). *Competitive strategy*. New York: Free Press.

Potargent, G. (1991). *Le marketing des produits verts: recommandations pour l'annonceur*. Louvain-la-neuve: IAG.

Pruden, H.O. (1978). 'The Kondratiev wave', *Journal of Marketing*, April, 63–70.

Quelch, J.A. and Hoff, E.J. (1986), 'Customizing global marketing', *Harvard Business Review*, **64**, May-June, 59–68.

Quelch, J.A. Buzzell, R.D. and Salama, E.R. (1991). *The marketing challenge of Europe 1992*. Reading, MA: Addison-Wesley.

Rapp, S. and Collins, T. (1990). *The great marketing turnaround*. Englewood Cliffs, NJ: Prentice-Hall.

Ries, A. and Trout, J. (1986). *Warfare marketing*. New York: McGraw-Hill.

Takeuchi, H. and Porter, M.E. (1986). Three roles of international marketing in global strategy, in *Competition in global industries* (ed. M.E. Porter). Boston: Harvard Business School Press.

de Woot, P. (1990). *High technology Europe*. Oxford: Basil Blackwell.

Chapter 3

Abbott, L. (1955). *Quality and competition*. New York: John Wiley.

Attali, J. and Guillaume, M. (1974). *L'anti-économique*. Paris: Presses Universitaires de France.

Baudrillard, J. (1968). *Le système des objets*. Paris: Gallimard.

Becker, G.S. (1965). 'A theory of the allocation of time', *The Economic Journal*, Sept, 494–517.

Berlyne, D.E. (1960). *Conflict, arousal and curiosity*. New York: McGraw-Hill.

Beirel, M. (1977). *Comment vivre sans tension?*. Bruxelles: Marabout.

Cotta, A. (1980) *La société ludique*. Paris: Grasset.

Duffy, E. (1957). 'The psychological significance of the concept of "Arousal" or "Activation"', *The Psychological Review*, **64**, Sept, 265–75.

FNGE, ESC Lyon, 1976. *Marketing industriel appliqué*, Cas Sedal.

Galbraith, J.K. (1971). *The affluent society*, 2nd edn. Boston: Houghton Mifflin.

Hebb, D.O. (1955). 'Drives and the C.N.S. (Conceptual Nervous System)', *The Psychological Review*, **62**, July, 243–54.

Jacquemin, A. and Tulkens, H. (1988). *Fondements d'économie politique*, 2nd edn. Brussells: De Boeck-Weesmael.

Kahle, L.R. (ed.) (1983). *Social values and social change: adaptation to life in America*. New York: Praeger.

Kahle, L.R., Poulos, B. and Sukhdial, A. (1988). 'Changes in social values in the United States during the past decade', *Journal of Advertising Research*, Feb–March, **00**, 35–41.

Katona, G. (1951). *Psychological analysis of economic behaviour*. New York: McGraw-Hill.

Keynes, J.M. (1936). 'Essays in persuasion – economic possibilities for our grandchildren', in *The collected writings of J. M. Keynes*, **9**. London: The MacMillan Press.

Kotler, P. (1991) *Marketing management*. Prentice-Hall International, 7th edition.

Lancaster, K.J. (1966). 'A new approach to consumer theory', *The Journal of Political Economy*, **74**, April, 132–57.

Maslow, H. (1943). 'A theory of human motivation', *The Psychological Review*, **50**, 370–96.

Murray, H.A. (1938). *Explorations in personality*. New York: Oxford University Press.

Nuttin, J. (1980). *Théorie de la motivation humaine*. Paris: Presses Universitaires de France.

Rokeach, M. (1973). *The nature of human values*. New York: Free Press.

Rosa, J.J. (1977). Vrais et faux besoins, in *L'économique retrouvé* (eds. J.J. Rosa and F. Aftalion). Paris: Economica.

Scitovsky, T. (1976). *The Joyless Economy*. Oxford: Oxford University Press.

Séguéla, J. (1982). *Hollywood lave plus blanc*. Paris: Flammarion.

Sheth, J.N., Newman, B.I. and Gross, B.L. (1991). *Consumption values and market choices: theory and applications*. Cincinnati OH: South-Western Publishing Company.

Valaskakis, K., Graham-Smith, J., Sindell, P. and Martin, I. (1978). *La société de conservation*. Montréal: Les Éditions Quinze.

Valla, J.P. (1980). 'Le comportement des groupes d'achat', in *L'action marketing des entreprises industrielles*, 22–38. Paris: Collection Adetem.

Webster, F.E. and Wind, Y. (1972). *Organizational buying behaviour*, Englewood Cliffs, NJ: Prentice-Hall.

Wundt, O. (1874), in Berlyne, D.E. (1960). *Conflict, Arousal and Curiosity*, 201. New York: McGraw-Hill.

Chapter 4

Abbott, L. (1955). *Quality and competition*. New York: Columbia Press.

Bauer, R.A. (1960). 'Consumer behaviour as risk taking', in *Proceedings of the Fall Conference of the American Marketing Association* (ed. A.S. Hancock), 389–98.

Becker, G.S. (1965). 'A theory of the allocation of time', *The Economic Journal*, Sept, 493–517.

Bank for International Settlements (BIS) (1990). Sixtieth Annual Report, Basle.

Bucklin, L.P. (1965). 'The informative role of advertising', *Journal of Advertising Research*, **5**.

Bulletin Financier de la BBL Inc. (1989). 'Taux d'épargne et endettement des ménages', **2233**, Sept – Oct.

Farley, J.V. (1964). 'Brand loyalty and the economics of information', *Journal of Business*, **37**, 370–81.

Fishbein, M. (1967). 'Attitudes and prediction of behaviour', in *Readings in attitude theory and measurement* (ed. M. Fishbein). New York: John Wiley.

Friedman, M. (1957). *A theory of the consumption function*. Princeton: Princeton University Press.

Green, P.E. and Wind, Y. (1975). 'New ways to measure consumers' judgments', *Harvard Business Review*, July–Aug, 107–17.

Haley, R.I. (1968). 'Benefit segmentation: a decision-oriented research tool', *Journal of Marketing*, July, 30–5.

Howard, J.A. and Sheth, J.N. (1969). *The theory of buyer behaviour*. New York: John Wiley.

Keynes, J.M. (1936). *The general theory of employment interest and money*. London: MacMillan.

Kirzner, I.M. (1973). *Competition and entrepreneurship*. Chicago: Chicago University Press.

Kuznets, S. (1946). *National product since 1869*. New York: National Bureau of Economic Research.

Lambin, J.J. (1976). *Advertising, competition and market conduct in oligopoly over time*. Amsterdam: North-Holland.

Lambin, J.J. (1989). 'La marque et le comportement de choix de l'acheteur', in *La marque* (eds. J.N. Kapferer and J.C. Thoenig). Paris: McGraw-Hill.

Lancaster, K.J. (1966). 'A new approach to consumer theory', *The Journal of Political Economy*, **74**, April, 132–57.

Lepage, H. (1982). *Vive le commerce*. Paris: Dunod, Collection L'oeil économique.

Levitt, Th. (1980). 'Marketing success through differentiation – of anything', *Harvard Business Review*, **58**, Jan–Feb, 83–91.

Lévy-Garboua, L. (1976). 'La nouvelle théorie des consommateurs et la formation des choix', *Consommation*, **3**.

Loudon, D.L. and della Bitta, A.J. (1984). *Consumer behavior: concepts and applications*, 2nd edn. New York: McGraw-Hill.

Myers, J.H. and Alpert, M.L. (1976). 'Semantic confusion in attitude research: salience versus importance versus determinance', in advances in consumer research proceedings of the 7th annual conference of the association of consumer research (ed. W.D. Perrecult). Oct, 106–110.

Nelson, D. (1970). 'Information and consumer behaviour', *The Journal of Political Economy*, **78**, 311–29.

Nelson, D. (1974). 'Advertising as information', *The Journal of Political Economy*, **82**, 729–54.

Newman, J.W. (1979). 'Consumer external research: amounts and determinants', in *An information processing theory of consumer choice* (ed. R. Bettman). Reading, MA: Addison-Wesley.

Pinson, C., Malhotra, N.K. and Jain, A.K. (1988). 'Les styles cognitifs des consommateur', *Recherche et Applications en Marketing*, **3** (1), 53–73.

Ratchford, B.T. (1975). 'The new economic theory of consumer behaviour', *Journal of Consumer Research*, **2**, Sept, 65–78.

Rosa, J.J. (1977). 'Vrais et faux besoins', in *L'économique retrouvé* (eds. J.J. Rosa and F. Aftalion). Paris: Economica, 155–92.

Roselius, T. (1971). 'Consumer rankings of risk reduction methods', *Journal of Marketing*, **35**, Jan, 56–61.

Rosenberg, M.J. (1956). 'Cognitive structure and attitudinal affect', *Journal of Abnormal and Social Psychology*, **53**, 367–72.

Tarondeau, J.C. (1982). 'Sortir du dilemma "flexibilité" – productivité', *Harvard-L'Expansion*, Spring, 25–35.

Waterson, M.J. (1992). 'International advertising expenditure statistics', *International Journal of Advertising*, **1**, 14–68.

Wilkie, W.L. (1990). *Consumer Behaviour*, 2nd edn. New York: J. Wiley and Sons.

Wittink, D.R. and Walsh, J.D. (1988). 'Conjoint analysis: in reliability, validity and usefulness', working paper, March. Ithaca, NJ: Cornell University, Johnson Graduate School of Management.

Chapter 5

Aaker, D.A. (1991), *Managing brand equity*. New York: Free Press.

Addelman, S. (1962). 'Orthogonal main-effect plans for asymmetrical factorial experiments', *Technometrics*, **4** (1), April, 21–46.

Allport, G.W. (1935). 'Attitudes', in a handbook of *Social psychology*, (ed. C.A. Murchison), 798–844. Worcester, MA: Clark University Press.

Assmus, G., Farley, J.U. and Lehman, D.R. (1984). 'How advertising affects sales: meta-analysis of econometric results', *Journal of Marketing Research*, **21**, Feb, 65–74.

Assael, H. and Day, G.S. (1968). 'Attitudes and awareness, predictors of market shares', *Journal of Advertising Research*, **8**, Dec, 10–17.

Bass, F.M. and Tarlarzyck, W.W. (1969). 'A study of attitude theory and brand preferences', *Journal of Marketing Research*, **9**, 93–6.

Bauer, R.A. (1960). 'Consumer behavior as risk taking', in *Proceedings of the Fall Conference of the American Marketing Association* (ed. A.S. Hancock), American Marketing Association, 389–98.

Beelson, B. and Steiner, G.A. (1964). *Human behavior: an inventory of scientific findings*. New York: Harcourt Brace Jovanovich, Ltd.

Boyd, H.W., Ray, M.L. and Strong, E.C. (1972). 'An attitudinal framework for advertising strategy', *Journal of Marketing*, **35**, April, 27–33.

Churchill, G.A. (1987). *Marketing research: methodological foundations*, 4th edn., 348–54. Chicago: Dryden Press.

Davis, H.L. and Rigaux, B.P. (1974). 'Perceptions of marital roles in decision processes', *Journal of Consumer Research*, **1**, 51–62.

Delta 2000 (1988). *L'impact de la presse quotidienne en Belgique*. May.

Festinger, L. (1957). *A theory of cognitive dissonance*. New York: Harper & Row.

Fishbein, M. (1967). 'Attitudes and prediction of behavior', in *Readings in attitude theory and measurement* (ed. M. Fishbein), 477–92. New York: John Wiley.

Green, P.E. and Rao, V.R. (1972). *Applied multidimensional scaling*. New York: Holt, Rinehart & Winston.

Green, P.E. and Srinivasan, V. (1990). 'Conjoint analysis in marketing research: new developments and directions'. *Journal of Marketing*, **54** (4), 3–19.

Herbst, P.G. (1952). 'The measurement of family relationships', *Human and Relations*, **5**, 3–35.

Herwats, B. (1986). *Etude de la sensibilité de la demande au prix des cigarettes blended*. Louvain-La-Neuve, Belgium: IAG.

Jarvis, L.P. and Wilcox, J.B. (1977). 'Evoked set, some theoretical foundations and empirical evidence', in *Consumer behavior: applications of theory* (ed. J.A. Howard). New York: McGraw-Hill.

Johnson, R.M. (1974). 'Trade-off analysis of consumer values', *Journal of Marketing Research*, **11**, 121–7.

Kapferer, J.N. and Laurent, G. (1983). *La sensibilité aux marques*. Paris: Fondation Jours de France.

Krugman, H.E. (1965). 'The impact of television advertising: learning without involvement', *Public Opinion Quarterly*, Autumn, 349–56.

Krugman, H.E. (1986), 'Low recall and high recognition of advertising', *Journal of Advertising Research*, Feb–Mar, 79–86.

Lambin, J.J. (1972). 'A computer on-line marketing mix model', *Journal of Marketing Research*, **9**, May, 119–26.

Lambin, J.J. (1976). *Advertising competition and market conduct in oligopoly over time*, Tables 6.2, 6.3. Amsterdam: North-Holland.

Lambin, J.J. (1988). 'Synthèse des études récentes sur l'efficacité économique de la publicité', *CESAM Working Paper*, July. IAG: Louvain-la-Neuve.

Lambin, J.J. and Peeters, R. (1977). *La gestion marketing des entreprises*. Paris: Presses Universitaires de France.

Lavidge, R.J. and Steiner, G.A. (1961), 'A Model for predictions measurement of advertising effectiveness', *Journal of Marketing*, **25**, Oct, 59–62.

Lewin, K. (1935). *A dynamic theory of personality*. New York: McGraw-Hill.

Morgensztern, A. (1983). 'Une synthèse des travaux sur la mémorisation des messages publicitaires', in *La publicité, nerf de la communication* (ed. S. Piquet). Paris: Les éditions d'organisation.

Nerlove, M. and Arrow, K.J. (1962). 'Optimal advertising policy under dynamic conditions', *Economica*, **29**, 129–42.

Nielsen Researcher, The (1981). *Utilizing UPC scanning data for new products decisons*, **1**. Northbank, A.C. Nielson City.

Parfitt, J.H. and Collins, B.J.K. (1968). 'The use of consumer panels for brand share prediction', *Journal of Marketing Research*, **5**, 131–45.

Palda, K.S. (1966). 'The hypothesis of a hierarchy of effects', *Journal of Marketing Research*, **3**, 13–24.

Pinson, C., Malhotra, N.K. and Jain, A.K. (1988). 'Les styles cognitifs des consommateurs', *Recherche et Applications en Marketing*, **3**, 53–73.

Pras, B. and Tarondeau, J.-C. (1981). *Comportement de l'acheteur*. Paris: Editions Sirey.

Ratchford, B.T. (1987). 'New insights about the FCB grid', *Journal of Advertising Research*, **27**, (4), 30–1.

Rogers, E.M. (1962). *Diffusion of innovations*. New York: Free Press.

Rosenberg, M.J. (1956). 'Cognitive structure and attitudinal affect', *Journal of Abnormal and Social Psychology*, **53**, 367–72.

Servais, M. (1988). *Le marché du gant industriel de protection en Belgique*. Louvain-la-Neuve: IAG.

Thurstone, L.L. (1959). *The measurement of values*. Chicago: University of Chicago Press.

Vaughn, R. (1986). 'How advertising works: a planning model revisited', *Journal of Advertising Research*, **26**, Feb–March, 57–66.

Watts, W.A. and McGuire, J.W. (1964). 'Persistence of induced opinion change and retention of inducing message content', *Journal of Abnormal and Social Psychology*, **68**, 233–41.

Wilkie, W.L. and Pessemier, E.A. (1973). 'Issues in marketing's use of multi-attribute attitude models', *Journal of Marketing Research*, **10**, 428–41.

Wittink, D.R. and Walsh, J.W. (1988). *Conjoint analysis: its reliability, validity and usefulness*. Ithaca, NY: Cornell University, The Johnson Graduate School of Management.

Zielske, H.A. (1958). 'The remembering and the forgetting of advertising. *Journal of Marketing*, **24**, 239–43.

Zielske, H.A. and Henry, W.A. (1980). 'Remembering and forgetting television ads', *Journal of Advertising Research*, **20**, April, 7–13.

Chapter 6

Abell, D.F. (1980). *Defining the business: the starting point of strategic planning*. Englewood Cliffs, N.J: Prentice-Hall.

Blanche, B. (1987). 'Le marketing global: paradoxe, fantasme ou objectif pour demain, *Revue Française du marketing*, **114**, 76.

Chamberlin, E.H. (1950). *The theory of monopolistic competition*. Cambridge, MA: Harvard University Press.

Day, G.S. (1990). *Market driven strategy*. New York: Free Press.

Dalrymple, D.J. and Parsons, L.J. (1976). *Marketing Management: text and cases*. New York: John Wiley and Sons.

Domzal, T. and Unger, L.S. (1987). 'Emerging positioning strategies in global marketing', *The Journal of Consumer Marketing*, **4**, Autumn, 23–40.

EUROSTAT (1991). *A social profile of Europe*. Luxembourg: Office for Official Publications of the European Community.

Farley, L.J. (1986). 'Going global: choices and challenges', *The Journal of Consumer Marketing*, **3**, Winter, 67–70.

Green, P.E. and Krieger, A.M. (1991). 'Segmenting markets with conjoint analysis', *Journal of Marketing*, **55**, Oct, 20–31.

Green, P.E. and Wind, Y. (1974). 'Some conceptual, measurement and analytical problems in life style research', in *Life style and psychographics* (ed. W.D. Wells). Chicago: American Marketing Association.

Haley, R.I. (1968). 'Benefit segmentation: a decision oriented tool', *Journal of Marketing Research*, **32**, July, 30–5.

Hassan, S.S. and Katsanis, L.P. (1991). 'Identification of global consumer segments: a behavioural framework', *Journal of International Consumer Marketing*, **3** (2), 11–29.

Hopkins, D.S. (1982). *The Marketing Plan*, New York: The Conference Board.

Kapferer, J.N. and Laurent, G. (1981). *Une analyse des relations entre les classifications socioculturelles et de style de vie et l'achat de produits courants*. Paris: Institut de recherches et d'études publicitaires, twenty-first Journal de l'IREP.

Lambin, J.J. and Hiller, T.B. (1990). 'Volvo Trucks Europe: a case study', in *The marketing challenge of 1992* (eds. J.A. Quelch, R.D. Buzzell and E.R. Salama), 348–67. New York: Addison-Wesley.

Plummer, J.T. (1974). 'The concept and application of life-style segmentation', *Journal of Marketing*, **38**, Jan, 33–7.

Porter, M. (1985). *Competitive advantage*. New York: Free Press.

Quelch, J. and Hoff, E.G. (1986). Customizing global marketing', *Harvard Business Review*, **64**, May–June, 59–68.

Ries, A. and Trout, J. (1981). *Positioning: the battle for your mind*. New York: McGraw-Hill.

Roisin, J. (1988). *Etude du concept d'une revue littéraire: une application de l'analyse conjointe*. Louvain-la-Neuve: IAG (unpublished term paper).

Shapiro, B.P. and Bonona, T.V. (1983). *Segmenting industrial markets*. Lexington, MA: Lexington Books.

Smith, W.R. (1956). 'Product differentiation and market segmentation as alternative marketing strategies', *Journal of Marketing*, **21**, July, 3–8.

Takeuchi, H. and Porter, M.E. (1986). 'Three roles of international marketing in global industries', in *Competition in global industries* (ed. M.E. Porter). Boston: Harvard Business School Press.

Valette-Florence, P. (1986). 'Les démarches de styles de vie: concepts, champs d'investigation et problèmes actuels', *Recherche et Applications en Marketing*, **1** (1 and 2), 93–102.

Valette-Florence, P. (1988). 'Analyse structurelle comparative des composantes des systèmes de valeurs selon Kahle et Rokeach', *Recherche et Applications en Marketing*, **3** (1), 15–34.

Wells, W.D. (1974). *Life style and psychographics*. Chicago: American Marketing Association.

Wells, W.D. and Tigert, D.J. (1971). 'Activities, interests and opinions', *Journal of Advertising Research*, **35**, 27–34.

Wind, J.Y. (1982). *Product policy: concepts, methods and strategy*. Reading, MA: Addison-Wesley.

Winkler, A.R. (1991). 'Euro-styles in panel analyses', *Europanel Marketing Bulletin*, 8–11.

Yankelovich, D. (1964). 'New criteria for market segmentation', *Harvard Business Review*, March–April, 83–90.

Yorke, D.A. (1982). 'The definition of market segments for banking services', *European Journal of Marketing*, **16**, 14–22.

Chapter 7

Barnett, F.W. (1988). 'Four steps to forecast total market demand', *Harvard Business Review*, July-Aug, 28–37.

Bishop, W.S., Graham, J.L. and Jones, M.H. (1984). 'Volatility of derived demand in industrial markets and its management implications', *Journal of Marketing*, **48**, Autumn, 95–103.

de Boisanger, P. (1988). 'Réduire l'imprévu à l'imprévisible'. *Futuribles*, March, 59–68.

Business International (1991). 'Indicators of market size for 117 countries', Weekly report, 8 July.

Cox, W.E. (1967). 'Product life cycles as marketing models', *Journal of Business*, **40**, Oct, 375–84.

Day, G.S. (1981). 'The product life cycle: analysis and application issues', *Journal of Marketing*, **45**, Autumn, 60–7.

Dhalla, N.K. and Yuspeh, S. (1976), 'Forget the product life cycle concept', *Harvard Business Review*, Jan–Feb, 102–12.

Eiglier, P. and Langeard, E. (1987). *Servuction*. Paris: McGraw-Hill.

Euroboromètre (1992). *L'opinion publique dans la Communanté Européenne*. Brussels.

Hinkle, J. (1966). *Life cycles*. New York: Nielsen.

Hunt, S.D. (1983). 'General theories and the fundamental explananda of marketing', *Journal of Marketing*, **47**, Autumn, 9–17.

Lambin, J.J. (1987). 'Le contrôle de la qualité dans le domaine des services', *Gestion 2000*, **1**, 63–75.

Levitt, Th. (1965). 'Exploit the product life cycle', *Harvard Business Review*, Nov–Dec, 81–94.

Levitt, Th. (1981). 'Marketing intangible products and product intangibles', *Harvard Business Review*, **59**, May–June, 94–102.

Makridakis, S. and Wheelwright, S.C. (1973). *Forecasting methods for management*. New York: John Wiley.

McCarthy, J. (1960). *Basic marketing: a managerial approach*, 1st edn. Homewood, ILL: R.D. Irwin.

Morris, M.H. (1988). *Industrial and organizational marketing*. Columbus: Merrrill Publishing Company.

Nielsen Researcher (1984). *Life beyond the life cycle*, **1**, 3.

Polli, R. and Cook, V. (1969). 'Validity of the product life cycle concept', *Journal of Business*, **42**, Oct. 385–400.

Porter, M.E. (1980). *Competitive strategy*. New York: Free Press.

Rink, D.R. and Swan, J.E. (1979). 'Product life cycle research: a literature review', *Journal of Business Research*, Sept, 219–42.

Sizer, J. (1972). 'Accountants, product managers and selling price decisions in multi-consumer product firms', *Journal of Business Finance*, **4**, Spring, 76.

Swan, J.E. and Rink, D.R. (1982). 'Fitting market strategy to varying product life cycles', *Business Horizons*, Jan–Feb, 72–76.

Taylor, J.W. (1986). *Competitive marketing strategies*. Radnor, PA: Chilton Book Company.

Tellis, G.J. and Crawford, C.M. (1981). 'An evolutionary approach to product growth theory', *Journal of Marketing*, **45**, Autumn 125–34.

Wasson, C.R. (1974). *Dynamic competitive strategy & product life cycles*. St Charles ILL: Challenge Books.

Weber, J.A. (1976). *Growth opportunity analysis*. Reston, VA: Reston Publishing.

Wilkie, W.L. (1990). *Consumer behaviour*, 2nd edn. New York: J. Wiley and Sons, 76–41.

Yale, J.P. (1964). 'The strategy of nylon's growth: create new market'. *Modern Textiles Magazine*, February, 72–79.

Zeithaml, V.A., Parassuzaman, A. and Berry, L.L. (1990). *Delivering Quality Service*. New York: Free Press.

Chapter 8

Abell, D.E. and Hammond, J.S. (1979). *Strategic market planning*. Englewood Cliffs, NJ: Prentice-Hall.

Abernathy, W. and Wayne, K. (1974). 'The limits of the experience curve', *Harvard Business Review*, Sept, 109–19.

Bialobos, C. (1982). 'L'hypermarché fait la loi', *L'Expansion*, 21 May– 3 June, 79–82.

Bon, J. and Louppe, A. (1980). *Marketing des services publics: l'étude des besoins de la population*. Paris: Les éditions d'organisation.

Boston Consulting Group (1968). *Perspectives on experience*. Boston: Boston Consulting Group.

Chamberlin, E.H. (1950). *The theory of monopolistic competition*. Cambridge, MA: Harvard University Press.

Clausewitz, von, C. (1908). *On War*. London: Routledge & Kegan.

Cournot, A.A. (1897). *Researches into the mathematical principles of the theory of wealth*. New York: The MacMillan Company.

Durö, R. and Sandström, B. (1988). *Le marketing de combat*. Paris: Les éditions d'organisation.

Hax, A.C. and Majluf, N.S. (1984). *Strategic management: an integrative perspective*. Englewood Cliffs, NJ: Prentice-Hall.

Kerin, R.A., Mahajan, V. and Varadajan, P.R. (1990). *Contemporary perspectives on strategic market planning*. Boston, MA: Allyn and Bacon.

Kotler, P. and Singh, R. (1981). 'Marketing warfare in the 1980s', *Journal of Business Strategy*, **2**, Winter, 30–41.

Kotler, P., Fahey, L. and Jatuskripitak, S. (1985). *The new competition*. Englewood Cliffs, NJ: Prentice-Hall.

Lambin, J. J. (1976). *Advertising, competition and market conduct over time*, 22–7. Amsterdam: North-Holland and Elsevier.

Lambin, J. J. (1983). 'La mesure du pouvoir de marché étude d'un cas concret', unpublished CESAM working paper, Louvain-la-Neuve University.

Lambin, J.J., Naert, P.A. and Bultez, A. (1975). 'Optimal marketing behaviour in oligopoly', *European Economic Review*, **6**, 105–28.

Lambin, J.J. and Peeters, R. (1977). *La gestion marketing des entreprises*. Paris: Presses Universitaires de France.

Lochridge, R.K. (1981). Strategies in the 1980s. *BCG Perspectives*, **241**. Boston: Boston Consulting Group.

Porter, M.E. (1980). *Competitive Strategy*. New York: Free Press.

Porter, M.E. (1985). *Competitive advantage*. New York: Free Press.

Ries, A. and Trout, J. (1986). *Warfare marketing*. New York: McGraw-Hill.

Sallenave, J.P., (1985). 'The use and abuse of experience curves', *Long Range Planning*, **18**, Jan–Feb, 64–72.

Wright, T.P. (1936). 'Factors affecting the cost of airplanes', *Journal of Aeronautical Sciences*, **3**, 16–24.

Chapter 9

Abell, D.E. and Hammond, J.S. (1979). *Strategic market planning*. Englewood Cliffs, NJ: Prentice-Hall.

Boston Consulting Group (1972). *Perspectives on experience*. Boston, MA: The Boston Consulting Group.

Buzzell, R.D., Gale, B.T. and Sultan, G.M. (1975). 'Market share, a key to profitability', *Harvard Business Review*, **53**, Jan–Feb, 97–106.

Calori, R. and Harvatopoulos, Y. (1988). 'Diversification: les règles de conduite', *Harvard-L'Expansion*, **48**, Spring, 48–59.

Chamberlin, E.H. (1950). *The theory of monopolistic competition*. Cambridge, MA: Harvard University Press.

Day, G.S. (1977). 'Diagnosing the product portfolio', *Journal of Marketing* **41**, April.

Drucker, P.F. (1981). 'The Five Rules of Successful Acquisition', *The Wall Street Journal*, 15 October, 16.

Galbraith, C. and Schendel, D. (1983). 'An empirical analysis of strategy types', *Strategic Management Journal*, **4**, 153–73.

Hamel, G. and Prahalad, C.K. (1985). 'Do you really have a global strategy?', *Harvard Business Review*, **63**, July–Aug, 139–48.

Hamermesch, R.G. (1986). 'Making planning strategic', *Harvard Business Review*, **64**, July–Aug, 115–20.

Hamermesch, R.G., Anderson, M.J. and Harris, J.E. (1978). 'Strategies for low market share businesses', *Harvard Business Review*, **56**, May–June, 95–102.

Haspeslagh, P. (1982). 'Portfolio planning: uses and limits'. *Harvard-L'Expansion'*, Summer, 58–72.

Henderson, B.B. (1970). *The product portfolio*. Boston, MA: The Boston Consulting Group (Perspectives).

Hussey, D.E. (1978). 'Portfolio analysis: practical experience with the directional policy matrix', *Long range planning*, **11**, August, 2–8.

Keegan, W.J. (1989). *Global marketing management*, 4th edn. Englewood Cliffs, NJ: Prentice-Hall.

Kotler, P. (1991). *Marketing management: analysis, planning and control*, 7th edn. Englewood Cliffs, NJ: Prentice-Hall.

Kotler, P. and Singh, R. (1981). 'Marketing warfare in the 1980s', *Journal of Business Strategy*, **2**, Winter, 30–41.

Kotler, P., Fahey, L. and Jatuskripitak, S. (1985). *The new competition*. Englewood Cliffs, NJ: Prentice-Hall.

Levitt, Th. (1980). 'Marketing success through differentiation – of anything', *Harvard Business Review*, **58**, 83–91.

Leroy, G. Richard, G. and Sallenave, J.P. (1978). *La conquête des marchés extérieurs*. Paris: Les Edition d'Organisation.

Oxenfeld, A.R. and Moore, W.L. (1978). 'Customer or competitor: which guide lines for marketing?', *Management Review*, Aug, 43–8.

Porter, M.E. (1980). *Competitive strategy*. New York: Free Press.

Ries, A. and Trout, J. (1986). *Marketing warfare*. New York: McGraw-Hill.

Wind, Y., Mahajan, V. and Swire, D.S. (1983). 'An empirical comparison of standardized portfolio models', *Journal of marketing*, **47**, 89–99.

Chapter 10

Ader, E. (1983). 'L'analyse stratégique et ses outils', *Futuribles*, **72**, December, 3–21.

Barreyre, P.Y. (1980). 'Typologie des innovations', *Revue Français de Gestion*, Jan–Feb, 9–15.

Bennett, R.C. and Cooper, R.G. (1979). 'Beyond the marketing concept', *Business Horizons*, **22**, June, 76–83.

Booz, Allen and Hamilton (1982). *New product management for the 1980s*. New York: Booz, Allen and Hamilton.

Choffray, J.M. and Dorey, F. (1983). *Développement et gestion des produits nouveaux*. Paris: McGraw-Hill.

Clarke, D.G. (1987). *Marketing analysis and decision making*. Redwood city, CA: The Scientific Press.

Cooper, R.G. (1979). 'The dimensions of industrial new products success and failure', *Journal of Marketing*, **43**, Summer, 93–103.

Cooper, R.G. (1981). 'The myth of the better mousetrap: what makes a new product a success?', *Business Quarterly*, Spring, 69–81.

Daudé, B. (1980). 'Analyse de la maîtrise des risques', *Revue Française de Gestion*, **24**, Jan–Feb, 38–48.

Davidson, J.H. (1976). 'Why do most new consumer brands fail?', *Harvard Business Review*, **57**, March–April, 117–22.

Eigler, P. and Langeard, E. (1987). *Servuction: le marketing des services*. Paris: McGraw-Hill.

Eskin, G.J. and Montgomery, D.B. (1975). *'Cases in computer and model assisted marketing'*. Palo Alto: The Scientific Press.

Garvin, D.A. (1987). 'Competing on the eight dimensions of quality', *Harvard Business Review*, **65**, Nov–Dec, 101–9.

Gordon, J.J. (1965). *Stimulation des facultés créatrices dans les groupes de recherche synectique'*. Paris: Hommes et Techniques.

Green, P.E. and Srinivasan, V. (1978). 'Conjoint analysis in consumer research: issues and outlook', *Journal of Consumer Research*, Sept, 103–23.

Groocock, J.M. (1986). *The chain of quality*. New York: John Wiley.

Horovitz, J. (1987). *La qualité de service*. Paris: InterEditions.

Kotler, P. (1991). *Marketing management, analysis, planning, implementation and control*, 7th edn. Englewood Cliffs, NJ: Prentice–Hall.

Lambin, J.J. (1987). Le contrôle de la qualité dans le domaine des services, *Gestion 2000*, **1**, 63–75.

Mansfield, E. (1976). *Business Week*, 8 June.

Mansfield, E. and Wagner, S. (1975). 'Organizational and strategic factors associated with probabilities of success in industrial R&D', *Journal of Business*, April, 181.

Mihaies, G. (1983). La stratégie japonaise de R&D, *Futuribles*, **68**, July–Aug, 59–69.

Nielsen Researcher, The (1971). 'New product success ratio', **5**, 4–9. Chicago: A.C. Nielsen Company.

O'Meara, J.T. (1961). 'Selecting profitable products', *Harvard Business Review*, **39**, Jan–Feb, 110–18.

Osborn, A.F. (1963). *Applied imagination*, 3rd edn. New York: Charles Scribner.

Parasuraman, A., Zeithaml, V.A. and Berry, L.L. (1985). 'A conceptual model of service quality and its implications for future research', *Journal of marketing*, **49**, Autumn, 41–50.

Parfitt, J.M. and Collins, J.K. (1968). 'Use of consumer panels for brand share prediction', *Journal of Marketing Research*, **5**, May, 131–45.

Rochet, L. (1987). *Diagnostic stratégique du potentiel d'extensions d'une marque de laque*. Louvain-la-Neuve: Institut d'Administration et de Gestion.

Saunders, J. (1990). 'Brands and valuations', *International Journal of Advertising*, **9**, pp. 95–110.

Stalk, G. (1988). 'Time–the next source of competitive advantage', *Harvard Business Review*, **66**, July–Aug, 41–51.

Takeuchi, H. and Nonaka, I. (1986). 'The new new product development game', *Harvard Business Review*, **64**, Jan–Feb, 137–46.

Tauber, E.M. (1973). 'Reduce new product failures: measure needs as well as purchase interest', *Journal of Marketing*, **37**, July, 61–70.

Taylor, D.W., Berry, P.C. and Block, G.H. (1958). 'Does group participation when using brainstorming facilitate or inhibit creative thinking?', *Administrative Science Quarterly*, **3**, 23–47.

Urban, G.L., Hauser, J.R. and Dholakia, N. (1987). *Essentials of New Product Management*. Englewood Cliffs, NJ: Prentice-Hall, Inc.

Wind, Y.S. (1982). *Product policy concepts methods and strategy*. Reading, MA: Addison-Wesley Publishing Company Inc.

Chapter 11

Boyd, H. W., Jr. and Walker, O.C., Jr. (1990). *Marketing management: a strategic approach*, 541. Homewood, ILL: Irwin.

Brown, M. P., Cardozo, R.N., Cunningham, S.M., Salmon, W.J. and Suetan, R.G.M. (1968). *Problems in marketing*, 4th edn., 332–345. New York: McGraw-Hill.

Ducrocq, C. (1991). *Concurrence et stratégies dans la distribution*. Paris: Librairie Vuibert.

Dupuis, M. (1991). *Marketing international de la distribution*. Paris: Les éditions d'organisation.

Dwyer, F.R., Schurr, P.H. and Oh, S. (1987). 'Developing buyer–seller relationships', *Journal of Marketing*, **51**, April, 11–27.

European Direct Marketing Association (1991). *Direct marketing in Europe: an examination of the statistics*, May.

Forsyth, D.P. (1988). Sales calls cost more according to McGraw-Hill. *Direct Marketing*, August, 67.

Jackson, B.B. (1985). *Winning and keeping industrial customers*. Lexington Books.

Kotler, P. (1991). *Marketing management: analysis, planning, implementation and control*. Englewood Cliffs, NJ: Prentice-Hall.

de Maricourt, R. (1988). 'Vers une nouvelle révolution de la distribution: de l'hypermarché à l'hyperservice', *Revue Française du Marketing*, **118**, 41–56.

Marshall, J.J. and Vredenburg, H. (1988). 'Successfully using telemarketing in industrial sales', *Industrial Marketing Management*, **17**, 15–22.

McCammon, B.C. (1970). 'Perspectives for distribution programming', in *Vertical marketing systems* (ed. L.P. Bucklin). Glenview ILL: Scott, Foresman and Co.

McGuire, E.P. (1971). *Franchised distribution*. New York: The Conference Board Report No. 523.

Monroe, K. B. (1979). *Pricing: making profitable decisions*. New York: McGraw-Hill.

Nielsen Company Belgium, A.C. (1990). *L'Univers alimentaire en Belgique*. Brussels: A.C. Nielsen, Belgium.

Quelch, J.A. and Takeuchi, H. (1981). 'Nonstore marketing: fast track or slow?', *Harvard Business Review*, **59**, July/Aug, 75–84.

Roscitt, R. and Parket, I.R. (1988). 'Direct marketing to consumers', *Journal of Consumer Marketing*, **5** (1), Winter, 5–13.

Rosenbloom, B. (1978). *Marketing channels: a management view*. Hinsdale, ILL: The Dryden Press.

Sallenave, J.P. (1979). *Expansion de votre commerce par le franchisage*. Gouvernement du Québec: Ministère du Commerce et du Tourisme.

Sanghavi, N. (1991). 'Retail franchising as a growth strategy for the 1990s', *International Journal of Retail & Distribution Management*, **19** (2), 4–9.

Stone, M. and Shaw, R. (1987). 'Database marketing for competitive advantage', *Long Range Planning*, **20** (2), 12–20.

Wortzel, L.H. (1987). 'Retailing strategies for today's mature marketplace', *Journal of Business Strategy*, **7** (4), 45–56.

Chapter 12

Assmus, G., Farley, J.V., and Lehmann, D.R. (1984). 'How advertising affects sales: meta-analysis of econometric results', *Journal of Marketing Research*, **21**, February, 65–74.

Blondé, D. (1964). *La gestion programmée*. Paris: Dunod.

Broadbent, S. (1980). 'Price and advertising: volume and profits', ADMAP, **16**, 532–40.

Business Week (1975). Detroit's dilemma on prices. January 20, 82–3.

Carlson, R.L. (1978). 'Seemingly unrelated regression and the demand for automobiles of different sizes: a disaggregate approach', *The Journal of Business*, **51**, April, 243–62.

Corey, E.R. (1991). *Industrial marketing: cases and concepts*, 4th edn. Englewood Cliffs, NJ: Prentice-Hall.

Dean, J. (1950). 'Pricing policies for new products', *Harvard Business Review*, November/December, **28**, 28–36.

Dorfman, R. and Steiner, P.O. (1954). 'Optimal advertising and optimal quality', *American Economic Review*. Dec, **44** (5), 826–33.

Hagerty, M.R., Carman, J.M. and Russel, G.J. (1988). 'Estimating elasticities with PIMS data: methodological issues and substantive implications', *Journal of Marketing Research*, **25**, February, 1–9.

Hanssens, D.M., Parsons, L.L. and Schultz, R.L. (1990). *Market response models: econometric and time series analysis*. Boston: Kluwer Academic Publishers.

Jacquemin, A. (1973). 'Optimal control and advertising policy', *Metroeconomica*, **25**, May–Aug, 200–207.

Kotler, P. (1991). *Marketing management: analysis, planning, implementation and control*. Englewood Cliffs, NJ: Prentice–Hall.

Lambin, J.J. (1976). *Advertising, competition and market conduct in oligopoly over time*. Amsterdam: North-Holland.

Lambin J.J. (1988). 'Sythèse des études récentes sur l'efficacité économique de la publicité', CESAM unpublished working paper, IAG, Louvain-la-Neuve, July.

Lambin, J.J., Naert, P.A. and Bultez, A. (1975). 'Optimal marketing behaviour in oligopoly', *European Economic Review*, **6**, 105–28.

Leighton, D.S.R., Fry, J.N., Johnson, C.B., Kennedy, J.R., Little, B., Navse, R.E.M., Taki, D.H. (1972). *Canadian problems in marketing*, 3rd edn. Toronto: McGraw-Hill Ryerson Limited.

Leone, R.P. and Schultz, R. (1980). 'A study of marketing generalizations', *Journal of Marketing*, **44** (1), 10–18.

Monroe, K.B. (1979). *Pricing: making profitable decisions*. New York: McGraw-Hill.

Nagle, T.T. (1987). *The strategy and tactics of pricing*. Englewood Cliffs, NJ: Prentice–Hall.

Nerlove, M. and Arrow, K.J. (1962). 'Optimal advertising policy under dynamic conditions', *Economica*, **29**, 129–42.

Neslin, S.A. and Shoemaker, R.W. (1983). 'Using a natural experiment to estimate price elasticity', *Journal of Marketing*, **47**, 44–57.

Oum, T.H. and Gillen, D.W. (1981). *Demand for fareclasses and pricing in airline markets*. Queen's University Belfast, School of Business working paper No. 80–12.

Oxenfeld, A.R. (1966). 'Product line pricing', *Harvard Business Review*, July/Aug, **44**, 137–44.

Porter, M.E. (1980). *Competitive strategy*. New York: Free Press.

Ross, E.B. (1984). 'Making money with proactive pricing', *Harvard Business Review*, Nov–Dec, **62**, 145–55, 631.

Shapiro, B.P. and Jackson, B.B. (1978). 'Industrial pricing to meet customers' needs', *Harvard Business Review*, **56**, Nov/Dec, 119–27.

Traylor, M.B. (1986). 'Cannibalism in multibrand firms', *The Journal of Consumer Marketing*, **3** (2), Spring, 69–75.

Tellis, G.J. (1986). 'Beyond the many faces of price: An integration of pricing strategies', *Journal of Marketing*, **50** (4), Oct, 146–60.

Tellis, G.J. (1988). 'The price elasticity of selective demand: a meta-analysis of econometric models of sales', *Journal of Marketing Research*, **25**, Nov, 331–41.

Chapter 13

Aaker, D.A. and Carman, J.M. (1982). 'Are you overadvertising?', *Journal of Advertising Research*, **22**, Aug–Sept, 57–70.

Assmus, G., Farley, J.U. and Lehman, D.R. (1984). 'How advertising affects sales: meta-analysis of econometric results', *Journal of Marketing Research*, **21**, Feb, 65–74.

Bell, D. (1979). 'L'avenir: la société de communication', *Harvard-L'Expansion*, **57**, Winter, 9–19.

Bogart, L. (1986). *Strategy in advertising*. Lincolnwood, ILL: NTC Business Books.

Bryk, C.S. and Davis, R. (1973). 'Ads work: Texasgulf proves in positioning campaign for acids', *Industrial Marketing*, **58**, Aug, 56–62.

Colley, R.H. (1961). *Defining advertising goals for measured advertising results*. New York: Association of National Advertisers.

Dalrymple, D.J. and Parsons, L.J. (1976). *Marketing management, texts and cases*. New York: John Wiley.

Darmon, R.Y., Laroche, M. and Petrof, J.V. (1982). *Le marketing, fondements et applications*, 2nd edn. Montreal: McGraw-Hill.

Davis, E., Kay, J.O. and Star, J. (1991). 'Is advertising rational?', *Business Strategy Review*, **2** (3).

Dhalla, N.K. (1978). 'Assessing the long term value of advertising?', *Harvard Business Review*, **56**, Jan/Feb, 87–95.

Dorfman, P. and Steiner, P.O. (1954). 'Optimal advertising and optimal quality', *American Economic Review*, **44** (5) Dec, 826–33.

European Advertising Tripartite (1991). *International advertising expenditure trends.*

Forsyth, D.P. (1987). Cost of a business-to-business sales call. McGraw-Hill Research *LAP Report 8013.9*, Laboratory of Advertising Performance.

Gross I. (1972). 'The creative aspects of advertising', *Sloan Management Review*, **14**, Autumn, 83–109.

Hanssens, D.M., Parsons, L.J. and Schultz, R.L. (1990). *'Market response models: econometric and time series analysis'*. Boston: Kluwer Academic.

Jacquemin, A. (1973). 'Optimal control and advertising policy', *Metroeconomica*, **25**, May, 200–207.

de Jaham, M.R. (1979). 'Le défi de la publicité institutionnelle', *Revue Française du Marketing*, **77**, 33–41.

Kapferer, J.N. (1985). 'Publicité: une révolution des méthodes de travail', *Revue Française de Gestion*, 53–54, Sept–Dec, 102–11.

Kotler, P. (1991). *Marketing management: analysis, planning, implementation and control.* Englewood Cliffs, NJ: Prentice-Hall.

Krugman, H.E. (1965). 'The impact of television advertising: learning without involvement', *Public Opinion Quarterly*, **29**, Autumn, 349–56.

Lambert, Z.V. (1968). *Setting the size of the sales force.* University Park: Pennsylvania University Press.

Lambin, J.J. (1969). 'Measuring the profitability of advertising: an empirical study', *Journal of Industrial Economics*, **17**, April, 86–103.

Lambin, J. J. (1972). 'A computer on-line marketing mix model', *Journal of Marketing Research*, May, 119–26.

Lambin, J.J., Naert, P.A. and Bultez, A. (1975). 'Optimal advertising behaviour in oligopoly', *European Economic Review*, **6**, 105–28.

Lambin, J.J. and Peeters, R. (1977). *La gestion marketing des entreprises.* Paris: Presses Universitaires de France.

Lavidge, R.J. and Steiner, G.A. (1961). 'A model of predictive measurement of advertising effectiveness', *Journal of Marketing*, **25**, October, 59–62.

Little, J.D.C. (1970). 'Models and managers, the concept of a decision calculus', *Management Science*, **16**, April, 466–85.

Maloney, J.C. (1961). 'Marketing decisions and attitude research', in *Effective marketing coordination*', (ed. G.L. Baker). Chicago: American Marketing Association.

Nelson, D. (1974). 'Advertising as information', *Journal of political Economy*, **82**, July–Aug, 729–54.

Ogilvy, D. (1964). *Les confessions de David Ogilvy*. Paris: Hachette.

Palda, K.S. (1963). *The measurement of cumulative advertising effects*. Englewood Cliffs, NJ: Prentice-Hall.

Reeves, R. (1970). 'Reality in advertising', in *Exploring advertising* (ed. O. Klepner and I. Settel). Englewood Cliffs, NJ: Prentice-Hall.

Rossiter, J.R. and Percy, L. (1987). *Advertising and promotion management*. New York: McGraw-Hill.

Séguéla, J. (1982). *Hollywood lave plus blanc*. Paris: Flammarion.

Semlow, W.J. (1959). 'How many salesmen do you need?', *Harvard Business Review*, **37**, May–June, 126–32.

Simon, J. (1983). 'Advertising sales effects can be measured and evaluated very well', *International Journal of Advertising*, **2**, Oct–Dec, 331–41.

Talley, W.J. (1961). 'How to design sales territories?', *Journal of Marketing*, **25**, Jan, 7–13.

Twedt, D.W. (1969). 'How to plan new products, improve old ones and create better advertising', *Journal of Marketing*, **33**, 53–7.

Van Hecke, Th. (1988). 'Avis aux mécènes: la brique est porteuse', *La Libre Belgique*, 11 June.

Variot, J.F. (1982). Huit strategies publicitaires pour gagner face à la crise. Paris: Les Editions d'Organisation.

Vidale, M.L. and Wolfe, H.B. (1957). 'An operation research study of sales response to advertising', *Operations Research*, **5**, June, 370–81.

Waterson, M.J. (1992). 'International advertising expenditures statistics', *International Journal of Advertising*, **11** (1), 14–67.

Xardel, D. (1982). 'Vendeurs: nouveaux rôles, nouveaux comportements', *Harvard-L'Expansion*, **25**, Summer, 59–75.

Chapter 14

Ansoff, H.I. (1984). *Implanting strategic management.* Englewood Cliffs, NJ: Prentice-Hall.

Barnoux, G. (1990). *L'audit marketing.* Paris: McGraw-Hill.

Business International (1991). 'The changing face of corporate planning in the 1990s', Bimonthly report, August 19.

Caeldries, F. and Van Dierdonck (1988). 'How Belgium businesses make strategic planning work', *Long Range Planning*, **21** (2), 41–51.

David, F.R. (1989). How companies define their mission, *Long Range Planning*, **22** (1), 90–7.

Day, G.S. (1986). 'Tough questions for developing strategies', *The Journal of Business Strategy*, **6** (3), 67.

Lagadec, P. (1991). *La gestion des crises.* Paris: McGraw-Hill.

Gilbreath, R.D. (1987). 'Planning for the unexpected', *The Journal of Business Strategy*, **8** (2), 44–9.

Greenley, G. (1987). 'An exposition into empirical research into marketing planning', *Journal of Marketing Management*, **3** (1), July.

Hamermesch, R.G. (1986). 'Making planning strategies', *Harvard Business Review*, **64**, July–Aug, 115–20.

Hapeslagh, P. (1982). Portfolio planning uses and limits', *Harvard Business Review*, **60**, Jan–Feb, 58–72.

Hopkins, D.S. (1981). *The marketing plan.* New York: The Conference Board.

Kotler, P. (1991). *Marketing management: analysis, planning, implementation and control*, 7th edn. Englewood Cliffs, NJ: Prentice-Hall.

McDonald, M.H.B. (1991). 'Ten barriers to marketing planning', *The Journal of Consumer Marketing*, **8** (2), Spring, 45–58.

Phelps, N.L. (1986). 'Setting up a crisis recovery plan', *The Journal of Business Strategy*, **6** (4), 5–10.

Porter, M.E. (1980). *Competitive strategy.* New York: Free Press.

Stevens, R.E. (1982). *Strategic marketing plan master guide.* Englewood Cliffs, NJ: Prentice-Hall.

Subject Index

Author Index